*EVELYN REED is an active par-
ticipant in the women's movement
and a veteran socialist.* She has lec-
tured on campuses and at feminist
meetings across the United States,
Canada, Australia, New Zealand,
and Japan and was keynote speaker
at the Southern Female Rights Union
conference in Mississippi in 1970.
Her Problems of Women's Liberation, *widely used as a text in wom-
en's studies classes, has been published in eight languages.* Woman's
Evolution *is the product of over
twenty years of research.*

WOMAN'S EVOLUTION

Evelyn Reed
WOMAN'S
from matriarchal clan

PATHFINDER PRESS, INC., NEW YORK

EVOLUTION
to patriarchal family

Copyright © 1975 by Pathfinder Press, Inc.
All rights reserved
Library of Congress Catalog Card No. 74-26236
ISBN: 0-87348-421-5 (cloth); 0-87348-422-3 (paper)
Manufactured in the United States of America

First edition, 1975

Pathfinder Press, Inc.
410 West Street
New York, N.Y. 10014

TO WOMEN
on the way to liberation

Contents

WOMAN'S EVOLUTION

Introduction

The early history of half the human species—womankind— has largely been hidden from view. To bring it to light requires a reinvestigation of anthropology, where the role and accomplishments of women in prehistoric society are buried. This book is a contribution to unveiling that remarkable record.

The resurgence of the women's liberation movement has thrown the spotlight on certain dubious assumptions and disputed questions regarding the past. Foremost among these is the subject of the matriarchy. Was there a period in history when women held a highly esteemed and influential place? If so, how did they lose their social eminence and become the subordinate sex in patriarchal society? Or is the matriarchy, as some say, a myth that has no historical basis?

The matriarchy is one of the most hotly contested issues in a hundred-year controversy between contending schools in anthropology. This book affirms that the maternal clan system was the original form of social organization and explains why. It also traces the course of its development and the causes of its downfall. Such partisanship on the side of the matriarchy would alone make this book controversial. But it contains other challenges to long-held opinions on prehistoric society.

Disagreements are to be expected in a field that covers so vast a stretch of human evolution, extending from the birth of our species to the threshold of civilization, and where the available data derived from biology, archaeology, and anthropology is fragmentary and uncoordinated.

Anthropology was founded as a distinct science in the middle of the nineteenth century. Most of the founding fathers (women entered the profession only later) had an evolutionary approach. Morgan, Tylor, and other pioneers regarded anthropology as the study of the origin of society and the material forces at work in its progress. They made brilliant beginnings in illuminating the main stages in human development.

Morgan delineated three great epochs of social evolution — from savagery through barbarism to civilization. Each was marked off by decisive advances in the level of economic activity. The most rudimentary stage, savagery, was based on hunting and food-gathering. Barbarism began with food production through agriculture and stock raising. Civilization crowned the development of the ancient world by bringing it to the point of commodity production and exchange.

These three epochs were of extremely unequal duration. Savagery lasted far longer than either of its successors. Although savagery is sometimes differentiated into an earlier "primeval" and a later "primitive" stage, both of these rested upon a hunting and gathering economy. Savagery had a span of a million-odd years, comprising more than 99 percent of human existence. Barbarism began about eight thousand years ago; civilization only three thousand years ago.

The early investigators of savage society, to their own surprise, came upon a social structure totally different from ours. They found a clan and tribal system based on maternal kinship and in which women played a leading role. This stood out in sharp contrast with modern society which features the father-family and male supremacy. Although they were unable to tell how far back the maternal system went, we propose to show that it dates from the beginning of humankind.

They made other astonishing discoveries. They observed that savage society had egalitarian social and sexual relations, arising from collective production and communal possession of property. These features too were at odds with modern society, based on private property and class divisions. Thus the maternal clan system, which gave an honored place to women, was also a collectivist order where the members of both sexes enjoyed equality and did not suffer oppression or discrimination.

Subsequently, these discoveries evoked doubts and resistance from the schools of anthropology that became dominant in the twentieth century. There arose a deep division between evolutionists and anti-evolutionists that has persisted to the present day. It is only through the evolutionary approach, however, that the concealed history of women—and of men—can be uncovered.

The principle of universal evolution had already been applied to the problem of the genesis of *Homo sapiens* with the publication in 1871 of Darwin's book *The Descent of Man.* After he demonstrated that the earliest subhumans, the hominids, arose out of the anthropoids, the question was posed: How did this transformation come about? In the following decades biology, archaeology, paleontology, and anthropology jointly assisted in the detective work required to clarify this problem.

The fossil evidence dug up by the archaeologists led the most astute among them to single out the use and fabrication of tools as the prime distinction separating the first hominids from other primates. Since tools are the basis of labor activities to produce the necessities of life, this would locate the dividing line between ape and human at the point where production was initiated. Such was the thesis of Frederick Engels in his unfinished essay, "The Part Played by Labor in the Transition from Ape to Human," written in 1876 but not published until 1896, a year after his death. The gist of his theory is that the activities and results of cooperative labor constituted the principal factor creating the distinctive capacities and characteristics of our species.

Thirty years later, in 1927, Robert Briffault's monumental three-volume work, *The Mothers,* demonstrated that prolonged maternal care in the higher apes was instrumental in spurring the female sex to become the trail-blazers in the advance to social life. The matriarchy was the necessary first form of social organization because women were not only the procreators of new life but also the chief producers of the necessities of life. Briffault's matriarchal theory dovetailed with Engels's labor theory. Together they pointed to the conclusion that women are to be credited with leading the humanization and socialization of our species.

Non-evolutionary anthropologists, whether they adhere to the diffusionist, functional, empirical-descriptive, or structural schools, reject the existence of a prehistoric matriarchy. They admit that matrilineal kinship still prevails in some primitive regions of the globe, but they do not explain how such matrilineal relations originated if they are not survivals from a previous matriarchal epoch.

Since the turn of the century, anthropology has amassed an immense stockpile of information about diverse cultures in various parts of the world. These descriptive studies are extremely valuable. However, this wealth of data has not been matched by an equivalent expansion in theoretical insight. Most academic anthropologists have turned away from the evolutionary viewpoint that launched the science, and reject attempts to systematize our knowledge and ascertain what stages society has passed through.

E.E. Evans-Pritchard writes that after delivering the Marett Lecture at Oxford in 1950 he ran "into a bad patch of anti-historical prejudice." This hostility to history, he says, has been dominant in England under the influence of Radcliffe-Brown and Malinowski. In the United States it has been the same. The late dean of American anthropologists, A.L. Kroeber, stated that fundamentally anthropology had been "anti-historical in tendency" (*Essays in Social Anthropology,* p. 46). At most, the bolder contemporary anthropologists, like Julian H. Steward, arrive at piecemeal evolutionary linkages, restricting their findings to parallels of limited occurrence.

(For an analysis of the wave of anti-evolutionism in the West, see the first chapter in the recent work by the Dutch scholar W.F. Wertheim, *Evolution and Revolution.*)

Today the basic facts of prehistory in their totality are not fitted into any broad, coherent pattern of social evolution as Morgan, Tylor, and their followers attempted. This failure to follow any consistent evolutionary line makes anthropology an anomaly among the sciences. Whereas biologists, archaeologists, and paleontologists construct their research and classification in an evolutionary manner, most schools of anthropology have gone off in a different and retrograde direction.

This aversion to the search for origins is usually justified on the grounds that the epoch of savagery, the one that includes most of human history, is inaccessible. It is presumed to be so inscrutable that deductions about its social institutions are purely speculative. E. Adamson Hoebel, head of the University of Minnesota's Department of Anthropology, states in his book *The Law of Primitive Man* that "no scientifically restrained anthropologist of today will ever hazard a statement as to what the specific details of any social institution may have been within the societies of early paleolithic men." This lopping off of most of savagery arbitrarily restricts the field of anthropology to the last ten thousand years or less.

Oddly enough, the same agnosticism does not prevail among the archaeologists who study the "paleolithic" epoch, which is only another name for the same million-year stretch of history known to evolutionary anthropologists as "savagery." On the contrary, they have not been so "scientifically restrained" as to prevent them from describing the whole prehistoric period from the time the anthropoids became hominids. They have arranged the data obtained from the excavated deposits of fossil bones and tools in chronological sequence and thereby marked off the main milestones in evolution from the *Australopithecines* of a million years ago to *Homo sapiens*.

However, tools and skulls have limited usefulness in the task of reconstructing primeval society. They cannot disclose the structure of social organization and shed little light on the customs, practices, and attitudes of our most ancient ancestors. For data of this kind we must turn to anthropology. Whereas archaeologists deal with the remains of extinct humans, anthropologists study primitive peoples still living in various parts of the globe who retain significant features of the savage or paleolithic mode of life. The mass of data accumulated by anthropologists in field studies is augmented by the reports of travelers, settlers, and missionaries over the past few centuries and even earlier.

This book adheres to the evolutionary and materialist method in utilizing these findings. It also presents a new theory about totemism and taboo, among the most enigmatic institutions of primeval and primitive society. Anthropologists of all persuasions have held the view that the ancient taboo on sexual intercourse with certain relatives, like our own taboo, arose out of a universal fear of incest. This book challenges that assumption. The ancient taboo existed — but it was primarily directed against the perils of cannibalism in the hunting epoch.

The elimination of the theory of a universal incest taboo removes one of the most serious obstacles to understanding other savage institutions, such as the classificatory system of kinship, exogamy and endogamy, segregation of the sexes, rules of avoidance, blood revenge, the gift-exchange system, and the dual organization of the tribe. It clears the way toward an understanding of how society arose—and why it arose in no other form than the maternal clan system or matriarchy.

The question of the matriarchy is decisive in establishing whether or not the modern father-family has always existed. The very structure of the maternal clan system precluded it. Instead of being the basic social unit from time immemorial, as most anthropologists contend, it is a late arrival in history, appearing only at the beginning of the civilized epoch.

*   *   *

The first two parts of this book deal with the matriarchal age—one from the standpoint of the mothers and the other from the standpoint of the brothers. The third part delineates the transition from matriarchy and matrifamily to patriarchy and father-family.

The terms "savage" and "primitive," often used in a derogatory, colonialist, or racist sense, are here used exclusively in a scientific way. "Savage" is simply a designation for our earliest ancestors. Without their colossal achievements over a span of a million years, humanity could not have walked the last mile to civilization.

To forestall other misunderstandings: This book does not suggest any return to a "lost paradise" of the matriarchy. The infancy of humanity with all its grandeur and limitations is behind us. All the same, that fundamental chapter of human evolution must be restored and take and honored place in our history. A correct understanding of the remote past can help us see ahead and move forward more surely.

This is especially true when we consider the outstanding role played by women in ancient times. The knowledge that female inferiority today is not biologically determined, that it has not been a permanent fixture throughout history, and that our sex was once the organizers and leaders of social life, should heighten the self-confidence of women who are today aspiring for liberation.

Evelyn Reed
October 31, 1974

Part I
The Matriarchy

1

Was the Primitive Sex Taboo an 'Incest' Taboo?

Animals satisfy their sexual needs without any self-imposed restrictions. An adult male can gain access to any receptive female, including the female that gave him birth (his mother) or the females born of the same mother as himself (his sisters). Such uninhibited sexual intercourse does not prevail among humans. "No known people regard all women as possible mates," observes Ruth Benedict (*Patterns of Culture,* p. 42). Restrictions upon sexual intercourse are therefore exclusively social and cultural.

The most stringent of all restrictions in civilized society is the prohibition against incest. For example, a man is forbidden to have sexual intercourse with or marry his mother and sisters. Such intermarriage of "blood relatives" is said to be not only immoral but injurious to the human species; the progeny of such unions may be born with physical or mental defects or both. This modern sex taboo is absolute and stands in a class by itself; it is clearly and specifically an "incest taboo."

It is usually assumed that there has never been any other kind of absolute sex prohibition than the incest taboo and that this goes all the way back to the beginning of human history. A reexamination of the subject, however, raises the question— was the primitive taboo directed against incest?

When the pioneer anthropologists of the nineteenth century took up their studies, they noted the central place occupied by the primitive sex taboo and the inordinate attention paid to its observance. However, they were struck by the fact that the primitive sex taboo had little resemblance to our incest taboo. The primitive prohibition applied to many more women than a man's own mother and sisters.

3

In our society, where the family circle defines the boundaries of the incest prohibition, the forbidden females are few in number. They consist of the mother and the sisters. However, in savage society where the unit was not the family but the maternal clan, a man had many "mothers" and "sisters." These were all the women who belonged to his own clan and to related clans. Under the "rule of avoidance" that implemented the taboo, clan kinsmen were obliged to maintain a distance from these forbidden females.

The rule of avoidance is not difficult to grasp since we still practice it to a certain degree. Nowadays a man must sexually avoid his mother and sisters though in other respects he has intimate association with them and normally lives in the same household with them until he becomes an adult. But in primitive society the rule of avoidance was wider and involved the physical separation of the sexes. The adult men lived in their own quarters or clubhouse separate and apart from the adult women and children who lived together in their own quarters. At puberty or even earlier, young males were removed from the residences of their mothers and sisters to reside henceforth with their adult male kinsmen.

J. J. Atkinson points out that in some languages the term "sister" is derived from a root meaning "avoidance" ("Primal Law," in *Social Origins and Primal Law,* p. 217). Andrew Lang, his collaborator, tells us that the term "sister" is identical with "taboo" and like taboo means "not to be touched." He emphasizes that these untouchables embrace a far larger group of women than the sisters of a man's family. He writes:

> In Lifu the word for "sister" means "not to be touched," and this is a mere expression of customary law. A man "must not touch" any one of the women of his generation whom the totem tabu and the rule of the exogamous "phratry" . . . forbid him to touch. All such women, in a particular grade, are his sisters. Many women, besides his actual sisters, stand to him in the degree thus prohibited. All bear the same name of status as a man's actual sisters bear, but the name does not *mean* "sisters" at all, in our sense of that word. . . . It means tabued women of a generation. ("Social Origins," in *Social Origins and Primal Law,* p. 100)

The women of a man's own generation were not the only forbidden females. Even more sacrosanct were the "elder sisters" or mothers, and the immature offspring, the "younger sisters." Mothers and children embodied the forbidden females in their sharpest expression.

Since in primitive society the term "mother" was not a family term but a functional clan term, females of every age level belonging to a man's own clan were tabooed. This peculiarity is noted by W. I. Thomas:

> . . . among the Chagga, they reinforce the sex tabu between brother and sister by making the sister the equivalent of the mother. Their expression is, "Sister is mother." Among the Bangala also, sister is called *mama* or *mama moti* (little mother). (*Primitive Behavior,* p. 192)

The rigidly enforced rule of avoidance broke down rapidly after the Europeans penetrated into primitive regions and introduced their own customs. According to Atkinson, it was "one of the very first customs to disappear after contact with whites, especially missionaries, being as it is in such extreme divergence with the economy of the European family" (*Social Origins and Primal Law,* pp. 216-17). He points out that, while thirty years earlier the avoidance was universal in New Caledonia, in many places it has become unknown even as a tradition among the younger aborigines.

In some regions, however, the reluctance of primitive peoples to adopt the civilized practices continued. According to E. Adamson Hoebel, an Ifugao questioned an American on the "indecent" behavior that permitted brothers and sisters to live and sleep in the same household. Although the American defensively explained that "our houses are very big," the Ifugao exclaimed:

> *"Nakayang!* If they are as big as a large village and if brothers and sisters sleep at opposite ends of them, it is perhaps not so bad. But the way the Fish-eaters (i.e. low-landers) do is a custom that stinks." (*Man in the Primitive World,* p. 241)

Atkinson regarded the rule of avoidance as a primordial law dating back to the formative stage of human evolution. As "the first factor in the ascent of man, it must have taken its rise whilst he was still some ape-like creature," he wrote, and added, "It ordained in the dawn of time a barrier between mother and son, and brother and sister, and that ordinance is still binding on all mankind" (*Social Origins and Primal Law,* p. 219).

The great antiquity of the sex taboo posed questions that have perplexed anthropologists. Assuming that the primitive sex taboo was an incest taboo, how could ancient hominids, not yet fully developed humans, have understood the scientific facts about inbreeding or have acquired the notion that it was injurious to the species? Even more incomprehensible, how and why did this apparent "incest" taboo come to be applied to a multitude of women extending far beyond the mother and sisters of a family circle?

Despite these difficulties, the theory that the primitive sex taboo was a prohibition against incest has acquired almost universal acceptance. Its upholders have invoked various arguments to buttress their contention. In examining these, let us begin with the one that seemed most plausible — the "inbreeding theory."

Weaknesses of the Inbreeding Theory

Early travelers, noting the horror aroused in aborigines at the very thought of violating their taboo, assumed that such a profound reaction could only spring from a recognition of the harmful effects of incest. As Robert Briffault observes:

> The older theorists and travellers who noted the customs of exogamous marriage so general among primitive peoples, and the horror with which incestuous relations are regarded by them, had no difficulty in accounting for those customs and beliefs. They unanimously expressed the view that, the evil effects accruing from the union of persons related by blood having obtruded themselves on the notice of the savages, the wise men among them had taken counsel about the matter and had appointed that such unions should in future be strictly prohibited. (*The Mothers,* vol. I, p. 241)

The assumption that inbreeding is injurious has been held by many distinguished men of science. It is not surprising that the concept was adopted by Morgan and other early anthropologists.

Toward the end of the last century, however, efforts were made to check this conception about the harmfulness of inbreeding and to substantiate it with hard data. "Those attempts have resulted in complete failure," says Briffault, who assembled a vast amount of documentation to prove this point (ibid., pp. 204-40).

To begin with, there is no fear of incest among animals, who mate without the slightest regard to inbreeding and with no sign of injury to their stock:

> All animal species propagate without regard to the closest inbreeding, and there exists no provision, either in the form of instincts or other devices, whereby any check is placed upon such inbreeding. Reproduction without any regard to relationship takes place habitually in animal species, such as rats, rabbits, and other rodents, which by their fertility and vitality have become obnoxious as vermin. Many animals appear to propagate exclusively by what we should term the closest incestuous unions. (ibid., p. 204)

Briffault gives examples of these close unions among animals from such authorities as Brehm-Strassen, Seton, Rengger, Darwin, Huth, and others.

Equally damaging to the theory of the harmfulness of inbreeding are the results of laboratory experiments testing this supposition, as well as prevailing practices in animal breeding. So long as other factors are taken into account, inbreeding is often the best way to produce uniformly high quality in animals such as prize breeding bulls, racehorses, and pedigreed dogs. Briffault writes on this point:

> All the most highly valued domestic stocks, and the individual animals which are esteemed most precious, are the outcome of such inbreeding carried often to the utmost limits. For example, a closely inbred prize bull is mentioned by Darwin, which was matched with its daughter, its grand-daughter, and its great-grand-daughter. . . . The resulting offspring was the realisation of the breeder's highest dreams of perfection. The English race-horse is one of the most closely inbred of existing animals. (ibid., p. 209)

From the data at his disposal Briffault observes: "It is no more than the soberest conclusion that there is not in the records of breeding from domesticated animals a single fact, alleged or verified, which indicates, much less evidences, that inbreeding, even the closest, is in itself productive of evil effects" (ibid., p. 215).

Similarly, laboratory experiments have produced no evidence of harmful effects from inbreeding. Among other authorities, Briffault cites P. Popenoe:

> Two series were inbred from two pairs of rats, brothers being mated regularly with sisters, and control breeds were kept which were allowed to reproduce at haphazard. "These laboratory rats, which have been inbred as closely as possible for twenty-two generations, are in every respect superior to the stock rats from which they took their start six years ago, and which have since been bred in the usual indiscriminate manner." The male inbred rats were 15 per cent heavier than the stock male rats, the females 3 per cent heavier. . . . The fertility of the inbred rats was nearly 8 per cent greater than that of the stock rats. (*The Mothers,* vol. I, p. 208)

Thus the argument on the dangers of inbreeding, which in the nineteenth century had furnished the basis for the incest theory, became seriously undermined, if not entirely invalidated, in the twentieth century. The most recent studies on the subject have also failed to substantiate this theory. Ernst Mayr in his book *Animal Species and Evolution,* which has been acclaimed as the most important work on biology since Darwin, writes that "loss of genetic variance through inbreeding occurs far more slowly than one might expect" and adds that "brother-sister matings can be continued in certain organisms for hundreds of generations without serious depression of viability and fertility. . . ." He gives numerous examples cited by Hutton (1897) who "pointed out long ago that the rather considerable amount of inbreeding in new colonies is not necessarily injurious" (p. 530).

Another factor that militated against the inbreeding theory was the ignorance of primitive peoples about biological relationships. It would require a high degree of scientific knowledge to understand the biological processes on which the supposed harmfulness of inbreeding is based. Even early civilized peoples a few thousand years ago had only the crudest notions about genetics, a science that began in our times. How, then, could our primeval ancestors, who had barely arrived at the stage of articulate speech, have grasped such a concept as inbreeding or incest?

Even if it could be proven that inbreeding is injurious, this could only be recognized by possessors of advanced scientific knowledge, and not by hominid or savage peoples. Darwin felt that ancient humankind was incapable of reflecting upon some distant injury to their progeny. Indeed, they had not yet reached the stage of domesticating and breeding animals, let alone assessing its results.

Other attempts to explain the primitive sex taboo have been even less satisfactory than the inbreeding theory. Among these are two arguments, one of which can be called the "instinctual" and the other the "psychological" approach. Neither succeeds in demonstrating a universal loathing of incest.

Instincts and Psychology

Edward Westermarck, L. T. Hobhouse, and Havelock Ellis were the foremost exponents of the proposition that the prohibition against incest arose from an innate revulsion at the idea of sexual intercourse with members of the same brood or family. If so, such an instinctive aversion must be implanted in the genetic structure not only of humans but also of animals. But the facts show there is no such aversion to inbreeding among animals.

The instinct of animals in the wild or in captivity is to mate with the nearest available member of the opposite sex, without regard to their possible close relationship. Those who have house pets, such as cats and dogs, know that animals frequently find their mates in the same brood. Pedigreed animals are encouraged or induced to do so.

Has humanity, then, acquired a type of instinct unknown in animals? The very existence of the taboo demonstrates the opposite. For if humans were provided with an instinctive barrier against incest, why was it necessary to erect so formidable a law against it? As Ralph Piddington cogently puts it, "Why should the most powerful forces of human society be mobilized in this way to prevent the individual from performing an act toward which he feels 'natural' indifference or even aversion?" (*An Introduction to Social Anthropology,* p. 134). Leslie A. White argues along the same line:

To say that prohibitions against incest are "instinctive" is of course to declare that there is a natural, inborn and innate feeling of revulsion toward unions with close relatives. But if this were the case, why should societies enact strict laws to prevent them? Why should they legislate against something that everyone already wishes passionately to avoid? (*The Science of Culture,* pp. 303-04)

The psychological theorists take a diametrically different position from the instinctualists. They proceed on the basis of natural attraction rather than instinctual aversion. Since the members of the same family circle, brought up in close intimacy over many years, are almost bound to develop a mutual attraction for one another, this necessitates the imposition of the incest taboo, they contend.

This thesis reached its most developed form after Freud and other depth psychologists of the early twentieth century disclosed the widespread character of secret incestuous desires among members of the same family circle. Strongest was the desire of a son for his mother. Reference to the most celebrated instance in Western literature of a man marrying his mother, the Greek legend of Oedipus, lent plausibility to the notion that incestuous desires were universal. The "Oedipus complex" has since become a generic term to express this seemingly everlasting trait in human nature.

Apart from the fact that the story of Oedipus is not connected in any way with secret incestuous desires — as will be explained later in this book — the prime error made by Freud and others was to assume that a phenomenon which asserted itself so prominently in nineteenth century social life has existed throughout all human history, reaching back into primordial times.

The secret incestuous desires of family members for one another in recent times have come from a special combination of circumstances. On one hand, the puritanical code of sexual ethics has insisted upon sexual suppression until marriage. On the other hand, marriage was founded upon economic, social, and status considerations and was therefore often postponed for many years after puberty. This conflict between biological need and social suppression actually resulted in certain family fixations and neuroses which have been erroneously called "Oedipal."

This peculiar pathology of modern society was absent from primitive life. So long as the rule of clan exogamy was observed, free sexual relations prevailed between the sexes. There were no sexual neuroses or "Oedipus complexes" among aborigines. Lord Raglan remarks:

> Let us now turn to the central feature of the whole system, the Oedipus complex — that every boy is subconsciously obsessed with a desire to kill his father and marry his mother. There seems to be no doubt that this complex occurs among European neurotics, and it may occur to some extent among normal Europeans; but even Freud's own followers have been unable to find it among savages, and have been reduced to the necessity of postulating a repressed repression in order to account for its apparent absence. It seems clear, however, that this complex, where it exists, is one of the numerous consequences of the simultaneous stimulation and repression of the sexual impulse which is one of the features of our social system. . . . Wherever a boy looks, whether in real life, in pictures, in books, or on the stage, scenes of sexual passion are thrust upon his sight and his imagination; yet the only woman whom he may kiss and fondle is his mother, so that he is liable to fall in love with his mother, and to be envious of his father, who has a prior claim on her attentions. Among savages, on the other hand . . . a boy . . . is usually, if not invariably, allowed opportunities for sexual gratification elsewhere, with the result that he no more thinks of falling in love with his mother than a young married European does of falling in love with his grandmother. (*Jocasta's Crime,* pp. 74-75)

Thus none of the familiar arguments, whether biological, instinctual, or psychological, can sustain the proposition that the primitive sex taboo was directed against incest. It has not been demonstrated through animal breeding or experiments that inbreeding is harmful to the species. In any case that kind of scientific knowledge was far beyond the grasp of primitive humanity. There is no instinctive aversion among animals to mating with members of the same brood. And if such an aversion had been present in human life, there would have been no need to enact strict laws to prevent incest. Finally, the assumptions made about modern family neuroses on the basis of a misinterpreted Oedipus legend are irrelevant to the subject.

However, the most damaging blow to the incest theory comes

from the anthropological data on the primitive kinship system. Savage concepts of kinship were so totally different from ours that it is difficult for us to grasp them. In our society, founded upon the individual family, kinship stems from biological or genetic relationship. But in ancient society, founded upon the collective clan system, kinship expressed a social relationship embracing the whole community.

Only a sex prohibition that forbids the known members of a family circle from mating can be called an "incest taboo." A sex prohibition that forbids a whole community of people from mating cannot be called an "incest taboo"; it is no more than a sex prohibition. This distinction can be seen more clearly when we examine the clan system of kinship, called the "classificatory system," which stands in sharp contrast to our family kinship system.

Classificatory Kinship

Lewis Morgan, who ascertained that the maternal gens or clan preceded the family in history, also discovered the classificatory system of kinship, which anthropologists today often call "social kinship." Under this system all members of the community were categorized according to sex and age, which also defined their occupations and social functions. While the sex divisions were fixed, the age divisions changed as the groups of females and males advanced from childhood to adulthood and old age. These classifications or "classes," as they are also called, were not based upon any family connections but upon clan, phratry, and tribal connections.

As W. H. R. Rivers says, "In nearly all peoples of low culture, the whole system of denoting relatives is so fundamentally different from our own that we have no real equivalent terms in our language for any one of the terms used by them, while, conversely, such people have no terms which are the exact equivalents of ours" (*Psychology and Ethnology,* p. 44). Elsewhere he spells this out more succinctly: "the essential distinction between the classificatory system and that used by ourselves is that the former is founded on the clan or other similar group while our own is founded on the family" (*The History of Melanesian Society,* vol. I, pp. 6-7).

Under the classificatory system a child will refer to a number of women as his "mothers," while in our family system of kinship only one woman can be the mother of a child—the woman that bore him. Moreover, under the classificatory system, where the term for mother is functional rather than biological, even female infants are called "mothers." Such oddities bring out the marked difference between the primitive and modern kinship systems.

To us a mother is an individual woman who bears a child; she does not become a mother until and unless she gives birth. But in primitive society motherhood was a *social* function of the female sex; thus all women were actually or potentially "the mothers" of the community. As adult women, all were equally responsible for the provision and protection of the children. Spencer and Gillen write about the Arunta:

> They have no words equivalent to our English words. . . . A man, for example, will call his actual mother *"Mia,"* but, at the same time he will apply the term not only to other grown women, but to a little girl child, provided they all belong to the same group. . . . the term *Mia* expressed the relationship in which she stood to him. (*The Native Tribes of Central Australia,* p. 58)

Frazer writes on the same subject:

> . . . we confuse our word "mother" with the corresponding but by no means equivalent terms in the languages of savages who have the classificatory system. We mean by "mother" a woman who has given birth to a child; the Australian savages mean by "mother" a woman who stands in a certain social relation to a group of men and women, whether she has given birth to any one of them or not. She is "mother" to that group even when she is an infant in arms. . . . It is not even necessary to suppose, as Dr. Rivers has suggested, the blood tie between a mother and her offspring may . . . have been forgotten in later life. . . . The true relation between mother and child may always have been remembered, but it was an accident which did not in any way affect the mother's place in the classificatory system, for she was classed with a group of "mothers" just as much before as after her child was born. (*Totemism and Exogamy,* vol. I, pp. 304-05)

This submersion of the individual within the collective group of mothers is expressed in some primitive languages surviving today which have no term to express the individual mother-child relationship. "Physical motherhood," says Hans Kelsen, "is nothing to these peoples. . . . The Australians, for instance, have no term to express the relationship between mother and child. This is because the physical fact is of no significance and not because of the meagreness of the language" (*Society and Nature,* p. 30).

It was not until the father-family made its appearance in history that the individual father and mother emerged from the undifferentiated maternal clan collective. This was noted by J. J. Bachofen as far back as 1861 with the publication of his book *Das Mutterrecht:*

> Every woman's womb, the mortal image of the earth mother Demeter, will give brothers and sisters to the children of every other woman; the homeland will know only brothers and sisters until the day when the development of the paternal system dissolves the undifferentiated unity of the mass and introduces a principle of articulation. (*Myth, Religion and Mother Right,* p. 80)

Thus the maternal clan which preceded the father-family was founded upon a collectivity of women who were sisters to one another and mothers to all the children of the community without regard to which individual mother bore any individual child. This is confirmed by the way aborgines describe themselves as social units; they are "brotherhoods" from the standpoint of the men and "motherhoods" from the standpoint of the women.

The Garos of Assam, for example, call their clans *machongs,* their term for "motherhoods" or, more simply, "the mothers." In Melanesia the term *veve* or *vev* means the same thing. As Lucien Levy-Bruhl describes this maternal clan:

> The kin is the *veve,* a child's mother is "they of the kin," his kindred. A man's kindred are not called his *veve* because they are his mother's people; she is called his *veve,* in the plural, his kindred, as if she were the representative of the kin; as if he were not the child of the particular woman who bore him, but of the whole kindred for whom she brought him into the world. . . . The mother is called . . . the sisters, the sisterhood, because she represents the sister members of the social group who are the mothers generally of the children. . . .
>
> *The absence of a family in our sense of the word* is on

all fours with the absence of the words corresponding with these ideas (of father and son). (*The "Soul" of the Primitive,* pp. 80-81, emphasis in the original)

How, then, in a society founded not upon individual family relations but upon social or community kinship, could the concept of incest have arisen? The elementary basis for understanding incest would be knowing the individual father and mother of each individual child. In the epoch of savagery, however, fathers were unknown, as the early scholars discovered. But even where the individual mother of a child was remembered, this fact was unimportant and irrelevant in a society founded upon the classificatory system of kinship.

Thus the very structure of the classificatory system, whether it is designated clan kinship, social kinship, or community kinship, itself provides a refutation of the incest theory. While it is undeniable that these classified kin observed a very strict sex taboo, that does not make it an incest taboo. A brief review of the vast number of women and girls included in this classification of forbidden women will demonstrate the absurdity of calling the primitive sex taboo an incest taboo.

A Multitude of Forbidden Females

The rule of exogamy is sometimes called the "marrying out" rule. In our society when a man "marries out" he marries out of a very small family unit including one mother and perhaps a sister or several sisters. But in tribal society when a man married out, it was not only out of his own clan, composed of many mothers and sisters, but also out of his own phratry, which represented a number of linked or related clans. This multiplied the number of mothers and sisters with whom a man could not have sexual relations since they were all forbidden females.

Morgan used the term "collateral" relatives to describe those who were not physiological relatives. Others have used the term "parallels" in place of the term "collaterals," and some have described them as "fictional" kin. Whatever the designation, a large number of women were forbidden to a man regardless of the fact that they had no genetic relationship to him.

In a community composed of two clans standing opposite each other for mating purposes, a man could not marry any woman in his own clan or *veve*. He had to marry an outsider, that is, a woman of the opposite clan or *veve*. The same was true of a tribe composed of two phratries standing opposite each other. A man could not marry any woman in any of the linked clans comprising his own phratry; he had to marry a woman of the opposite phratry. Since both phratries were composed of a number of linked clans, there were a multitude of women who were forbidden females to a man. Each man was restricted to the women of a specific clan on the opposite side.

Even this does not exhaust the restrictions on mating. Within the opposite clan or phratry a man was restricted to women of his own age level or generation. His mate's mothers, older sisters, and younger sisters were forbidden. A man's "marriage class," as it is usually called, limited to the women of his own generation in one clan of the opposite phratry of the tribe, was thus very narrow. Some scholars have observed that in the world of primitive man, half the women were his sisters and the other half eligible as wives. This ratio is incorrect. As Briffault remarks of the aborigines of Australia, Melanesia, and other very primitive peoples, "The savage lives in such societies in the midst of females the great majority of whom are inaccessible to him under penalty of death" (*The Mothers,* vol. I, p. 612).

This exaggerated situation prevailed only at the peak of the enforcement of the sex taboo. Subsequently it broke down; a man could then marry a woman in any of the clans of the opposite phratry. Later even the prohibition between the linked clans of his own phratry was dissolved and a man could marry a woman in any other clan than his own. Morgan observed this breakdown of the old rigid sex taboo occurring during the period of his studies. Frazer describes the breakdown of this "bloated" system of restrictive marriage classes as follows:

> The history of exogamy is the history first of a growing and afterwards of a decaying scrupulosity as to the marriage of near kin. . . . the barriers reach their greatest known height in the eight-class system of the Australian aborigines, which practically shuts the door for every man upon seven-eighths of the women of the community. . . . Having reached its culminating point in the bloated systems of eight classes and the like, exogamy begins to decline. . . . The last stage of decay is reached when the exogamy of the clan breaks down also, and henceforth marriage is regulated by the prohibited degrees alone. (*Totemism and Exogamy,* vol. IV, pp. 152-53)

Such facts deliver the most damaging blow to the incest theory. A taboo marking off the great majority of women as forbidden to a given man can be called a sex taboo, but it cannot be called an incest taboo.

It is understandable that in the nineteenth century when both biology and anthropology were infant sciences the pioneer anthropologists should have believed that the primitive sex taboo was an incest taboo. But it is quite another matter to keep repeating this error for the next hundred years when considerably more information has been made available in both these sciences to help overcome this misconception.

This is all the more inadmissible since many anthropologists who have accepted the incest theory are dissatisfied with it and even skeptical of its correctness. They are aware that direct inquiries made of aborigines with regard to the sex taboo have failed to shed light on its origin or meaning. Aborigines merely state that their ancestors laid down the prohibition which they have undeviatingly observed ever since. Similarly, a study of primitive myths, legends, and traditions furnishes no clues on the subject. As Cora Du Bois writes:

> The material on incest is obviously trivial. It was practically impossible to get data, not because the informants seemed shocked, but rather because they showed so little interest and had so little to say about it. The myths and autobiographies are similarly lacking in this theme. (*The People of Alor,* p. 105)

It is not surprising that aborigines have so little to say about incest since it is a phenomenon that preoccupies civilized peoples but conveys no meaning to the savage mind. Even when explained it is usually misunderstood by aborigines. The term "incest" is not their term for their taboo; it is a term introduced by civilized people who made wrong assumptions about the nature of the taboo.

The uncritical acceptance and last-ditch defense of the incest theory has led to another absurdity. This is the attempt to twist the definition of the term "incest" into something different from its real meaning. By definition the term "incest" refers only to sexual intercourse between biologically or genetically related individuals. Since this does not match the reality in the primitive world, Robert H. Lowie and other anthropologists have decided to "lump" together relatives and nonrelatives and thus stretch the definition of the term "incest," even if by doing so they cancel out its meaning.

A characteristic illustration of the illogical logic that results can be found in Hoebel's presentation:

> Mating with any person who is *socially defined* as a genetic relative is forbidden. Any such prohibited mating is incestuous.
>
> Incest taboos are universal among all peoples, because incest is repugnant to the least as well as to the most civilized people.
>
> This broadening of relationship categories has been aptly called *lumping* by Lowie. It is the usual characteristic of relationship systems that are identified as *classificatory*. Because most primitive systems are classificatory, many individuals are embraced within the incest prohibitions by the simple fiat of a social system that dubs them as "father," "mother," "brother," or "sister" when in biological fact they are no such thing. (*Man in the Primitive World,* pp. 191-92, emphasis in the original)

This turns the matter upside down. The classificatory system of social kinship preceded the family kinship system just as the clan preceded the family in history. Thus primitive peoples did not "lump" together nonrelatives with family relatives. Theirs was exclusively a social or communal system of kinship; they were unaware of and indifferent to individual family ties. It was only in the course of time that the old classificatory system gave way to the family kinship system.

A good analogy to the classificatory system of kinship can be made with the fraternal organizations and trade unions of our day, where men are called "brothers" and women are called "sisters." They are perfectly aware that this *social* designation does not mean that all of them or even any of them are genetic brothers and sisters. Suppose, therefore, that a law was passed declaring that all the "brothers and sisters" of a labor union composed of thousands of members could not marry one another. We would certainly call this a sex taboo. But it would not be an incest taboo. For even if a few members of this large organization happened to be genetic brothers and sisters, this would be immaterial to a rule governing the whole unrelated body of union members.

Stretching the term "incest" into an opposite meaning does not help solve the problem of locating the origin and meaning of the taboo. On the contrary, it serves as a stumbling block in the path of solving the riddle. For until we realize that incest was not involved we cannot get to the heart of the question: What was the taboo directed against?

The Importance of the Problem

Since the various premises of the incest theory cannot stand up under sharp scrutiny and must be declared invalid, why pursue the matter further? Why make so much fuss over the regulation of sexual relations in primitive society which happens to differ from ours when there are so many other aspects of primitive social organization that should claim attention?

The fact is that until the real reason for the taboo is found we cannot fathom a series of other questions in primitive life that are still poorly understood. Without an accurate answer to this question we cannot know why primitive society arose as a maternal clan system instead of a father-family system. We cannot fully understand the origin and meaning of exogamy and endogamy; of the dual organization of society; or of the various aspects of the classificatory system of kinship. Insight into the reasons for the taboo is not only the key to understanding primitive social institutions but also assists us in reconstructing a continuous history of humankind from the beginning up to civilization.

The taboo is no trivial or incidental feature of primitive society. It occupies the central place in social custom. "The exogamic system," says Briffault, "is regarded by the great majority of societies in the more primitive stages of culture as the most important, the most inviolable principle of social organization" (*The Mothers,* vol. I, p. 202). Investigation has disclosed that the ruder the economy, the greater is the fear of any transgression of the taboo and its law of exogamy. There are authenticated reports of savage hunters and warriors dying of fright at even an unintentional infringement of it. This alone would indicate that the taboo is something more than a mere sexual prohibition; it is a social law of supreme force.

This is borne out by the savage attitude toward the taboo and any violation of it. Such a violation, in fact or in imagination, is regarded not simply as an individual misdeed for which the individual alone is responsible. On the contrary, the punishment is believed to fall upon the whole community, often threatening its very survival. As a social prohibition the taboo is regarded as specifically instituted to ward off some dreaded community disaster. Nothing less than the annihilation of the community is held to be the consequence of violating the taboo.

The taboo is often called a "categorical imperative," a law of such sweeping scope and power that no laws promulgated by civilized society can compare with it. Lord Raglan, citing Captain Rattray's observations of the Ashanti, gives their cataclysmic view of the matter.

> Had such an act been allowed to pass unpunished, then, in the words of my informants, "hunters would have ceased to kill animals in the forest, the crops would have refused to bear fruit, children would have ceased to be born, the spirits of the dead ancestors would have been infuriated, the gods would have been angered, clans would have ceased to exist, and all would have been chaos in the world."
> (*Jocasta's Crime,* p. 3)

Hutton Webster describes the taboo system as "systematized fear" which runs the whole gamut of emotional reactions from "awful to awesome." He writes:

> The authority of a taboo is unmatched by that of any other prohibition. There is no reflection on it, no reasoning about it, no discussion of it. A taboo amounts simply to an imperative thou-shalt-not in the presence of danger apprehended. That the breach of the prohibition was unintentional or well-intentioned matters nothing, no allowance is made for either the ignorance or praiseworthy purpose of the taboo-breaker. . . .
> Death — certain, sudden, and in terrible form — is not seldom the fate which is announced to the taboo-breaker. In the midst of Eden grows the tree of knowledge of good and evil, and God has forbidden man to eat of its fruit, saying "In the day that thou eatest thereof, thou shalt surely die." As a matter of fact, the taboo-breaker does often die, so acute is the fear aroused by even an involuntary transgression. (*Taboo: A Sociological Study,* pp. 17, 24)

The incongruity of such systematized fear surrounding a mere sexual prohibition — and this in a society where, apart from the forbidden females, complete sexual freedom prevailed — has perplexed the most acute thinkers who have studied the problem. "What can be the great social wrong which was supposed to result from incest?" Frazer asks. "How were the guilty persons believed to endanger the whole tribe by their crime? . . . I must confess to being completely baffled" (*Totemism and Exogamy,* vol. IV, pp. 157, 160).

Freud was similarly bewildered:

> We surely would not expect that these poor naked cannibals should be moral in their sex life according to our ideas, or that they should have imposed a high degree of restriction upon their sexual impulses. And yet we learn that they have considered it their duty to exercise the most searching care and the most painful rigour in guarding against incestuous sexual relations. In fact, their whole social organization seems to serve this object or to have been brought into relation with its attainment. (*Totem and Taboo,* pp. 4-5)

Andrew Lang, observing the multitude of women brought under the so-called incest prohibition, expressed complete frustration at trying to solve the problem:

> . . . scientific curiosity has long been busy with the question, why should the least civilised of human races possess the widest list of prohibited degrees? What is the origin of the stringent laws that, among naked and far from dainty nomads, compel men and women to seek their mates outside of certain large groups of real or imagined kindred? . . . all attempts to solve the problem must be provisional. New knowledge may upset even the most recent theory. . . . (*Social Origins and Primal Law,* p. 2)

Some contemporary anthropologists confess to being equally baffled. Fifty years later Ashley Montagu despairs of ever finding the answer: "The origin of the incest prohibition has puzzled anthropologists for many years. . . . We shall probably never be able to ascertain the origin of the incest prohibition" (*Man: His First Million Years,* p. 118).

Is the situation really so hopeless? Possibly investigators

have been looking in the wrong direction and overlooking clear signals from another direction. The taboo existed, to be sure, but was it only a sex taboo? According to Briffault, "Nothing approaching to a satisfying explanation has been offered" thus far. He also suggests, "That failure seems to point to some radical fault in our method or in our assumptions" (*The Mothers,* vol. I, p. 203).

One assumption that is demonstrably in error is the notion that the taboo was directed against incest. But the broader assumption that the prohibition was directed only against certain categories of sexual activities is equally wrong. A closer look at the taboo shows that it was a double prohibition. Only one clause was connected with sex. Its other and far more important clause was connected with food. It was, in fact, a taboo against cannibalism.

2

Taboo Against Cannibalism

The survival of a species, whether human or animal, depends upon the fulfillment of two basic needs: food and sex. Food takes priority; without regular nourishment the animal dies. But mating is also mandatory if the species is to continue. These twin needs are the dynamic in the behavior and evolution of mammalian species.

Hunger is the organic mechanism worked out in natural evolution to prod species into action to satisfy these needs. It has two forms: hunger for food and hunger for mates. Driven by these imperatives, animals seek out the closest available sources to satisfy both hungers. In one species alone, the human species, survival came to depend upon social controls over these biological needs.

This is the underlying meaning of the primitive institution of totemism and taboo. It represents the earliest form of social control over food and sex hungers, classifying that which is forbidden in both realms. The sex clause is well known; under totemic law a man could not mate with any woman belonging to his totem-kin group. Under the food clause, a man was prohibited from killing or eating totem-kin animals.

This peculiar prohibition, which involves humans in its sex clause and animals in its food clause, has made totemism and taboo almost unintelligible to many investigators of the subject. Freud formulates the riddle this way:

> The oldest and most important taboo prohibitions are the two basic laws of *totemism:* namely not to kill the totem animal, and to avoid sexual intercourse with totem companions of the other sex. . . .

It would therefore seem that these must have been the oldest and strongest desires of mankind. We cannot understand this. . . . (*Totem and Taboo,* p. 44)

One reason for the enigmatic character of the food taboo is that the prohibition is framed in terms of the "totem animal." However, as we shall see, there were totem humans in the totemic system who were not originally recognized as humans or were thought to be only quasi-humans. This had the effect of concealing the essence of the food prohibition as a taboo against cannibalism.

Morgan was among the first to discover that humanity had passed through an epoch of cannibalism. However, he thought it was a fully conscious practice due to the shortage of other foods. He wrote, "From the precarious nature of all these sources of food, outside of the great fish areas, cannibalism became the dire resort of mankind. The ancient universality of the practice is being gradually demonstrated." Subsequently, "the acquisition of farinaceous food in America and of domestic animals in Asia and Europe, were the means of delivering the advanced tribes, thus provided, from the scourge of cannibalism . . ." (*Ancient Society,* pp. 22, 24). Morgan was wrong in thinking that ancient mankind was consciously cannibalistic, but he was right about the former universality of the practice.

The idea that humanity had passed through a cannibalistic era was offensive to most people, and few studies of the subject were undertaken. In 1958 Garry Hogg's book *Cannibalism and Human Sacrifice* was published. He states that the Royal Anthropological Institute had no comprehensive work on the subject and "subsequent inquiries at the British Museum met with the same result: on the 80 miles of shelves in that incomparable library of 8,000,000 books, there is no single work in the English language that covers the immense field of cannibalism and human sacrifice" (Pan Books ed., p. 7).

Material scattered through many books and periodicals indicates its former universality. J. A. MacCulloch writes in his article on cannibalism in Hastings's *Encyclopedia of Religion and Ethics:*

Cannibalism, anthropophagy, or man-eating, is a custom which at once inspires horror in the civilized mind. But, though the present range of the practice is somewhat restricted, it was much wider within even recent times, and there is every probability that all races have, at one period or another, passed through a cannibalistic stage, which survived occasionally in ritual or in folk-custom, or was remembered in legend or folk-tale. (vol. III, p. 194)

Julius Lippert, citing R. Andree's studies, states that "all extant anthropophagy seems only a remnant of a once universal practice." He adds:

It radiates far and wide from the heart of Africa and from Australia. It is widespread over the whole of Oceania as far as Malaysia, and in America it extends from south to north, reaching its climax in the civilized states of the center. Only Asia and Europe, the classic ground of true pastoral culture and the civilizations arising therefrom, are free from the custom in historical times. Here, where the grave-escort is indigenous, cannibalism became extinct at an early date. Otherwise it once covered the entire earth, as Andree correctly concluded. But even Europe and Asia were not always exempt. (*The Evolution of Culture,* p. 421)

The usual argument raised against the theory of an ancient epoch of cannibalism is that all species have an instinctual abhorrence against eating their own kind. Investigations of the habits of carnivorous animals do not warrant this assumption. MacCulloch, citing Brehm's *Thierleben,* says, "Among the lower animals eating of their own kind occurs as a habitual or occasional practice with most of the carnivores, feline and canine, and with some rodents, the young or weak falling victims to the rapacity of others" (*Encyclopedia of Religion and Ethics,* vol. III, p. 194). Our rejection of cannibalism, therefore, is not innate; it is a social acquisition.

It is difficult to detect the ancient practice of cannibalism for two main reasons. First, since apes are fruit eaters, the question of cannibalism does not arise in any examination of the conditions of life of our anthropoidal predecessors. Second, by the time recorded history came into existence, the main centers of the world had so long ago abandoned this practice that its former existence had been forgotten. Although numerous survivals of cannibalism were found in primitive regions, these seemed to be only ritualistic peculiarities. Thus the epoch of cannibalism was "boxed off" at both ends; it was absent in primate life and behavior, and vestiges of it were no longer evident in civilized life and behavior.

To dig out this chapter of prehistory, we must begin with the fact that mankind became carnivorous only after our species had emerged from the primates. Although apes in captivity can learn to eat some meat, in the wild state they do not. The change of diet to meat-eating is regarded by some scholars as one of the major dividing lines between humans and apes. Kenneth P. Oakley has said:

> All known races of man include a substantial percentage of flesh in their diets unless, for some secondary cultural reason, they have become vegetarians. . . . Meat-eating is, as one might say, as old as man.
>
> From the endowment of nature, we should be vegetarians. We lack the teeth evolved by true carnivores, and we have the long gut associated with a herbivorous diet. (*An Appraisal of Anthropology Today*, pp. 236-37)

Hoebel writes on the same subject, "Man is omnivorous by nature. This more than any other single trait distinguishes him from his vegetarian anthropoidal relatives. When or how the revolutionary meat-eating habit first took hold in the evolutionary development of man we do not know." But this new diet led to the development of a whole series of assault weapons for bringing down prey. Hoebel writes:

> Thus he uses clubs, spears, darts, arrows, deadfalls, pitfalls, snares, nets, weirs, hooks, axes, knives, and poisons to accomplish his ends. . . . Whatever the device he may use, hunting techniques are those of assault (shooting, spearing, clubbing, axing, stabbing), trapping and snaring, the pitfall and poisoning. Shooting, while the most commonly preferred technique among recent primitives, was probably the last of these methods to appear in human prehistory. The bow was not invented until Late Paleolithic or Early Neolithic times. Neandertal man had clubs, spears, and hand axes. (*Man in the Primitive World*, pp. 102-03)

Although the cannibalistic era was essentially over by the time of written history, it has left its traces in the evolutionary sequence of fossil mankind.

The Fossil Trail of Cannibalism

The trail of cannibalism extends from the beginning of the paleolithic era to its end or, put another way, from the beginning of savagery to its end. At the beginning there is *Australopithecus,* the man-apes, sometimes called the "Dawn men." Higher in the evolutionary sequence, and perhaps representing the midway mark, are *Pithecanthropus* and *Sinanthropus,* also known as Java man and Peking man. Ascending still higher, to about a hundred thousand years ago, we reach Neanderthal man, now considerably more human than ape, and shortly afterward we arrive at full-fledged humans or *Homo sapiens.* Since there were various lines of hominid development, some of which died out before reaching human status, this presentation is not unilateral nor rigidly fixed. But it provides an approximation of the sequences in hominid evolution.

Evidence of cannibalism has been found on each of these levels, although the practice recedes as the hominids advance toward mature human stature. Beginning with *Australopithecus,* we learn from Raymond Dart:

> Australopithecus lived a grim life. He ruthlessly killed fellow Australopithecines and fed upon them as he would upon any other beast, young or old. He was a flesh eater and as such had to seize his food where he could and protect it night and day from other carnivorous marauders. . . . Life was bought at the price of eternal vigilance. (*Adventures with the Missing Link,* pp. 191, 193)

Java man and Peking man are related to each other, but more data is available on the latter. They lived about 500,000 years ago or, according to Robert J. Braidwood, about 350,000 years ago. The Choukoutien cave dwellers in Peking were tool-makers, fire-makers, hunters of large game—and also cannibals. Braidwood writes:

> Peking man had fire. He probably cooked his meat, or used the fire to keep dangerous animals away from his den. In the cave were bones of dangerous animals, members of the wolf, bear, and cat families. Some of the bones belonged to beasts larger than tigers. There were also

bones of other wild animals: buffalo, camel, deer, elephants,
a horse, sheep, and even ostriches. . . .

Peking man also seems to have eaten plant food. . . .
His tools were made of sandstone and quartz and sometimes of a rather bad flint. . . . There are also many split
pieces of heavy bone. . . .

Now hold your breath! Many of these split bones were
the bones of Peking man himself! . . . There is nothing
like a burial; all of the bones are scattered. . . . It's pretty
clear who the people were. Peking man was a cannibal.
("Prehistoric Men," in *Readings in Anthropology,* p. 35)

William W. Howells says that not only Peking man but also
Solo man, a member of the Java family tree, was cannibalistic
(*Man in the Beginning,* p. 80).

With Neanderthal man we find two significant changes: the
growing practice of burial and the dwindling of the former
full-scale practice of cannibalism. According to Kenneth P.
Oakley:

There is evidence to show that they were sometimes cannibals, with a predilection for human brain; and occasionally these men buried their dead in shallow holes
scraped in the ground or in the floor of their cave, close
to the hearth. (*Man the Tool-Maker,* p. 56)

The decline of cannibalism at this stage is also noted by
Grahame Clark:

Cannibalism certainly continued in Upper Paleolithic times,
although not in so full-blooded a manner as previously.
Partial cannibalism appears to have been linked with head-
hunting. (*From Savagery to Civilization,* pp. 60-61)

By the time we reach *Homo sapiens* and the primitive hunters
in the later period of savagery, cannibalism fades away. In
some regions it has been reduced to a ritualistic custom; in
others it has all but disappeared. Howells says of these hunters:

They are not natural-born killers. Cannibalism is practically unheard of among these hungriest of men (except
for instances of magical nibbling), and the Bushmen will
not even eat the baboon, because he is so like a man.
Head-hunting is also unknown. . . . Nor are such people
merely one step away from apes in their general exis-

tence. . . . human hunters are an aeon away from apes, because they are human and have culture. (*Man in the Beginning,* p. 133)

To MacCulloch, more significant than the existence of cannibalism in the primordial stage of human development was its ultimate conquest by our primitive ancestors. He writes:

> . . . the men of Paleolithic times were cannibalistic. . . . better that it should have begun at a time when there existed no ethical or aesthetic reason to hinder it, and that, with increasing civilization, men should have begun to give it up, than that we should seek its origin at a later age when its commencement would involve the shifting of already formed higher feelings. (*Encyclopedia of Religion and Ethics,* vol. III, p. 194)

However, most of these writers fail to see that ancient men, still possessing many traits in common with animals, were unaware that they killed and ate other humans along with animals. In their own sights they were never man-eaters; they ate only animals. Why was this so?

The Savage Ignorance of Cannibalism

Our definition of cannibalism is based upon scientific knowledge of the distinctions between species, above all the demarcation between ourselves as humans and all other mammalian species. Savages did not have such knowledge. This is especially true of the primordial period which preceded the primitive period. Before hominids had attained their own fully human characteristics, the lines between diverse creatures made of flesh and blood were not at all clear to them.

It may seem incredible that humans at any stage of development could fail to see the essential differences between themselves and animals. But in remote ages men and animals were closely associated; they lived together in the primal forest and their necessities were the same to a large extent. Even at a higher stage of evolution, savages continued to credit animals with an intelligence and capability similar to their own. As Frazer writes:

> This incapacity to distinguish between a man and a beast, difficult as it is for us to realize, is common enough, even

among savages who have not the totemic system. A Bush-
man, questioned by a missionary, "could not state any difference between a man and a brute—he did not know but
a buffalo might shoot with bows and arrows as well as
a man if it had them." When the Russians first landed on
one of the Alaskan Islands the natives took them for cuttle
fish "on account of the buttons on their clothes." (*Totemism
and Exogamy,* vol. I, p. 119)

Unable to draw the dividing line between humans and
animals through biological criteria, our earliest ancestors were
obliged to invent other means for making the distinction. They
did this through their social kinship system. This began as
totem kinship before it evolved into the higher form, the classificatory system of kinship. Those who were of the same kin
were of the same kind, human beings. Outsiders, non-kin,
were members of a different kind, i.e., animals. This kinship
criterion established the boundaries of cannibalism. The lives
of all members of the horde or kin-community were sacred
and inviolable; kinsmen could never kill or eat other kinsmen. They could only kill and eat outsiders or non-kin who
were regarded as animals.

As Leo Frobenius says, to primitive peoples the "other species"
began "at the neighbouring village, so that his neighbours
are for him 'fair game.'" He adds, "When it comes to a question
of capturing a head, then every inhabitant of the neighbouring
village already belongs to 'another species,' and that is true
not only in the matter of head-hunting, but also as regards
cannibalism" (*The Childhood of Man,* p. 476). A similar comment is made by Julius Lippert: "Each tribe regarded its neigh-
bor as a herd of wild animals from which a piece of meat
might be obtained if opportunity presented" (*Evolution of Culture,* p. 89).

This crude notion that kinsfolk alone belonged to the human
species is borne out by the fact that each kin-group called
itself "the people" or "the human beings." R. H. Codrington in
the last century noted that "people discovered in isolation from
others call themselves merely 'men' without a name for their
race or nation, as if they thought themselves the only men in
the world" (*The Melanesians,* p. 21).

A. W. Howitt writes with regard to the Wotjobaluk peoples
of Southeast Australia, "The tribal name is taken from the
word *Wotjo* meaning 'man' and *baluk* meaning 'people,' the

latter word being in its extended form *Wot-jo-ba-laiuruk,* that is 'men' and 'women'" (*The Native Tribes of South-East Australia,* p. 54). Similarly William Graham Sumner writes:

> When Caribs were asked whence they came, they answered, "We alone are people." The meaning of the name Kiowa is "real or principal people." The Lapps call themselves "men," or "human beings." . . . As a rule it is found that nature peoples call themselves "men." Others are something else — perhaps not defined — but not real men. In myths the origin of their own tribe is that of the real human race. They do not account for the others. (*Folkways,* p. 14)

Ruth Benedict comments on the difference "in kind" between the aborigines' view of "my own" closed group and the "outsider":

> All primitive tribes agree in recognizing this category of the outsiders, those who are not only outside the provisions of the moral code which holds within the limits of one's own people, but who are summarily denied a place anywhere in the human scheme. A great number of the tribal names in common use, Zuni, Dene, Kiowa, and the rest, are names by which primitive peoples know themselves, and are only their native terms for "the human beings," that is, themselves. Outside of the closed group there are no human beings. (*Patterns of Culture,* pp. 21-22)

Lippert observes that, when a tribe calls itself "the men" or "the people," "such a name is spoken with a suggestion of pride. Every tiny tribe regards itself as the association of the first men, as the center of the visible world. Round about it lies the wilderness . . . the opposite of 'humanity'" (*Evolution of Culture,* p. 90).

Under these circumstances savages were not cannibalistic according to their comprehension of what constituted human beings. Since kinsmen never killed or ate other kinsmen, this was equivalent to a total taboo on cannibalism. When we speak of cannibalism in the epoch of savagery we must bear in mind this limited conception of humanity which made the men of those days unwitting or innocent cannibals.

Early investigators, coming upon clear evidence of cannibalistic practices, were puzzled by the outraged reactions of aborigines to accusations on this score. Each group vigorously

denied that they were man-eaters or people-eaters. Only those who were "animals" were capable of killing and eating "people."
Spencer and Gillen write:

> As usual, in regard to customs such as this, it is by no means easy to find out exactly what takes place, as the natives of one part of the country will assure you that they do not indulge in the habit, but that they know that those of other parts do. When the accused are questioned, they in turn lay the same charge against their accusers and so on, often from group to group. (*Native Tribes of Central Australia,* p. 475)

A. P. Elkin gives a similar report with regard to the Australian aborigines:

> A more striking manifestation of the tribal sentiment is seen in the attribution of "evil" practices to other tribes, attribution which increases with distance. Thus the cannibals and the savage treacherous natives are always those of the next tribe or the next but one, though when the investigator visits and studies them, he finds them quite as peaceable and courteous as those he just left, but now it is the latter who are credited with savage attributes. (*The Australian Aborigines,* p. 37)

In his visits to tribes in the Americas, George Catlin looked for evidence of cannibalism but could not find it. He tells of an amusing encounter with some Tupinambas of South America who assured him they were not man-eaters. They said they knew some such characters living down the river who were so lost to all human decency as to feed upon "their own kind." According to the native who gave him this information, the cannibals down the river were white men like Catlin:

> "Yes, tell the white man, there are some such persons farther down the river. He will find some white men living in two or three wigwams on the left bank of the river, who eat the flesh of their own relations, and what was worse, they sell their skins!"

Catlin hurried down the river to see these cannibals and describes what he found:

. . . we found these cannibals, several Frenchmen and Americans killing monkeys and sending their skins to Paris for the manufacture of ladies' gloves; and living, as they told us, entirely on the flesh of those poor brutes!

Catlin wrote about the monkey episode, "This was the nearest approach to cannibalism that I have ever discovered in my travels amongst North or South American Indians. Books are full of it, but the wilderness is without it! I have traveled and lived fifteen years amongst Indians, and I have not found it" (*Life Among the Indians,* pp. 280-81).

Cannibalism existed, however, even though savages may have expressed it with an ambiguous term like "man-eater," which is applicable to animals as well as humans. It appears that the term "cannibal" is relatively recent. According to Mac-Culloch it came into existence only after Columbus came to the Caribbean Islands:

The word "cannibal" is derived from *Carib.* When Columbus visited Cuba he heard of the "Canibales" (Caribs) as man-eaters. At Hayti they were called "Caribes". . . . The name of this particular man-eating people was then extended as a popular term for all man-eaters, or for any bloodthirsty race. . . . By the end of the 16th cent. the word was in common use as a generic term. . . . (*Encyclopedia of Religion and Ethics,* vol. III, p. 194)

Only after anthropology was established did some scholars come to understand this contradictory aspect of primitive society, which was founded upon the solidarity of kin-humans but excluded non-kin as being of a different species. As Briffault observes, "The solidarity of the primitive group . . . is applicable to the clan-brotherhood only; beyond the group it has no meaning. Thus it is that in tribal society, not only in its primitive, but also in its advanced stages, we come upon what appear strange contrasts of extreme devotion, self-sacrifice, sympathy, and utter ferocity and callousness" (*The Mothers,* vol. II, p. 492).

E. B. Tylor points out that, in their relations with one another, "*kindred* and *kindness* go together"—two words whose common derivation represents "one of the main principles of social life." He adds, "In the West Indian Islands where Columbus first landed lived tribes who have been called the most gentle and benevolent of the human race" (*Anthropology,* p. 249).

Behind these sharp contrasts are the realities of survival in the period when humankind was emerging from the animal world. The first hominids were obliged to learn everything the hard way; they had no one to teach them. They had to learn how to master a new diet of flesh foods while at the very same time learning to abstain from eating certain animals. These prohibited foods represent the heart of the totem and taboo system, the first social institution created by humankind. What is the nature of this remarkable institution?

Totemism and Taboo

The riddle of totem and taboo preoccupied some of the foremost scholars of the late nineteenth and early twentieth centuries, among them Spencer, Frazer, Lang, Rivers, N. W. Thomas, Thurnwald, Graebner, Gomme, Father Schmidt, van Gennep, Durkheim, Wundt, and Freud. But, although few topics have provoked more heated controversies, in recent years there has been a tendency to downgrade the subject as having little or no value to anthropology. In fact, it is centrally important in uncovering the origin of social life.

Since totemism and its taboos permeated the whole of savage society and passed through a long evolution, it cannot be explained by a single definition. However, a good starting point is its connection with the matrilineal kinship system. In a summary article on the subject, E. Sidney Hartland writes:

> The word "totem" is derived from *ototeman,* which in the Ojibwa and cognate Algonquian dialects means "his brother-sister kin." Its grammatical stem *ote,* meaning the consanguine kinship between uterine brothers and sisters, the group of persons recognized by birth or adoption collectively related together as uterine brothers and sisters who cannot intermarry, is never used alone. The word was introduced into the English language by J. Long in the form of *totam.* (*Encyclopedia of Religion and Ethics,* vol. XII, p. 393)

Counting kinship through the female line, the "sister-brother" kin relationship is also described as "a man's clan" or "his own kin" or "his own flesh" or "his flesh-and-blood kin." All these definitions, however, are usually placed in the context of the taboo on sexual intercourse between the man and woman belonging to the same totem-kin group. This leaves out the taboos surrounding the male occupation of hunting and the numerous prohibitions connected with the eating of certain foods.

Despite this one-sidedness, an excellent beginning was made by the early anthropologists who delved into the subject. J. F. McLennan was the first to call attention to both totemism and exogamy. The great service he rendered, said Frazer, was to raise the right questions although he was unable to answer them correctly. Even Frazer, who undertook one of the most exhaustive studies in his *Totemism and Exogamy,* was unable to penetrate into the innermost core of the phenomenon. But these and other scholars brought forward basic data upon which later investigators could make further inroads into the subject.

It is unfortunate that later anthropologists, turning away from the subject because of its complexities and difficulties, began its systematic liquidation in university circles. Claude Levi-Strauss approves of this effort. He dismisses the subject as "speculations which eventuated in the totemic illusion." He believes that Goldenweiser's derogation of totemism of about 110 pages, published in 1910, will "exercise a more lasting theoretical influence than the 2,200 pages in Frazer's four volumes" of *Totemism and Exogamy.* Levi-Strauss's review of the demolition of totemism as a social reality appears in his book *Totemism* (1962).

Among the liquidators standing with Goldenweiser and Levi-Strauss are Lowie, Kroeber, Boas, and other anti-evolutionists. On the opposite side are evolutionists such as Frazer, Rivers, Durkheim, and Tylor. Totemism is one of the issues marking the deep division between opposing schools of thought.

It is not easy, however, to erase so deep-rooted a phenomenon as totemism from the prehistoric record. Innumerable reports from early travelers, settlers, and anthropologists show that totemic practices and principles survived in virtually every primitive region of the globe from Australia to Africa, from the Americas to Asia, and throughout Oceania. In some places totemism was found in full-blooded form; in others it was in various stages of decay. In civilized Europe the inhabitants had so completely shed their totemic past that they had no notion of its former universality. Nonetheless, crests containing birds and animals, adopted by families and nations, remain as tokens of their totemic past.

Far from being irrelevant or incidental, as Levi-Strauss implies, the study of totemism is indispensable for any investigator of social origins, and the documentation assembled by the pioneer scholars is the starting point for such a study.

The enigmatic character of the totem is lodged in the fact that it appears as an incongruous assortment of unrelated and conflicting phenomena. The totem is usually described as a species of animal, less often of plants, sometimes even as a natural object such as a stone. This is in addition to the definition of the totem as "his own kin" in the female line. There is also a sex-totem representing each of the sexes as well as an individual totem. Further, the totem represents both a man's ancestors and a joint "brotherhood" of men and animals.

Finally, the totem is always taboo. Not only is everything connected with the totem tabooed; the term "totem" itself means "taboo." How can all these disparate elements be analyzed and synthesized? To do this, we must take a closer look at the general problems connected with food and the particular problem connected with cannibalism.

It is curious that while the subject of sex in ancient society has received no little attention, the same cannot be said of the primary requirement for human survival, food. Audrey I. Richards points this out:

> Nutrition as a biological process is more fundamental than sex. In the life of the individual organism it is the more primary and recurrent physical want. . . .
> Yet in current sociological theory man's nutritive needs play a very insignificant role. While discussions on sex are thrust constantly before us, both by the scientist and the man of practical affairs, the proportion of serious attention devoted to nutrition is almost fantastically small. (*Hunger and Work in a Savage Tribe,* p. 1)

In his preface to Richards's book, written in 1932, Bronislaw Malinowski hails her pioneering venture. He writes:

> It is extraordinary what an uneven treatment has been meted out in all studies of mankind to the twin impulses of sex and hunger respectively. . . . We are enjoying now a surfeit of sex — I alone have to plead guilty to four books on the subject. . . .

Common sense tells us that nutrition is an independent impulse, more important, if anything, than sex. And yet what do we know of nutrition as a creative force in human societies and cultures?

In comparative works an accidental, scrappy and unsatisfactory account is given of it; while in the records of field-work we mostly look in vain even for a mention of the manner in which people eat their food, and its influence on social life. . . . (ibid., pp. x-xi)

This neglect is all the more a handicap when we consider the question of cannibalism in the earliest period of human evolution. Survival depended upon making tools and using them to secure food and other necessities. This in turn required the close cooperation of the whole group. All its members had to rely on and have full confidence in one another. Even the slightest possibility that men hunting animals could turn upon other men in the group to kill and eat them would shatter the solidarity of the "primal hordes" in which budding society was organized. Nothing less than an absolute, inviolable food taboo could serve to avert such a disaster, and this was the task of totemism, the earliest social institution.

Frazer ruled out the notion that totemism was a religious institution, an opinion that he had himself held but subsequently corrected. He wrote:

Thus it is a serious, though apparently a common mistake to speak of a totem as a god and to say that it is worshipped by the clan. In pure totemism, such as we find it among the Australian aborigines, the totem is never a god and is never worshipped. . . . The system is thoroughly democratic; it is simply an imaginary brotherhood established on a footing of perfect equality between a group of people on the one side and a group of things (generally a species of animals and plants) on the other side. No doubt it may under favourable circumstances develop into a worship of animals or plants, of the sun or the moon, or the sea or the rivers . . . but such worship is never found amongst the lowest savages, who have totemism in its purest form; it occurs only among peoples who have made a considerable advance in culture . . . a product of the disruption and decay of totemism proper. (*Totemism and Exogamy,* vol. IV, pp. 5-6)

The essence of the totemic taboo was that it eradicated any possibility that a kinsman would hunt, kill, or eat another kinsman. MacCulloch sees this aspect:

> One result of totemism was certainly to make tabu the eating of the animal or plant which was the totem of the group of kinsmen, because, in effect, it was a kinsman. . . . If it is wrong to kill and eat one's totem-animal because it is of kin to one, it is equally wrong to eat a kinsman. . . . The animal kinsman being tabu, not to be killed or eaten, the human kinsman must have been so too. (*Encyclopedia of Religion and Ethics,* vol. III, p. 195)

According to W. Robertson Smith, the concept of the sacred character of human life originated not through any recognition of the distinctiveness of human life as such, but through the totemic taboo which protected all the "kin," both animal and human:

> Early man had certainly no conception of the sacredness of animal life as such, but neither had he any conception of the sacredness of human life as such. The life of his clansman was sacred to him, not because he was a man, but because he was a kinsman; and in like manner, the life of an animal of his totem kind is sacred to the savage, not because it is animate, but because he and it are sprung from the same stock and are cousins to one another. (*The Religion of the Semites,* p. 285)

Once instituted, totemism not only checked cannibalism but produced a broader beneficial effect. It tended to protect animal and plant life in general in a period when unregulated plunder of food supplies could have produced results almost as antisocial as cannibalism. Under temporary taboos nothing could be touched until it had grown to maturity and the taboo had been formally lifted by the elders in authority. Under permanent taboos some animals or plants could not be eaten by those who raised them but had to be reserved for gift-exchange with other groups. Even the eating of permissible foods was tightly organized; certain individuals could eat only a certain portion of an animal while different portions were reserved for others.

Frank B. Jevons observes that it is not by consuming everything in sight but by abstaining from eating certain things at certain times that species are preserved, permitted to grow to maturity, and allowed to multiply. It is not by consuming every ear of corn but by abstaining from doing so that plants are enabled to grow and furnish larger sources of food. The same is true of animals. Jevons says, "The whole species is reverenced, protected and allowed to increase and multiply over the whole area traversed by the tribe." And he adds, "The savage required no teaching in the art of consumption, it is the lesson of abstinence which it is hard for him to learn. That lesson he was incapable of teaching himself, but totemism taught him" (*An Introduction to the History of Religion,* pp. 114-15).

Even after totemism faded away, the protectorate remained as a system of wildlife conservation. J.H. Driberg writes that "some tribes indeed like the Baganda and Keyu say definitely that the system was introduced to give every animal a measure of protection in order that it should not be exterminated by hunters" (*At Home with the Savage,* p. 108). But the crowning achievement of totemism was to save the human hunters themselves from extermination.

Those proto-human groups in which these controls were most effective had a competitive advantage and larger survival coefficient which enabled them to reproduce more successfully over the generations. Thus, contrary to the superficial view of Levi-Strauss, totemism was indispensable in liberating humans from the hazards of primeval existence, enabling them to join together as sisters and brothers in social life and labor. And once the system was established within a horde, totemism could then be extended to alien hordes, bringing them together in fraternal alliances leading to ever larger and stronger tribal communities.

Frazer noted the effectiveness of totemism and taboo in bringing about this social cooperation. He writes:

> If totemism has apparently done little to foster the growth of higher forms of religion, it has probably done much to strengthen the social ties and thereby to serve the cause of civilisation, which depends for its progress on the cordial co-operation of men in society, on their mutual trust and good-will, and on their readiness to subordinate their personal interests to the interests of the community. A society thus united in itself is strong and may survive; a society rent by discord and dissension is weak and likely to perish. . . . The tendency of totemism to knit men to-

gether in social groups is noticed again and again by the writers who have described the institution from personal observation. (*Totemism and Exogamy,* vol. IV, p. 38)

Even after the totemic era had drawn to a close and cannibalism had largely been conquered, the taboo on killing the kinsman remained. A good description is given by George Thomson:

> Throughout the history of tribal society, clan kinship is of all ties the most sacred. The horror excited by homicide within the clan is well described by Groenbech, writing of the primitive Norsemen. . . . "from the moment we enter into the clan, the sacredness of life rises up in absolute inviolability, with its judgment upon bloodshed as sacrilege, blindness, suicide. The reaction comes as suddenly and unmistakably as when a nerve is touched by a needle."
>
> Among the Norsemen, the man who had killed a fellow clansman was cursed and cast out of the clan. He became an outlaw. Unless, as sometimes happened, he was adopted into another clan, he ceased to exist as a member of society. Cut off from the clan, in which alone he had had his being, he went mad and died of starvation. So in Greece. The man who had killed a fellow clansman was hounded out of the community, pursued by the curses of his kinsfolk, or, as they expressed it, by his victim's avenging spirits, the Erinyes or Arai, who drove him mad and sucked his blood until he was nothing but a heap of bones. (*Aeschylus and Athens,* pp. 34-35)

Food Avoidances: Survivals of Cannibalism

Certain food avoidances that have come down to the historic period and even persist to the present have aroused curiosity as to their origin and meaning. According to William Graham Sumner, "Our intense abomination for cannibalism is a food taboo, and is perhaps the strongest taboo which we have inherited" (*Folkways,* p. 329). Apart from human flesh, however, there are many animals, birds, and fishes whose flesh is abhorred by peoples in various parts of the world. At least some of these must also be survivals of the ancient totemic taboos. Sumner cites this list:

. . . a Phoenician or an Egyptian would sooner eat man's flesh than cow's flesh. A Jew would not eat swine's flesh. A Zoroastrian could not conceive it possible that any one could eat dog's flesh. . . . The Banziris, in the French Congo, reserved dog's flesh for men, and they surround meals of it with a solemn ritual. . . . The inhabitants of Ponape will eat no eels, which "they hold in the greatest horror." . . . Dyaks eat snakes, but reject eels. . . . South African Bantus abominate fish. Some Canary Islanders ate no fish. Tasmanians would rather starve than eat fish. The Somali will eat no fish. . . . They also reject game and birds. . . . Some Micronesians eat no fowl. . . . Tuaregs eat no fish, birds, or eggs. (*Folkways,* p. 339)

Frederick J. Simoons examines food avoidances in the Old World in his book *Eat Not This Flesh* (1961). He observes that animal, not plant, foods are the usual object of disgust and revulsion. Among the most frequently avoided foods are pork, beef, chicken flesh and eggs, horse flesh, dog flesh, and camel flesh. He sees a connection between these food avoidances and the ancient totemic taboos:

> The totemic relationship, which may exist between an animal and a group, whether tribe, clan, lineage, or other unit, is commonly said to have arisen because in the past the animal helped the group in some way. The observances connected with the totemic animal take a great variety of forms, but usually the group shows honor and affection for the totem and places restrictions on killing it. (p. 118)

As the practice of cannibalism receded, it left a survival in the form of blood-drinking rituals that brought alien men together in fraternal relations. Men formed a blood covenant by opening their veins and drinking a little of each other's blood. This was a pledge that they would not kill or injure one another. As Lippert remarks, "The survival to which cannibalism most frequently shrivels is the drinking of blood" (*Evolution of Culture,* p. 428).

Gradually the poured blood was diluted with other drinks, such as red wine where this was a common beverage. In the end, blood-drinking was entirely eliminated, and the drinking of wine or other beverages became the pledge of friendship. This symbolic act is observed to the present day when people drinking wine or liquor raise their glasses and clink them together. This is called a toast or "drinking to one's health."

Tylor remarks on this "very absurd, though universal custom of drinking people's health. Can there be anything in the world less relative to any other man's health, than my drinking a glass of wine?" (*The Origins of Culture,* p. 95). Ancient history provides the answer. To drink one another's health with wine is a vast departure from the practice of eating the flesh and drinking the blood of humans under the erroneous notion that, because they were not kin, they were not people. From this standpoint drinking toasts is not absurd; it is a tribute to the human victory over cannibalism.

*   *   *

The theory of cannibalism illuminates one clause of the taboo, the food clause. However, it was a twofold prohibition covering sex as well as food. As Frazer spells out this combination:

> Corresponding to the two sides of the system are two rough-and-ready tests or canons of Totemism; first, the rule that a man may not kill or eat his totem animal or plant; and second, the rule that he may not marry or cohabit with a woman of the same totem. (*Totemism and Exogamy,* vol. I, p. 101)

To explain this puzzling duality of the totemic taboo we must see its inseparable connection with the specialization and divergences of female and male in the transition from primate to human.

3
Female Biology
and the Double Taboo

Since the system of totemism and taboo represents the earliest social regulator of human needs, the question arises: Who instituted it and by what means? Did males place upon themselves the prohibitions on killing and eating certain animals and mating with certain women? Or did females create the institution to protect themselves and their offspring? These questions take us into the thorny thicket of the biological differences between the sexes to determine which sex was by nature equipped to take the lead in founding this social institution.

Humans arose out of a branch of the higher apes that had developed certain biological organs and functions preadapted for social life. Primary among these are the flexible hand, which led to tool-using and tool-making, the enlarged brain, upright posture, stereoscopic vision, and vocal organs that made speech possible. As William W. Howells describes the human, "In body and brain he is simply a made-over ape with no fundamental distinctions at all; his organization and all his parts go back, lock, stock, and barrel, to the anthropoids, and beyond them to those earlier ancestors in whom those parts first appeared" (*Mankind So Far,* p. 2).

However, while both sexes possess all the above bodily features, another biological requirement for mammalian and human existence was possessed by the female sex alone: the organs and functions of motherhood. Despite their fundamental importance in perpetuating the species, attention is rarely given to woman and her biology in the development of social life and labor. The transition from ape to human is almost always labeled as the ascent of "man" or "mankind" out of the

primates. This omission is due in part to serious misinterpretations of animal life and behavior.

Since men hold the dominant place in all spheres of modern
social and cultural life, while women have been reduced to a
narrow, dependent life in home and family, a false proposition
has been set forth to account for this. Woman's social inferiority
is attributed to her faulty biology. Childbearing is represented
as the eternal handicap of the female and the source of her
status as the second sex.

To buttress this, a corollary myth is circulated. Reference
is made to the "dominant male" in the animal world as evidence
of the eternal superiority of the male sex. Males have always
held power over females, it is said, because they are physically
stronger, more aggressive, better fighters, and more intelligent
than females. This misrepresents the biological differences between the sexes.

It is undeniable that our society has taken advantage of woman's capacity to bear children to place serious obstacles in the
path of her development. But childbearing as a "disability" is
relatively recent and exclusively social. It did not exist in primitive society and does not exist among animals. Woman's subordination is thus not the result of a predetermined biological
handicap.

In reality the opposite is the case. A careful study of animal
life and behavior shows that it is not the female animal but the
male animal that suffers from a biological liability. This stems
from the violent characteristics of male sexuality in nature,
propelling males to strive for "dominance" over other males
and limiting their ability to cooperate with one another. Females, on the other hand, far from being handicapped by
their maternal functions, acquired from them the very traits
conducive to advancing from animality to human life and
cooperative labor. Insofar as the sexes were unequally endowed
by nature, the biological advantages for humanizing the species
were on the side of the females, not the males.

To demonstrate this, let us examine the biology first of females and then of males.

The Female Sex and Mother-Care

In *The Mothers* Robert Briffault showed how mother-care in
the animal world laid the groundwork for a broader and
higher development in the human world that can be called

"social care," the mutual concern of all members of the horde or clan for one another's welfare and security. To put it in other terms, the nurturing instincts of the females enabled them to lead the way in the modification of animal impulses and to gradually replace them with socialized behavior.

Animal behavior, fashioned by nature's mode of survival, is preponderantly individualistic and competitive. Since there is not enough food to sustain all the organisms reproduced, each individual organism struggles against the others for its own survival. As Darwin pointed out, this is true not only between different species; the struggle is even more intense among members of the same species, which have similar needs and rely on the same territory to provide them with food and mates.

Food competition varies, depending upon the type and abundance of the supplies. Herbivorous animals can tolerate one another in the same tracts and associate together in herds. Carnivores, on the other hand, are more wary and solitary. They not only prey upon other animals but are themselves in danger of being killed and eaten by one another. These animals do not form herds and even their smaller packs, where these exist, are loose and easily dispersed.

Whether the competition is more or less intense, each adult animal forages for its own food and provides for itself without regard to the needs of others. With the exception of the provision made by the female for her offspring there is no cooperation among animals in getting or sharing food. Wolves and wild dogs, which are sometimes held up as examples of cooperation because they often form packs, are "conspicuously individualistic and selfish" according to the authorities cited by Briffault. While they may engage in concerted action to bring down large prey, they fight furiously among themselves over the spoils, and the strong ones are "ever ready to kill the weaker ones and eat them." As soon as the food is secured they scatter in different directions (*The Mothers,* abr. ed., pp. 1-2).

Even among primates, cooperation is virtually nonexistent. As Marshall Sahlins observes, "Monkeys and apes do not cooperate economically; monkeys cannot even be taught by humans to work together, although apes can. Nor is food ever shared except in the sense that a subordinate animal may be intimidated into handing it over to a dominant one" ("The Origin of Society," *Scientific American,* vol. 203, no. 3, p. 86).

On the same point Solly Zuckerman writes:

In their behaviour at feeding times, monkeys and apes
display the most conspicuous selfishness. With few exceptions, every monkey or ape living in captivity tries to obtain as much for itself and to take as much as it can from
its fellows. . . . It is a common experience that when food
is passed into a cage of monkeys, the more dominant
members come forward to accept it, pushing aside their
weaker fellows, who may have preceded them. (*The Social
Life of Monkeys and Apes,* p. 295)

Thus, apart from the maternal brood, individualism and
competition represent the general rule of behavior in the animal world. As Briffault sums this up:

Every society is characterized by some form of division
of labour and of cooperation. The various needs of each
individual, male and female, are provided for not by his
or her exertions alone, but, directly or indirectly, by the
joint action of various other individuals whose behaviour
is more or less coordinated. Except as regards the care
of their brood by females, those conditions do not exist
anywhere in the animal kingdom outside humanity. Every
adult animal, male or female, fends for itself so far as
regards its economic needs. Even among primates no instance is known of one individual adult being dependent
upon another for the means of subsistence. There is no
known instance of cooperation and coordination in procuring food. (*The Mothers,* abr. ed., p. 1)

However, while male animals have only themselves to consider, the females also have to provide for their offspring.
This exception to individualism became the starting point for
the modification of animal traits and the development of new
habits required for socializing the species.

The highly developed mother-care of the primates is the
end product of tens of millions of years of slow and precarious
development. In the lowest species such care is nonexistent.
Among some fishes nature is exceedingly wasteful in its reproductive processes; a female may spawn millions of eggs and
thereafter do little or nothing to provide for them or protect
them from an egg-hungry world. V. Gordon Childe points
out that some fish species maintain the numbers required for
survival only through "a prodigious fecundity." A pair of cod
produces 6 million eggs, a pair of ling as many as 28 mil-

lion eggs. The sea is not a mass of ling because only two or three eggs hatch and come to maturity with each batch. Most are eaten (*Man Makes Himself,* p. 17).

Reptiles stand higher than fish in the evolutionary scale. Yet here too, according to Briffault, "out of some 2,600 existing species of reptiles not half a dozen — one or two crocodiles and a couple of snakes — devote any attention to their young, either before or after hatching." Even among birds, which are often upheld as models of parental care, such care is ephemeral. As soon as the nestlings become self-sufficient, they are driven away as though they were strangers and foes (*The Mothers,* vol. I, p. 113).

Mother-care really begins with the mammal. It is least developed among the herbivores, where the offspring mature rapidly and require care for only a short time. A higher degree of maternal function is found among the carnivores, where the cubs have a more protracted period of helpless infancy. The peak of such care is reached with the primate species and is far more developed among the higher apes than among the monkeys. The baby gibbon, according to F. Wood Jones, clings to its mother for about seven months, and the young orangutan is dependent upon mother-care for about two years (*Arboreal Man,* p. 186).

The basic factors in the rise of mother-care are a reduction in the number of young born at one time and a prolonged period of dependency of the infant. With the protraction of infancy and maternal care there grows a tendency toward relying less on instinct and learning more from experience. Filial responses to the other members of the brood also occur, and these help set the stage for the rise of group-conditioned behavior.

In the maternal broods of the carnivores, the cubs and kittens display attachment to one another and to their mother during their early period of growth. These attachments, along with a far higher development of mental capacities, reach their peak with the primates. As Briffault puts it:

> "Monkey-love," "Affenliebe," is a common expression in German for doting maternal fondness, and pages could be filled with descriptions of its manifestations. The tense and watchful anxiety of the mother monkey, and the pathetic gravity with which she will sit for hours contemplating her offspring, have often been noted. Baboon mothers take their young to a stream to wash them, and Rengger watched

a Cebus carefully driving away the flies which plagued its infant. "So intense is the grief of female monkeys for the loss of their young that it invariably caused the death of certain kinds kept under confinement by Brehm in North Africa." (*The Mothers,* vol. I, p. 115)

The essence of socializing the animal is to break the absolute dictation of nature and replace purely animal instincts with conditioned responses and learned behavior. Humans today have shed their original animal instincts to such a degree that most have vanished. A child, for example, must be taught the dangers of fire, which animals flee instinctively. According to Ralph Linton, these "unlearned reactions" have now been reduced to "such things as the digestive processes, adaptation of the eye to light intensity and similar involuntary responses." He adds:

> The fewer instincts a species possesses, the greater the range of behaviors it can develop, and this fact, coupled with the enormous capacity for learning which characterizes humans, has resulted in a richness and variety of learned behavior which is completely without parallel in other species. (*The Tree of Culture,* p. 8)

Although both sexes were equally endowed with the hand, brain, and other anatomical preconditions required for human activity, it was the female that led the way over the bridge from animality to humanity. The mothers alone were equipped with the maternal and affective responses that were extended into the human world in the form of social collaboration.

Some scholars see a connection between the emergence of the first humans and the advent of the great Ice Age, both occurring about a million years ago. Gordon Childe describes this change in the environment as so drastic that many species perished while new species came into existence better adapted to the harsher conditions of life. At this juncture, he says, there emerged the first humans, so radically different from humans today that they are called "hominids, 'men-like creatures'" (*What Happened in History,* p. 29).

William W. Howells likewise writes, "It is extraordinary that the sudden, severe Age of Ice, a mere pinpoint in time, should have coincided with the very period, also short, when man at last was rapidly becoming what he is today" (*Mankind So Far,*

p. 113). This is probably more than mere coincidence. After a very long period of favorable climate, the severe conditions drove our female ancestral anthropoids into more determined efforts to survive through new methods. They began to use and make tools. In so doing they changed from nature's mode of survival on an individualistic, competitive basis to the new and human mode of survival through social cooperation in productive labor.

With only a slight correction in the name of the sex, we can agree with Sherwood L. Washburn that:

> Man began when populations of apes, about a million years ago, started the bipedal, tool-using way of life that gave rise to the man-apes of the genus *Australopithecus*. Most of the obvious differences that distinguish man from ape came after the use of tools. ("Tools and Human Evolution," *Scientific American,* vol. 203, no. 3, p. 63)

Before humans could domesticate animals they first had to domesticate themselves. As Howells puts it, "In domesticating animals we feed them regularly (or else lead them to food), protect them against natural enemies, and oversee their breeding, and we began by doing this for ourselves first of all" (*Mankind So Far,* pp. 126-27). All we need add is that the mothers, through their role in maternal care, started the process of domestication that led to socialization and culture. "It is in the maternal, not in the sexual, association," says Briffault, "that the growth of the so-called 'social instinct' takes place" (*The Mothers,* vol. I, p. 188).

This is confirmed from the other side when we turn from the female sex and its functions to the male sex and its striving for dominance.

The "Dominant Male" — Fact and Fiction

The phenomenon called the "dominant male" exists in the animal world; it is the product of the individualistic and competitive character of male sexuality. Each male competes with other males for sexual access to the female or females in his vicinity. This makes males the combative sex, fighting one another not only for females but also to secure the dominant place in the tract or territory occupied by the females.

The most naked expression of what is sometimes called "jungle law" is this unmodified male animal behavior. The antagonism and strife of male animals is an antisocial force which prevents them from banding together in cooperative groups for mutual provision and protection.

Male combats are often ascribed to "jealousy," although it is not jealously in our sense of the term, which implies a desire for a particular female. Such selective individual preference is exclusively a feature of human culture and does not exist among animals. In nature's wasteful mode of propagating the species, males have few functions other than serving as studs. The combats that occur among male animals are not for any particular female but for access to females in general, and to as many as possible during the rutting season. Briffault writes:

> The struggles and contests of male animals are not for possession of particular females, but for access to females in general; they commonly take place in the absence of all females. Male animals fight for the opportunity of reproduction as they fight for food; to speak of that competition as 'jealousy' is as appropriate as it would be to describe their desire for food as 'love.' When in possession of a female they may fight for retention of that possession, as a dog fights to retain possession of a bone; they may fight also to gain access to as many females as possible. (*The Mothers,* vol. I, p. 182)

Zuckerman observes:

> The pugnacity of rutting animals is an expression of their physiological condition and is not necessarily determined by the presence of females. . . . Stags have been observed fighting during the mating season in the total absence of females, while bull seals fight each other not for females, but for territory in the rookery or mating ground. (*Social Life of Monkeys and Apes,* p. 69)

Many of the physical features developed by males, such as exaggerated canine teeth, claws or horns, larger muscles, more vivid plumage in birds, are the result of the competitive struggle between males to attract females. According to Alexander Wetmore, among the special weapons developed by birds are "the spurs of male gallinaceous birds, the sharp claws of coots, the knob-like projections on the wings of geese." It is generally the male, he says, who "at the approach of the nesting season selects some tract" and "defends it against encroachments from other males of his kind. . . . These battles often lead to the serious injury or even the death of one of the contestants. Feathers fly and blood is drawn, and the struggle may be prolonged until both birds are exhausted. . . ." He gives this illustration of combativeness even in the absence of females:

> Sometimes the seasonal antipathy of male for male becomes ridiculous and may even lead to the injury of the bird, as when a robin or cardinal becomes obsessed with fury at his own reflection in a window-pane, and returns day after day to struggle futilely with a phantom antagonist against which he beats and struggles until he falls exhausted. This shadow fighting sometimes becomes so aggravating that the householder is forced to screen his window. (*Warm-Blooded Vertebrates,* Smithsonian Scientific Series, vol. IX, pp. 68-70)

This easily triggered combativeness is commercially exploited by men today in the form of cock fights. Such exploitation is not possible with hens but only with cocks, condemned as they are by nature to strut about and fight other members of their own sex. Since this combativeness is present in mammalian males also, it represented a biological handicap at the beginning of human life.

Investigators concerned with the question of social origins have emphasized the numerous hazards that confronted the early hominids. They had to cope with a hostile environment and win mastery over the larger and fiercer beasts. It is seldom pointed out, however, that early man also had to win mastery over his own animal impulses and convert them into a new humanized nature. In particular, males were obliged to conquer their own easily aroused animosity against other males of their own species and learn to cooperate with one another. The combativeness associated with male sexuality had to be overcome and replaced by fraternal and social relations.

Against this reality, many writers translate the "dominant male" of the animal world into modern terms and see him as a patriarchal sultan, served by a harem of submissive females. Sometimes he is portrayed less flamboyantly as the father of a family, standing at the head of a wife and children, controlling their lives and destiny. In both instances the females are pictured as weak, helpless, and dependent upon a male for the support of themselves and their offspring.

This is a flight of fancy appropriate to science fiction but not to science. One of the most explicit purveyors of such fiction is Robert Ardrey, author of *African Genesis* (1961). Since his views are a clearcut expression of this whole school of writers, he furnishes a good example of how they distort biology.

To Ardrey, the dominant male is the "overlord" of his wife. Females preen and flutter around him, each hoping for the honor of his sexual attention. These male animals are rated by the females according to the amount of territorial "property" they possess; the hero who owns the most property is the most sexually desirable. When an insignificant female wins out in the competitive scramble for husbands, she is portrayed as honored beyond her desserts. He writes about one jackdaw female: "All in a happy hour the scrubby little female had become the President's wife" (p. 93).

Ardrey implies by such distortions that, just as women in class society have to compete with one another for husbands of wealth and rank, the same is true of animal females; they, too, struggle against one another for sexual access to males. This is a falsification of animal sexual behavior, where competition is peculiar to the male sex.

Crudities of this type are not usually present in the works of more serious biologists although they, too, are prone to glorify the "aggressive" traits of males over what they call the "passive" characteristics of the females. But when they refer to a "pecking order" among some birds or animals, this is only another way of describing the competitive male and his striving for dominance. Although the stronger males are ever ready to fight and drive the weaker ones out of the vicinity, if the weaker ones submit to the dominant males they can be tolerated and remain in the same area.

So far as the females are concerned, no male, including the dominant male, can control their lives and sexual activities. When a female is not in heat she avoids males and they do not approach her without receiving a sexual signal from her. When she is in heat she takes a male or males as she sees fit. She is not forced to restrict herself to any particular male.

Ardrey is obliged to recognize this fact, and he even gives an example. After portraying the male ape as an "overlord" dominating his "wife," he cites from a study of baboons:

Bolwig observed a female on one spectacular occasion copulate thirty times in one hour with six different males, then disappear into the bush with the youngest of the six. Her overlord had taken his turns but had otherwise watched unmoved. He apparently considered the gay proceeding no challenge to his dominance. We shall encounter the same indifference in heavily-dominant mountain gorillas. (*African Genesis,* p. 99)

What he calls "indifference" is more accurately the inability of male animals to dominate females in the wild, a refutation of his "overlord" thesis. Sahlins writes of the New World monkeys that when a female is in heat "she does not become attached to a specific male, but, wearing them out in turn, goes from one to another" (*Scientific American,* vol. 203, no. 3, p. 81).

The essence of male sexual dominance in our society, which is founded upon the father-family, is the husband's exclusive possession of his wife who, by law, must restrict her sexual activities to him alone. Serious penalties are imposed on a wife who violates this legal injunction with even one other man. The sexual freedom of female apes and other animals who mate at their own will and with any number of males they choose testifies that, in nature, males do not dominate females. Male domination is expressed only in relation to other males.

Nor are animal females rendered helpless and dependent upon a male for their sustenance because of their procreative functions. In some bird species the males participate with the females in hatching the eggs and feeding the young. This is not because of the helplessness of the females but because male sexuality is temporarily suppressed at those times and such male "maternal" assistance becomes possible. However, the transference of some maternal functions to males in some species does not demonstrate any disabilities in females at times of giving birth. In the great majority of species they perform their maternal functions without any assistance from males.

The animal "family" is no more than a maternal brood, with the mother alone providing for herself and her offspring. Even among monkeys and apes, adult males do not provide food for females and juveniles. This is true of mammals in general. There is no "father-family" in the animal world; males do not provide for a pregnant female or for her offspring.

The contrary is the case. It is a general habit among mammals for the female to separate herself from all males, including the dominant male, when she reaches advanced pregnancy, and to remain segregated throughout the period of giving birth and nursing her offspring. During this retreat the female is entirely capable of providing for her own needs as well as the needs of her young.

This segregation is one of the most pronounced features of animal life. Among chimpanzees, according to Yerkes, "when the females have retired to bring forth young or when they are engaged with their newly born progeny," the precincts they occupy are left entirely to them and no male ventures near them (*The Great Apes,* p. 271). Even Ardrey is impressed by this fact, for he writes:

> It is standard behaviour among baboons that when a pregnant female's time arrives, she seeks and receives complete privacy. I cannot think of an observation of baboon childbirth ever recorded in the wild; success at achieving privacy is that complete. (*African Genesis,* p.100)

All female mammals, not simply primates, seek seclusion at the time of giving birth and caring for the offspring. The mother provides for herself during these periods, as she does throughout her life generally, without assistance from any male. If food is occasionally brought near the lair of a female by a male, this is episodic and incidental; it does not alter the self-reliance of the female. As Briffault describes this maternal brood:

> The animal family is the product of the maternal instincts and of those alone; the mother is the sole centre and bond of it. The sexual instincts which bring the male and the female together have no part in the formation of the group. . . . The male has no share in forming the animal family; he is not an essential member of it; he may join that maternal group, but commonly does not do so. When he attaches himself to the animal family his association with it is loose and precarious. . . . There is no division of labour between the sexes in procuring the means of subsistence. The protective functions are exercised by the female and not by the male. (*The Mothers,* vol. I, pp. 188-89)

Those who attempt to portray animal life and behavior in patriarchal terms not only become involved in contradictions but often produce absurdities. This is the case with Ardrey and his lion pride. He portrays the solitary male attached to the group of females and cubs as their lord and master, upon whom they are dependent for their sustenance. He writes, "A lion pride is a hunting unit, and this would seem to be the sole reason for its existence. And it is the extraordinary dominance of the male lion, and little else, that welds the society together" (*African Genesis*, p. 101).

What Ardrey calls a "lion pride" is actually a pack of lionesses who have permitted a male access to their group. On his own, the male lion hunts and kills his own food, but when he is attached to a group of females they are in charge of the hunt. As Ardrey puts it, "The male lion rarely makes the kill. Such entertainments he leaves to the lioness. His normal position in a hunting pride is in the centre with lionesses spread out on either flank considerably in advance " (ibid.).

If, as Ardrey says, the "sole reason" for the lion pride is hunting and providing food, the male is not an indispensable member since he does neither. The females are the huntresses, providing food for themselves and their cubs and even feeding the male they have permitted in their group. Contrary to Ardrey's opinion, the pride of lionesses is welded together not by the "extraordinary dominance" of the male but by the maternal functions of the females.

Ardrey may wish to glorify the image of the solitary male hero who might otherwise cut an ignominious figure, surrounded as he is — and controlled — by a formidable pack of lionesses. But for all his handsome mane and noble mein, King Lion is not the master of a harem of lionesses; he is no more than a stud for their convenience in the mating season. He remains with the group only as long as they wish and during his good behavior. At any time he can be replaced by a younger and stronger "dominant male" who succeeds in usurping his place — or the pack of females may desert him and go off on their own.

Thus male dominance in the animal world, far from being a mark of superiority, is a serious liability. Unable to join together in mutual cooperation and protection, males are the expendable sex. In the competitive struggle of males to win a place in the female group only a few can achieve this objective. The others are condemned to wander about as "loners" attempting from time to time to find a place in a group. Many die off or are killed in competitive struggles.

Even Ardrey, who is so enamoured of this masculine trait of dominance, is struck by the losses it brings about in the males of a species, not simply in the wild but also on reservations. He writes:

> The appalling death rate of juvenile lions, for example, as recorded in the Kruger reserve, can scarcely be regarded as in the long-run interests of natural selection or in the short-run interests of the pride. Yet the death-rate results from the conflict of juvenile appetites with the rigorous dominance of their elders. (ibid., p. 103)

Here, then, is the reality of the phenomenon called the "dominant male" in nature. He is not, as frequently portrayed, a self-satisfied patriarch dominating wife and family. At best he is a tolerated member of a female group; at worst he is an outcast relegated to a solitary life. Far from being the superior or ruling sex, as men are in our society, animal males are the secondary sex, the incidental sex, and, where they are too numerous, the expendable sex.

Another fallacy about animal behavior is the popular notion that sexual attraction involves love or affection. The fusion of love with sexual desire is a human acquisition that does not exist among animals. As Briffault explains, tender sentiments, the rudiments of love, exist only in the maternal brood (*The Mothers,* vol. I, p. 131). These maternal and filial sentiments were eventually extended in the human world to sexual partners, producing sex-love. But with animals sex is no more than a raw hunger.

Briffault comments on the brutal character of the sex drive in the animal world, "It would be more accurate to speak of the sexual impulse as pervading nature with a yell of cruelty than with a hymn of love" (*The Mothers,* vol. I, pp. 119-20). His description of animal "love-making" is instructive:

> The male animal captures, mauls and bites the female, who in turn uses her teeth and claws freely, and the "lovers" issue from the sexual combat bleeding and mangled. Crustaceans usually lose a limb or two in the encounter. All mammals without exception use their teeth on these occasions. Pallas describes the mating of camels; as soon as

impregnation has taken place, the female, with a vicious snarl, turns round and attacks the male with her teeth, and the latter is driven away in terror. Rengger remarks that the sexual union of a pair of jaguars must be a formidable conflict, for he found the forest devastated and strewn with broken branches over an area of a hundred feet where the fierce "love-making" had taken place. (ibid., p. 119)

The sex urge, as Briffault says, can be "as cruel as hunger." And among the carnivorous animals the distinction between the two forms of hunger is frequently effaced. He writes:

All carnivorous animals and rodents are cannibalistic. Lions and tigers, which furnish favourite examples of mating among carnivora, commonly kill and devour their mates. Andersson describes how a lion, having quarrelled with a lioness over the carcass of a springbok, "after killing his wife, had cooly eaten her also," and the same thing has been reported by other observers. A female leopard which had been wounded, but had got away, was found a few days later with her hind-quarters half eaten by her mate. Half-grown tiger cubs, orphaned by their mother being killed, are attacked and eaten by their father. . . . Wolves commonly kill and eat their mates. (ibid., pp. 118-19)

Such incidents also occur in captivity. In the Griffith Park Zoo of Los Angeles, a polar bear who had killed two previous mates killed his third mate even though "they had shared the same grotto for the past eleven years without trouble," according to the *Los Angeles Times* of April 26, 1963. An Associated Press dispatch of August 9, 1967, likewise reported that "a female lion named Norma died of a broken neck at the Portland Zoo after her mate, Caesar, grabbed her with his jaws and 'shook her like a rag doll,' zoo officials said."

Despite the fact that animals in captivity are regularly fed and cared for, which tames them to a certain degree, zoo officials have learned to recognize the danger of allowing the sexes to associate. Briffault gives the following illustration:

A jaguar in the Zoological Gardens at New York, to whom it was desired to give a female companion, showed every sign of delight and of extreme fondness for her while she was safely kept in an adjacent cage in order to habituate the animals to one another's company; the male jaguar purred, licked the female's paws, and behaved like the most love-sick admirer. When at last the partition between the cages was removed and the male was united with the object of his affection, his first act was to seize her by the throat and kill her. The same thing happened when a female was introduced to a grizzly bear. (ibid., pp. 118-19)

"The circumspection which is exhibited by many animal females in yielding to the male," says Briffault, "the haste which is shown by most to separate as soon as impregnation has taken place, would appear to be due in a large measure to the danger attending such relations rather than to 'coyness'" (p. 120).

The same factors that operate against the development of tenderness between the sexes also prevent the formation of the father-family in the animal world. As Briffault demonstrates, the two sexes are specialized for different functions: the male for sex and the female for maternity. This specialization was eventually overcome in the human world with the extension of maternal care functions to males. But in the animal world there is a basic antagonism between sex and maternity because of the violence of male sexuality.

Not only among the carnivores but also with the herbivores the segregation of the sexes rather than their permanent union into pairs is the rule. In most species they meet only for sexual congress in the mating season, after which they separate. Where cohabitation occurs it is for a brief period only, during the rutting season. This is true of herding animals, such as antelope, reindeer, and buffalo, where females form into separate herds from males after the breeding season. It is true of the more solitary carnivores as well as the higher apes and monkeys. Briffault gives the following illustrations:

Among bats the sexes live entirely separate; the males are driven off after sexual congress, and no male is ever found in a band of females. Elephant cows, after they have been impregnated, likewise form bands from which males are driven off; the cow, which carries for nearly two years, does not receive the male until eight or twelve months after calving. . . . The young males remain with their dams only until they are full-grown. . . . Seals and walruses separate into male and female herds after the breeding season. . . . The wild boar consorts with the female at the breeding season only. . . . With the orang-utan the sexes never live together. In bands of gorillas the sexes keep separate, the females and young forming one group, the males keeping to themselves. . . .

. . . Bears do not cohabit after sexual congress. . . . The jaguar cohabits with the female during one month of the year only; and the cougar during a few weeks. The leopard male and female live entirely separate. (ibid., pp. 123-24)

A closer examination of this widespread segregation of the sexes in nature shows it to be perhaps the most effective of the various safeguards developed by the female sex to carry out her primary function, maternity.

Nature's Safeguards for Females

It is misleading to picture the sexual life of animals in terms of human sexuality. Like everything else in nature and society, sex has undergone an evolution. Aeons ago the sexual form of reproduction did not yet exist. After it came into existence it went through many modifications until it attained its higher forms. The most drastic change in the evolution of sex came about in the human world when it became fused with sentiments of tenderness and love, and took on a new dimension apart from its procreative function.

Today the sexual natures of human males and females are essentially different from animals. Men are not governed by their sexual drive alone, nor are they mere studs for impregnating females. They do not normally become violent through the operation of the sex impulse as animals do. Where violence occurs in the human world it is exclusively due to serious social dislocations and psychological mutilations, and these pathological compulsions are by and large a relatively recent phenomenon. In any case the behavior of men is the product of social and cultural developments, not blind instincts.

An evolution of a different type has taken place in female sexuality. In the animal world female sex need is directly tied to her procreative functions and does not assert itself apart from these functions. Women today are liberated from this restricted form of sexuality. Although sex is still required for procreation, the sexual desires of human females have a broader range, independent of their connection with the bearing of offspring. Thus in considering the sexual life of animals we must bear in mind the different characteristics of sexuality in nature, where each sex is rigidly specialized, the one as stud, the other as procreatrix.

Among mammals, once a female has entered her maternal cycle, sexual desire ceases and she manifests an aversion to the male sex. This is the period when she retreats from the orbit of males to give birth and tend her offspring. The more protracted the helpless infancy of the young, the longer is the period of segregation of the female from the male. This is the case with the primates, where a greater disparity exists between maternal functions and female sexuality than exists in the lower species.

A study by Phyllis C. Jay shows this disproportion between sex needs and maternal functions in most primate females. "Her primary focus . . . is motherhood," she writes.

> She raises one infant after another from the time she assumes adult roles at the age of about three to four years, until the time she dies. In other words, more than two-thirds of her life, and probably much more, is spent nurturing and protecting her infants. . . .
>
> Sexual behavior actually plays a very small part in the life of an adult female. A female is sexually receptive only when she is in estrus. This lasts from five to seven days a month when she is not pregnant or lactating. . . . This is in contrast to the human female, who is continually sexually receptive. . . . Births in many species such as langurs in India are spaced at approximately two-year intervals. In these species a female is sexually receptive on less than approximately 5 per cent of the days in her adult life, and in reality is sexually active on less than 3 per cent. If we were able to figure out exactly the number of hours during which she was sexually active, it would be far less than 1 per cent. ("The Female Primate," in *The Potential of Woman,* pp. 3-6)

This characteristic of female sexuality among primates is often overlooked because on those days when she is sexually active she is exceedingly vigorous and can wear out a number of males. "During estrus," says C. R. Carpenter, "a female's capacity for copulation greatly exceeds that of any one male" ("Societies of Monkeys and Apes," in *Primate Social Behavior,* pp. 44-45). The same point has been stressed by other observers. However, this intensity during estrus does not alter the fact that female sexuality among primates is exceedingly underdeveloped compared to their maternal functions, to which they devote the greatest portion of their lives.

The estrus period, which is exclusive to the animal world, represents one of nature's safeguards for females. Unlike humans who can mate all year round, animals restrict their mating to the rutting or estrus season. In most species the male sexual drive is roughly adjusted to female sexual receptiveness. According to Zuckerman:

> This seasonal alternation from sexual to completely asexual behaviour is outside the range of human experience. It is as if an animal were periodically castrated and then, after an interval, subjected to the operation of implanting a functional gonad. (*Social Life of Monkeys and Apes,* p. 63)

Thus the non-estrus season is a period of quiescence for both sexes, and during these periods the female can pursue her maternal functions without being pursued by the male. Only when the female is in heat again does she give the sexual "signal" which inaugurates a new estrus season for the species.

Another safeguard for females is that male animals do not normally attempt to mount an unreceptive female. As Phyllis Jay says of the primate female, "She is the sole initiator of sexual activity, and she is not mounted unless she solicits the attention of the male" (*Potential of Woman,* p. 5). The same point is made by Carpenter, who says that the female is the "initiator" of sexual responses, with the male reacting to the female's needs.

This means that rape does not exist among animals in nature. Males do not attempt to mount immature or unreceptive females. According to Zuckerman, there can be no serious doubt that rape is exclusively a human practice. He writes:

> It is well known that potent males react differently to oestrus and anoestrus females. The bitch in heat is a magnet for all dogs in her neighborhood. Rams wander in and out of a flock of ewes, stopping to mate only with those in

heat. . . . Every female laboratory animal except apparently the rabbit, allows the male to mount and copulate only
when she is in oestrus. The only non-laboratory animals
which are said to copulate outside oestrus are the llama
and the camel. (*Social Life of Monkeys and Apes,* p. 126)

It is true that in captivity or in the absence or breakdown
of natural safeguards for females, rape can occur in some species. But under normal conditions the female is not mounted
when she is unreceptive. In addition she has a choice of retreats in which she can segregate herself from males. This
segregation is the safeguard par excellence in nature, and even
in captivity females retain their predisposition to move away
from males during birth and the vulnerable infancy of their
offspring. Briffault, citing various sources, writes:

> The mammalian female is extremely particular, and even
> capricious, as to the choice of an abode, and is careful
> to select a well-concealed, dark, and protected spot; she
> constantly changes it both before and after the birth of
> the young, and invariably at the least sign of danger. In
> menageries it is found advisable to provide a choice of at
> least two retreats for a young-bearing female, "for the moth-
> er, even if she be not disturbed, is restless after the cubs
> are born, and frequently will carry them from one place
> to another until she finds a nook to her liking." The male,
> who is prone to mistake the cubs for articles of food, is
> usually driven away, and is allowed to return only after
> a few days, when the nature of the brood has become more
> evident. (*The Mothers,* vol. I, pp. 191-92)

Our knowledge of animal life has progressed slowly, and
there is still much to be learned. Great mistakes have been
made by zoo officials and others concerned with preserving
and studying animals by assuming that their mode of life
and their relationships are analogous to ours. One of the most
instructive examples is the London Zoo experiment.

The London Zoo Catastrophe

While in the lower mammals the males become quiescent
in the non-estrus season, primate males are potent all year
round. On the other hand, we have seen that the maternal func-

tions, which are most highly developed among female primates, preoccupy them for vastly longer periods than is the case with lower mammals. This means that the disparity between sex and maternity is greatest among the primates. It would follow that the safeguards provided for females in nature would be just as imperative, and even more so, in captivity. The failure to understand these safeguards brought about the London Zoo catastrophe.

An experiment was conducted by the London Zoological Society upon a colony of about a hundred Hamadryas baboons in a rockwork enclosure called "Monkey Hill." Originally the colony was all male, but it was decided to introduce females to the Hill to cohabit with the males, thus furnishing an opportunity to study their behavior. The experiment, conducted over a five-year period beginning in 1925, was reported by Solly Zuckerman in *The Social Life of Monkeys and Apes.*

Despite what seemed to be optimum conditions, a "natural" environment with food and care provided, the results were disastrous. There were continuous fights among the males for possession of the females to the point of the virtual extermination of the females and young.

The greatest number of deaths occurred in 1925 and 1927 when the main consignments of females were introduced. In the latter year fifteen of the thirty females were killed within a month. In 1928 fifteen more females were killed in one month. In the fights over females, males were also killed. By 1930 there were thirty-nine males and nine females left, and only one young baboon surviving of all those bred on the Hill.

The injuries were of all degrees of severity. Limb bones, ribs, and skulls were fractured; wounds penetrated chest or abdomen, and many animals showed extensive lacerations in the ano-genital region. At least four of the females killed were immature; two adult females died after miscarriages precipitated by the fighting. In one case four males fought over a single female.

Fourteen of the fifteen baboons born on Monkey Hill perished. In most cases death occurred within six months of birth. One nursing mother dropped her baby in a fight; it was seized by a male who made off with it, and it died. Another death was caused by a male who transferred his attentions from the female to her baby, injuring it severely in the loins.

The sexual fights often went on for days, with a female mounted by every male that could gain access to her. During these periods she suffered continuous physical torment and was unable to get food. After death the fights often continued over her dead body with males still treating her as a sexual object. So protracted and repellent was the last fight that by 1930, when the experiment was declared a failure, the five remaining females were removed and Monkey Hill once again became an all-male colony.

Anthropologists as well as zoologists have puzzled over the behavior of these male primates since it bears no resemblance to the behavior of animals in the wild. It was recognized that a zoo enclosure, no matter how skillfully constructed, can be only a rough approximation of the natural environment. The regular supply of food, it was thought, may have released energies in the males that would otherwise have been expended in foraging over a large tract. But the most important factors leading to the disaster went unrecognized: the preponderance of males over females in the enclosure and the absence of retreats for the females.

Zuckerman saw one aspect of the problem, the destructive fights between males for access to the females in which a considerable number of males were injured or killed. "Confined to a small area, animals cannot separate from one another as they would in a natural environment," he wrote; thus "a baboon worsted in a fight is unable to escape from his aggressors" (p. 217). But the females too were trapped in the same area, which lacked retreats for them; outnumbered and overwhelmed by the males, they were exterminated along with their offspring.

It has been said that the apes who committed the rape, murder, and mayhem in the London Zoo were abnormal or "depraved." Such behavior would not have occurred, however, if wrong assumptions had not been made about animal life. Sex in the animal world does not bring females and males together in love relationships or father-family units because of the antagonism between male sexuality and female maternal functions. The attempt to reproduce a mirror-image of human relationships among animals can only lead to disastrous errors.

Such errors are all the more unwarranted since most animal breeders and stock raisers are aware of the violence of male sexuality in the natural state. They know that the males' striving for dominance sets off the fights among them and that damage can result from having more than one potent male in a herd of females. Stock raisers use the expedient of castrating most males, leaving only the number required for servicing the females. According to Chapple and Coon, among many peoples who keep herds of sheep, reindeer, and cattle, the majority of males are castrated, and "the ratio is as low as one male to thirty females" (*Principles of Anthropology,* p. 194).

Apart from the absence of retreats for the females, the worst mistake made by those in charge of the London Zoo experiment was to introduce a small number of females into an overwhelmingly male enclosure. In the wild this ratio is just the reverse, giving females the advantage of numbers.

Among trooping primates females outnumber males, and in some species this disproportion is very high. Marshall Sahlins writes:

> There are typically more adult females than adult males within the horde, sometimes, as in the case of the howler monkey, three times as many. This may be in part due to a faster maturation rate for females. It may also reflect the elimination of some males in the course of competition for mates. These males are not necessarily killed. They may lead a solitary life outside of or on the fringes of the horde, attempting all the while to attach themselves to some group and acquire sexual partners. (*Scientific American,* vol. 203, no. 3, p. 81)

Carpenter also gives figures on the preponderance of females over males in primate species. Among the howler monkeys one group consisted of three males to eight females; a spider monkey group had eight males to fifteen females; a macaque group two males to six females. He cites examples where the disparity is very high; one rhesus monkey group contained six adult males and thirty-two females; another only seven males and eighty-five females (*Primate Social Behavior,* pp. 29, 31, 32, 40).

Females and young generally comprise a separate pack, with the males forming a loose periphery around the group. If a disturbance occurs or an alarm is sounded by one of the animals, the whole troop may react. But in nature each adult animal defends its own life either by fight or by flight, the sole exception being the female who will fight to defend her offspring or carry it off with her if she flees.

The study of biology is of great importance in the task of reconstructing our social origins and understanding the problems that had to be surmounted before human life could begin. We cannot know what these problems were nor how they were solved if animals are portrayed as quasi-human. To mis-represent animal relations by modeling them upon family life is a disservice to science. This is especially true with respect to the question of nature's specialization of the sexes. Precisely because this specialization has vanished from modern human life, it becomes all the more imperative to uncover it in our past history.

Serious anthropologists have not romanticized the animal trait of male dominance and rivalry; they have recognized it as an obstacle in the path of human progress. In the last century Engels wrote that mutual toleration among adult males was "the first condition for the building of those large and enduring groups in the midst of which alone the transition from animal to man could be achieved" (*The Origin of the Family, Private Property, and the State*, p. 49). Today Sherwood L. Washburn says virtually the same thing: "One of the essential conditions for the organization of men in cooperative societies was the suppression of rage and of the uncontrolled drive to first place in the hierarchy of dominance" (*Scientific American*, vol. 203, no. 3, pp. 69-71).

Perhaps the most graphic portrayal of the problems posed by the striving for dominance is given by Atkinson:

> In a state of society where literally every male creature's hand was against the other, and life one continual uproar from their contending strife; where not only was there no instant's truce in the warfare, but each blow was empha-sized (fatally) by the intellectual finesse which now directed it, it became a question of forced advance in progress or straight retreat in annihilation as a species. . . . A forward step was somehow taken, some road out of the maze was somehow found. . . . ("Primal Law," in *Social Origins and Primal Law*, p. 227)

That forward step was taken through totemism and taboo, which instituted social controls over natural needs and drastical-ly altered the violent character of male sexuality. Marshall Sahlins writes on this point:

> Sex is not an unmitigated social blessing for primates. Competition over partners, for example, can lead to vi-cious, and even fatal strife. It was this side of primate sexuality that forced early culture to curb and repress it.

The emerging human primate, in a life-and-death economic struggle with nature, could not afford the luxury of a social struggle. Co-operation, not competition was essential. Culture thus brought primate sexuality under control. More than that, sex was made subject to regulations, such as the incest tabu, which effectively enlisted it in the service of co-operative kin relations. (*Scientific American,* vol. 203, no. 3, p. 80)

Sahlins feels that the "decisive battle" was waged on the field of sex curbs. Our argument is that, in view of the hazards of cannibalism, food restrictions were even more imperative. This brings us back to the question: Which sex was biologically better equipped to take the lead in instituting these totemic controls which were required for the transformation of the ape into the human?

Woman's Role in the Transition from Ape to Human

Because men are today conditioned by a highly individualistic society to compete with one another in all spheres of life, they are often said to be "nothing but" animals with a few extra skills. Misanthropic writers portray them as blindly following their instincts and obeying the uncontrollable forces of their biological makeup. This is a gross error.

It was impossible to pass from nature's jungle to the modern man-made jungle in one leap. The first task before our anthropoid ancestors was to become humanized and socialized. This could not be done by perpetuating the antisocial forces that operate in nature but by radically changing them. Such a conquest could be made only by establishing a brotherhood of men, a communal society, in which all the members cooperated in producing the necessities of life and made them available on an equal basis. In other words, long before men could become enmeshed in their own social competition, they first had to win total liberation from the competitive struggle characteristic of animals and become social. As Sahlins writes:

The liberation of human society from direct biological control was its great evolutionary strength. Culture saved man in his earliest days, clothed him, fed him and comforted him. . . . The remarkable aspect of culture's usurpation of the evolutionary task from biology was that in so doing it was forced to oppose man's primate nature on many fronts and to subdue it. It is an extraordinary fact that primate urges often become not the secure foundation of human social life, but a source of weakness in it. (*Scientific American,* vol. 203, no. 3, pp. 77-78)

"Culture," however, did not create itself; it was the creation of human beings who, in producing the means of life, also produced a cultural superstructure. The prime agent in this process was womankind, who "saved man in his earliest days, clothed him, fed him and comforted him," beginning in his infancy when he was nurtured and protected by the mothers.

Whatever features humans still retain in common with animals, they are primarily the product of their own social and cultural evolution, and this was promoted by the institution of totemism and taboo. It has seldom been asked which sex instituted totemism. Most anthropologists have simply assumed it was the male sex. Frazer, for example, thought men had invented the taboo and law of exogamy to preserve the sexual purity and morality of women. He wrote:

The scheme no doubt took shape in the minds of a few men of a sagacity and practical ability above the ordinary, who by their influence and authority persuaded their fellows to put it in practice. . . . each successive step . . . added at once to the complexity and to the efficiency of the curious machinery which savage wit had devised for the preservation of sexual morality. (*Totemism and Exogamy*, vol. IV, p. 121)

We are not told, however, how these men acquired their exceptional sagacity and morality or how they restrained their own sexual violence and competition at a time when, as Atkinson puts it, man was "still some ape-like creature," and "his speech was yet as halting as his gait, only less brutish than his moral state" ("Primal Law," in *Social Origins and Primal Law,* p. 219).

Frazer correctly went beyond the sexual question to the need for food and cooperation in food-getting as a prime concern of totemic law, but here again he sees it in a male-oriented manner. He writes:

You cannot do men a deeper injury than by preventing their women from bearing children and by stopping their supply of food. . . . crimes which imperil the production of children and the supplies of food deserve to be punished by any society which values its existence with the utmost rigour of the law. (*Totemism and Exogamy,* vol. IV, p. 157)

It is far more likely, however, that in the beginning it was the females, not the males, who reacted to any perils involving their offspring and sustenance. So long as males remained hobbled by individualism, competition, and striving for dominance over other males, they could not respond to the need for group preservation. But the females, already equipped by nature with their highly developed maternal functions and, moreover, capable of cooperating with other females, could achieve the self-restraint and foresight required to take the measures necessary for group survival. They instituted taboo.

Through the sex clause of the totemic taboo the women initiated the rules of avoidance that forbade men access to certain women. The males of the group worked in economic collaboration with the women, but they could no longer seek sexual access to any women totemized and classified as their mothers and sisters. In other words, nature's safeguard for females — their periodic segregation from males — was extended in the human world to a permanent segregation of specific categories of male and female kin. By this means struggles between kinsmen for access to women were avoided.

The question of who instituted the food clause of the totemic taboo is even more obscure because so few studies have been made on two important topics. One is the subject of cannibalism. The other is the uneven development of the sexes in adopting the new carnivorous diet. It is commonly assumed that wherever men led the way, women automatically followed; thus when our branch of the primates passed over into hominid life and men became hunters and eaters of flesh foods, women also adopted the flesh diet. But this assumption is unproven.

To begin with, it conflicts with the original division of labor between the sexes, which centers on food. A number of investigators have puzzled over this sharp divergence in food-getting, the women collecting vegetables while the men hunted meat. The theory of the handicapped biology of the female sex seemed to take care of the problem. The men were the flesh hunters because the women, tied down by childbearing functions, were unable to go on hunting expeditions and therefore stayed close to the campsite foraging for the less important roots and vegetables.

Both the male occupation of hunting and the male taste for meat have been presented as attributes befitting the superior male sex. As Grahame Clark puts it:

> The acquisition of carnivorous tastes necessitated a form of activity for which adult males were particularly adapted, and so laid the basis for that economic specialization of the sexes which until modern times dominated society. Against a background of women and children engrossed, like their simian forebears, in the collection of vegetable food, there emerged the resplendent figure of Man the Hunter, prototype of Man the Warrior! (*From Savagery to Civilization*, p. 8)

Clark's exaggerated appreciation of male splendor as hunters and meat-eaters leaves out of account the hazards of cannibalism in an epoch when the distinctions between hominids and animals were still unclear. The fact that females, like their ape forebears, continued to collect vegetation instead of hunting and killing animals may have played a highly salutary role under the circumstances. Before weapons took the place of canine teeth in hunting, the earliest animals to be hunted would have been the small, weak, and helpless. The nonhunting females, therefore, were strategically situated to set up the totemic barriers for the protection of these animals — and their own offspring — from hunters.

It is true, as Clark says, that the males were particularly adapted to the occupation of hunting. They were not inhibited by any maternal functions or sentiments, and the canine teeth they developed in the primate stage had become the flesh-tearing teeth of the hominid stage. Sherwood L. Washburn writes on this point:

> In all the apes and monkeys the males have large canine teeth. The long upper canine cuts against the first lower premolar, and the lower canine passes in front of the upper canine. This is an efficient fighting mechanism, backed by very large jaw muscles. I have seen male baboons

drive off cheetahs and dogs, and according to reliable reports male baboons have even put leopards to flight. The females have small canines, and they hurry away with the young under the very conditions in which the males turn to fight. (*Scientific American,* vol. 203, no. 3, p. 69)

Among the carnivores, lionesses and tigresses are equipped with canine teeth just as the males are, and they too are hunters and flesh-eaters. Humans, however, stem from the non-carnivorous primates where only the males, through their competitive combats, had evolved the large jaw muscles and canine teeth which pre-adapted them for hunting. Thus, even apart from the female's maternal functions, there was this added biological difference between the sexes.

The first division of labor between the sexes or, more accurately, the "food division" of labor, grew up logically in the human world out of the biological disparity between the sexes carried over from the animal world. Only the females possessed maternal functions and sentiments, and this probably caused them to lag behind in their diet, retaining the vegetable food of the primates. Only in the course of time did they gradually acquire the practice of eating meat.

Apparently it was a long, slow process. Even up to our times there are still many primitive regions where women do not eat meat as a regular part of their diet; they eat morsels of flesh only on certain occasions, as in rituals. This persistence of a preponderantly vegetarian diet for women after so many millennia has captured the attention of a few antropologists. J. A. Driberg presents the following hypothesis as to its significance:

> The question of nutrition has not been sufficiently studied as yet, but it appears likely that experiment has demonstrated the value of certain vegetables and herbs for the feminine organism, especially during pregnancy and lactation, which has led to a differentiation in the menu. Thus, among the Akikuyu the women have certain dishes of which the men do not usually partake . . . and only boys below the age of six may eat these women's dishes. Among the Masai, again, the men are almost entirely dependent on milk, blood and meat for their food, although there is a further distinction that the old men may eat vegetables,

whereas the women are to a large extent vegetarian. Consequently, it follows as a necessity that with menus so diverse they are almost compelled to eat apart. (*At Home with the Savage,* p. 66)

This is not a satisfactory explanation. It was not simply women in pregnancy and lactation who restricted themselves to vegetable dishes. Such foods were the preference of primitive women at all times except for ritual occasions, when it seems to have been far more a duty than a desire for the women to swallow morsels of meat. Nor can we be satisfied with the explanation that "with menus so diverse they are almost compelled to eat apart."

Only when we consider the question of cannibalism can we make sense out of the long-drawn-out resistance of women to eating meat or even eating together with men who were eating meat. Without this clue there can only be unconvincing hypotheses. For example, when some investigators noted that primitive women ate little or no meat, they drew the conclusion that men appropriated the "best" food, meat, for themselves, giving women only the "worst" and "poorest" foods, vegetables. As this thesis is usually stated, women were "forbidden" to partake of "man's foods."

The same thesis is presented to explain why the cannibal feast was reserved for men only. According to J. A. MacCulloch, "Women were not allowed to take part in the cannibalistic meal; it was taboo to them." Citing Crawley, he adds, "The prohibition against women's eating human flesh is doubtless nothing but an instance of that universal sexual tabu in connexion with eating which forbids men and women to eat together or to eat the same kind of food" (*Encyclopedia of Religion and Ethics,* vol. III, p. 206). In a similar vein Julius Lippert writes:

> Among many cannibal tribes it is customary to debar women and children entirely from the enjoyment of human flesh, or else to silence them with only a trifle. The cannibal repast is in its origin a meal of men only. (*Evolution of Culture,* p. 424)

Such reasoning results from the conception that men have always been the superior sex. Hunting is regarded as the superior occupation because men do it, and flesh foods are regarded as the best foods because they were eaten by the hunters themselves. Even the cannibal feast is upheld as another testimonial to eternal male supremacy. It does not occur to these writers that women may have excluded themselves from having anything to do with a food that repelled them. Their subjective approach can only derail the study of totemism and taboo and the part played by women in its origin.

The double taboo must be placed in the context of the twin hazards that confronted early humanity. On the one hand there was the violence of male sexuality, on the other the problem of cannibalism. It is improbable that the males imposed the necessary restraints upon themselves in their hunt for food and mates. Rather, it was the females, with their highly developed maternal functions and their inhibitions with respect to eating meat, who led the way.

Thus, far from being handicapped by its biology, the female sex was in fact the biologically advantaged sex. To be sure, primate males are often larger and stronger than females and possess fighting equipment in their canine teeth. But the females, with a capacity for cooperation and collective action, had a strength superior to that of any single individual. In addition, as mothers, they wielded their socializing influence over the young males for a longer period than among anthropoids. These advantages enabled women to institute the prohibitions and restraints required for social life.

Through totemism and taboo, men were reconditioned to overcome the handicaps imposed upon males in nature. Their combative traits were channeled into useful services in regulated hunting and in defending their communities from predators. The "motherhood," as primitive people call their maternal clan system, furnished the model for the "brotherhood," the male economic arm of the clan. Something new arose in human life that does not exist in nature—the cooperative horde of men capable of working together for their mutual provision and protection. Briffault describes this profound transformation:

In human societies there always exist means of establishing understandings and guarantees, and there are bonds of fellowship and brotherhood which are absent and impossible among animals. Hence primitive humanity, owing to its social character, is not under the same necessity to secure the satisfaction of its sexual instincts by sheer competitive struggle. . . . There is thus between the operation of sexual hunger in primitive human social groups and among animals the same momentous difference as in regard to the operation of food-hunger. Animals tear their closest associates and even their sexual mates to pieces in the struggle for food; the member of the rudest and most primitive social group will starve rather than not share his food with his fellow-members. Those circumstances constitute the fundamental differentiating character between human society and animality. So likewise in no human society, however primitive, is a lawless scramble for the possession of females to be found. (*The Mothers,* vol. II, p. 118)

A correct understanding of the hazards connected with food and sex that confronted budding humanity is the starting point for answering the puzzling question: Why did society begin not with the father-family but with the maternal clan as its unit? The first requisite for human economic and social life was to create a brotherhood of men able to cooperate with one another and with women. Under the conditions prevailing in the primeval period, society could not be based upon the sexual union of married pairs in individual father-families. It had to begin with the nonsexual economic union of sisters and brothers in a horde governed by the mothers. The women gained a degree of social control precisely through sexual segregation, and thereby set in motion the process of creating the required brotherhood.

4

The Maternal Clan
and Sex Segregation

Through various avenues of research the pioneer anthropologists discovered that a maternal form of social organization had preceded civilized patriarchal society. Bachofen described it as a period of "mother-right" as opposed to the "father-right" of later times (*Das Mutterrecht*, 1861). This became popularized in the term "matriarchy." Morgan, more fundamentally, uncovered the maternal gens or clan as the unit of primitive society (*Ancient Society*, 1877). Other nineteenth-century investigators added to the data sustaining the priority of the matriclan system.

These discoveries came as a jolt to the long-held doctrine that the father-family and patriarchal society had always existed. As Hartland remarked, "The mother as the sole foundation of society is so alien from the habits of thought of civilized nations of European descent that . . . at most it was dismissed as an aberrant system practised by very few peoples" (*Primitive Society,* p. 2). Controversy raged as to whether or not the father-family was a late development in history and had been preceded by the maternal clan.

Although the founders of anthropology had produced substantial data to support that thesis, they were themselves surprised by their discovery and puzzled by many aspects of the matriclan structure. At that early stage of investigation they were unable to answer all the questions that were posed by their findings. Among these was the question: Why did society begin with the maternal clan rather than the father-family?

In the absence of an adequate answer there developed a tendency to doubt or deny the findings of the pioneers. New schools of anthropologists came forward in the twentieth century to reassert the doctrine of the eternal father-family. Edward

Westermarck, one of the leaders of this retrogressive trend, insisted that the institution of marriage and the family was so ancient and deep-rooted that it could be traced back to the animal world. He wrote:

> It is found among many of the lower animals, it occurs as a rule among the anthropomorphous apes, and it is universal among mankind. It is closely connected with parental duties; the immediate care of the children belongs chiefly to the mother, whilst the father is the protector and guardian of the family. . . . the marriage of the Primates seems to be due to the small number of young and the long period of infancy. Later on, when mankind became chiefly carnivorous, the assistance of an adult male became still more necessary for the subsistence of the children, as the chase everywhere devolves on the man. The suggestion that in olden times the natural guardian of the children was not the father, but the maternal uncle, has no foundation in fact; neither has the hypothesis that all the males of the tribe indiscriminately were their guardians. (*The History of Human Marriage,* pp. 537-38)

This deliberate retreat from the disclosures of the pioneer anthropologists affected the further search for social origins. A few investigators attempted to develop a theory that would not conflict with the concept of the eternal father-family. By introducing the father-family into the primeval epoch where it did not exist, they blocked themselves off from deciphering the maternal kinship structure of ancient society. They were thrown further off course by accepting the usual explanation for segregation of the sexes — that it was designed to prevent in-family marriage. Instead of a logical exposition of human beginnings, they arrived at what may be called the "incest theory of social origins."

Father-Son Jealousy and Incest Reform

Some scholars are aware of the violent character of male sexuality in the animal world, which manifests itself in the striving for "dominance." But they go astray when they reduce this general biological problem to a "jealous father" fighting off his "sons" to prevent them from gaining access to his females. This has led to the concoction of fanciful tales about human beginnings, of which Freud's is probably the best known.

Freud's thesis of father-son jealousy and incest reform as the starting point of social life has influenced every generation since his time. His flight of fancy is all the more incredible since he correctly points to the need for an "association of men" capable of cooperating with one another as the first requirement for social life. He writes:

> The Darwinian conception of the primal horde does not, of course, allow for the beginning of totemism. There is only a violent, jealous father who keeps all the females for himself and drives away the growing sons. This primal state of society has nowhere been observed. The most primitive organization we know, which to-day is still in force with certain tribes, is *associations of men* consisting of members with equal rights, subject to the restrictions of the totemic system, and founded on matriarchy, or descent through the mother. Can the one have resulted from the other, and how was this possible? (*Totem and Taboo*, pp. 182-83, emphasis in the original)

It was inconceivable to Freud that an association of women, the matriarchy, could have furnished the prototype for the association of men in what can be called the "fratriarchy." Instead he begins with the jealous father of a family as the dominant male and weaves his famous tale of how a pack of fighting sons reformed themselves into the first association of men, or the brotherhood.

According to Freud, the jealous father, determined to keep the females to himself, expelled all his sons when they reached sexual maturity and threatened his exclusive possession. Freud writes that the sons loved and admired their father but also hated him because he "stood so powerfully in the way of their sexual demands and their desire for power" (ibid., p. 184). One day the expelled sons joined forces, killed their father and then ate him, putting an end to the father-horde. "Together they dared and accomplished what would have remained impossible for them singly. Perhaps some advance in culture, like the use of a new weapon, had given them the feeling of superiority" (ibid., p. 183).

Indeed, just the ability to band together in collective action would have given the group of sons superiority over the solitary father. But this leaves unexplained how rival, fighting males, each striving for the dominant place occupied by the father, could have arrived at collective action in the first place. Freud admits that "in the fight of each against the other the new organization would have perished." But he resolves the problem through a psychological explanation.

After the crime, the murdering, cannibalistic sons were filled with a sense of guilt and remorse. Thereupon they reformed themselves into the first brotherhood of men. They "undid their deed," says Freud, by creating the two fundamental taboos of totemism: never again to seek sexual access to their mother and sisters, and never again to commit the crime of father-killing. Thus out of parricide and incest, totemism and taboo were born, and along with this human cooperation and culture.

Other investigators, dubious about Freud's thesis, attempted a more plausible explanation of how society got its start despite the antisocial character of male sexuality. But wherever they began with the father-family as the original unit of society, they too ended up in a blind alley.

This was the case with Atkinson, who also viewed the problem in terms of a jealous father and his rival sons. However, he doubted that an act of parricide could lead to such momentous results as the beginning of society and its culture. He felt that the more likely result of killing the father would have been the unleashing of fratricidal strife among the sons as each sought to take the father's place. Atkinson therefore saw the mother and her tender influence bringing father-son enmity to a close.

One day a clever, farsighted mother, noting that the patriarch was growing old, prevailed upon him to allow her last male child to remain at home rather than be banished at adolescence as was customary. As Atkinson describes the drama:

> Pure maternal love triumphed over the demons of lust and jealousy. A mother succeeded in keeping by her side a male child, and thus, by a strange coincidence, that father and son, who, amongst all mammals, had been the most deadly of enemies, were now the first to join hands. So portentous an alliance might well bring the world to their feet. The family group would now present, for the first time, the till then unknown spectacle of the inclusion with-

in a domestic circle, and amidst its component females, of an adolescent male youth. It must, however, be admitted that such an event, at such an epoch, demanded imperatively very exceptional qualities, both physiological and psychological, in the primitive agents. The new happy ending to that old world drama which had run for so long through blood and tears, was an innovation requiring very unusually gifted actors. (*Social Origins and Primal Law,* pp. 231-32)

Unlike Freud, who sees only males as actors on the stage of prehistory, Atkinson gives credit to feminine influence in starting social life and behavior. But the net result is the same; the family circle is cleaned up by bringing father-son enmity to an end and prohibiting incest. He writes, "For the first time in the history of the world we encounter the factor which is to be the leading power in future social metamorphosis, i.e., *an explicit distinction between female and female as such,* namely, that certain females are now to become sacred to certain males" (emphasis in the original). He concludes:

This, then, the primal law — avoidance between a brother and sister — with appalling conservatism has descended through the ages. . . . It ordained in the dawn of time a barrier between mother and son, and brother and sister, and that ordinance is still binding on all mankind. . . . Between these for ever, a bit was placed in the mouth of desire, and chains on the feet of lust. (ibid., pp. 236, 238)

Thus Atkinson, like Freud, winds up with the incest theory of social origins. He overlooks the fact that the "distinction between female and female as such" was not restricted to a few women in a family circle. The sex taboo covered multitudes of women who were made inaccessible to certain categories of men. The question that has to be answered is why all these women were made into forbidden females under the same sex taboo.

The only way to cope with this quandary within the framework of the father-family thesis is to expand the definition of incest to cover all these unrelated clanswomen, even though this renders the term "incest" meaningless. This is the course taken by Ralph Piddington, who writes.

Because of its importance in human evolution, sex is a powerful force, but one whose frustration lets loose the most disruptive of human passions. On the other hand, these passions must be controlled in the interests of social order. Nowhere is this so true as in the family whose intimate system of domestic and economic co-operation necessitates harmonious relationships between its members. Paternal love and filial respect cannot be maintained if father and son are rivals for the sexual favours of the same woman. Family life would be impossible if brothers were always quarrelling, as they would be if they were allowed access to their sisters. The same interpretation applies to wider kinship groups such as the clan. Here, again, the need for harmonious cooperation in economic, political and religious activity is threatened by the disruptive forces of sex, and this leads to the rules of exogamy and the prohibition of clan incest. This is one of the extensions of family sentiments, in this case of a negative order, which lie at the base of the classificatory system of relationship. For example, by calling all female members of his clan "sister," a man establishes a relationship of fictional kinship with them which precludes, ideally at least, marriage or sexual intercourse. (*Introduction to Social Anthropology,* pp. 134-35)

Piddington too became trapped in the incest theory of social origins. These investigators began with a correct premise, that the antisocial character of male sexuality in nature presented an obstacle to budding humanity. But they fell into the error of reducing this tremendous social problem to a family affair involving father-son jealousy and incest.

Human beings did not start out with a concern about incest in a family circle. They began with the imperative necessity to create a social organization in which men cooperated with other men and with women in collective labor activities to produce the necessities of life and furnish mutual protection for one another. This required the suppression of animal competition and violence not simply in the sex hunt but also in the hunt for food.

It was this double requirement that brought into existence the totemic taboos which, in turn, produced the clan — and not the family — at the start of human life. Society's initial stage of development, far from featuring the father-family and sexual union in marriage, was exactly the opposite. It started

with the maternal clan, a unit composed of nonsexual partners, the mothers and brothers (or sisters and brothers). They
were closely united as clan-kin but rigorously separated with
respect to both food and mating.

Let us examine this double segregation of the sexes in the
prefamily epoch of history.

Eating and Mating Restrictions

In its internal structure the clan was composed of the "close
kin," the sisters, brothers, mothers, and mothers' brothers.
Although sexually separated, they were the economic and social partners who jointly provided for all members of the clan
community. Thus they had what may be called a "close
separation."

On the other hand, there was a "far separation" of these
sisters and brothers from their mates, who lived in different
and sometimes distant matriclan communities together with
their own clan brothers and sisters. By the time anthropologists began their studies, matrimonial unions and even some
cohabitation of pairing couples were found in most primitive
regions. But in the early stage of matrimony the inclusion of
a husband or wife in a group did not alter the essential structure of the clan, which remained a sister-brother matriclan.

The matriclan structure was divided by sex divisions and
age categories. Under the classificatory system the sex divisions are called "male and female classes," a term introduced
by Morgan. Although the sisters and brothers lived together
in the same campsite or community, they occupied separate
sectors. The women and young children lived, ate, and slept
in the female sector; the adult males lived, ate, and slept in
the men's sector. The older sisters (mothers) were in charge
of the younger sisters (female children) and trained them in
their future occupations, while the older brothers (mothers'
brothers) were the tutors and guardians of the younger brothers
(male children).

Infants and very young children of both sexes lived with
the mothers in the female sector. At this period of their lives
the male children were lumped together with the female children. As J. H. Driberg describes it, the young boy was barred
from consorting with adult males. "He is still tied to his
mother's apron strings and his friends are boys of his own

age and little girls with whom he is classified" (*At Home with the Savage,* p. 63).

At a certain age, in some regions as early as six, in others at eight or ten, the young males were transferred to the male sector, reclassified as men, and trained as hunters and warriors. They were also instructed in new rules of behavior. Most important were the rules of avoidance now imposed upon the male youth with respect to the mothers and sisters with whom they had formerly lived. Henceforth they had to maintain a strict reserve toward these forbidden females.

A description of this separation of brothers from sisters, as it was found in the New Hebrides, New Caledonia, and elsewhere, was given by Frazer (*Totemism and Exogamy,* vol. II, p. 77) and has been used by many anthropologists for illustrative purposes. The boy leaves his maternal home at a fixed age and moves to the "clubhouse" where he regularly sleeps and takes his meals. Thereafter if brother and sister meet by chance, she turns aside or he runs away. If he recognizes certain footprints in the sand as his sister's he is not to follow them. He will not mention her name and will guard against using any word if it forms part of her name. The young man may still visit his home to ask for food, but if a sister is about he goes away before he has eaten. If no sister is visible he may sit down to eat the food that is set outside the door for him. A mother is also reserved in her manner toward him, using the formal address, and if she brings him food she sets it out without having any direct contact with him.

The separation of the boys from their mothers and sisters is almost always interpreted as merely designed to prevent sexual intercourse between them. In actuality, it was even more stringently a food separation. Once the boys were transferred from the female sector to the male sector, they were also transferred from the female food division to the male food division. Formerly they ate female foods, cooked by the women on their fires, and ate together with the women and girls. Now they would eat men's foods, cooked by them at their own fires, together with the adult men.

A few anthropologists have noted the stringency of this food segregation. Ernest Crawley, for example, writes:

> In the Society and Sandwich Islands as soon as a boy was able to eat, his food was kept distinct from that of his mother, and brothers and sisters were not allowed

to eat together from the earliest age. In Uripiv boys from a few days after birth are supposed to eat with the male sex only. . . . The fact of suckling, however, is overlooked. In Fiji brothers and sisters may not speak to each other, nor eat together. (*The Mystic Rose,* vol. I, p. 262)

Audrey I. Richards observes a similar custom among the Southern Bantu:

The first step in this separation of the boy from his mother is the prohibition laid on their eating together, and it is interesting to note that, in Kafir society at any rate, the boy is forbidden to eat with the women for some years before he ceases to sleep in the women's part of the hut. . . .
From henceforth, therefore, the way of the boys and the girls divides, and even when the children combine at harvest-time to scare the birds off the crops, the sex division is most rigorously observed in the preparation of the meals to be eaten in the fields. (*Hunger and Work in a Savage Tribe,* p. 70)

While most anthropologists have centered their attention upon the sexual segregation of clan brothers and sisters, they have overlooked the significance of the food segregation. Yet, as Ernest Crawley exclaimed, "the most widely spread and the most stringent of all sex-taboos has nothing to do with sexual functions — this is the prohibition against eating together" (*The Mystic Rose,* vol. I, pp. 84-85).

Along with other evidence, this food segregation of the sexes refutes Westermarck's thesis that the father has always been the provider of food for his wife and offspring because the chase devolved upon the hunter. Since neither women nor young children depended upon meat for their food, they were not dependent upon male hunters for their subsistence. Even male children were fed first with mother's milk and then with vegetable mash. Only when the young males were transferred to the men's sector did they begin to eat flesh.

The food segregation of the sexes was even more pronounced between mates or "husbands and wives," as they are usually called, than between sisters and brothers. The spouses belonged to different clans. Under the classificatory system the term "marriage division," also called "marriage class," was more importantly the "food division" to which each of the spouses

belonged. The wife belonged to her food division in her matriclan, the husband to his food division in his matriclan. Thus
even though a husband had sexual intercourse with a woman
he could have no food intercourse with her.

Crawley gives an example among the Damaras, where the
word for "marriage division" is *Oruzo*, which "refers to food,
and these divisions are described as 'dietaries'" (ibid., vol.
II, p. 227). But he did not understand why all men, both
brothers and husbands, were barred from having food intercourse with women. He asks, "Why, according to a very general
custom, are husbands and wives, brothers and sisters, required
to avoid each other in one or more ways, and why, in particular, may they not eat together?" (vol. I, p. 2).

The answer is that the food segregation of the sexes is only
the most conspicuous part of the general segregation of the
hunters from the mothers and children in the epoch of cannibalism.

Segregation of Hunters from Mothers

Some anthropologists have observed that in the beginning
little distinction was made between hunting and warfare. They
point out that the same weapons and techniques were used in
both the animal hunt and the man hunt. The same lack of distinction can be found in the totemic regulations that were imposed on both activities. The hungers and warriors were obliged
to submit to certain struct rules that began even before the
hunting or fighting expedition, and afterward they were subjected to rigorous rituals of purification before they could return
to normal life in the community.

The most prominent and inflexible rules concerned women
and the avoidance of both food and sex intercourse with them.
At the start of every hunting and fighting expedition men were
restricted from certain foods for specified periods; they were
also prohibited from having any contact with women, including
their mates. In many accounts, the sexual aspect of this double
prohibition is described as "continence" or "sexual abstinence"
or even "celibacy" temporarily imposed upon the men on these
occasions.

The following is a portion of Crawley's summary, drawn
from numerous authorities, showing the universality of this
practice:

On a war party, the Maoris are taboo "an inch thick" and may not go near their wives until the fighting is over and peace proclaimed. . . . The Moanus of the Admiralty Islands must observe continence for five days before he goes fishing with large nets, for two or three days before he goes to war. . . . Before the departure of an expedition the Trobrianders abstain from their wives for two days. The Motumotu of Freshwater Bay in New Guinea have to observe continence before hunting, fishing or warlike expeditions. . . . In south-east New Guinea, similarly, men are taboo for some days before fighting and are not allowed to see or approach women. . . . In Assam "warriors, both before and after a raid, may not cohabit with their wives, and may not eat food cooked by a woman." . . .

The Indians of Nootka Sound in British Columbia, for three or four weeks before setting out on a military expedition, must abstain from sexual intercourse and undergo painful purifications. . . . The North American Indians generally "will not cohabit with women while they are out at war; they religiously abstain from every kind of intercourse even with their own wives, for the space of three days and nights before they go to war, and so after they return home." . . . The Western Tinneh leaves his marriage bed for ten days before he goes on a marten-hunt and for a month in the case of a bear-hunt. . . .

In South Africa, before and during an expedition, men may have no connection with women. Before a war the South African Bantus perform ceremonies for sexual purification and practise continence. Of the Zulu warriors a native said that "no one among them is able to associate with his wife." . . . The Negrillos also practise continence before fighting. . . . The fishers and hunters of the Bangala on the Upper Congo have to observe continence. . . . The natives of (German) East Africa do not approach their wives for some days before an elephant hunt. (*The Mystic Rose*, vol. I, pp. 66-71)

The explanations given by the aborigines themselves for this strict avoidance of women during hunting periods were, as usual, vaguely formulated and easily misinterpreted. They said that any infringement of the taboos would at the very least result in an unsuccessful hunt; at worst, it would bring down upon the hunter some horrible calamity and even death.

From this, many investigators concluded that savage hunters
and warriors feared the "weakening" influence of women at such
times; contact with women would "contaminate" a man with
feminine weakness and thus bring about bad luck. Frazer
fell into this error when he wrote:

> Why exactly so many savages have made it a rule to
> refrain from women in time of war, we cannot say for
> certain, but we may conjecture that their motive was a
> superstitious fear lest, on the principles of sympathetic
> magic, close contact with women should infect them with
> feminine weakness and cowardice. . . . Indeed the Kayans
> of Central Borneo go so far as to hold that to touch a
> loom or woman's clothes would so weaken a man that he
> would have no success in hunting, fishing, and war. Hence
> it is not merely sexual intercourse with women that a
> savage warrior sometimes shuns; he is careful to avoid
> the sex altogether. (*The Golden Bough*, Part II, *Taboo
> and the Perils of the Soul*, pp. 164-65)

Frazer subsequently changed his mind and thought that the
rule of avoidance was due not so much to the supposed
weakening effect of women upon men but rather to the belief
that the animals they were hunting would fail to come out
and let themselves be caught (ibid., p. 196). But he failed to
explain why contact with women would produce such a result.

In the absence of a satisfactory explanation for the practice,
the male-oriented theme that the women were a contaminating
influence upon the men became crystallized. However, the voluminous data indicates that it was just the other way around.
The men were obliged to go through elaborate purification
rituals to cleanse them of the impurities they had acquired in
their bloody occupations of hunting and fighting. After every
expedition, before the men could return to any kind of association with women, they had to be decontaminated of the blood
they had shed, the flesh they had eaten, and the blood they
had drunk in the hunt or fight.

Jevons writes on this point:

> Naturally, therefore, the shedder of blood is regarded as
> taboo. Amongst the Yumas of Colorado the manslayer
> is taboo for a month, during which time he must fast;
> and the Kaffir is "unclean" after a battle. Animal blood

produces the same effects. The Hottentot after a hunt must purify himself from the blood of the animals he has slain. (*Introduction to the History of Religion*, p. 74)

There are numerous descriptions of the rituals through which the men had to pass after the hunt or the battle. They were isolated in cabins outside the community. While in quarantine they were gradually released from their fast by being given weak gruel or vegetable mash. Sometimes the hunter was fed by an old woman who maintained her distance by putting the food at the end of a long stick and delivering it to his mouth in that manner. Hutton Webster describes these practices among some tribes:

Among the Thonga the slaying of enemies in battle entails great glory for the slayers, but also great danger to them. "They have killed. So they are exposed to the mysterious and deadly influence of the *nuru* and must consequently undergo medical treatment. What is the *nuru? Nuru* is the spirit of the slain which drives them to take revenge on the slayer. It haunts him and may drive him to insanity; his eyes swell, protrude and become inflamed." He will go out of his mind, be attacked by giddiness, and the thirst for blood may even lead him to fall with murderous intent upon the members of his own family. To avoid such terrible consequences the slayers are placed under many taboos. They put on old clothes, eat with special spoons, and from special plates and broken pots. They are not allowed to drink water. Their food must be cold; if it was hot it would make them swell internally, because, say the natives, "they are hot themselves, they are defiled." Sexual relations are absolutely forbidden them. After some days a medicine man comes to purify them and remove their "black." When this has been accomplished, all the implements used by the slayers during their seclusion and all their old garments are tied together, hung upon a tree and left there to decay. (*Taboo*, pp. 210-11)

Most anthropologists have made two basic errors: first, believing that men had imposed the rules of avoidance upon themselves as a protection against the "contaminating" woman, and, second, regarding the taboo as primarily a sexual prohibition. Rather, it was the women who laid down the edict that they were not to be approached at times when the men were

engaged in the dangerous and contaminating occupation of
hunting and killing.

And it was more than a mere sexual avoidance. It was a
total taboo that prevented men from having any kind of association with women. Its object was to prevent hunters or
warriors from coming into contact with women and children
whenever they were embarked upon killing expeditions. Even
more fundamental than sexual intercourse was the rule of
avoidance of food intercourse, for it was primarily against
cannibalism that the taboo was directed.

There is some evidence that originally the terms for food
did not refer to flesh and, further, that those who did not eat
flesh were regarded as more "human" than those who did.
Gladwin and Sarason, for example, write that "the general
word for food in Trukese is more specifically applied only to
cooked starch foods." Since women were originally and traditionally the collectors of vegetables and roots, the starch foods,
they obviously were the eaters of "human" foods — unlike the
hunters, who ate "animal" foods.

In a Rorschach experiment made upon some young Trukese,
one youth associated an ink splotch with the fruit bat and
described it as follows:

> "This is a picture of fruit bats; they just eat breadfruit,
> coconuts and papaya. . . . They also eat bananas. They
> are very like humans, because they just eat human food,
> they cannot eat animal's food. They are very good ani-
> mals. If we get them small and keep them as pets in the
> house, they just eat papayas, breadfruit and bananas;
> they don't eat all kinds of food." (*Truk: Man in Paradise*,
> p. 631)

Strict rules were imposed upon males with respect to what
flesh they could or could not eat and under what conditions
they could eat it. These food laws were inculcated into young
males at the time of their transfer from the female to the male
sector of the community. Some were temporary avoidances;
others were permanent. The most forbidden was the flesh of
certain birds and animals associated with the female sex. Crawley writes that among the Kurnai of Gippsland "men may
only eat the males of the animals they use for food," and in
western Victoria "boys are not allowed to eat any female quad-
ruped" (*The Mystic Rose*, vol. I, p. 207).

Along with the food taboos, boys were instructed about the
rules governing the segregation of the sexes. Frazer writes:

> In New South Wales . . . the novice during his proba-
> tion is not permitted even so much as to look at a wom-
> an or to speak to one; and even, for some time after, he
> must cover his mouth with his rug when one is present. . . .
> The Kurnai youth is not allowed to eat the female of any
> animal, nor the emu, nor the porcupine. (*Totemism and
> Exogamy,* vol. I, p. 41)

The ancient segregation of the sexes survives in the form of
the segregation of "milk" from "meat" foods. Frazer gives the
following illustration of what are often called dietary laws:

> Thus the Masai are at the utmost pains to keep milk from
> touching flesh. . . . they will not suffer milk to be kept in
> a pot in which flesh has been cooked, nor flesh to be put
> in a vessel which has contained milk, and consequently
> they have two different sets of pots set apart for the two
> purposes. The belief and practice of the Bahima are simi-
> lar. . . . if milk were poured into a pot in which flesh
> had been boiled, the cow that had yielded the milk would
> die.
> But it is not merely in a pot that milk and flesh may
> not come into contact with each other; they may not meet
> in a man's stomach, because contact there would be equally
> dangerous to the cow whose milk was thus contaminated.
> Hence pastoral tribes who subsist on the milk and flesh
> of their cattle are careful not to eat beef and milk at the
> same time. . . . Similar, though somewhat less stringent,
> rules as to the separation of flesh and milk are observed by
> the Israelites to this day. (*Folklore in the Old Testament,*
> abr. ed., pp. 370-71)

Although the savage hunters and warriors did not look upon
women as the "contaminating" sex, it is correct to say that
they regarded women as the "dangerous" sex. Women were
extremely dangerous if their taboos and rules of avoidance
were violated. This fear of women is reflected in the male
avoidance of female flesh as food, as MacCulloch points out
in his article on cannibalism in the *Encyclopedia of Religion
and Ethics:*

> A similar extension of the sexual tabu, which regards wom-
> an as potentially or actually dangerous to man, will also

explain the fact that, while the flesh of men is freely eaten, that of women was abhorred or regarded as poisonous. (vol. III, p. 206)

Thus the primitive sex taboo, which was far more fundamentally a food segregation of the sexes, testifies to the threat posed by cannibalism in the hunting epoch. One of the surprising features about this segregation is its duration. In regions where cannibalism has survived up to recent times, even though only in ritualistic form, the segregation of the men from the women after a hunt or a fight is protracted, often extending for a year or more. Webster writes:

The Kwakiutl of British Columbia, with whom cannibalism was a ceremonial rite, subjected the eaters of human flesh to many restrictions. They were not allowed to work, gamble, or approach their wives for the space of a year, and for four months of this had to live alone in their bedrooms. (*Taboo*, p. 213)

Where cannibalistic practices had ceased, the period of segregation after hunting or fighting was greatly reduced; to a few weeks, then a few days, until it faded out of history. One survival of the ancient practice is the separation of the sexes at mealtimes, a custom that can be found in some regions even at the present day.

Mealtime Separation of Spouses

The practice of husbands and wives eating their meals apart from each other is found both in primitive regions retaining matriarchal customs and in regions with fully entrenched patriarchalism. Since the origin of the custom was unknown to them, anthropologists have generally failed to see that the patriarchal version is completely changed from the former matriarchal custom.

As the practice is usually described, the man ate first, alone or with his male friends, while the wife and children ate together afterwards. Although the wife often served the food to her husband, she never sat down at table with him. This has correctly been interpreted as signifying the inferior position of the wife in a patriarchal household. It is incorrect, however, to think that the practice had the same meaning in the savage era. Originally this custom was part of the food segregation of the sexes in the period of cannibalism.

The gap in understanding the origin of mealtime separation has produced confused and conflicting reports on the practice. In some instances it is reported that women were forbidden to eat with men; in others that men were forbidden to eat with women. Whichever way it is expressed, there is no doubt about the universality of the custom. The following is a portion of Crawley's data on the subject:

Amongst the Braknas of West Africa husbands and wives do not eat together. Fulah women may not eat with their husbands. In Ashanti and Senegambia, amongst the Niam-Niam and the Barea, the wife never eats in the presence of her husband. . . . In Eastern Central Africa each village has a separate mess for males and females. This prohibition is very general throughout Africa. . . .

Amongst the Kurds husband and wife never eat together. . . . A Hindu wife never eats with her husband. . . . So in Ancient India, according to Manu, "let him not eat in the company of his wife.". . . The men and women of Kumaun eat separately. Amongst the hill tribes near Rajmahal in Bengal, the women are not allowed to eat with the men. Amongst the Todas men and women may not eat together. . . . In Cochin a wife never eats with her husband. A Siamese wife prepares her husband's meals, but dines after him. . . . In the Maldive Islands husband and wife may not eat together. The same rule is in force amongst the Khakyenas. In China . . . the wife neither eats with her husband nor with her male children; she waits upon them at table. . . . In Korea men and women have their meals separately, the women waiting on the men.

Amongst the Indians of Guiana husbands and wives eat separately. Macusi women eat after the men. . . . In ancient Mexico each person had a separate bowl for eating; the men ate first and by themselves, the women and children afterwards. In Yucatan men and women ate apart. "So far as I have yet travelled in the Indian country," says Catlin, "I have never yet seen an Indian woman eating with her husband. Men form the first group at the banquet, the women and children and dogs all come together at the next." Amongst the Iroquois tribes the men ate first and by themselves, then the women and children took their meals alone. . . . So amongst many other tribes of North Indians. . . . Amongst the Natchez the husband used a respectful attitude towards his wife, and addressed her as if he were her slave; he did not eat with her. An Eskimo wife dares not eat with her husband. Amongst the California Indians husbands and wives eat separately; they may not even cook at the same fire.

The rule is general throughout Australia that husband and wife must eat separately. . . . Thus in Victoria males and females have separate fires at which they cook their own food. . . . In Melanesia generally, women may not eat with men. . . . In the Banks Islands all the adult males belong to the men's club, *Suge,* where they take their meals, while the women and children eat at home. . . . In Malekula men and women cook their meals separately, and even at separate fires, and all female animals, even hens and eggs, are forbidden articles of diet. A native told Lieutenant Somerville that a mate of his had died from partaking of a sow. . . . In Fiji husband and wife may not eat together, nor brother nor sister, nor the two sexes generally. Young men may not eat of food left by women. . . . A female child (in the Sandwich Islands) from its birth until death was allowed no food that had touched the father's dish. "From childhood onwards, no natural affections were inculcated, no social circle existed." (*The Mystic Rose,* vol. I, pp. 202-11)

In some primitive regions the old separation between meat as man's food and vegetables as woman's food has been retained along with the mealtime separation of the sexes. Katherine Routledge writes about the Akikuyus:

Men and women do not eat together. A woman is not allowed to see a man eat meat; still less does she cook it for him. . . . Women eat meat only on special occasions . . . making a stew of boiled meat and vegetables. The women make flour and all sorts of vegetable cookery. All cooking, except that of meat is done by the women. (*With a Prehistoric People, the Akikuyu of British East Africa,* p. 61)

Those who interpret the mealtime separation of the sexes according to patriarchal principles believe that men imposed the rule upon women; that it is an expression not only of the inferior status of women but of men's fear of being contaminated. Webster writes:

> This sexual separation in eating may sometimes be simply an outcome of the inferior status of the female sex; the men satisfied their hunger first and with the best of the food. In other cases, the custom has been dictated by dread of woman's uncleanness. The custom, whatever its origin, is widespread. (*Taboo,* p. 111)

Observing that meat was man's food, and interpreting this in patriarchal terms, Webster says of certain tribes in New Guinea that the "menu" is so arranged that "the good things, the dainties are reserved for the men." He condemns the "male selfishness" that humiliated and degraded women and "put a handicap on women over and above that imposed by their physical inferiority to men."

Cora Du Bois also believes that women did not eat meat because it was reserved for men. In her studies of an East Indian tribe she wrote:

> The meat at feasts is always distributed to the women but only in terms of the males in their household. That is, women get meat for their husbands and sons but not for themselves or their daughters. This is consistent with the theory that flesh food is the property of men. . . . The system of meat distribution helps to reinforce early in life, and on a very basic level, the role of masculine prestige in the culture. Men are not the providers, in fact, they are quite the contrary. They are the ones provided for, but they are also the purveyors of a delicacy. (*The People of Alor,* pp. 57-58)

If women are the "providers" of food for the community, and the men are the ones "provided for," it does not seem likely that women were deprived of meat by men but rather that they did not regard it as a delicacy. Meat may have become the property and prerogative of men in patriarchal society, but in the matriarchal period women decided for themselves whether they would eat meat, and usually they did not.

Some anthropologists have observed that, of all the unfamiliar customs introduced to primitive peoples by European con-

querors and settlers, the one that caused the greatest consterna-
tion was the custom of eating together. Morgan wrote with
regard to the Iroquois:

> After intercourse commenced with whites, the Iroquois grad-
> ually began to adopt our mode of life, but very slowly.
> One of the difficulties was to change the old usage and ac-
> custom themselves to eat together. It came in by de-
> grees. . . . There is a tradition still current among the
> Seneca-Iroquois, if the memory of so recent an occurrence
> may be called traditional, that when the proposition that
> man and wife should eat together, which was so contrary
> to immemorial usage, was first determined in the affirma-
> tive, it was formally agreed that man and wife should sit
> down together at the same dish and eat with the same
> ladle, the man eating first and then the woman, and so
> alternately until the meal was finished. (*Houses and House-
> Life of the American Aborigines,* pp. 99-100)

Some primitive peoples have not adopted the custom of eating together even today. Meyer Fortes's study of the Ashanti
gives one example of the retention of mealtime segregation of
the sexes, although Fortes is not clear about the meaning
of the custom:

> The most striking feature of Ashanti domestic life appears
> vividly in one of the common sights in any village or
> township. As night falls young boys and girls can be seen
> hurrying in all directions carrying large pots of cooked
> food. One can often see food being carried out of a house
> and a few minutes later an almost equal amount of food
> being carried into it. The food is being taken by the chil-
> dren from the houses in which their mothers reside to those
> in which their fathers live. Thus one learns that husband
> and wife often belong to different domestic groups, the chil-
> dren perhaps sleeping in their mothers' houses and eating
> with their fathers. ("An Ashanti Case Study," in *Social
> Structure,* pp. 63-64)

Some primitive women retreat to an "outhouse" at mealtime,
where they eat their food apart from men. This custom arose
after the practice of matrimony began and husband and wife
occupied the same household. It then became necessary, dur-

ing periods when the segregation of the sexes was in order, for women to use a separate house to maintain this segregation. However, there is nothing to indicate that the women retreated to the "outhouse" through any dictates other than their own.

A far more pronounced retreat to the "outhouse" occurs in some areas during women's menstrual periods and when they give birth. This practice also originated in the taboo system by which the "hunters" were segregated from the "mothers."

Childbirth and Menstruation Taboos

The segregation of females from males at the time of giving birth has a very long history; as we have seen, it antedates human life. The female mammal finds a suitable nook or retreat where she secludes herself during birth and nursing. Should an adult male of her own species happen to venture near, he would be repelled by the mother in the same manner that she would fight off any other animal that might harm her young.

This pattern of female behavior was carried over into the early human world, where the instinctive reaction of the animal female was superseded by a formulated rule of avoidance. Briffault writes:

> The repulse of the male by the female presents the analogue, and the only one, of a "prohibition" among animals. . . . It is at the human level only, through the medium of language, that a prohibition can acquire the status of a recognised principle. And if I am right in considering that in the earliest human groups the influence and authority of the female were paramount, that order of prohibitions must inevitably have been one of the first, or rather the very first to come into operation. (*The Mothers,* vol. II, p. 365)

The tenacity of this most ancient prohibition can be seen in its survival to the present day in some primitive regions, where no man, including the husband, may approach a lying-in woman. Its stringency is illustrated by Fortune, writing about the Dobuans:

> At his own birth a male is for the first and the last time present at birth. He is unavoidably present. Thereafter his presence in any house where a woman is in labour is avoidable, and he is excluded. (*Sorcerers of Dobu,* p. 273)

A curious feature of this rule of avoidance is that it applied not simply to women in labor but also to women in their menstrual periods. As Briffault sums it up: "All the world over, not only among savages, but also among peoples on a far higher cultural plane, the forms of tabu attaching to menstrual women are similar; and those which refer to women in childbed are practically identical with those which apply to menstruation" (*The Mothers,* vol. II, p. 366). How did this come about?

To us there is a great distinction between menses and giving birth. But to primitive peoples, who were extremely sensitive to blood, there was a similarity between the two because on both occasions women were in a bloodied condition. Since the bloodshed, and hence segregation, occurred more frequently in the menstrual periods, anthropologists drew the conclusion that it was primarily a "menstrual taboo." In fact, it was a taboo on women whenever they were in a condition of shedding blood.

The extreme fear of savage men at approaching or even looking at a woman in her menses has been widely reported, from the earliest writers to the most recent field investigators. Although under direct questioning the aborigines could give only vague explanations as to the source of this fear, these were very similar to the reasons they gave for avoiding women during hunting and killing expeditions: even an unwitting violation of the rule of avoidance would result in the worst calamities and even death. To cite a few examples:

> Among the Bacas and other South African tribes, "should a man touch a woman during the period, his bones become soft, and in future he cannot take part in warfare or any other manly exercise." The Bushmen believe that a glance from a menstruating woman could cause men to become fixed in whatever position they happened to be, and turn into trees. In New Guinea, if a lochial woman were so much as seen by a man, his body would swell up and he would surely die; and the natives of Mowat and Daudai are convinced that slow death would follow any relations with a menstruous woman. The islanders of Wetar, in the

Malay Archipelago, believe that if a man were to tread on a drop of menstrual blood terrible misfortunes would befall him in war or any other enterprise, and that no precautions could avail to save him from his fate. The Orang Belanda believe that contact with a menstruous woman will deprive a man of his manhood. In Australia the natives of Queensland believe that if they were to approach the place where a woman stayed during her period of seggregation they would surely die. . . . (ibid., pp. 386-87)

Once again these vague explanations by the aborigines were misinterpreted by male-oriented investigators. They assumed that savage men were motivated by feelings of disgust and repulsion at the sight of blood in general, and in particular the loathsome menstrual blood of women. But how likely is it that such squeamishness existed among cannibalistic hunters? As Briffault comments:

When a savage manifests disgust, it is almost invariably the suggestion of the breach of some tabu, such as eating some food, maybe quite appetising, that is prohibited by his customs, which calls forth those manifestations; the tabu is the cause, not the effect of, his disgust. . . .
    The awful character ascribed to a menstruating or lochial woman has been set down to a supposed primitive "horror of blood." M. Durkheim has elaborated a far-reaching theory which has met with wide acceptance. . . . But there is no evidence of any such horror among primitive peoples. On the contrary; far from his manifesting a horror of blood, the savage appears to have a passionate predilection for it. Blood is everywhere regarded as a delicacy. . . . Human blood is constantly drunk by savages in their rites and blood covenants, and partaken of as a tonic medicine. . . . There is no instance known of blood, in general, being regarded with horror by any uncultured people. (ibid., pp. 397-99)

Savage men's horror of menstrual blood was connected with their dread of women and of infringing women's taboos, which in the first instance prohibited men from shedding the blood of women. Briffault, citing Kingsley, writes, "Blood from a woman is held in high horror." She was told about a man who, from some cause or other, became so weak that he could hardly crawl; he ascribed his condition to having seen the blood of a woman who was killed by a falling tree. It was not merely menstrual blood but any blood from a woman that inspired this fear. To locate the source of this reaction we must bear in mind the ignorance of savages about biological processes.

Primitive peoples did not know the facts about life and death. They did not know that a child was conceived through the sexual intercourse of a man and woman. Among other naive views they held on the subject was the notion that the child was conceived spontaneously through a woman's magical powers or through something she ate. Similarly, they did not know that death could occur through natural or accidental causes. They thought all deaths were the result of a hostile act on the part of an enemy.

They were also ignorant of the causes and character of menstruation. As Crawley observes, "Ignorance of the nature of female periodicity leads savage men to consider it as the flow of blood from a wound" (*The Mystic Rose,* vol. I, pp. 230-31). The wound is usually attributed to some animal, bird, or snake. These totemic disguises, however, conceal the fact that a man found in the vicinity of a woman shedding blood would be regarded with suspicion as the possible attacker and suffer the consequences.

The safest policy for men was to adhere to the rule of avoidance of women not only during their periods but even more strictly during childbirth, lest they be held responsible if the child died. Thus, although the taboos and rules of avoidance were instituted by women for their convenience, these also furnished protection to those men who abided by the rules and stayed away from women and children whenever they were tabooed.

Since woman's blood was taboo, daubing with blood became the mark or insignia of the tabooed condition. "Blood is not only the object of various tabus," says Briffault, "but the 'sign of blood' is the most general symbol and mark of a tabu" (*The Mothers,* vol. II, p. 412). In the course of time, red ocher came to serve as a substitute for blood. According to Spencer and Gillen, the deposits of red ocher found in various parts of Australia are said by the aborigines to have been caused by the flow of blood from women's vulvas in the most ancient times, which they call Alcheringa. Briffault writes on this point:

The Australian blacks pour blood over their sacred stones and poles, and paint their "churingas" with red ochre. They paint themselves red after the performance of the intichiuma rites. They moreover volunteer the strangely significant information that this red paint is really the menstrual blood of women. . . . The Bushmen and Hottentots . . . appear to associate, like the Australian aborigines, their ceremonial red paint with menstrual blood. (ibid., pp. 416-17)

Red ocher as a substitute for blood has been used in virtually every primitive region of the globe. Chapple and Coon write, "The list of peoples who use red ocher is practically a list of the peoples of the world" (*Principles of Anthropology*, p. 597). It has been found daubed on the fossil bones dug up by archaeologists. "In Aurignacian times," says Hocart, "it was sprinkled over the remains of the dead, sometimes in such profusion that the skeleton of Paviland is known as the 'Red Lady of Paviland'" (*The Progress of Man*, p. 143). Even in death the sign of blood marked woman off as taboo—"untouchable."

When savage women painted themselves or their infants red, this was a public signal that the rule of avoidance was in operation. The following examples are from Briffault's data:

The condition of women in a tabu state is itself commonly indicated by their painting themselves red. Thus among the Dieri and other Australian tribes, menstruating women were marked with red paint round the mouth. Among the tribes of Victoria a menstruating woman is painted red from the waist upwards. Among the Tapuya tribes of Brazil a menstruating woman is also painted red. In some parts of the Gold Coast women painted themselves red when menstruating. Kaffir women, when they are pregnant, paint themselves with red ochre. In India the condition of a menstruating woman is indicated by her wearing round her neck a handkerchief stained with menstrual blood. . . .

Mothers among the Tlinkit Indians, in order to safeguard their children against evil influences and cause them to grow strong, paint their noses red. (*The Mothers*, vol. II, pp. 414-15)

The color red as the mark of taboo was extended beyond women and children to everything forbidden or dangerous. Among the people and objects placed under the taboo by being daubed, painted, or sprinkled with blood or red paint were corpses, man-slayers, war-chiefs, brides, sacred trees, and stones. To the present day the color red is the official signal of danger.

The segregation of women from men at the time of child-birth was even more pronounced and of longer duration than during the menstrual period. It resembled more closely the segregation of the men from the women after a hunting or fighting expedition. As Crawley sums up these two periods of intense taboo, they were connected with "men at war and women at child-birth" (*The Mystic Rose*, vol. I, p. 85).

Even after matrimony was well established, on the occasion of childbirth the woman left the house where she normally lived with her husband and retreated to a hut, lodge, or other "outhouse" erected for that purpose at a distance from the house. There she remained to give birth and tend her offspring, assisted only by women. Webster's illustrations are typical:

> A Herero woman who has given birth to a child lives in a special hut which her female companions have constructed for her. Both the hut and the woman at this time are "sacred." Men are not allowed to see the lying-in woman until the navel string has separated from the child, otherwise they would become weaklings and when later they went to war they would be killed. . . .
>
> A Huron or an Iroquois mother never gave birth in her own hut but always in a little house outside the village. She remained secluded for some time—for 40 days in the case of a first child. (*Taboo*, pp. 73, 75)

This segregation of women during childbirth and menstruation has been even more misunderstood than their segregation during the hunting and fighting expeditions of the men. In both instances anthropologists have assumed that men laid down the groundrules that kept women at a distance from them, and that the object was to prevent the men from becoming "contaminated." And the worst menace was assumed to be connected with the menstruating woman because her blood would defile the men.

This thesis of the "contaminating woman" has had a growing

vogue in twentieth-century anthropology. Even women anthropologists have submitted papers at conventions describing the subject in these terms. It is even suggested that this biological stigma of unclean, impure blood is the source of woman's social degradation.

This thesis stems from modern interpretations of the term "taboo," which is said to mean unclean, impure, or polluting. However, the word "taboo" also has a diametrically opposite meaning — sacred, pure, holy. Given these opposite meanings, it is as appropriate to say that the blood shed by woman at menstruation or childbirth is polluting as it would be to say that the blood shed by hunters and drunk by cannibals is pure and undefiling.

Moreover, in its original sense the term "taboo" meant "forbidden" or "untouchable" and extremely dangerous if the rule of avoidance was violated. The most untouchable were children in those periods when they were marked off as taboo, and the most dangerous were the women if their rules of avoidance were violated. As Briffault points out:

> Primitive man dreads to have anything to do with what is tabu much as a person is unwilling to handle a loaded infernal machine. The deterrent motive is dread of the consequences. The only vague thing about the sentiment with which the tabu is regarded by primitive man, is his ignorance of the exact causes of the peril and of the exact form which the dreaded consequences may take; and that very ignorance is a powerful factor in increasing the magnitude of his dread. (*The Mothers*, vol. II, p. 362)

In the epoch of savagery it was not the mothers but the hunters and eaters of flesh who represented the "contaminating" sex, as evidenced by the purification rituals they were obliged to perform. This was turned into its opposite after the patriarchal takeover. To justify the degradation of women that now occurred for the first time in human history, the blame was placed upon woman's biology in general, and in particular upon her "contaminating" blood. A few examples will show this upside-down patriarchal picture of brave, clean men and repulsive, unclean women.

Crawley cites the early patriarchal Hindu Laws of Manu, which state, "The wisdom, the energy, the strength, the right,

and the vitality of a man who approaches a woman covered
with menstrual excrement, utterly perish." This attitude is well
expressed, Crawley says, in a rhyme quoted by Havelock Ellis:

> Oh! menstruating woman, thou'rt a fiend
> From whom all nature should be closely screened.
> (*The Mystic Rose,* vol. I, p. 77)

Briffault cites the Hindu Institutes of Vishnu, where it is
laid down that "if a woman in her courses should touch an
Aryan, she shall be lashed with a whip." Similarly, in ancient
Persia, the Zoroastrian sacred books say that "the very glance
from the eye of a menstruous woman was regarded as polluting
whatever thing it fell on, 'for a fiend so violent is that fiend
of menstruation that, where another fiend does not smite anything with a look, it smites with a look.'" And in the Old Testament it is written:

> "If a woman have an issue, and her issue in her flesh be
> blood, she shall be put apart seven days; and whosoever
> toucheth her shall be unclean until even. And everything
> that she lieth upon in her separation shall be unclean;
> everything also that she sitteth upon shall be unclean. And
> whosoever toucheth her bed shall wash his clothes, and
> bathe himself in water, and be unclean until the even . . .
> and the priest shall make an atonement for her before
> the Lord for the issue of her uncleanness." In ancient Arabia
> similar precautions were observed, and the menstruous
> woman was isolated in a special hut. (*The Mothers,* vol.
> II, pp. 375-76)

Thus did the formerly forbidden woman become the "unclean" woman, lashed by the male lords and masters of society for contaminating men. Under patriarchal rule women
suffered punishments and hardships totally unknown in the
matriarchal epoch. Where formerly the tabooed woman was
surrounded, protected, and comforted by other women, now
the "unclean" woman was avoided even by members of her
own sex. There are reports of women fleeing in stormy weather
and snow to give birth alone, often in the open without any
kind of hut or outhouse in which to take refuge. Briffault gives
other examples:

In Bokhara the women are reputed impure for forty days after their delivery; "they would not even dare to pray to God while that supposed impurity lasts." In the Caucasus, among the Chevsurs, there is at some distance from every village a rough stone hut thatched with straw; thither every Chevsur girl or woman betakes herself for two days when she is menstruating. She wears her oldest clothes; and her provisions are brought to her and put down at some distance from the hut. For her confinement a special shelter is built for her by other women, at a distance of two or three "versts" from the village; she is delivered there on straw entirely unattended; women bring food, which is left in front of the hut, for on no account must they hold any communication with her. The hut and its contents are afterwards burnt. Those customs are general throughout the Caucasus; Circassian women are also invariably delivered on a bed of straw. In Russia a woman, after delivery, is regarded as being in a state of impurity and may not hold any communication with others until she has been purified by a priest; in the province of Smolensk she is confined in a barn or in a hut at some distance from the house. In Serbia, likewise, birth takes place invariably out of doors, no matter what the weather or the severity of the season. When she feels the first indications of labour, a woman "quietly and silently departs in order not to pollute the house. She returns, after the separation of the afterbirth, with the baby in her apron. (ibid., pp. 374-75)

Under these circumstances it was the fortunate woman who found refuge with patriarchal man's most valuable property, the domesticated animals he protected from the elements in warm stables and barns. Here at the hour of delivery the woman could lie down on the straw in the manger and give birth. The sheep, horses, and cows provided the comfort denied her by fellow humans. We are told that Mary, the most famous of mothers, gave birth in this fashion.

One of the most conspicuous features of egalitarian maternal society was the deference of men toward the female sex. Indeed, so carefully did they abide by the taboos and rules of avoidance laid down by women, and so extended were the periods of time in which they were segregated from women, that primitive man's knowledge about the work and general activities of women was extremely limited. Some anthropologists have lamented the fact that most investigators have been men, receiving their information from savage men who were poorly informed about the activities of women. Much valuable documentation has been irretrievably lost because women anthropologists have been so few and have entered this field of study quite late. This dearth of information about savage women has compounded the errors made by anthropologists imbued with modern patriarchal notions.

Prominent among these errors was the insistence by Sir Henry Maine, Westermarck, and others that the father was indispensable in providing for his helpless wife and children. They could not see that in the period of the maternal clan, when men were preoccupied with hunting and fighting, women were the principal producers of the necessities of life for all the members of the community, as their labor record shows.

5

The Productive Record
of Primitive Women

Production and procreation are the twin pillars upon which all human society has been founded. Through labor humans provide themselves with the necessities of life; through reproduction they create new life. However, only one of these is an exclusively human activity. Procreation is a natural function that humans share with the animals; production is uniquely a human acquisition. The use and making of tools, therefore, marks the great dividing line between human society and animal existence.

It is sometimes objected that primates, like humans, can make and use tools. A primate may grasp a twig, defoliate it, and then utilize it to get at insects under a stone. In captivity, under human influence, these animals can be very clever; sometimes they fit sticks together to extend their reach or stack boxes one on the other to climb up for food. But these are only incidental and episodic acts. Their existence does not depend on learning them. Humans, on the other hand, cannot survive except through systematic labor.

Further, in the course of their productive activities humans generate entirely new needs that go beyond the biological needs of animal existence. From the first chipped stone or digging stick to the jet plane and space ship, the history of human production is the continuous emergence of new needs and of the technology for satisfying them. Gordon Childe defines society as "a co-operative organization for producing means to satisfy its needs, for reproducing itself—and for producing new needs" (*What Happened in History,* p. 17).

It is commonly believed that because men are the principal producers in modern society this has always been the case. In fact, the opposite was true in the earlier and longer epoch before civilization; the larger share of work devolved upon women. This is borne out in the oft-cited statement of a Kurnai aborigine in Australia, who said that man's work was to hunt, spear fish, fight, and then "sit down." Woman's work was to "do all else." Let us examine what is incorporated in the succinct "all else."

Control of the Food Supply

The quest for food is the most compelling concern of any society. No higher development of society is possible unless and until people are fed. Moreover, while animals can live on a day-to-day basis, humans had to win some measure of control over their food supply if they were to progress. Control means not only sufficient food for today but a surplus for tomorrow, and the ability to preserve and conserve stocks for future use.

From this standpoint human history can be divided into two main epochs: the food-gathering epoch which extended over hundreds of thousands of years and the food-producing epoch which began with agriculture and stock-raising about eight thousand years ago, laying the foundation for civilization. Between these two periods was a transitional stage of small-scale garden culture or horticulture.

From the beginning there is a continuous record of the work of women in procuring and developing the food supply, discovering new sources and kinds of food, and gaining knowledge about its preservation. The prime tool in this work was the digging stick, a long stick with a pointed end used by the women to dig up roots and vegetables from the ground. To this day, in some parts of the world, the digging stick remains as inseparable from the woman as her baby. The white settlers called the Shoshone Indians of Nevada and Wyoming "The Diggers" because they still employed this ancient technique.

Except for a few areas in the world at certain historical stages, the most reliable sources of food were not animal but vegetable. Alexander Goldenweiser writes:

> Everywhere the sustenance of this part of the household is more regularly and reliably provided by the efforts of the home-bound woman than by those of her roving hunter husband or son. It is, in fact, a familiar spectacle

among all primitive peoples that the man, returning home from a more or less arduous chase, may yet reach home empty-handed and himself longing for food. Under such conditions, the vegetable supply of the family has to serve his needs as well as those of the rest of the household. (*Anthropology,* p. 101)

Through long experience in digging-stick activities, women eventually learned the art of cultivating the soil. Frazer gives a description of his process among the Australian aborigines:

Again, among the natives of Western Australia "it is generally considered the province of women to dig roots, and for this purpose they carry a long, pointed stick, which is held in the right hand, and driven firmly into the ground, where it is shaken, so as to loosen the earth, which is scooped up and thrown out with the fingers of the left hand, and in this manner they dig with great rapidity. But the labour, in proportion to the amount obtained, is great. To get a yam about half an inch in circumference and a foot in length, they have to dig a hole above a foot square and two feet in depth; a considerable portion of the time of the women and children is, therefore, passed in this employment. . . . In fertile districts, where the yams . . . grow abundantly, the ground may sometimes be seen riddled with holes made by the women in their search for these edible roots. . . . Among the aborigines of central Victoria. . . . The implement which they used to dig up roots with was a pole seven or eight feet long, hardened in the fire and pointed at the end, which also served them as a weapon both of defence and of offence. . . .

In these customs . . . we may perhaps detect some of the steps by which mankind have advanced . . . to the systematic cultivation of plants. For an effect of digging up the earth in the search for roots has probably been in many cases to enrich and fertilise the soil and so to increase the crop of roots or herbs. . . . Moreover, the winnowing of the seeds on ground which had thus been turned up by the digging-sticks of the women would naturally contribute to the same result. . . . It is almost certain that in the process of winnowing the seeds as a preparation for eating them many of the grains must have escaped and, being wafted by the wind, have fallen on the upturned soil and borne fruit. Thus . . . savage woman was unconsciously preparing for the whole community a future and more abundant store of food. . . . (*The Golden Bough*, Part I, *Spirits of the Corn and of the Wild*, vol. I, pp. 126-29)

In the course of their work not only was the quantity assured; the quality of the plants was also improved. New types and better varieties came into existence. Chapple and Coon refer to the turnip, which gave rise to "such diverse vegetables as cabbage, Brussels sprouts, broccoli, and cauliflower." And, "in Melanesia, people grow cultivated yams six feet long and a foot or more thick; the miserable root which the Australian digs wild from the ground is no more voluminous than a cigar" (*Principles of Anthropology*, pp. 174-75).

According to Otis Tufton Mason, "Long before the days of discoverers and explorers who wrote about them, women in America, Africa, and the Indo-Pacific were farmers, and had learned to use the digging stick, the hoe, and even a rude plough" (*Woman's Share in Primitive Culture*, pp. 24-25).

Gordon Childe tells us that "every single cultivated food plant of any importance has been discovered by some nameless barbarian society," among them wheats, barleys, rice, millet, maize, yams, manioc, squashes and other plants that are not cereals at all. To accomplish this neolithic revolution, he says, "mankind, or rather womankind, had not only to discover suitable plants and appropriate methods for their cultivation, but must also devise special implements for tilling the soil, reaping and storing the crop, and converting it into foods" (*What Happened in History*, pp. 56-58).

It is not surprising that primitive men came to look upon women as possessing magical powers in the growing of food, akin to their powers in growing children. Crawley tells how the Orinoco Indians explained this to a missionary:

When the women plant maize the stalk produces two or three ears; when they set the manioc the plant produces two or three baskets of roots; and thus everything is multiplied. Why? Because women know how to produce children, and know how to plant the corn so as to ensure its germinating. Then, let them plant it; we do not know so much as they do. (*The Mystic Rose*, vol. I, p. 62)

In addition to cultivating plants, women also collected grubs, bugs, lizards, molluscs, and small animals such as hares, marsupials, birds, and the young of many animal species. They protected, fed, and cared for many of these animals as well as the young animals brought back alive by the hunters to the campsite.

This care and protection on the part of the women provided the basis for the first experiments in animal taming and domestication. Not infrequently a field investigator has encountered a woman suckling a puppy or other animal infant at one breast, her own baby at the other. The specific characteristics of each animal were studied, and those which grew up to be dangerous were kept in cages. Mason writes on this subject:

> Now, the first domestication is simply adoption of helpless infancy. The young wolf, or kid, or lamb, or calf, is brought to the home of the hunter. It is fed and caressed by the mother and her children, and even nourished at her breast. Innumerable references might be given to the caging and taming of wild creatures. The Eskimos and the Indians south of them capture the silver fox, and the women feed them until such time as is best for stripping off their hides. The Pueblo people cage eagles and hawks for their feathers, and the women feed them. Every native hut in Guiana is the abode of many species of birds, kept for their bright plumage. The great domestic animals left off the ferine state so long ago that no one knows their aboriginal home. Women were always associated especially with the milk-and-fleece-yielding species of these. (*Woman's Share,* p. 151)

Control of the food supply involved sparing young animals, which could grow up and multiply. Some animals and birds were not used for food at all while others were used only at certain times and under certain conditions. This preservation of animals, which requires the exercise of restraint, is at once the cause and the consequence of domestication.

While one aspect of woman's work, soil cultivation with the digging stick, was leading in the direction of agriculture, another was leading toward the domestication of stock animals. This combination of techniques laid the foundation for elevating humanity out of savagery, through barbarism, and into civilization. It was only later that men took over what women had developed, becoming the principal farmers and stock raisers.

In the process of gaining control of the food supplies women were also obliged to invent a whole collateral series of techniques and equipment for the preservation of food. Mason describes how the manifold industries of women grew up out of this necessity:

> Wherever tribes of mankind have gone women have found out by and by that great staple productions were to be their chief reliance. In Polynesia it is taro and bread fruit. In Africa it is the palm and tapioca, the millet and yams. In Asia it is rice, in Europe the cereals, and in America corn and potatoes, and acorns or pinions in some places. The whole industrial life of woman is built up around these staples. From the first journey on foot to procure the raw material until the food is served and eaten there is a line of trades that are continuous and that are born of the environment. (ibid., p. 15)

Among the requirements were vessels and containers for carrying, cooking, serving, and storing food and drink. Depending upon the materials at hand in the environment, these containers were made of wood, bark, fibers, skins, and so on, until finally women learned how to make pots and vessels out of clay, hardening them in the fire.

Even the discovery of the uses of fire was connected with women's labor activities. From the first digging stick, with its point hardened in the fire, there is a continuous development in the uses of fire by women.

The Use of Fire in Cooking and Industries

All animals fear fire and flee from it; even the smell of smoke is sufficient to cause a stampede. Humans are capable of controlling and utilizing fire. According to Childe, this achievement marks a major distinction between humans and animals. Here is how he describes this great conquest:

> . . . in mastery of fire man was controlling a mighty physical force and a conspicuous chemical change. For the first time in history a creature of Nature was directing one

of the great forces of Nature. And the exercise of power must react upon the controller. The sight of the bright flame bursting forth when a dry bough was thrust into glowing embers, the transformation of the bough into fine ashes and smoke, must have stimulated man's rudimentary brain. . . . in feeding and damping down the fire, in transporting and using it, man made a revolutionary departure from the behavior of other animals. He was asserting his humanity and making himself. (*Man Makes Himself*, p. 46)

A.M. Hocart points out that invoking some "lucky accident" such as two branches rubbing against each other in the wind and catching fire is no explanation for the domestication of fire. More likely, it came about in the course of labor activities; "given a craftsman whose chief material is wood, not stone, and who shapes his works by friction, fire is bound to result sometimes" (*The Progress of Man*, p. 115). Since the females were the first "craftsmen," this suggests that in the course of her labor activities woman discovered how to rekindle fire and learned how to use it.

Both the preparation and conservation of food required the use of controlled fire and directed heat. The basic cooking techniques — broiling, boiling, roasting, baking, steaming, etc. — were developed by women. Through the application of fire and directed heat, they also preserved stocks of vegetable, fish, and animal foods for future use.

Fire was also used in the collateral equipment that women made for cooking, preserving, and storing food. One of the remarkable achievements of the women was the making of wooden vessels for cooking that were both leak-proof and fireproof. From Mason's description we can see how the same principles could have been applied to the manufacture of the first canoes and other water craft:

> . . . they burned out the cavity of the future boiler. They carefully watched the progress of the fire, and when it threatened to spread laterally, they checked its course in that direction by means of strips of green bark or mud or water. As soon as the ashes and charred wood prevented the further action of the fire, this marvellous Gill-at-all-trades removed the fire and brushed out the *debris* with an improvised broom of grass. Then, by means of a scrap-

er of flint which she had made, she dug away the charcoal until she had exposed a clean surface of wood. The
firing and scraping were repeated until the "dugout" assumed the desired form. The trough completed, it was ready
to do the boiling for the family as soon as the meat could
be prepared and the stones heated. (*Woman's Share,*
pp. 32-33)

In this remarkable conversion of natural substances through
the application of fire, wood, which is normally consumed by
fire, was fashioned into fire-proof vessels for cooking. In the
same way the "dugouts" could be enlarged to make leak-proof
vessels for travel on the water.

Through the use of fire and directed heat women even converted some substances that are poisonous in the natural state
into food staples. Manioc, one of the best known, was made
edible through a complicated process of squeezing out its poisonous properties in a basketry press and driving out the
residue by heating. According to Mason, "There are in many
lands plants which in the natural state are poisonous or extremely acrid or pungent. The women of these lands have all
discovered independently that boiling or heating drives off the
poisonous or disagreeable element" (ibid., p. 24).

The Medicine Woman

The original "medicine men" in history were actually women.
Briffault writes on this subject, "The connection of women with
the cultivation of the soil and the search for edible vegetables
and roots made them specialists in botanical knowledge, which,
among primitive peoples, is extraordinarily extensive. They
became acquainted with the properties of herbs, and were thus
the first doctors." He adds:

The word "medicine" is derived from a root meaning "knowledge" or "wisdom"—the wisdom of the "wise woman." The
name of Medea, the medical herbalist witch, comes from
the same root. . . . "The secret of the witch," said an Ogowe
native, "is knowing the plants that produce certain effects,
and knowing how to compound and use the plants in
order to bring about the desired result; and this is the
sum and essence of witchcraft." In the Congo it is noted
that woman doctors specialise in the use of drugs and herb-

al pharmacy. In Ashanti the medicine women are "generally preferred for medical aid, as they possess a thorough knowledge of barks and herbs." In East Africa "there are as many women physicians as men." (*The Mothers*, vol. I, p. 486)

Dan McKenzie, in *The Infancy of Medicine* (1927), lists hundreds of ancient remedies, some of which are still in use without alteration, while others have been only slightly improved upon. Among these are substances used for their narcotic properties. A fleeting review indicates the astounding scope of these medicinal products. Useful properties were developed from acacia, alcohol, almond, asafetida, balsam, betel, caffeine, camphor, caraway, chaulmoogra oil (a leprosy remedy), digitalis, gum barley water, lavender, linseed, parsley, pepper, pine tar, pomegranate, poppy, rhubarb, senega, sugar, turpentine, wormwood, and hundreds more. These came from regions all over the globe— South America, North America, Africa, China, Europe, Egypt, etc. Not only vegetable but animal substances were made into remedies; snake venom, for example, was converted into a serum to be used for snake bites, the equivalent of today's antivenin.

According to Marston Bates, very little had been added to this remarkable ancient collection of medicine, until the discoveries of sulfa and antibiotics. "How primitive man discovered the ways of extracting, preparing and using all of these drugs, poisons and foods, remains one of the great mysteries of human prehistory," he writes (*The Forest and the Sea*, p. 126). But it is not so mysterious when we look in the direction of the female sex and become acquainted with the hard work, vast experience, and nimble wits of primitive womankind, preoccupied with every aspect of group survival.

Not only medicine but the rudiments of various other sciences grew up side by side with the craft and know-how of women. Childe points out that to convert flour into bread requires a knowledge of biochemistry and the use of the yeast microorganism. This substance also led to the production of fermented liquors and beer. Childe also gives credit to women for "the chemistry of pot-making, the physics of spinning, the mechanics of the loom, and the botany of flax and cotton" (*What Happened in History*, p. 59).

As one need was satisfied, new needs arose, and these in turn were met in a rising spiral of newly emerging needs and

newly acquired skills. Since woman's labors in primitive industries are usually credited to "man" or "mankind," it is worth
examining the great variety of handicrafts that originated in
the hands and heads of women before they were taken over
by men in the higher stages of industry.

From Cordage to Textiles

Cordage may appear to be a very humble trade, yet this
was the beginning of a whole chain of crafts that culminated
in the great textile industry. The technique of making and
plaiting cordage requires not only manual dexterity but a
knowledge of selecting, treating, and manipulating the materials used. Chapple and Coon write:

> All known peoples make some use of cordage, whether
> it is for binding haftings on implements, making rabbit
> nets and string bags, or tying ornaments about their necks.
> Where skins are much used, as among the Eskimo, this
> cordage may consist mostly of thongs cut from hides, and
> animal sinews; people who use few skins and live in forests
> use vegetable fibers, such as rattan, hibiscus fiber, and
> spruce roots, which come in such long units that, like
> thongs and sinews, no secondary treatment is necessary
> to make them serviceable.
>   Other fibers, however, are short, and must be twisted
> together into a continuous cord or thread if they are to
> be used. (*Principles of Anthropology,* p. 112)

The technique of plaiting led to the basket industry. Depending upon the available materials, these were made of bark,
grass, bast, skins, roots. Some were woven, others sewn. The
variety of baskets and other woven articles is immense. Robert
H. Lowie lists some of these: burden baskets, water bottles,
shallow bowls, parching trays, shields (in the Congo), caps
and cradles (in California), fans, knapsacks, mats, satchels,
boxes, fish-creels. Some of the baskets are so tightly woven that
they are waterproof and used for cooking and storage (*An
Introduction to Cultural Anthropology,* p. 124). Briffault tells
us:

> The weaving of bark and grass fibres by primitive women
> is often so marvellous that it could not be imitated by any

man at the present day, even with the resources of machinery. The so-called Panama hats, the best of which can be crushed and passed through a finger-ring, are a familiar example. . . . (*The Mothers,* vol. I, p. 465)

Women utilized every resource that the environment placed at their disposal for this craft. In areas where the coconut is found, a superior cordage was made from the fibers of its husk. In the Philippines an inedible species of banana furnished the famous manila hemp for cordage and weaving. In Polynesia the paper mulberry tree was cultivated for its bark. After the bark was beaten out by the women it was made into cloth, and from this cloth they made shirts for men and women, bags, straps, and so on.

All this led to the textile industry, which emerged in the neolithic period. According to Childe:

> Among the remains of the earliest neolithic villages of Egypt and Hither Asia we find the first indications of a textile industry. Manufactured garments, woven out of linen, or later wool, begin to compete with dressed skins or skirts of leaves as protection against cold and sun. For this to be possible another complex of discoveries and inventions is requisite; a further body of scientific knowledge must be practically applied. . . . A textile industry thus not only requires the knowledge of special substances like flax, cotton, and wool, but also the breeding of special animals and the cultivation of special plants. (*Man Makes Himself,* pp. 79-80)

The loom was a new creation brought about by the requirements of the textile industry. Childe writes about its importance:

> Now a loom is quite an elaborate piece of machinery — much too elaborate to be described here. Its use is no less complicated. The invention of the loom was one of the great triumphs of human ingenuity. Its inventors are nameless, but they made an essential contribution to the capital stock of human knowledge. . . . (*Man Makes Himself,* p. 80)

When we turn to the dressing and tanning of hides, we find an equally astonishing performance on the part of primitive women.

Leather-Makers and Tanners

Carleton Coon writes on the subject of hunting, which was man's work:

> Hunting is fine exercise for body and brain. It stimulates and may have "selected for" the qualities of self-control, cooperation, tempered aggressiveness, ingenuity, inventiveness, and a high degree of manual dexterity. Mankind could have gone through no better school in its formative period. (*A Reader in General Anthropology*, p. 590)

However, hunting and killing animals does not involve more mental effort and physical dexterity than is required for converting the hides and other by-products of the chase into useful articles. It was the women who dressed the skins, tanned them into leather, and made a great variety of new products out of them.

Leather-making is a long, difficult, and complicated process. Lowie describes the earliest form of this work as it was still being practiced by the Ona women of Tierra del Fuego in recent times. He writes:

> When an Ona has flayed a guanaco hide, his wife stretches it for drying and after several days lays it out on the ground, wool side down. She kneels on the stiff rawhide and laboriously scrapes off the fatty tissue and the transparent layer below it with her quartz blade. After a while she kneads the skin piecemeal with her fists, going over the whole surface repeatedly and even bringing her teeth into play until it is softened. If the hair is to be taken off, that is done with the same scraper. (*An Introduction to Cultural Anthropology*, p. 118)

The chipped stone scraper and the digging stick are the two most ancient implements. This fact alone establishes women as the inventors and users of the first tools and thereby the pioneers in labor activities. Briffault sums up the evidence as follows:

> In order to carry out those industrial processes, primitive woman has devised various implements. The "scrapers," which form so large a proportion of prehistoric tools,

were used and made by women. In the days when Boucher de Perthes's discoveries of the palaeolithic tools of European humanity were being discussed, much controversy took place as to the possible use of those "scrapers." The fact which went farthest toward silencing scepticism was that the Eskimo women at the present day use instruments identical with those which their European sisters have left in such abundance in the drift gravels of the Ice Age. The scrapers and knives of the Eskimo women are often elaborately and even artistically mounted on handles of bone. In South Africa the country is strewn with scrapers identical with those of palaeolithic Europe; and Mr. E. S. Hartland learnt from the testimony of persons intimately acquainted with the Bushmen that those implements were manufactured by the women. (*The Mothers,* vol. I, p. 461)

Mason holds the same view:

These stone scrapers, universal in present savagery, were once the favorite implement with our grandmothers many times removed. The Aryan peoples, both in Asia and in Europe, once clothed themselves in the same fashion as the American aborigines of to-day. If you were to visit their camp sites you would pick up among the implements of flint, scrapers in abundance. In the pile dwellings of Switzerland and Italy fragments of leather have been found, and the Britons were clad in skins in the days of Julius Caesar. . . . The scraper is the oldest implement of any craft in the world. The Indian women of Montana still receive their trade from their mothers, and they, in turn, were taught by theirs, in unbroken succession, since the birth of the human species. (*Woman's Share,* pp. 77-78)

Leather-making required more than manual dexterity. Since tanning is essentially a chemical alteration of the raw hide, women had to learn the secrets of such chemistry. They learned how to apply one substance to effect a transformation in another.

Among the Eskimos, writes Lowie, this chemical change is achieved by steeping the skins in a basin of urine. In North America the Indian women soaked the skins in a preparation made with the brains of animals (*Introduction to Cultural Anthropology,* p. 119).

Directed heat was also part of the process of leather-making. To toughen the leather, women smoked it over a smoldering fire. The shields of the North American Indians were so tough that they were not only arrow-proof but sometimes even bullet-proof.

Leather products cover as broad a range as basketry. Lowie lists some of these: Asiatic nomads used leather for bottles; East Africans made shields and clothing. North American Indians used leather for robes, shirts, dresses, leggings, moccasins, tents, cradles, and shields. They stored smoking outfits and sundries in buckskin pouches and preserved meat in rawhide cases. The elaborate assortment of leather products made by the North American Indian women excites the admiration of visitors to the museums in which they are collected.

Briffault points out that the women had to know the nature of the particular hide they were preparing and had to decide beforehand the type of product for which it was best suited:

It varies infinitely according to the use for which the leather is intended; pliable skins smoothed out to a uniform thickness and retaining the layer to which the hair is attached; hard hides for tents, shields, canoes, boots; thin, soft, wash-leather for clothing — all require special technical processes which primitive woman has elaborated. (*The Mothers,* vol. I, p. 460)

Regarding the vast assortment of skins utilized by women in this industry, Mason tells us:

On the American continent alone women skin dressers knew how to cure and manufacture hides of cats, wolves, foxes, all the numerous skunk family, bears, coons, seals, walrus, buffalo, musk ox, goat, sheep, antelope, moose, deer, elk, all kinds of whales, squirrels of thirty species, beaver, gopher, muskrat, porcupine, hares, opossum, crocodile, tortoise, birds innumerable, and fishes and reptiles.

If aught in the heavens above, or on the earth beneath, or in the waters wore a skin, savage women were found on examination to have had a name for it, and to have succeeded in turning it into its primitive use for human clothing, and to have invented new uses undreamed of by its original owners. (*Woman's Share,* p. 71)

Decorative art was developed by women in connection with their crafts. This can be seen in the colorful designs woven into their baskets and leather products. This artistry was carried forward in pot-making, where woman's productive skill reached a higher plateau.

Pot-Makers and Artists

Pot-making, according to Childe, signifies a leap in the conscious control of fire and the knowledge of how to achieve chemical changes. He writes:

> Pot-making is perhaps the earliest conscious utilization by man of a chemical change. . . . The essence of the potter's craft is that she can mold a piece of clay into any shape she desires and then give that shape permanence by "firing" (i.e., heating to over 600 degrees C). To early man this change in the quality of the material must have seemed a sort of magic transubstantiation — the conversion of mud or dust into stone. . . . In the process of firing, the clay changes not only its physical consistency but also its color. . . . Thus the potter's craft even in its crudest, most generalized form, was already complex. It involved an appreciation of a number of distinct processes, the application of a whole constellation of discoveries. Only a few of these have even been mentioned. . . . The constructive character of the potter's craft reacted on human thought. Building up a pot was a supreme instance of creation by man. (*Man Makes Himself*, pp. 76-79)

Although Childe, in his lengthy description of the intricacies of pot-making, repeatedly refers to the potter as "she," he concludes with "man" as the creator of pots. George Thomson, on the other hand, gives a picturesque description of how primitive women, the pot-makers, viewed their own endeavors:

> To them it was an act of creation — a woman's mystery, at which no man might be present. When one of them finished a model she held it up for the others to admire, and called it a "created being." After drying it in the sun, she tapped it with her scraper, and it chimed. This was the creature speaking. When she put it in the oven, she laid

food beside it. If it cracked in the firing — and it did if there was not enough sand or grit in it — the loud clang was the creature's cry as it escaped. This was shown by the fact that a cracked jar never chimed again. Hence, in striking contrast to their usual practice, the women never sang at this work for fear that these creatures they had brought into being might be tempted to respond and so break the pots. To them, therefore, the finished article was something more than a pot. It was a living vessel with a voice and a will of its own. (*Studies in Ancient Greek Society,* vol. II, p. 48)

With the development of the potter's wheel, which came late in history, pot-making was taken over by men. But Briffault gives a roundup of data from every portion of the globe indicating that "the original potter was a woman," and so was the original artist-decorator:

The origin of ceramic ornament may be clearly seen in the polychromatic designs of Maidu basket-work, which for beauty even surpass many products of Greek ceramic decoration. Fifty entirely different schemes of design have been distinguished. At the present day "the knowledge of those designs is almost exclusively confined to the older women." Similarly, the extremely intricate designs of Tunisian pottery differ in every family of women-potters, and are transmitted from mother to daughter. In Guiana the women not only decorated the pots they made, but also all other articles, and even the posts of the huts. It would thus appear that decorative art originated with the women, the first decorators of clothes, of plaited basketry, of pottery. (*The Mothers,* vol. I, p. 477)

It is easier for us to associate women with the artistic work of making pottery than with engineering and construction, but in their earliest stages these, too, were once part of woman's work.

Architects and Engineers

The construction of storehouses for food and of houses for people were once closely connected; in the opinion of some, storehouses came before dwellings. Various types of bins and even elaborate structures were made by women for storing food. Some of the granaries and caches were dug in the ground and lined with straw. On wet, marshy lands they built storehouses on poles above the ground. Mason gives illustrations ranging from the little wicker basket in a northern California hut for preserving acorns to large granaries in Mojave country. One can see the origin of Islamic domes in the African structures made by women as receptacles for storing corn.

Mason also credits women with taming the cat to keep food free of vermin. "Woman tamed the wild-cat for the protection of her granaries. . . . Already at the dawn of written history in Egypt the cat was sacred to Sekhet, or Pasht, daughter of Ra and wife of Ptah" (*Woman's Share,* pp. 17-18).

Women developed their skills far beyond the building of granaries. They built elaborate houses and even whole pueblos or towns. Briffault assembled voluminous data on this aspect of woman's work as architect and engineer, of which the following is a portion:

> The huts of the Australian, of the Andaman islanders, of the Patagonians, of the Botocudos, the rough shelters of the Seri, the skin lodges and wigwams of the American Indian, the black camel-hair tent of the Bedouin, the "yurta" of the nomads of Central Asia, are all the exclusive work and the special care of the women. Some of those more or less movable dwellings are extremely elaborate. The "yurta," for example, is sometimes a capacious house built on a framework of poles pitched in a circle and strengthened by a trellis-work of wooden battens, the whole being covered with thick felt, forming a dome-like structure; the interior is divided into several apartments. "With the exception of the wood, all its component parts are products of the industry of the Turkoman woman, who busies herself also with its construction and the putting together of the various parts. . . . When Mr. Bogoras was studying the language of the Chukchi, he enquired from some men the names of the various parts of the framework of the house. But they were quite unable to inform him on that point; "I don't know," they would answer, "that is woman's business."
>
> . . . The earth-lodges of the Omahas were built entirely by the women. The "pueblos" of New Mexico and Arizona recall the picturesque sky-line of an Oriental town; clusters of many-storied houses rise in terraced tiers, the flat roof

of the one serving as a terrace for that above. The upper stories are reached by ladders or by outside stairs, and the walls are bordered with ornamental crenellated battlements. Courtyards and piazzas, streets and curious round public buildings serving as clubs and temples, form part of those towns. . . . Those edifices are built exclusively by the women. Among the Zuni at the present day the men assist with the heavier work of timbering; among the Hopis the work is still done entirely by the women. (*The Mothers,* vol. I, pp. 478-79)

The Spanish priests who settled among the Pueblo Indians were astonished not only at the beauty of the churches and convents built for them but by the fact that women built them. One priest observed in a report to his European countrymen that "no man had ever set his hand to the erection of a house." He added:

"Those buildings have been erected solely by the women, the girls, and the young boys of the mission; for among these people it is the custom that the women build the houses. . . . When first a man was set by the good padres to building a wall, the poor embarrassed wretch was surrounded by a jeering crowd of women and children, who mocked and laughed, and thought it the most ludicrous thing that they had seen that a man should be engaged in building a house." (ibid., p. 479)

Transportation, like construction, also began with women. This is especially instructive in view of the myth that women have always been physically weaker than men.

On Women's Backs and Heads

Before domesticated animals were utilized for carrying loads, women were the main haulers of goods and equipment. They not only conveyed the raw materials used in their industries but moved entire households of goods from one place to another. On every migration Indian women took down the tents, wigwams, or huts and put them up again. In everyday life they were the carriers of firewood, water, food, and other necessities.

Mason points out that the "burden bearer" is an essential part of primitive industrial life. "Clay and fuel must be brought to make pottery, and pottery, in turn, has to be shaped to carry water and food, so the potter and the carrier are sisters" (*Woman's Share,* p. 116). In many instances a child is part of the load. He writes:

> In British New Guinea . . . it is a common occurrence to see the mother carry on her back a basket of food, a large bundle of firewood — both being supported by a band extending round the forehead — and on top of all her little two-year-old baby. The women are habituated from early life to carrying enormous burdens. (ibid., p. 120)

The Routledges discovered that among the Kikuyus of British East Africa, forty pounds was considered a fair load for a man. But "a woman, fetching home firewood a distance of five to ten miles, of her own accord makes up her load to quite 100 pounds. A Kikuyu man is quite unequal to carrying a load that his women think nothing of" (*With a Prehistoric People,* p. 105).

It has been noted that the greater physical strength of men over women today is a cultivated product of modern life and attitudes about "masculinity" and "femininity." In primitive society the physical differences between the sexes were far less pronounced, according to numerous observers. In some instances the women were found to be superior in physical strength to the men. Here is part of Briffault's documentation on the subject:

> Among the Adombies of the Congo "the women are often stronger than the men and more finely developed." Among the Ashira "the men are not nearly so finely built as the women." The Bashilanga women are "strikingly more muscular than the men," who are weak by comparison. In Dahomey "the women are generally tall, muscular and broad". . . . The women of Ashanti "are of a stronger make than the men." The Wateita women are described as being much more muscularly developed than the men. "In muscular strength and endurance, the women of the Somals are far superior to their lords." . . .
>
> The Kru women "are robust and strong, and capable of carrying immensely heavy burdens on their heads. Every

evening they may be seen trudging home with large water-
pots or a bundle of wood of a hundred pounds weight
on their heads, and perhaps a child slung on their backs.
They can in this way walk for miles without raising their
hand to steady or adjust their heavy burden." . . .

Champlain remarks on the "powerful women of extraordinary strength" among the Canadian Indians; and an
Indian chief declared that a woman "can carry or haul
as much as two men can do." . . . Among the Fuegians
"in general the female sex is much sturdier and stronger
than the male sex." Arab and Druse women are said to
be as tall and as strongly developed as the men; and so
are the women of Afghanistan. Tibetan women are described
as being taller and stronger than the men. . . . The Khasi
women of Assam "can carry loads which Hindus are unable to lift." (*The Mothers,* vol. I, pp. 443-45)

The impressive labor record of women is obscured by the
usual description of it as "household" work. This gives the impression that primitive women, like housewives today, were
preoccupied with the small chores of individual homes, isolated
from one another and having no part in social production.
In reality the opposite was the case.

Women's Social Production

Because women began their labors in so humble a fashion
it is customary to describe their work as mere "handicrafts."
But before machines, everything was made by hand. And
before guilds and factories, the home was the site of all production—that is, not individual homes but the community
household. Without these beginnings the guilds of the Middle
Ages could not have come into existence, nor, at a later stage,
the whole modern complex of mechanized industry. Gordon
Childe writes on this point:

The neolithic crafts have been presented as household industries. Yet the craft traditions are not individual, but
collective traditions. The experience and wisdom of all
the community's members are constantly being pooled.
In a modern African village the housewife does not retire
into seclusion in order to build up and fire her pots. All

the women of the village work together, chatting and comparing notes; they even help one another. The occupation is public; its rules are the result of communal experience. . . . And the neolithic economy as a whole cannot exist without cooperative effort. (*Man Makes Himself,* p. 81)

Cooperative effort — or social production — goes far beyond the solitary efforts of isolated individuals. The experience and knowledge of the whole community can be pooled and transmitted to new generations of producers. As Childe points out:

Even the simplest tool made out of a broken bough or a chipped stone is the fruit of long experience — of trials and errors, impressions noticed, remembered, and compared. The skill to make it has been acquired by observation, by recollection, and by experiment. It may seem an exaggeration, but it is yet true to say that any tool is an embodiment of *science*. For it is a practical application of remembered, compared, and collected experiences of the same kind as are systematized and summarized in scientific formulas, descriptions, and prescriptions. (*What Happened in History,* p. 9)

It was in and through the development of cooperative labor that speech and language also came into existence. Here again, the decisive contributions to early language came from women as a result of their manifold productive activities. Mason writes about the original female "linguist":

Women, having the whole round of industrial arts on their minds all day and every day, must be held to have invented and fixed the language of the same. . . . Indeed, the Mexicans say, "A woman is the best dictionary." This unpremeditated confession is based upon an early induction made by the aborigines of that country centuries ago. Savage men, in hunting and fishing, are much alone, and have to be quiet, hence their taciturnity; but women are together, and chatter all day long. Away from the centres of culture women are still the best dictionaries, talkers, and letter writers. (*Woman's Share,* pp. 189-90)

The first women, the "feminids," began their labor activities without any teachers. They had to learn everything the hard way, sustained only by persistence, courage, wits, and collective ingenuity. They learned some things from close observation of living creatures in nature. As Mason sees it, both sexes probably learned in this manner, but as different sexes they learned different things.

About the male sex he writes: "In contact with the animal world, and ever taking lessons from them, men watched the tiger, the bear, the fox, the falcon — learned their language and imitated them in ceremonial dances." Then he adds:

> But women were instructed by the spiders, the nest builders, the storers of food and the workers in clay like the mud wasp and the termites. It is not meant that these creatures set up schools to teach dull women how to work, but that their quick minds were on the alert for hints coming from these sources. . . . It is in the apotheosis of industrialism that woman has borne her part so persistently and well. At the very beginning of human time she laid down the lines of her duties, and she has kept to them unremittingly. (ibid., pp. 2-3)

Through these manifold labor activities, the minds of women developed at a more rapid pace than those of men. Already more alert because of their maternal functions, women speeded up their intellectual capacities through their ramified social production. Briffault writes:

> The primitive human female, like the animal female, is far more wary, sagacious and ingenious than the male, who is dull and stupid by comparison. Her maternal functions have in the course of a long evolution developed an alertness, a circumspection, an ingenuity, a constructive aptitude, which are foreign to masculine development. The female is accordingly in primitive conditions, not only the equal intellectually of the male, but often his actual superior. . . . it is no wonder that the savage habitually goes to his women-folk for advice. (*The Mothers,* vol. I, p. 490)

The productive record of primitive women has been underestimated and neglected because of the assumption by many anthropologists that man's work has always been the most important. This has resulted in a distorted picture of primitive life and labor. Pages are filled with descriptions of the hunting and fighting activities of men, their blood rites, their games and ceremonies, while the activities of the women are slighted.

As W.I. Thomas explains this, the "unusual esteem" paid to "the destructive activities of the male" is due to the fact that man's exploits were "of a more striking and sensational character, appealed to the emotions more, and secured the attention and the admiration of the public more than the 'drudgery' of the woman" (*Sex and Society,* p. 131). It is a common mistake to conceive of primitive woman's work as "drudgery" in the modern sense of the exploitation and oppression of working women.

The fact is that in primitive communalist society there was no forced or alienated labor, male or female. As Briffault comments:

> It was a pervading fallacy of earlier accounts of primitive social conditions that wherever women were seen working hard, their status was judged to be one of slavery and oppression. No misunderstanding could be more profound; the significance of such evidence is the exact reverse. Generally speaking, it is in those primitive societies where women toil most that their status is most independent and their influence greatest; where they are idle and work is done by slaves, the women are, as a rule, little more than sexual slaves." (*The Mothers,* vol. I, p. 328)

In contrast to this degraded position of women in patriarchal societies, Briffault writes, "In the great majority of uncultured societies women enjoy a position of independence which would appear startling in the most feministic modern civilized society" (ibid., p. 311).

Primitive men did not share the disdain of modern men for the work of women. It was precisely through the technological advances made by women that men were finally liberated from reliance on hunting and moved to higher forms of labor activities. As soil cultivation advanced from garden culture to agriculture, and with the extension of animal domestication to the raising of stock animals, men became farmers and herders while hunting was reduced to a sport.

At first, men did the unskilled labor as assistants to the women. They cleared away the brush, felled trees, and prepared the ground for cultivation by the women. Gradually they became skilled workers, participating in the numerous crafts of the women. Men eventually began to initiate improvements in a whole series of industrial techniques. With the potter's wheel, for example, men took over pot-making and made it one of their specialized trades. They took over the ovens and kilns invented by women and developed these into forges where they smelted the earth's metals — copper, gold, iron. And with the Metal Age we enter the civilized epoch.

Woman's activities in tool-making and productive labor have left their traces in some ancient legends. Tylor cites one in which the moral is that the man who refuses to work will revert to the animal condition. Significantly, the most basic work is not conceived as hunting and killing animals but rather as digging and tilling the soil to make food grow. Here is the legend:

The Zulus still tell the tale of an Amafeme tribe who became baboons. They were an idle race who did not like to dig, but wished to eat at other people's houses, saying, "We shall live, although we do not dig, if we eat the food of those who cultivate the soil." So the chief of that place, of the house of Tusi, assembled the tribe, and they prepared food and went out into the wilderness. They fastened on behind them the handles of their now useless digging picks, these grew and became tails, hair made its appearance on their bodies, their foreheads became overhanging, and so they became baboons, who are still called "Tusi's men." (*The Origins of Culture,* pp. 376-77)

Social labor is the prime feature distinguishing humans from animals. In the beginning this was largely in the hands of the women. They were, so to speak, the first farmers and industrialists; the first scientists, doctors, nurses, architects, and engineers; the first teachers, artists, linguists, and historians. The households they managed were not merely kitchens and nurseries; they were the first factories, laboratories, clinics, schools, and social centers.

Far from being "drudgery," woman's work was supremely creative; it created nothing less than the human species. According to E. Sidney Harland, the term for "mother" in some primitive languages can be translated as "producer-procreatrix."

This expresses the essence of the matriarchal period of social organization. Women then were not simply the procreators of new life, the *biological mothers*. They were the prime producers of the necessities of life: the *social mothers*.

6

Women and Men
in the Matriarchal Commune

The resistance against accepting the matriarchy is due in part
to a false image of "female rule" over men, an inverted version of modern male domination over women. This misconception comes from a failure to take into account the diametrically different nature of the two social orders.

Sexual inequality is one of the diverse manifestations of
discrimination and oppression that are bound up with the
private ownership of property and division of society into
classes. Neither sexual nor social inequalities could exist in
the matriarchal epoch when society was both communalist
and egalitarian. Briffault writes on this point:

> In the most primitive human societies there is nothing
> equivalent to the domination which, in advanced societies,
> is exercised by individuals, by classes, by one sex over
> the other. . . . Neither the notion of economic domina-
> tion through the ownership of private property, nor the
> notion of privileged right or authority, is a primitive idea
> or has any place in truly primitive forms of society. (*The
> Mothers,* vol. I, pp. 433-34)

When the matriarchy was first discovered over a hundred
years ago it was unclear how far back in history it went. The
high status of women is most visible during the early period
of agriculture, which marked the end of savagery and the
first stage of barbarism. Women's preeminence as cultivators
was registered in the fertility rites and other practices conducted by the female sex, as well as in their glorification as

"goddesses." It appeared to some that the matriarchy was limited to the short period of the beginnings of agriculture. This gave rise to the belief that at most there had been only a "partial matriarchy."

In fact, the maternal clan system is as old as humanity itself. The earliest feminids who plied their digging-sticks to get at roots and grubs eventually learned how to cultivate the soil, advancing from gardening in the last stage of savagery to agriculture in the first stage of barbarism. The so-called partial matriarchy of this period is in reality the high point of its development. The second stage of barbarism saw its decline and fall.

The matrilineal kinship system testifies to the priority of the matriarchy no less than does the labor record of women. The discoverers of the matrikinship system correctly inferred it to be a survival from a prefamily period when, as some put it, "fathers were unknown." They reasoned that cases where kinship ties and the line of descent passed through the mothers, without recognizing fathers, were evidence that the matriclan had existed before the father-family. The matrikinship system persists up to our times in many primitive regions, even where fathers have become known.

Although the majority of anthropologists today concede the existence of matrikinship, they deny that it originated in a matriarchal epoch. This leaves unanswered two embarrassing questions: How did this one-sided mother-kinship system come into existence in the first place? And why is it found only among the most primitive peoples and not in civilized nations?

The most formidable barrier to recognizing the priority of the matriarchy is the reluctance to accept the maternal clan as the unit of society that preceded the father-family. Such an acknowledgment would invalidate the claims that male supremacy has always existed because men are physically stronger and thereby socially superior to women, and that women as child-bearers are the weak and helpless sex and have always been dependent on men for the support of themselves and their children.

These assumptions are not borne out by the anthropological record. Women have always borne children, but there was a time when this did not interfere with their economic independence, as their productive record shows. Communal production was accompanied by collective child care. Women were not always beholden to husbands and fathers; before marriage and the family existed, their coworkers were the brothers and mothers' brothers of the clan.

Moreover, even after husbands and fathers made their appearance in the clan system, it took a long time before marriage and the father-family were solidly instituted. Evidence for this can be seen in the segregation of wife from husband and of father from child.

The Prefamily Epoch

Since primitive women did not have access to scientific methods of birth control, it is assumed that they were obliged to bear one child after another throughout their reproductive years. A succinct expression of this widespread misconception is given by Vern L. Bullough:

> During the prime of their lives, women were usually pregnant, probably at least every other year until the menopause. The long periods of gestation cut them off from the freedom to roam and help account for the male monopoly on hunting and fishing. Even through there was a high proportion of miscarriages and a high infant mortality in the past, still the continued pregnancies and the slow development of the child from infancy to puberty curtailed the scope of feminine activities. Men on the other hand were free to leave the home, to roam at will in the forest, to hunt, to fight, even to contemplate. . . . This does not mean that women were not productive in advancing civilization. They were. . . . Still women were subordinate and their very subordination is demonstrated by the fact that once agriculture developed and specialization occurred, most of the tasks previously done by women were taken over by men. (*The Subordinate Sex,* p. 5)

In the final chapter of this book his collaborator, Bonnie Bullough, concurs that women's biology is responsible for their subordination to men. She writes that women have "never" held a position of equality with men and that this is due to their "unlimited fertility" (ibid., p. 335). But the assertion that primitive women bore large numbers of children is not borne out by the data. George Catlin, who traveled widely throughout North and South America, made the following observation:

It is a very rare occurrence for a woman to be *"blessed"* with more than four or five children during her life; and generally speaking, they seem contented with two or three; when in civilised communities it is no uncommon thing for a woman to be the mother of ten or twelve, and sometimes to bear two or even three at a time; of which I never recollect to have met an instance during all my extensive travels in the Indian country, though it is possible that I might occasionally have passed them. (*North American Indians,* vol. II, p. 258)

According to Hutton Webster, primitive peoples were shocked when they learned that in civilized nations one woman bore as many as ten or more children. He writes:

I heard of a white man, who being asked how many brothers and sisters he had, frankly said "ten." "But that could not be," was the rejoinder of the natives, "one mother could scarcely have so many children." When told that these children were born at annual intervals and that such occurrences were common in Europe, they were very much shocked, and thought it explained sufficiently why so many white people were "mere shrimps." (*Taboo,* pp. 69-70)

Contrary to what might be expected, at a time when the earth was most sparsely populated women limited themselves to a very small number of children. This cannot be explained, as some have attempted to do, as the result of miscarriages or high infant mortality. In fact, increased mortality occurred in some regions after modern customs corroded ancient practices. Where this did not occur, both the birth rate and infant mortality rate are lower than in civilized nations.

Katherine Routledge discovered this in the studies she and her husband conducted among the Akikuyus of Africa early in this century. She was surprised by the average figure of births per mother, which came to less than four. She was even more surprised when she found that their infant death rate was only 84 per thousand as against 138 per thousand in the imperial England of her day. This was so upsetting that she thought there might be something wrong with her calculations or information.

The low birth rate of primitive women is not surprising when we consider the prolonged periods of segregation of the sexes each time a child is born. The farther back we go in prehistory, the longer is the period of segregation. In the more primitive regions it covers a period of ten to twelve years; in the more advanced regions from two to three years.

The usual formula for expressing this astonishing fact is that a woman "may not" have sexual intercourse with her husband, or any other man for that matter, after giving birth to a child. The prohibition is said to continue throughout the period that the mother is "nursing" or "weaning" her child. This is a very long period. Whereas children are today normally weaned at from three to nine months after birth, in primitive society it was a protracted process covering from three to nine *years* or more. The following is from Briffault's documentation:

> It is a very general rule that all cohabitation must cease when a woman becomes pregnant, or at any rate during the later months of pregnancy, and the separation between her and her husband is commonly observed during the whole time that she is nursing the child. The latter period is very much longer among uncultured peoples than with European women. Children practically wean themselves. It is no uncommon thing for a youngster who is running about and taking part in the games of other children and even in the occupations of the men to be still unweaned. To suckle her children for over four years, and even five, six, or seven years is quite usual for a primitive woman. From two to three years is the most general duration of nursing. Throughout the greater part of that time marital relations among many uncultured peoples, cease entirely. (*The Mothers,* vol. II, pp. 391-92)

Other anthropologists have made brief references to the same phenomenon. W.I. Thomas observes that "the child is frequently suckled from four to five years, and occasionally from ten to twelve" (*Sex and Society,* p. 56). William Graham Sumner cites a report about the Plains Indians: "It has long been the custom that a woman should not have a second child until her first is ten years old" (*Folkways,* p. 315). The same is reported from other primitive regions. But in these perfunctory references we do not learn the reasons for the custom.

C.L. Meek's report is more revealing. He writes that Nigerian women kept their bodies smeared with red earth throughout the entire period as a public announcement that they were bearing, nursing, and weaning a child. As he explains it:

The original object of the practice was probably to ward off evil influences, but it serves as a public announcement that she is weaning a child, an announcement which is advisable, as a woman may not have sexual relations during the lactation period, which among the Katab is reckoned as three years. (*Tribal Studies in Northern Nigeria,* vol. II, p. 40)

We know that women made themselves taboo and inaccessible to men during hunting and fighting expeditions and that the same segregation took place when women were in their menstrual periods or in a maternal cycle. But the number of years of such segregation at times of child rearing has received surprisingly little attention. Is this because it damages the assumption that marriage is the normal and eternal state of man-woman relations?

The essential feature of modern marriage is that the husband has control over his wife. If a woman today made herself sexually inaccessible to her husband for years at a time he could insist upon his marital rights or divorce her. But when the savage woman daubed herself with red paint and segregated herself, no man approached her until she gave the signal that she was again sexually available. This is more reminiscent of primate behavior, with the female segregating herself from males throughout her maternal cycle, than it is of modern marriage.

But it raises questions about the evolution of female sexuality. The lengthy segregation of savage women far exceeds that of the primates during their maternal cycle. In fact, the complete cessation of sexual intercourse for periods of up to twelve years has no analogue either in the animal world or in the modern human world. It is a practice that stands in a class by itself.

Women today are just as capable of a continuous sex life as men; there are even suggestions that women may be more vigorous in this respect than men. Cessation of sexual intercourse after childbirth may occur for a short period of time — a few weeks, more or less, depending on the circumstances. But nowadays a woman who shunned all sexual intercourse for many years after the birth of a child would be regarded as abnormal. Yet for savage women this was the norm. How is it to be explained?

It would be absurd to suggest that a husband prohibited

his wife from having sexual intercourse with him for years at a time because he feared contamination from her impurities after childbirth. And it is highly unlikely that savage women were puritans who consciously repressed their sexual desires. The terms "abstinence" or "continence," so frequently used by anthropologists, are misleading because they imply such suppression. The conclusion to be drawn is that savage women felt minimal sexual desires or perhaps none at all during those periods when they segregated themselves.

This indicates a sharpening divergence in the early evolution of female and male sexuality which far exceeds the divergence between the sexes in the animal world. The nonsexual season common to lower species vanished with the primates, where males are potent all year round, and this trait continued in the human world. With females, however, a change took place in the opposite direction. Their sexual needs, already reduced in the primate stage compared to lower species, shrank still further in the human world. What was the reason for this drastic drop in female sexuality?

Here we must bear in mind that the disparity between the sexes in sexual activity also existed in the food realm. In the animal world both sexes eat the same food. Male and female herbivores feed upon grass and other vegetation. Among the carnivores both sexes are hunters and eaters of flesh. But in the human world, with the advent of the "omnivorous" diet, there is a sudden, unexplained divergence between the sexes both in occupation and diet. The males are the hunters and eaters of flesh foods; the females the collectors and eaters of vegetable foods.

No matter how these divergences came about, the fact remains that they prevailed in the epoch of cannibalism, the very period when the totemic taboos were erected by women as social controls over both food and sex. Is this the reason for the sharp drop in female sexuality? Was it the result of the struggle against cannibalism and the responsibility placed upon the female sex for the survival of the species? Was this one of the means by which women were able to organize the nonsexual union of sisters and brothers in the maternal clan system? We do not yet know whether social stress produced this biological result in women.

In any case, the prolonged periods of segregation of the sexes testifies to the absence of marriage and father-family in the epoch of savagery. This is not the view of most anthropologists, who believe that marriage has always existed; they differ only on whether or not it was monogamous. Some see in the prolonged separation of man and wife the seedbed of polygamous marriage. Hutton Webster writes: "The prohibition of sexual intercourse between husband and wife helps to account for the custom of polygyny. A man with one wife must remain continent perhaps for a long time, unless sexual relations outside of wedlock are permissible" (*Taboo,* p. 69). Hoebel writes on the same point:

> Primitive mothers are usually continent during pregnancy and nursing, which may be prolonged for years. In this situation, the husband who can manage it will find multiple wives advantageous — a need the woman does not face on this basis. (*Man in the Primitive World,* p. 233)

In fact, there was neither polygamous nor monogamous marriage in savage society. Just as a man could not determine his mate's sexual practices, neither did she place restrictions on his. Some anthropologists, among them Webster, have observed that the "wife" favored the idea of her "husband" having many other wives besides herself.

Katherine Routledge gives an interesting picture of a "polygamous household" among the Akikuyu. The women have their separate huts ringed around the kraal, which they occupy with their children. The women cook their food at their own fires, and the husband does not eat with any of them nor do any of them cook for him. With each woman having her "independent establishment," as Routledge calls it, this "places the whole on the footing of a village under one head man."

Most surprising to Routledge was the absence of jealousy among the "wives." The aboriginal women were equally surprised that English women could be jealous of one another over the sexual attentions of a man. They gave Routledge a message to take back to the women in England: "We do not marry any one we do not want to," and "we like our husbands to have as many wives as possible." She adds: "The poverty stricken condition of the 'rich' white man in respect of wives aroused unfailing interest. My husband's attempted explanation 'that a white woman preferred to have a husband to herself,' fell extremely flat" (*With a Prehistoric People,* pp. 124, 133-34).

This so-called polygamous household is actually a little maternal clan of women and children to which a headman is attached who is in charge of the male defensive services for the village. This is hardly the same as the polygamous establishment of a patriarchal overlord who has absolute control over his wives and concubines. Harem women are subservient to the will and wishes of their master; they are not allowed to follow their own sexual inclinations, and above all may not have sexual intercourse with any man but the master.

In the maternal village, however, the headman may have served as a husband to any of the women who made themselves sexually available, but this was not mandatory for the women. There is no evidence that all the women restricted their sexual relations to the one man. If they did so, it was voluntarily and not under any compulsion from him. As they told Routledge, they were not compelled to "marry," i.e., have sexual intercourse with anyone if they did not wish to do so, and when they did have intercourse it was with a man of their own choice.

This freedom of women to follow their own sexual inclinations distressed settlers and missionaries in primitive regions, who tried to change things according to their own customs. Audrey Richards, writing about the Southern Bantu peoples, notes that sexual relations are strictly forbidden until the second or third year after the birth of a child. She observes, "The problem has obvious practical bearings for those missionaries and others who insist on strict monogamy among these tribes" (*Hunger and Work in a Savage Tribe,* p. 39). Indeed, it is difficult to enforce monogamy upon a man who has only a sometime sex partner. The aboriginal women were more realistic about their community "husband," encouraging him to have many "wives."

Where a wife segregates herself from her husband for years at a time, occupies her own independent household with her children, does not cook for the man or eat with him, we cannot speak of marriage in the true sense of the term. The attempt to force the marriage institution—whether monogamous or polygamous—upon a period of prehistory where it did not exist misrepresents the real relations that prevailed between the sexes. In savage society the man was only an occasional or temporary sex partner of the woman.

The segregation of man and woman also meant the segregation of the man from his mate's children. In the earliest period a man had little or no contact with the child of a woman with whom he had sexual intercourse. Later on, when certain relations between father and son were permitted, these were restricted and did not include his presence at the time of birth — or for some years thereafter.

Although this phenomenon is reported often enough, it is mentioned in a perfunctory manner as though it were perfectly normal for a father to be kept at a distance and treated like a dangerous enemy of the woman's child. The following by Webster is typical:

> A Bavenda mother remained secluded until the child's umbilical cord dropped off, about four months after her confinement. Her husband was informed of the birth of the child and its sex, but he might not see or touch it until the mother's seclusion was over. (*Taboo*, p. 73)

Briffault gives data from various continents and islands where segregation of father and child lasts for years, in others for months. In some regions the man could not see his wife or child until the baby could crawl; in others the ban was lifted only when the child could walk. Elsewhere the segregation was even enforced for four or five years. The practice persisted up to recorded history. Briffault writes, "The rule mentioned by Herodotus that a man might not see his own child until he was five years old, probably refers to such a lengthy exclusion of the man from the house of his wife" (*The Mothers*, vol. II, pp. 393-96, 376). A whittled-down segregation of up to forty days continues to the present day in some regions.

The segregation of "father and child" was originally a segregation of children still in the care of their mothers from adult men, who were hunters and warriors. It cannot be understood except as a survival of the epoch of cannibalism.

The dangers to the children are reflected in the curious rituals performed around the lying-in mother and child. As usual, these rituals are explained by the aborigines in vague terms as designed to ward off "evil influences" or the "evil eye," or to protect the child against some undefined hostile force. In positive terms, the rituals are said to make the child grow up strong and healthy.

The exact peril feared for the newborn infant is only implicit in the rituals themselves. For example, why did the women attending a lying-in mother rush out of the house where the birth had taken place to flail the air with weapons of some kind? Were the invisible "evil eyes" they feared so much the eyes of dangerous animals — or men? And what is the meaning of the barricade of fire that encircled the mother and infant in their lying-in period? Survivals of this ancient practice in more modern societies include the small flame kept burning under or beside the bed upon which the mother and child are lying. Frazer writes about this fire ritual:

> Among the Bogos, to the north of Abyssinia, when a woman has been brought to bed, her female friends kindle a fire at the door of the house, and the mother with her infant walks slowly round it, while a great noise is made with bells and palm-branches for the purpose, we are told, of frightening away the evil spirits . . . to protect the mother and her newborn babe against the assaults of demons. So in Greek legend the Curetes are said to have danced round the infant Zeus, clashing their spears against their shields, to drown the child's squalls, lest they should attract the attention of his unnatural father Cronus, who was in the habit of devouring his offspring as soon as they were born. We may surmise that this Greek legend embodies a reminiscence of an old custom observed for the purpose of protecting babies against the many causes of infantile mortality which primitive man explains by the agency of malevolent and dangerous spirits. (*Folklore in the Old Testament,* abr. ed., p. 434)

However, before men came along to explain the causes of infant mortality as due to malevolent "spirits," women were confronted with the real problem of protecting infants and children from hungry predators, both animal and human. They solved the human part of the problem by segregating themselves and their offspring under the protection of their institution of totemism and taboo.

This sheds a different light on the simplistic formula given to explain the segregation of the sexes — that a women "may not" have sexual intercourse with her husband throughout her "lactation period." It is highly unlikely that any woman nursed her child for ten or twelve years. Rather, the fact that she was a woman, in a tabooed condition, furnished protection for the child so long as it was in contact with her. The tabooed woman, her child, and everything else she rendered taboo were "untouchable."

Where the husband is not free to associate with his wife whenever he wishes, and a father is treated like a dangerous enemy of a child, we cannot speak of the everlasting father-family. The evidence shows that it developed only after a very long and precarious evolution. The farther back we go in prehistory, the less we see of the union of the sexes and the more we see of their segregation. The following illustrations are from Crawley:

A peculiarity of conjugal life in New Caledonia is that men and women do not sleep under the same roof. The wife lives and sleeps by herself in a shed near the house. "You rarely see the men and women talking or sitting together. The women seem perfectly content with the companionship of her own sex. The men, who loiter about with spears in a most lazy fashion, are seldom seen in the society of the opposite sex.". . .

In the Pelew Islands there is "a remarkable separation of the sexes." Men and women hardly live together and family life is impossible. . . .

In Seoul, the capital of Korea, "they have a curious curfew law called *pem-ya*. A large bell is tolled at about 8 p.m. and 3 a.m. daily, and between those hours only women are supposed to appear in the streets. In the old days men found in the streets during the hours allotted to women were severely punished, but the rule has been greatly relaxed of late years." Apart from this rule "family life, as we have it, is utterly unknown in Korea." (*The Mystic Rose,* vol. I, pp. 46-50)

Struck by the implications of his voluminous data on the segregation of the sexes, Crawley exclaims, "Men and women are as ignorant of each other as if they were different species. . . . every woman and every man are, as men and women, potentially taboo to each other" (ibid., p. 86). Leo Frobenius cites the following legend bearing on the same subject:

One of the most curious legends that have come down to us from very ancient times describes the earliest sex relations of mankind and states that in the beginning men and women lived separately and knew nothing of each other. The legend continues to relate that at the first accidental meeting of members of these two sexes, the women defended themselves like men in battle, so that it came to a decisive combat, and only then did the difference in sex become apparent. These legends come from northwest Africa and in a variety of forms travel eastward right down to the Pacific. ("Marriage and Matriarchy," in *The Book of Marriage*, p. 77)

If such battles took place, and it is entirely plausible in that primeval dawn of human development, the objective of the woman was to lay down the inviolable totemic taboos and rules of avoidance by which the safety of women and children was assured. Put another way, the objective was not to establish a little father-family but to effect the creation of a brotherhood of men modeled in the image of the motherhood and sisterhood of women.

The women were not only biologically endowed to bring this about; through their labor activities they had acquired the decisive means for their victory. They had discovered fire.

Woman and Fire

How fire was discovered and for what original purposes it was put to use is a topic of endless fascination to scholars concerned with social origins. Fire in industrial crafts is recognized as the "tool of tools." But the discovery of fire goes back very far in history, more than half a million years, even before the development of *Homo sapiens*. What was the original driving need for the control and use of fire?

Julius Lippert writes, "The extraordinary importance of fire in human history has two aspects; one social and the other technical." He suggests that the social aspect is the earliest. "The use of fire in the mechanic arts is very late, and even its employment in the preparation of food is not original." In his view, "What fire provided first of all was protection from cold and from the nocturnal attacks of carnivorous animals." Fire became "a dependable watchman before the campsite, whether in a cave or in the open field," and this enabled humans to extend their habitat "into wildernesses dominated by animals and into bleak highlands and the frigid north" (*Evolution of Culture*, pp. 148, 130).

The original need for fire as a protection against cold has been questioned. Even to the present day there are primitive peoples who go about almost naked in cold, mountainous regions where warm coverings could easily be made, and who swim in icy waters with no discomfort. The use of fire for warmth, like clothing, probably developed later. But there can be no doubt about the need for fire as a protection against dangerous animals — or humans.

Thus before fire became the tool of tools for technical uses, it was the "weapon of weapons" in social life. Fire could serve both defensive and offensive purposes. The blazing bonfire furnished a barrier; in the form of a fire stick it became an offensive weapon against a threatening or charging animal.

In both its aspects, as tool and weapon, fire added a whole new dimension to budding human life. Tamed and controlled for social and industrial uses, it helped bring the human species to its feet. Benjamin Farrington quotes Pliny's picturesque description of the dual aspects of fire: "O fire, thou measureless and implacable portion of nature, shall we rightly call thee destroyer or creator?" (*Greek Science,* vol. I, p. 42).

Primitive legends record both aspects of fire. The most ancient myths single out fire as marking the dividing line between humans and animals. Radcliffe-Brown gives examples from the legends of the Andaman Islanders. "It is the possession of fire that makes human beings what they are," he writes, and it is "the lack of ability to make use of fire that makes animals what they are, that cuts them off from participation in human life." According to the aborigines, "It was on account of the fire (i.e. of the possession of fire) that the ancestors became alive" (*The Andaman Islanders,* pp. 342-43).

Frazer cites the Papuan legend about the first human pair that appeared on earth. Their minds were imperfectly developed. Ignorant of fire, they "lived like beasts . . . without feeling the need of communication with each other by speech." At the first sight of the crackling of flames in the bamboos, they uttered their first cry of fear and wonder, and so "unloosed their tongues. Henceforth they could speak." To this day the hole in the ground from which these human ancestors emerged is a sacred area; "everything that runs or flies or grows there, is holy" (*Folklore in the Old Testament,* vol. I, pp. 38-39).

This refers not only to the beginning of human life but to the oldest institution governing society — totemism and taboo.

Where totemism exists, there also we find the tabooed woman, the woman in authority. The close association of woman with both fire and the totemic system is embedded in primitive languages as well as in legends. W. G. McGee points out that among the Seri Indians the term *Km-kaak* not only means Great Mother, but "the designation is made to cover tutelary animals of the tribe, and fire, as well as human folk" (*The Seri Indians,* p. 123).

The domestication of fire is usually attributed to men. But traditions of primitive peoples indicate that women were the makers of fire before the technique was turned over to men. In the Torres Straits, New Guinea, according to Frazer, the operation of making fire with two sticks is called "mother gives fire"; the horizontal stick is named "mother" and the upright stick "child."

The hearth fire has always been associated with woman and with the domestication of man. The renewers of fire, the tenders of fire, and the transporters of fire were from the most ancient times women. Even as late as Roman civilization the Vestals were the tenders of perpetual fires.

The theme that women were the first possessors of fire is prominent in Frazer's extensive assemblage of legends on its origin. According to these stories, woman "had" fire; woman alone could make fire; she kept fire in various places, often in the end of her yam stick or digging stick. She kept fire in the fingers or nails of her hands. An old woman had six fingers; in the sixth she carried fire. Another old woman obtained fire from lightning; she lost it, then regained it by rubbing two sticks together (*Myths of the Origin of Fire,* pp. 54-58).

The desire of the woman or the ancestress to keep fire for herself and conceal it from a man or men figures heavily in these themes. There are pronounced differences between the sexes in their relationship to fire; some are openly expressed, others concealed behind totemic animals and birds. The women are connected with the taming and use of fire, the concealment of fire, the protection of fire, and the salvaging of some precious sparks after a catastrophic holocaust or flood. Men, on the other hand, wittingly or unwittingly, are connected with some misuse of fire or "theft" of fire that results in catastrophe.

There are legends of great conflagrations or "deluges of fire" which almost brought the world to an end. In some instances this entailed a reversion from human life to animal conditions of existence. Tylor cites a myth of the Mbocobis of South America which indicates such a relapse. "In the great conflagration of their forests a man and a woman climbed a tree for refuge from the fiery deluge, but the flames singed their faces and they became apes" (*The Origins of Culture,* p. 377).

In later legends there emerges a new male figure, a mother's son or grandson, the culture-hero who brings many benefits to mankind. These include bestowing the blessings of fire, received from some unseen source, upon all humankind. The legend of Maui, the culture-hero of the Maoris of New Zealand, is a well-known illustration.

According to the versions reported by Sir George Grey in 1855, the youth "set about to extinguish and destroy the fires of his ancestress Mahuika." This aged woman gave him fire by pulling it out of a nail on her hand. The youth played tricks on her and continued to ask for more fire. But after pulling fire out of all the nails on her fingers and even toes, she had none left.

At this point the conflagration occurred. There was no place of refuge on earth with its blazing forest fires, and even the seas became boiling hot from the flames. Maui and the old woman almost perished in the holocaust. Fortunately, through the intervention of other ancestors, floods were unleashed which quenched the flames and both were saved. The old woman Mahuika, now called "the goddess of fire," managed to save a few sparks before all was lost, and this gave them a new start in life. After that terrifying experience, Maui went on to perform many good deeds for humanity. This is the "creation" myth of the Maoris ("The Creation According to the Maori," in *Source Book in Anthropology,* pp. 454-56).

Radcliffe-Brown cites legends connected with Biliku, the ancestress of the Andaman Islanders, who is closely associated with yams and other vegetable foods and is "the first possessor of fire." He writes:

> *Biliku* as the source from which comes the fire is also the source of life. This view of *Biliku* is certainly to be found in all parts of the islands, though it has been developed more in the South than the North. *Biliku* thus becomes responsible for the beginning of society, and since the whole universe centres in the society, of the whole universe. She becomes the being who created or arranged the order in which men live. (*The Andaman Islanders,* p. 372)

In this region too there are tales of a great fire catastrophe which overwhelmed the ancestors and transformed them into animals. In many versions fire was almost lost; sometimes it was salvaged by being carried in a cooking pot into a cave. In the end there came the culture-hero and a restoration of the creative uses of fire.

These tales indicate that woman in the primeval epoch was more than the gentle tender of the hearth-fire usually associated with the "domestication" of men and animals. Radcliffe-Brown is puzzled by the dual character of woman presented in these legends; she is not only portrayed as a great "benefactress" but also as "hostile to mankind." She is a wielder of lightning and a sender of storms and cyclones. What this duality suggests is that in the earliest period, in view of the hazards that confronted developing humanity, the struggle for social survival could not have been achieved through pacific means alone. Having led the way in creating the human world, women were prepared to defend their creation against any attempts to destroy it.

The fire rituals at times of childbirth that come down to the present day in various forms are survivals from the ancient period when fire was applied as a defensive weapon. Frazer tells about "the extraordinary custom in Lao and Siam of surrounding a mother after childbirth with a blazing fire within or beside which she has regularly to stay for weeks after the birth of the child." He thought this "impassible girdle" of fire was designed to protect the "fluttering soul" of the child at the most critical period of its life. However, to mothers living in the primeval period of roaming carnivores, both animal and human, the dangers were not mystical but real.

Long after the original reasons for the fire barriers had vanished, the rituals persisted. Frazer speaks of the "continual and continuous circle of fire," and writes:

> A survival of this custom is seen in the old Scottish practices of whirling a fire candle three times around the bed on which the mother and child lay. . . . In Sonnenberg a light must be kept constantly burning after the birth, or the witches will carry off the child. . . . Amongst the Albanians a fire is kept constantly burning in the room for forty days after the birth; the mother is not allowed to leave the house all this time, and at night she may not leave the room; and anyone during this time who enters the house by night is obliged to leap over a burning brand. (*Garnered Sheaves,* pp. 26-27)

In Malinowski's report of the fire ritual in the Trobriand Islands, the practice is attributed to the "beneficial" effects this has upon the health of the child:

Mother and baby spend the greater part of their time during the first month on one of the raised bedsteads with a small fire underneath. This is a matter of hygiene, as the natives consider such baking and smoking to be very beneficial for their health, and a sort of prophylactic against black magic. No men are allowed into the house. . . . (*The Sexual Life of Savages in North-Western Melanesia*, p. 232)

By extension, the fire rituals that helped children to grow up healthy and strong were adapted to a new use in the agricultural period to ensure that the crops would grow and yield an abundance of food. On the subject of vestal fires and fertility rites, Briffault points out:

The practice of lighting fires or of carrying lighted torches round the newly-sown fields is one form of the rites in which fire is associated with the success of agriculture, and which have assumed so many significances and associations that their original intention is often forgotten and undiscoverable. (*The Mothers*, vol. III, pp. 4-5)

Along with her "magical" arts in causing the earth to yield an abundance of food, woman gave the signal when the crops could be picked and eaten. According to Briffault, at the corn feast of the American Indians women "exercise almost unlimited authority. The oldest and most respected mother prepares for and conducts the ceremony. She also claims the privilege of informing her children, as she calls the tribe, when they may commence eating the green corn; nor do the younger ones ever anticipate her permission." He adds, citing Father Hennepin, "They have great reverence for those old witches" (vol. II, p. 519).

The term "witch" was originally not a derogatory designation for woman. The witch and the sorceress were predecessors of the goddess. In primitive society women were witches because of their mysterious powers of production and procreation. They could bear children and make crops grow; they could control fire, establish settlements, and make rules for the disciplined social behavior of men. "The power of witchcraft," says Briffault, "is universally regarded as appertaining specifically to women. The witch is a woman, the wizard is but a male imitation of the original wielder of magic power. . . . every woman, wherever magic powers are believed in, is credited with the possession of those powers because she is a woman" (vol. II, p. 556).

With the rise of patriarchal influences some of the witches became transformed into goddesses, the subordinate wives or companions of the gods. In the transitional period from matriarchy to patriarchy, former female deities were even replaced by male figures. This is the case with Ishtar, the Babylonian or Assyrian goddess, who is said to have originated as a primitive Semitic divinity. However, "as society passed from the matriarchal to the patriarchal organization," she changed from female to male. Ishtar became a male, Ashtar (*Encyclopedia of Religion and Ethics,* vol. VII, pp. 428-33).

In some regions where the complete changeover did not occur, investigators become confused by the ambiguity of the sex of the leading mythological figure. Radcliffe-Brown, for example, is puzzled by the conflicting views in the Andaman Islands of Biliku, the female creatrix of the world. She is closely associated with, and not yet displaced by, Puluga, a male figure.

Where the full shift took place, the male culture-hero of the matriarchal epoch evolved into the patriarchal god. A prominent example is Dionysus, the god of the vine and of wine, who makes his appearance along with the new patriarchal order in the region called the "cradle of civilization." After this shift, the mythical world was no longer populated by mothers and their culture-hero sons and grandsons but by the gods and their sons (the sun-gods). The goddesses were by and large reduced to wives bearing sons for the gods.

Along with this, myth-history and tradition were framed in male terms. The tributes formerly paid to the woman creatrix of the world now went to a male creator. One illustration can be found in the Indian Rigveda, which attributes the beginning of Aryan life to the discovery of fire by the Angiras gens. According to S. A. Dange, "The revolution was so great that all later Aryan life is ascribed to fire, revolves round it and is centered on it. Creation, existence, growth, wealth, happiness, all proceed from fire (*Agnil*)." Along with fire there came the "art of domestication of animals" which produced wealth in cattle and people. The great "leader" in this creation of the world was a male, Agni, who was also the smelter of ores. Dange writes:

> Hence the *Rigveda* calls fire the leader and protector of the settlements of man. He is the Vishpati, *Vish* meaning set-

tlement. He alone made households possible. He is the oldest and greatest friend of mankind, sent by the gods for man. (*India: From Primitive Communism to Slavery,* pp. 44-45)

But *woman's* discovery and use of fire, *her* settlements and organization of social life, have left traces that cannot be ignored. The sixth edition of Webster's New Collegiate dictionary described the Roman deity Vesta as the "goddess of the hearth and its fire, and hence of cookery," and added: "Her temple symbolized the hearth of the city and contained a fire, rekindled on the day (March 1) beginning the new year. . . ." Thus the hearth was originally the heart of an entire settlement and reached its apex in the temple of the goddess before dwindling to the household hearth of the modern family. In Peru the vestal priestesses are still called *mama-cuna* or "the mothers" according to Briffault (*The Mothers,* vol. II, p. 16).

The clay products made by women in their kilns, some in the form of pots and some as images of woman herself, are additional artifacts indicating the priority of the matriarchy. Female figurines have been found by the hundreds in the neolithic and chalcolithic deposits of Central Europe, the Mediterranean region, and the Near East — regions that comprise the cradle of civilization. Along with those made of terra-cotta some have been found carved in stone. The oldest statue is known as the Venus of Willendorf.

Not simply the figurines but even the pots made by women came to be regarded as "goddesses." The term "pot" was not so long ago used to refer to a woman as a dull drudge and housewife. But originally, as Briffault writes:

> "The Mother Pot is really a fundamental conception in all religions," observes Dr. Elliott Smith, "and is almost worldwide in its distribution. The pot's identity with the Great Mother is deeply rooted in ancient belief through the greater part of the world." In Peru a deity called Sanacmana was worshipped throughout the country in the form of a pot. Among the aboriginal races of southern India, as in Greece, goddesses are commonly represented by pots. . . . In Canara there was a special Pot Goddess, called Kel Mari. Goddesses are similarly worshipped in the form of pots by the Dayaks of North Borneo, and in the Philippine Islands. (ibid., vol. I, pp. 474-75)

There are survivals of the same reverence for the Fire Mothers as for the Mother Pot in some primitive regions. In an article on the Ainus of Japan, J. Batchelor writes:

> The personal essence of fire, that is to say, its supposed spirit, when upon the hearth, is said to be of the feminine gender, and, besides being called *Fuji*, *Unji*, or *Huchi* as the case may be . . . is also named *Iresu-Kamui*, *i. e.* "the divine being who rears us," and *Iresu-Huchi*, i. e. "the ancestress who rears us" — *Fuji* or *Huchi* meaning "grandmother" or "ancestress," and *Iresu* "to sustain" or "to bring up." She is the chief in her sphere and class, and is sometimes spoken of as a disease-destroying and body-purifying spirit. As she is of so great importance, and holds so high a position, it is not surprising to find that fire is in comparison most often worshipped. Indeed, so high is she supposed to be that she is sometimes spoken of as the "Governor of the world." (*Encyclopedia of Religion and Ethics*, vol. I, p. 242)

Given the diversified record of women's work through the ages, it is not surprising that the female sex bears so many names. As Mother Earth or the Goddess of Fertility, women bring forth abundance of food from the earth and also bear children. In their cooperative groups they are known as "The Fates," the spinners and weavers of the destiny of mankind, as well as "The Graces," and "The Charities." But whatever the specific names given to women — whether Pot or Venus, witch or goddess — in the beginning they were the mother-governesses of the matriarchy.

The record of primitive man's reverence for the creativity of women is so impressive that even those who believe that women have invariably been the second sex are struck by it. Such is Alexander Goldenweiser, who cites Radin's report of the Kagaba of Colombia. They have a "female deity and a profession of faith that should satisfy even the most exacting monotheist," he writes, and presents it as follows:

> The mother of our songs, the mother of all our seed, bore us in the beginning of things and she is the mother of all types of men, the mother of all nations. She is the mother of thunder, the mother of the streams, the mother of trees and all things. She is the mother of the world and of the

older brothers, the stone-people. She is the mother of our younger brothers, the French, and the strangers. She is the mother of our dance paraphernalia, of all our temples and she is the only mother we possess. She alone is the mother of the fire, and the Sun, and the Milky Way. She is the mother of the rain and the only mother we possess. And she has left us a token in all the temples — a token in the form of songs and dances. (*Anthropology*, p. 228)

The Matriarchal Brotherhood

Those who fail to understand the position of women in primitive society also misinterpret the position, attitudes, and behavior of the men. This comes from overlooking or denying the communal, egalitarian character of savage society and viewing it as a little duplicate of modern class society with its male supremacy and the subordination of women.

Thus, when they observe the central position occupied by the "brothers" in savage society they do not see them as members of a communal "brotherhood" but as "dominant" males, standing over their sisters just as husbands and fathers stand over their wives in patriarchal society. Since the anthropological data does not sustain this assertion, their argumentation is based upon the superior physical strength of the male together with the fact that men are the armed sex.

W. I. Thomas, for example, writes, "From the standpoint of physical force, man was the master, and was often brutal enough." He adds:

> In view of his superior power of making movements and applying force, the male must inevitably assume control of the life direction of the group, no matter what the genesis of the group. It is not a difficult conclusion that, if woman's leaping, lifting, running, climbing, and slugging capacity is inferior to man's by however slight a margin, her fighting capacity is less in the same degree; for battle is only an application of force, and there has never been a moment in the history of society when the law of might, tempered by sexual affinity, did not prevail. (*Sex and Society,* p. 67)

This theme of the "brutal brother" is made even more explicit by Goldenweiser:

The fact that the warrior or fighter, who is skilled in the wielding of weapons, is always a man, inevitably stands for a certain social pre-eminence. It is in fact likely, though difficult to prove, that one of the earliest incentives for the sociopolitical disfranchisement of woman came in consequence of her helplessness when confronted with her armed male brother, whose natural physical superiority was thus further enhanced in a most emphatic and — shall we say with her? — dangerous way (*Anthropology,* p. 140)

The labor record of primitive women does not warrant the assertion that they were physically weak or helpless. While variations occur in the size and strength of the sexes, the advantage is not always on the side of the males, as the documentation on this subject shows. More significant than these variations, however, are the different uses to which the sexes put their strength.

In the first division of labor, women were involved in food collecting, crafts, construction, portage, gardening, and many other productive activities. This gave them a high degree of endurance and the strength to lift heavier loads than men. On the other hand, men, as the hunters and fighters, developed the kind of musculature that comes from running, leaping, throwing, and so on. But male muscles did not, as Goldenweiser says, give primitive men social preeminence over women.

In fact, Goldenweiser contradicts his own thesis. On the one hand he asserts that the physical superiority of men rendered women helpless. On the other hand he says that "the economic discrimination against woman, which threw her out of many professions and made her dependent upon man, is conspicuous among primitives by its absence" (ibid., p. 140). This means that the social oppression of women, the hallmark of our society, did not exist in savage communal society.

Thomas likewise cannot sustain his thesis that because men were able to "apply force" they have always had control over social life. However important the running, leaping, and slugging movements of men were, they were secondary to the productive labor activities of the women. Thomas admits as much in the following statement, which is a fairly good thumbnail sketch of what the term "matriarchy" signifies:

Man did the hunting and fighting. He was attached to the woman, but he was not steady. He did not stay at home.

The woman and the child were the core of society, the fixed point, the point to which man came back. There consequently grew up a sort of dual society and dual activity. Man represented the more violent and spasmodic activities, involving motion and skilled coordination, as well as organization for hunting and fighting; while woman carried on the steady, settled life. . . . her attention was turned to industries, since these were compatible with settled and stationary habits. Agriculture, pottery, weaving, tanning, and all the industrial processes involved in working up the by-products of the chase, were developed by her. She domesticated man and assisted him in domesticating the animals. She built her house, and it was hers. She did not go to her husband's group after marriage. The child was hers, and remained a member of her group. The germ of social organization was, indeed, the woman and her children and her children's children. The old women were the heads of civil society, though the men had developed a fighting organization and technique which eventually swallowed them up. (*Sex and Society,* pp. 227-29)

The opinion that women have always been subordinate to men stems from the attempt to transfer conditions of modern life to savage society where they did not exist. Precisely because women were not the roaming hunters and warriors, they could become the settlement-makers, cultivating the soil, producing useful articles, domesticating animals and men. Men, on the other hand, were armed for their occupation of hunting and defending their communities from outside predators; they were not armed for assault upon or domination over their brothers, and least of all over their sisters and mothers. Under the savage system of totemism and taboo the life of the kinsman was sacred and that of the tabooed woman even more so.

Different kinds of society produce different kinds of men, and the men of the matriarchy were conditioned by the communal, egalitarian society that had been established by the women. The primitive "brother" was a member of a large tribal "brotherhood" based on these relationships. Morgan's description of the Iroquois is a good example:

All the members of an Iroquois gens were personally free, and they were bound to defend each other's freedom; they were equal in privileges and in personal rights, the sachem and chiefs claiming no superiority; and they were a brother-hood bound together by the ties of kin. Liberty, equality, and fraternity, though never formulated, were cardinal principles of the gens. (*Houses and House-Life of the American Aborigines,* p. 8)

As part of the male division of labor, certain community functions were given to headmen, sachems, or chiefs. Their actions, however, especially in such matters as war and peace, were decided through the collective deliberations of the whole community, whether it held formal councils or not. Tyrannical male authority was incompatible with the egalitarian character of primitive society.

Radcliffe-Brown writes about the Andaman Islanders: "The affairs of the community are regulated entirely by the older men and women. . . . The respect for seniority is kept alive partly by tradition and partly by the fact that the older men have had a greater experience than the younger. It could probably not be maintained if it regularly gave rise to any tyrannical treatment of the younger by the elder." He says the authority of all chiefs, from head chief to sub-chiefs, is extremely limited, and adds: "The words 'chief' and 'authority' seem to imply some sort of organised rule and procedure, and of this there is nothing in the Andamans" (*The Andaman Islanders,* pp. 44-47).

Similar reports on the limited powers of chiefs come from all parts of the primitive world. Thomas says of the Orokaiva of New Guinea that there is no well-defined chieftainship; it is therefore difficult to find a word which would correspond with our idea of the "chief," since that term is "too pretentious" for even their most important leaders (*Primitive Behavior,* p. 418). The Eddystone Islanders are similar, according to W. H. R. Rivers; "the so-called chiefs exerted none of the social functions which we ordinarily associate with chieftainship" (*Social Organization,* p. 161).

The real role of savage chiefs has been distorted by numerous reports depicting them as patriarchal rulers possessing wealth, rank, and coercive power. But primitive peoples had no understanding of abject obedience to rulers. Briffault gives the following illustrations:

The Iroquois and Delawares "know no magistracy, laws, or restraint. Chiefs are nothing more than the most respected among their equals in rank." Their principal duties were to conduct negotiations with other tribes and with Europeans, and to hold themselves responsible for the carrying out of any agreement thus entered into. For a small mistake they were severely reprimanded; for any neglect of their duties they were cashiered. They "laugh when you talk to them of obedience to kings." A trader in the employment of the Hudson's Bay Company relates the perplexity of the Indians when he spoke of the directors of the Company as his "chiefs." They asked, "Who are thy chiefs and what makes them superior to other men?" He explained that their influence was owing to their great wealth; "but the more I said in their praise, the more contempt I brought upon myself, and if ever I regretted anything in my life it was to have said so much." (*The Mothers,* vol. I, p. 494)

In a communal society there is no obeisance of men to other men by virtue of their superior wealth, rank, and power; by the same token, there is no subordination of women to the "superior" male sex. On the contrary, the influence of women upon men was far more pronounced than the influence of men upon women. Early settlers and observers were perplexed by these attitudes, which stood in such sharp contrast to the attitudes of people conditioned by patriarchal class society.

This is highlighted in the remark made by W. W. Rockhill in his book *The Land of the Lamas,* cited by Briffault. "'By what means,' remarks Mr. Rockhill, 'have those women gained such complete ascendancy over the men, how have they made their mastery so complete and so acceptable to a race of lawless barbarians who but unwillingly submit to the authority of their chiefs, is a problem well worth consideration'" (ibid., p. 327). To this writer the egalitarian savage was "lawless" and his respect for women unfathomable.

The "mastery" exercised by primitive women was not achieved by force of arms, for men were the armed sex. The women were the most respected sex because the communal society they had created was beneficial to the whole community, men as well as women. Even those anthropologists who doubt or deny the existence of the matriarchy are obliged to recognize the influential place occupied by primitive women. Thomas writes, "There was never such a system as a matriarchate, properly speaking, where women were as a class the rulers, but . . . under the matrilineal-matrilocal system the women were sometimes in control of 'domestic relations.'" However, the illustration he gives, taken from J. W. Powell's report on the Wyandot government, goes much further than his watered-down view of the matter.

Powell showed that the tribal councils were "composed one-fifth of men and four-fifths of women." The chief was chosen by women councillors who consulted with the other women and the men of the community; he was installed by the women and held accountable to the women for his actions and behavior. These were not small "domestic" chores but important social and political functions that were in the hands of the women.

Goldenweiser describes the "maternal" Iroquois organization, one of the largest and best-known matriarchal societies. This huge League of Tribes had an overall council of fifty sachems or chiefs. Yet the influence of women was paramount, not only in the clans, but in the tribes and in the League. The "matrons" played the deciding role both in electing chiefs, including the highest, and in deposing them if they failed to perform their duties to the satisfaction of the women. Goldenweiser reports:

> It will be clear from what was said that even though no woman, so far as known, ever occupied the position of a regular chief in the Iroquois Confederacy, women were more influential than men both in the election of chiefs and in their deposition. In other words, the public opinion of the clan and maternal family was involved in the limited choice of these chieftains, and that public opinion was more significantly that of the women than of the men of the group. . . .
> The matrons of all the maternal families of the League, as a group, also functioned as a unit in a socially constructive direction, by exercising as a body a restraining influence upon the behaviour of the young warriors whenever such restraint seemed to them desirable. . . . many a devastating war must have been averted by wise counsel of the matrons, who would warn the young and impetuous warriors, before it was too late, against dangerous attacks or discourtesies and thus prolong the duration of peace. (*Anthropology,* pp. 364-65)

If men molded by patriarchal concepts could not understand the deference of savage hunters and warriors toward women, the savages could not understand the male supremacy of the "civilizers" and their contempt for women. Two examples from Briffault's data point up this contrast.

He quotes the report of the missionary J. F. Lafitau, who writes about the matriarchal American Indians in patriarchal terms:

"Nothing is more real than this superiority of the women. It is in the women that properly consists the nation, the nobility of blood, the genealogical tree, the order of generations, the preservation of families. It is in them that all real authority resides; the country, the fields, and all the crops belong to them. They are the soul of the councils. the arbiters of war and peace." (*The Mothers,* vol. I, p. 316)

On the other hand, the address made by "Good Peter," the chosen orator of the Iroquois in their negotiations with Governor Clinton, was an appeal to the patriarchal rulers to have more respect for the Iroquois women:

Brothers! Our ancestors considered it a great offense to reject the counsels of their women, particularly of the Female Governesses. They were esteemed the mistresses of the soil. Who, said our forefathers, brings us into being? Who cultivates our lands, kindles our fires, and boils our pots, but the women? Our women, Brother, say that they are apprehensive. . . . They entreat that the veneration of our ancestors in favor of the women be not despised; the Great Spirit made them. The Female Governesses beg leave to speak with the freedom allowed to women and agreeable to the spirit of our ancestors. They entreat the Great Chief to put forth his strength and to preserve them in peace. For they are the life of the nation. (ibid., pp. 316-17)

Just as the relations between men and women in savage society were totally different from ours, so were the relations of men with other men. On this point Tylor makes the following generalization:

Among the lessons to be learnt from the life of rude tribes is how society can go on without the policeman to keep order. It is plain that even the lowest men cannot live quite by what the Germans call "faust-recht," or "fist-right,"

and we call "club-law." The strong savage does not rush
into his weaker neighbour's hut and take possession, driving the owner out into the forest with a stone-headed javelin
sent flying after him. Without some control beyond the
mere right of the stronger, the tribe would break up in
a week. . . . In the West Indian islands where Columbus
first landed lived tribes who have been called the most
gentle and benevolent of the human race. Schomburgh,
the traveler, who knew the warlike Caribs well in their
home life, draws a paradise-like picture of their ways,
where they have not been corrupted by the vices of the
white men. . . . the civilized world, he says, has not to
teach them morality, for though they do not talk about
it, they live in it. (*Anthropology*, pp. 249-50)

The inequalities and discriminations that came forward in
civilized society did not and could not exist at a time when
human survival depended upon the closest solidarity among
men. Thus, apart from personal articles which were regarded
more as parts of one's body than as individual wealth, all
land and property were held in common and utilized for the
benefit of all the members of the clan. This gave savages a
sense of security and trust in their fellows that is noticeably
absent in our society.

The striking contrast between the behavior of savages and
civilized men has been observed from the time that the first
contacts were made with aborigines. Father Jacob Baegert,
who settled among the California Indians about two hundred
years ago, described them as follows:

I can assure the reader that . . . they live unquestionably
much happier than the civilized inhabitants of Europe. . . .
Throughout the whole year nothing happens that causes
a Californian trouble or vexation, nothing that renders his
life cumbersome and death desirable. . . . Envy, jealousy,
and slander embitter not his life, and he is not exposed to
the fear of losing what he possesses, nor to the care of
increasing it. . . . the Californians do not know the meaning of *meum* and *tuum,* those two ideas which, according
to St. Gregory, fill the days of our existence with bitter-
ness and unaccountable evils. (*Reader in General Anthropology,* pp. 77-78)

Briffault presents numerous reports about the American Indians in general, of which the following is a portion:

"These savages," writes La Hontan, "know nothing of mine and thine, for it may be said that what belongs to one belongs to another. When a savage has been unsuccessful in beaver-hunting, his fellows succour him without being asked. . . . It is only those who are Christians and dwell at the gates of our towns who make use of money. The others will not touch it. They call it the 'Snake of the French.' They say that amongst us folks will rob, slander, betray, sell one another for money; that husbands sell their wives, and mothers their daughters, for this metal. They think it strange that someone should have more goods than others, and that those who have more should be more esteemed than those who have less. They never quarrel and fight amongst themselves, nor steal from one another, or speak ill of another." "What is extremely surprising in men whose external appearance is wholly barbarous," says Father Charlevoix, "is to see them treat one another with a gentleness and consideration which one does not find among common people in the most civilised nations. This, doubtless, arises in part from the fact that the words 'mine' and 'thine,' which St. Chrysostom says extinguish in our hearts the fire of charity and kindle that of greed, are unknown to these savages." "I have seen them," says Heckewelder, "divide game, venison, bear's meat, fish, etc., among themselves, when they sometimes had many shares to make; and cannot recollect a single instance of their falling into a dispute or finding fault with the distribution as being unequal or otherwise objectionable. They would rather lie down themselves on an empty stomach than have it laid to their charge that they neglected to satisfy the needy; only dogs and beasts, they say, fight amongst themselves." (*The Mothers,* vol. II, pp. 496-97)

Rivers gives the following report of an interview he had with some aborigines in the Polynesian Islands:

I was travelling on a boat with four inhabitants of Niue or Savage Island, and took the opportunity of inquiring into their social organization. At the end of the sitting they said they would like now to examine me about my

customs, and using my own concrete methods, one of the
first questions was directed to discover what I should do
with a sovereign if I earned one. In response to my somewhat lame answers, they asked me point-blank whether I
should share it with my parents and brothers and sisters.
When I replied that I would not usually, and certainly
not necessarily do so, and that it was not our general
custom, they found my reply so amusing that it was long
before they left off laughing. Their attitude towards my
individualism . . . revealed the presence of a communistic
sentiment of a deeply seated kind. (*Social Organization,*
p. 108)

It has been noted that individualism was so poorly developed
in primitive society that there was no term to express the individual as an entity apart from the group. This led to serious
errors on the part of some investigators, who translated the
aboriginal term meaning "we" into "I" and believed that the
primitive outlook was no different from ours. Lucien Levy-
Bruhl writes on this point:

A native so thoroughly identifies himself with his tribe
that he is ever employing the first personal pronoun. In
mentioning a fight that occurred possibly ten generations
ago he will say: "I defeated the enemy there," mentioning
the name of the tribe. In like manner he will carelessly
indicate 10,000 acres of land with a wave of his hand,
and remark: "This is my land." He would never suspect
that any person would take it that he was the sole owner
of such land, nor would any one but a European make
such an error. When Europeans arrived on these shores
many troubles arose owing to the inability of the Maori
to understand individual possession of land, and land
selling. (*The "Soul" of the Primitive,* p. 68)

Hans Kelsen emphasizes that the primitive "lack of ego-
consciousness" is evidenced in their language, where the "pos-
sibilities of expression in the first person are comparatively
underdeveloped." He writes, "If the Maori speaks in the first
person, he does not necessarily speak of himself but of his
group, with which he naturally identifies himself. He says, 'I'
have just done this or that, and means thereby that my tribe

has done it. 'My soil' means the land of the tribe" (*Society and Nature,* p. 11).

Briffault points out that the group solidarity of the primitive commune was not "imposed from without by legislation on an unwilling people." Rather, savages genuinely felt that "if one member of the clan suffered, all the members suffered, not in sentimental phraseology, but in real fact" (*The Mothers,* vol. II, p. 496). In other words, every man was literally his brother's keeper because they knew that only through such solidarity could they maintain their well-being. The results can be stated in Morgan's words: "It would be difficult to describe any political society in which there was less of oppression and discontent, more of individual independence and boundless freedom" (*League of the Iroquois,* p. 139).

To be sure, as Briffault says, in many primitive regions, "after a few years of contact with Europeans primitive man becomes entirely transformed," and "the chief and most powerful cause of his transformation is the acquisition of private property" (*The Mothers,* vol. II, p. 500). Where this occurs, primitive men can become as domineering over women as civilized men. However, this does not prove that women have always been the inferior, subjugated sex. It simply means that with the downfall of the communal, egalitarian society men too became debased along with women.

Since early society was initiated and consolidated by the female sex, it bore the stamp of the maternal side of the clan system. However, it was more than a matriarchy; it was a matriarchal brotherhood. This requires a closer examination of the male side of primitive society and the evolution of the fratriarchy.

Part II
The Fratriarchy

7

Forging Fratrilineal Kinship

Unlike the basic, much-used term "matrilineal kinship," the term "fratrilineal kinship" is conspicuously absent from anthropological writings. Yet it was the male corollary of the female line of kinship in the period of the maternal clan system that preceded patrilineal kinship. This deficiency has held back a comprehensive study of how the first human group, the primal horde, evolved into the network of "brother" clans and phratries that marked the peak of development of the tribal system.

By the time anthropologists began their studies in the last century, the patrilineal relationship had made its appearance in almost all surviving primitive regions of the globe. This was seized upon by opponents of the matriarchy as evidence that the father-family (and patriarchy) had always existed. To bring to light fratrilineal kinship and the fratriarchy, as the male counterparts of matrilineal kinship and the matriarchy, is therefore the best way of upholding the prior existence of both.

The pioneer scholars, with their evolutionary approach, had observed that the patrilineal relationship was a recent development in numerous regions. In some areas it emerged under their very eyes in the course of their investigation. In each instance the maternal form was superseded by the paternal form and not the other way around.

Among those who regarded this as evidence of the priority of the matrilineal system is E. Sidney Hartland. He wrote: "A consideration of the evidence relating to the whole of the Australian race leads to the conclusion that at one period all the tribes were organized on the basis of matrilineal descent" ("Matrilineal Kinship and the Question of Its Priority," in

Memoirs of American Anthropological Association, 1917, vol. IV, p. 86).

In his book *Primitive Society,* Hartland concluded that the shift from matrilineal to patrilineal kinship had taken place in other areas at different times. "Patriarchal rule and patrilineal kinship have made perpetual inroads upon mother-right all over the world; consequently matrilineal institutions are found in almost all stages of transition to a state of society in which the father is the centre of kinship and government" (p. 34). He suggested that patrilineal kinship was only a "half-way house" to the ultimate goal, the father-family (p. 100).

Franz Boas, an avowed antimatriarchalist, tried to find an exception. He came up with a reverse movement among the Kwakiutl Indians of the northwest coast of the United States. But his evidence was so dubious that most anthropologists have been unable to accept it. According to Moret and Davy, "Transformations of uterine into patriarchal clans have been many times observed, while not a single case of the inverse transformation is known, those alleged by Boas among the Kwakiutl being, in fact, pure conjecture" (*From Tribe to Empire,* p. 30).

Even Frazer, who did not support the matriarchal theory, objected to the example given by Boas. He declared, "Whenever we find a tribe wavering between female descent and male descent we may be sure that it is in the act of passing from mother-kin to father-kin, and not in the reverse direction, since there are many motives which induce men to exchange mother-kin for father-kin but none which induce them to exchange father-kin for mother-kin" (*Totemism and Exogamy,* vol. IV, p. 132). In a more expanded treatment he explains why:

> . . . the theory that a people who once possessed paternal descent afterwards exchanged it for maternal descent would require very strong evidence in its support to make it probable, since both intrinsic probability and analogy are strongly against it. For it seems very unlikely that men who had once been accustomed to transmit their rights and privileges to their own children should afterwards disinherit them and transmit these rights and privileges to their sisters' children instead; and in point of fact, while there are a good many symptoms of a transition from maternal to paternal descent in other parts of the world there is, so far as I know, none whatever of a transition in the reverse direction from paternal descent to maternal. (*Totemism and Exogamy,* vol. III, p. 320)

It would indeed be difficult to find examples of a man in a patriarchal culture disinheriting his own son in favor of a sister's son; all the more so since such paternal inheritance is fixed by law in nations founded upon private property and the father-family. As Hartland, in the article previously cited, sums up the case on the priority of matrilineal kinship, this throws the burden of proof not upon those who accept the evidence on the priority of matrilineal kinship, but upon those who deny it (p. 87).

Hartland and others who argue for the precedence of matrilineal kinship make no mention of its male counterpart, fratrilineal kinship. This aspect of the matter comes forward in a somewhat different way, through their descriptions of the central role played by the mothers' brothers. Their preeminent position, not only in matrilineal regions but even where patrilineality is firmly entrenched, is sometimes cited as proof that the maternal clan was the earlier form of organization. Hartland writes:

> The social importance of the maternal uncle, when it appears in a patrilineal community too, is not to be accounted for by patrilineal institutions; but it suggests the former existence of a matrilineal society, with the conditions of which it is almost invariably present. (*Primitive Society*, p. 34)

In an article on "Mother-Right," W. H. R. Rivers draws the same conclusion:

> In a state of typical mother-right a person would belong to his mother's social group. He would not recognize the existence of any kind of social duty except towards his mother's relatives, and would ignore the relatives of his father; property, rank and office would pass solely through the women. (*Encyclopedia of Religion and Ethics*, vol. VIII, p. 851)

Before marriage and the family came into existence, the mothers' brothers performed the "paternal" functions for their clan sisters' children that were later taken over by the fathers of families. It is significant that even those who reject the matriarchy admit the important role of the mothers' brothers wherever matrilineal communities still exist. Among them is E. Adamson Hoebel, who describes the Dobuan *susu*, which means "the mothers" or "mother's milk," as follows:

The nuclear basis of the susu is the brother-sister relationship. The husband does not enter into it at all. His role, except as procreator, is replaced in part or wholly by the mother's brother. . . . The main burden of educating the boys in men's work falls on the mother's brother. His nephews inherit most of their goods from him. . . . He passes on his social prerogatives to his nephew, not to his son. Where the susu organization is highly institutionalized the father, as we know him, is almost entirely ruled out of the picture. (*Man in the Primitive World*, pp. 242-43)

In the ancestral realm also, the mother's brother preceded the father. Ralph Piddington writes:

Thus the effective head of a matrilineal lineage is usually its senior living male member, while among dead forebears it is often the brother of an ancestress rather than the ancestress herself who is emphasized in religion and mythology. But the matrilineal principle is strictly observed — the individual in question owes his importance to his relationship through a female to the lineage as a whole. (*Introduction to Social Anthropology*, p. 144)

Malinowski makes the same point forcefully in speaking about Trobriand origin myths:

What interests us most in them is that the first ancestral groups whose appearance is mentioned in the myth consist always of a woman, sometimes accompanied by her brother, sometimes by the totemic animal, but never by a husband. . . . Thus instead of the creative force of a father, the myths reveal the spontaneous procreative powers of the ancestral mother. . . .
Nor is there any other role in which the father appears. In fact, he is never mentioned, and does not exist in any part of the mythological world. . . . There is not a single myth of origins in which a husband or a father plays any part, or even makes his appearance. (*Sex and Repression in Savage Society*, pp. 101-03)

In another book Malinowski reiterates the essential feature of primitive origin myths: that the world began on the basis of a sister-brother partnership, not on the basis of a father-family. He writes:

According to native tradition, mankind originated from underground, whence a couple, a brother and a sister, emerged at different specified places. According to certain legends, only women appeared at first. Some of my commentators insisted upon this version: "You see, we are so many on the earth because many women came first. Had there been many men, we would be few." Now, whether accompanied by her brother or not, the primeval woman is always imagined to bear children without the intervention of a husband or of any other male partner. . . . (*Sexual Life of Savages*, p. 182)

Because of the repeated discovery of the primacy of the mothers' brothers in primitive regions, Frazer challenged Westermarck on his thesis that the father-family had existed throughout human history:

If the normal human family from the earliest times down to the present day has been the monogamous patriarchal family with the father as the guardian of his children, how comes it that throughout a large part of mankind, especially among the savages, descent has been traced through the mother and not through the father; that property, where it exists, has been inherited from her and not from him; and that the guardian of the children has not been their father but their mother's brother? To these questions Dr. Westermarck makes no satisfactory answer. . . . The system of mother-kin and the position of the mother's brother in savage and barbarous society are formidable obstacles. (*Totemism and Exogamy,* vol. IV, p. 99)

The role of the mothers' brothers demonstrates that not only matrilineal but also fratrilineal kinship preceded patrilineal kinship and the father-family in history. This furnishes the starting point for investigating the main building blocks of solidarity among men upon which the fratriarchy was constructed.

Indigenous or "Milk and Blood" Brothers

In the course of its long evolution the term "brother" came to be applied to more and more groups of men. This poses the problem of distinguishing between different categories of brothers; those who were most closely related belonged to one category, while those with whom fraternal alliances had been made belonged to a separate category. From this standpoint the primal horde or individual clan consisted of what may be called indigenous or "milk and blood" brothers.

They are also "born" brothers, but on this point we must distinguish between the savage concept of birth and ours. In our contemporary family system of kinship the term "brother" signifies that a man is a member of a specific family and that he is "blood-related," i.e., biologically related, to the other members of the family. Under the primitive classificatory system of kinship the term did not mean either of these relationships. It signified only that the child was a "born" member of a group of mothers, his matrilineal kin, and a group of mothers' brothers, his fratrilineal kin.

W. H. R. Rivers puts it this way: "A term like that of brother which, except in the mataphorical sense, is limited among ourselves to the male children of our own parents, is in the classificatory system extended to all the male members of the clan of the same generation" (*History of Melanesian Society*, vol. I, p. 7). Such an all-inclusive grouping of genetically unrelated males who regard one another as "blood brothers" demonstrates that this was not "blood" brotherhood in our sense of the term — that is, it was not family brotherhood.

This raises the question: What was the basis of the savage concept of close kinship if it was neither family nor blood kinship as we understand it? Serious mistakes have been made by assuming that the savage concept of kinship, like ours, involved a genetic relationship. It meant something quite different.

Some probers into this subject have pointed out that common residence, common food, and common motherhood were the original factors in establishing the bonds of matrilineal kinship. Tyloı emphasizes residence as the key factor, while Briffault emphasizes food and motherhood. "Common food means, as primitive man understands it, kinship and common generation," Briffault writes. "He regards himself as being one with the group not because of any genealogical kinship, but because he is actually of the same substance" (*The Mothers*, vol. II, p. 490).

Being of the same substance means being of the same "flesh" and of the same "blood" in the most literal sense. A community of children are born in the blood of their mothers. They are fed from the flesh of their mothers in the form of mother's milk. The combination makes them "flesh-and-blood kin."

According to Frazer, in the Wotjobaluk tribe of Australia the term *yauerin* means "flesh" and also "totem"; it signifies kinship through the female line. A man may not marry a woman of his *yauerin* (*Totemism and Exogamy,* vol. I, p. 458). On the same point Briffault writes, "In Arabic and in Hebrew one and the same word signifies 'flesh,' 'kindred,' or 'clan.' In China kindred in the female line is expressed by the term 'of the same flesh.' The same nomenclature is used in Tibet, and in India among the Santals" (*The Mothers,* vol. I, p. 491).

The same concept of literal flesh-and-blood kinship is reported by Malinowski among the matrilineal Trobriand Islanders. He writes:

> That the mother contributes everything to the new being to be born of her is taken for granted by the natives, and forcibly expressed by them. "The mother feeds the infant in her body. Then, when it comes out, she feeds it with her milk." "The mother makes the child out of her blood." "Brothers and sisters are of the same flesh, because they come of the same mother." This and similar expressions describe their attitude towards this, their fundamental principle of kinship. (*Sexual Life of Savages,* p. 4)

W. I. Thomas gives the following description of the "milk" bond that ties together mother-sister-brother kin:

> The Chickasaw Indians have a term "itibapicili," "those who suck together," used for brothers and sisters collectively, and those who suck together and the one who gives suck and the protector of the suck-giver and the sucklings are in a unique relation of intimacy. They represent a group personality and the status of all is affected by the behavior of each. (*Primitive Behavior,* pp. 189-90)

It was not the individual biological relationship between mother and child but the collective motherhood of all the women to all the children of the group that made them the closest kin. In accord with this principle, every nursing mother might participate in feeding an infant. To take a few examples from Briffault:

> In the care and rearing, and even in the nursing of children, the closest cooperation takes place. . . . Among the Andamanese, a child is petted and nursed " . . . by everyone in the village; a woman with a nursed child will often give suck to the children of other women." In Indonesia, likewise, it is usual for sisters and female relatives to assist in the suckling of a child when the mother is occupied. . . . "A very common, and indeed almost universal custom," says Dr. Siebert, "is that a child should be suckled not only by its mother, but also by its grandmother and likewise by other near female relatives." (*The Mothers,* vol. I, pp. 597-98)

These facts help to bring out the essential distinctions between the primitive concept of kinship and ours. To us the term "brother" is applicable only to those individuals born of the same mother and father. But in primitive society, where the facts about biological relationship were unknown and irrelevant to the communal mode of life, kinship was exclusively social. For example, the Dobu term *susu,* which is sometimes translated as "the motherhood" or "mother's milk," is also translated as the "milk brotherhood" when it refers to the males of the group.

While we can understand the primitive practice of the collective suckling of an infant, it is far more difficult to grasp the notion that a child which visibly emerges from one woman's womb could be viewed as collectively "borne." In primitive society, however, to collectively "bear" a child it was only necessary for all the women of the group to take turns lifting the infant up and holding it for a while. Rivers describes such a ceremony:

> In the island of Motlav, and similar customs probably exist elsewhere in the group, all the women of the island assemble in the house where a woman has been delivered of her first-born child. At the end of twenty days a ceremony is performed in which the women sit in a circle and the child is handed round to them, each woman holding the child for a time, after which it is returned to the mother. . . . it suggests a survival of a condition in which the women of the community had the right to assist in the care and nurture of the child. . . . (*History of Melanesian Society,* vol. II, pp. 139-40)

Under such circumstances even men could "bear" and raise children. In primitive languages the mother's brother is also called a "male mother," a term that has perplexed some anthropologists. Radcliffe-Brown tells us that "in South Africa the common term for the mother's brother is *malume* or *umalume,* which is a compound formed from the stem for 'mother"—*ma*—and a suffix meaning 'male.'" An equivalent term, he says, is found in the Friendly Islands of Polynesia. He is astonished by the fact that the same phenomenon occurs in widely dispersed regions whose languages are not related (*Structure and Function in Primitive Society,* p. 19).

C. L. Meek reports that a youth in Nigeria will say that his maternal uncle or "male mother" is the man who "bore" him (*Tribal Studies in Northern Nigeria,* vol. II, p. 34). This curious statement has a basis in fact. Certain rituals performed upon each generation of male youth appear to be survivals of an ancient practice when mothers' brothers "bore" their clan sisters' children.

Spencer and Gillen describe such a ritual among the Australian aborigines, the first in a series of rites. It is called "Throwing the Boy Up in the Air." It takes place when a group of boys have reached a certain approximate age, and registers their transfer from the female to the male sector of the community. On this occasion the boys "are taken one by one and tossed in the air several times by the men, who catch them as they fall, while the women dance round and round the group swinging their arms and shouting loudly. . . . This over, the boys are painted on their chests and backs" (*Native Tribes of Central Australia,* p. 214).

In this instance the men who throw the boys up in the air belong not to their own maternal group but to the maternal group of the future wives of the boys. But it suggests a time when male children were "borne" first by their mothers and then by their mothers' brothers.

Max Gluckman writes that among the Barotse of Africa the mother's brother "is grouped with his sister and called 'male mother.'" He illustrates this with the following account:

Once when I was working in Barotseland during the war, a new District Commissioner told me that he had had an inquiry from the Army about a Barotse soldier who had overstayed his leave. The soldier's excuse was that while he was at home his mother had died, and he had stayed for her funeral. The District Commissioner had found that it was the soldier's mother's brother who had died. I explained that the Barotse called the mother's brother 'my male-mother', or more simply even 'my mother'. The mother's brother was a very close relative whose funeral a man should attend. So the District Commissioner wrote to the Army: 'Please ask the soldier if his mother was a woman or a man. If he says his mother was a woman, he is lying; if he says his mother was a man, he is telling the truth.' (*Custom and Conflict in Africa,* p. 62)

Thus unlike female children, who were born once of their mothers, in ancient times male children were born twice — once of their mothers and then of their "male mothers." This may be the forerunner of the "twice-born" sons of the "high-born" castes of a later patriarchal era. But in the beginning the second birth was no more than a method of transferring the male children to the tutorship and guardianship of the mothers' brothers.

This transfer is usually described as an "initiation ceremony" marking the beginning of the changed status of the young men. As this is put, they were formerly classified with the females, but now they are "men." Henceforth they may not continue their close contact with the women and girls for as men they are now hunters and warriors. One point that is insufficiently analyzed in this transfer is the change of diet that accompanies it. Formerly the youth ate women's foods with the women. Now they eat men's foods. Thus they have been transferred not only to a different residential sector but also to a different "food division."

This apparently resulted in an additional type of blood brotherhood exclusive to men only. These blood kin were those who hunted and ate the same food together. By the same token they would never under any circumstances hunt, kill, or eat one another. As Robertson Smith puts it, "Those who sit at meat together are united for all social effects; those who do not eat together are aliens to one another . . . without reciprocal social duties" (*Religion of the Semites,* p. 269).

As "blood brothers" they were brought under the double taboo: just as they could not kill or eat their own kin, they could not mate with their own kin. All hunting, whether for food or for mates, was expelled from the community. The brothers had to go outside the community of kin to hunt "animals"; they could eat only "strange flesh." Curiously enough, the term "strange flesh" applied also to mates, i.e., women who were not of their own kin.

Frazer observed this in the Wotjobaluk tribe of Australia, where the term for flesh was *yauerin.* At marriage the first question was, "What is the *yauerin* of the two persons?" The term meant "class" and "totem" as well as "flesh," and no marriage could take place between persons closely related by "flesh." Hence, he writes, a man was forbidden to marry a woman of the same place as his mother; he had to go to some place where "there was no flesh (*yauerin*) near to his" (*Totemism and Exogamy,* vol. I, p. 458).

Indigenous "blood brotherhood," which demarcated the in-group or kin from all outsiders or strangers, was the first building block in the construction of the fratriarchy. It was indispensable in eradicating any possibility of cannibalism or violent struggle over females within the primal horde. At the same time, since it was restricted to the in-group and excluded out-groups, the kinship was one-sided and limited. Unavoidably it polarized kin against non-kin, brothers against strangers.

Many anthropologists have commented on this polarization. Within the kin group there was trust, peace, generosity, and the greatest consideration for the needs and rights of others. But toward those belonging to the outside world there was deep suspicion, distrust, and hostility. As L. T. Hobhouse observes, the typical primitive community was "a little island of friends amid a sea of strangers and enemies" ("Class Relations," in *The Making of Man,* p. 828). Others write that an unidentified stranger was regarded as little more than a wild animal, a danger to the community who had to be killed on sight.

Some writers refer to this sharp contrast in attitude as a dual system of "morals." Others think of the phenomenon in psychological terms, as a dislike of anything "strange," which they call xenophobia and regard as an eternal trait of human nature. This is Hoebel's view. "Human beings in general," he says, "prefer to associate with their own kind. They incline to be suspicious of differences and to give warm approval to likenesses of themselves" (*Man in the Primitive World,* p. 70).

The primitive barriers between kin and non-kin, however, came from the dangerous conditions of life in the primeval epoch. Our earliest ancestors, just emerging from the animal world, were unable to distinguish between themselves and other animal species. Since kinship alone marked the dividing line between humans and animals, those who were non-kin were non-human and therefore dangerous to the humans. Under these conditions life was inviolable only for members of the kin-group. As Robertson Smith sums this up:

> To the primitive man all other men fall under two classes, those to whom his life is sacred and those to whom it is not sacred. The former are his fellows; the latter are strangers and potential foemen, with whom it is absurd to think of forming any inviolable tie unless they are first brought into the circle within which each man's life is sacred to all his comrades. (*Religion of the Semites,* p. 272)

In view of this, how was the "blood kinship" tie extended from one horde to another, bringing them together as affiliated clans?

Here the system of social kinship showed its advantages over family kinship. Whereas the latter is rigidly restricted to genetic relatives, members of the same family circle, the kinship of the maternal clan was capable of broad and expanding inclusiveness. Through the interchange of totem-kin ties, distinct hordes could be joined together in a larger, more secure organization.

These alliances were of two main types. The earliest, modeled on the pattern of the indigenous blood brothers, produced what may be called "parallel" brother-clans. The second type, which came later, produced "cross-cousins" — a wholly new kind of brother, the brother-in-law.

Let us examine the parallel brothers, the first systematic expansion of fraternal kinship ties.

Parallel Brothers and the Blood Covenant

Although the primitive concept of sisters and brothers had a broad, all-inclusive application, it became apparent to the early anthropologists that aboriginal peoples had several categories of sisters and brothers; some very close, others not so close. One of the problems in uncovering this differentiation has been the lack of equivalent terms in modern languages. This has resulted in futile attempts to distinguish between family and nonfamily members of the clan.

Lewis Morgan singled out what he called "own" brothers and sisters from "collaterals." Since Morgan himself stated that the family was a late arrival in history, his attempt to designate family members in the prefamily epoch of history conflicted with his own thesis and created considerable confusion. It played into the hands of those who insisted that the family had always existed.

The term "collateral" kin fell into disuse. Subsequently the term "fictional" kin was used by some anthropologists to distinguish family brothers and sisters from the others. But this too was misleading since it posited family relationships in a period when they did not yet exist.

Family kinship terms came into existence late in history with the advent of the family institution itself. To be sure, the terms "mother," "brother," and "sister" as family terms grew up out of the equivalents in clan terminology. But this occurred only after the clan system broke apart and was succeeded by the family.

In our society, whatever else a man is, he is a member of a family, usually born of a known father and mother and deriving his social identification and status through his family line. But in savage society men were identified collectively, not by their family connections but by their clan and tribal connections. Each individual was a member of the brothers and sisters in his own clan. And he was also affiliated to the brothers and sisters in clans that were allied or "linked" to his own. I have found it useful to refer to these as "parallel" clans and to their members as "parallel" sisters, brothers, and other kin.

The special feature of the "parallel" kin is that they were governed by exactly the same food and sex taboos as were the indigenous kin. Under the food taboo, which was also an occupational taboo, the men of one clan could not hunt, kill, or eat the brothers in their parallel clans any more than they could the brothers in their own clan. Under the sex taboo a man could no more have sexual access to the women in a parallel clan than he could the women in his own clan.

The parallel brotherhood represents the second building block in constructing the fratriarchy. The term "parallel brothers" does not appear in anthropological works; the only references are to "parallel cousins," usually only to show the difference between them and a totally different kind of cousin called "cross-cousin." The difference between them is important. Cross-cousins are not only permitted but enjoined to marry and therefore are "mating cousins." Parallel cousins, also called "ortho-cousins," are strictly prohibited from mating, just as are brothers and sisters. This suggests that originally the parallel cousins were parallel brothers and sisters who evolved into cousins at a later period.

This hypothesis corresponds to the original need and function of the parallel kinship system; it was an extension of brotherly relations from one horde to another to prevent the hunters in both from killing and eating any of their parallel kin. In the earliest epoch of cannibalism the first linkages between alien clans would have been the most difficult to accomplish. It would have been easier to proliferate sister-brother relations on the model already established within each horde than to initiate the wholly new relationship of cross-cousin.

A close examination of the ritual called the "blood covenant" confirms this hypothesis. In this ceremony men who were formerly strangers became bound together as "blood brothers." The ritual went through many changes in the course of its very long evolution, but always retained its original key feature — a pact of mutual assistance between men.

As with other controversial findings in anthropology, opinions differ on the origin and functions of the blood covenant. Among the disputed issues is the question of whether it was a group alliance or an individual bond between men. The evidence shows that it originated as a group-to-group alliance in which each individual man participated as a member of the group. It is our argument that originally these blood covenants converted separate hordes into parallel brother-clans. However, in the course of time, as the parallel brotherhood itself disappeared, the blood covenant also changed and became a pact between individual men. Survivals of the blood pact are usually found in individual form, although there are some examples of the more ancient group covenant.

As it is described, two men can become blood brothers by opening their veins and sucking a little of each other's blood. Variations of the ritual occur when the men smear a little of their own blood upon each other, or upon a food article that they then eat together. Once the ritual has been performed, the men are assured that each will do no injury to the other and will come to his assistance if necessary.

Robertson Smith cites the rite described by Herodotus in which the blood exchanged between two individuals is sufficient to bind together their entire groups:

The rite described by Herodotus has for its object the admission of an individual stranger to fellowship with an Arab clansman and his kin; the compact is primarily between two individuals, but the obligation contracted by the single clansman is binding on all his "friends," i.e. on the other members of the kin. The reason why it is so binding is that he who has drunk a clansman's blood is no longer a stranger but a brother, and included in the mystic circle of those who have a share in the life-blood that is common to all the clan. Primarily the covenant is not a special engagement to this or that particular effect, but a bond of troth and life-fellowship to all the effects for which the kinsmen are permanently bound together. (*The Religion of the Semites,* pp. 315-16)

E. Sidney Hartland writes on the same subject:

The blood covenant is a very common ceremony. . . . It consists in the transfusion of blood between two or more individuals, either directly, or by drinking, or in some symbolic manner. By this means the persons who go through the rite and those whom they represent become of one blood, and are entitled to all the privileges and liable to all the duties of blood-kinship, exactly as if they had been born to them. (*Primitive Law,* p. 36)

One of the best-preserved relics of the ancient blood covenant can be found in a report on the Chagga by Gutmann, cited by W. I. Thomas. It is particularly significant in that the blood covenant is preceded by a milk covenant, indicating not only the most ancient form of the covenant but also the part played by women in it.

The report states that "the establishment of a blood-brotherhood always joined two groups, never two individuals only." It describes the milk ritual as follows:

First of all the sib brothers join in the milk brotherhood. A bowl is filled with thick milk into which a nursing mother of the sib lets drop some of her own milk. In doing so she utters an incantation: "Whosoever among you brings himself to slander his brother, whoever accuses him or commits treachery against him, into his body may this

milk bring sickness and boils, so that men will say of
him: 'The brotherhood milk brings this plague upon him.'
But if you are loyal to your brother and stand by his
side in times of need, may it preserve and keep you—
hawu!" The bowl thus adjured is now held out to each
participant for a drink. While his lips are on the vessel
each individual is addressed, "Should you betray your
brother or his children, if you desert him in the battle . . .
hofa—then die! But if you love him and help him and
stand by him, may you be kept and preserved—*hawu!*"
(*Primitive Behavior,* pp. 164-65)

Following the milk ritual, which occurs inside the hut, the
blood exchange takes place outside the hut on a spread-out
oxhide.

The officiating old man and the woman who previously
gave her milk grasp the hide, swing it and say: "You, the
brothers of one sib, have agreed to bind yourselves more
securely. Whosoever acts against this brotherhood—may
he become as barren as this hide. . . . may he fall into
the abyss! All that will be said is: 'It is the hide of the
brotherhood that killed him.' But if you are loyal to this
brotherhood, etc. may you be preserved and kept—*hawu!*"
(ibid.)

The elaborate ceremonies included the slaying and roasting
of a goat and an exchange of blood through incisions made
in the arm, as well as eating goat meat upon which the blood
of the participants had been smeared.

In another reference to the Chagga we are told that "a man
may not marry the sister of a man with whom he has exchanged blood" (ibid., p. 180). This was the prime deficiency
of the parallel blood brotherhood. From the standpoint of the
males the blood covenant brought men together as brothers
who had formerly hunted and killed one another. However,
so long as the sex taboo remained an integral part of the
taboo against killing and eating, it had the effect of increasing the number of forbidden females. Among the Chagga,
for example, we are told that "from the blood brotherhood
of the clans a blood brotherhood for provinces was evolved"
(ibid., p. 168).

This deficiency ultimately led to the abandonment of the blood covenant and its replacement by a more advanced method of joining men in fraternal relations — the familiar "peace pact."

Both types of alliances — the parallel blood covenant and the peace pact — appear in the anthropological record. Often no clear distinction is made between them. The distinction can be deduced, however, in the context of the particular union; if it is required that the women shall be sisters when the men become brothers, it is a parallel blood covenant. Examples of both types of alliance appear in the following comments by Crawley:

> Peace is made after war by eating food mingled with the blood of the parties. The people of Luang-Sermata make peace by drinking together. In the Babar Islands the blood of the two parties is mingled with liquor and drunk, both when peace is made between two villages and when two persons form a league of friendship. . . . In the islands, Leti, Moa and Lakor, when a man has cursed another the injury is put away by the two eating together at a feast made for the purpose; on these occasions a stick is broken in two and each party keeps a piece. In the ceremonial words uttered at this time, the phrase is used, "Our women shall be sisters and our men brothers. ". . . At peacemaking in Wetar the parties exchange presents and eat together; when a bond is made between two individuals or villages, the parties drink each other's blood as a mark of union. The members of such villages may not after this ceremony intermarry. . . . The Ceramese habitually make alliance of friendship by exchanging presents, especially of food; moreover, quarrels between two villages are settled, and peace made after war, in the following way: gifts are exchanged, and a feast is made in one village to which members of the other are invited. The chiefs of both parties drop some of their own blood into a dish of food in which swords and other weapons are dipped — this food they now alternately eat. . . . Many villages have been through the ceremony which is called *pela*, and "those who have taken part therein may not intermarry, but must help each other in war." A similar process is gone through by parties who are going "headhunting" together. (*The Mystic Rose*, vol. I, pp. 295-96)

According to some scholars, blood exchange is itself a derivative of an even more basic exchange involving food. J. A. MacCulloch writes on this point:

> Probably the idea that kinship means blood-relationship — a relationship which can be produced by the blood-covenant — is not primitive. More primitive is the idea that contact, eating and drinking together, exchange of names, garments, weapons, and the like, will produce a close bond, whether involving identity or relationship between two un-related persons. (*Encyclopedia of Religion and Ethics*, vol. III, p. 207)

The giving and receiving of food was fundamental throughout the entire evolution of these fraternal unions, from the earliest blood covenant up to the tribal peace alliance. In the epoch of cannibalism, no doubt, it operated on the principle that "if I give you food and you give me food, we bind ourselves to a pledge not to regard each other as food."

The blood covenant, in which men drink a little of each other's blood, has been recognized by some investigators as a relic from the period of cannibalism. But long after cannibalism had faded out of history, the food bond remained the most basic pledge of trust and friendship between men; it was the peace symbol without peer. Robertson Smith gives an example:

> Among the Arabs every stranger whom one meets in the desert is a natural enemy, and has no protection against violence except his own strong hand or the fear that his tribe will avenge him if his blood be spilt. But if I have eaten the smallest morsel of food with a man, I have nothing further to fear from him; "there is salt between us," and he is bound not only to do me no harm, but to help and defend me as if I were his brother. (*Religion of the Semites*, pp. 269-70)

As peace alliances increasingly displaced the more ancient blood-brotherhood covenants, the sex taboo that had prevented a man from mating with parallel sisters became more and more corroded. As usual when new customs collide with old practices, this breakdown was accompanied by many difficulties. In some regions survivals of certain rituals called "cutting kinship" or "killing the relationship" testify to these problems. Old women or old men had to decide questionable cases, and if the decision was favorable, the cutting ritual was performed to signify that the pair was no longer kin and therefore could marry. The following from Evans-Pritchard is an example:

> If a proposed union is a borderline case a gourd may be ritually broken in half to end kinship. They then say *Bakena mar,* "We break kinship," and *Ba bak ne kir,* "It (kinship) is broken with a gourd." . . .
> Cases arise in which there is disagreement whether or not the genealogical distance between a suitor and the girl wom he wishes to marry is wide enough to permit marriage. If it is permitted a beast will be sacrificed to cut what kinship there may be held still to be between them. ("Nuer Rules of Exogamy and Incest," in *Social Structure,* pp. 86, 90)

The widespread "elopement" phenomenon in primitive society is probably connected with the difficulties involved in the severance of kinship between a pair. In most instances the elopement is followed by a more or less ritualistic storm of public disapproval and even a mild punishment of the pair when they are located. Subsequently, however, they are accepted as a married couple.

Anthropologists who fail to take into account the vast distinction between classified kin and family kin are unable to analyze this severance of ties between parallel sisters and brothers. Yet here we find the answer to a problem that has vexed some anthropologists, namely, how a "brother" came to marry his "sister." Their usual explanation that these were "incestuous" marriages contradicts their central thesis that fear of incest is universal and the taboo against it so stringent it could never be violated.

The fact is that these parallel brothers and sisters were not family kin but classified kin. They were not genetic relatives when they were prohibited from mating, and they were not genetic relatives when the prohibition was lifted. The so-called brother who married his sister was merely marrying a woman who, under the changed conditions, was no longer his parallel sister.

Hans Kelsen correctly observes that since primitive kinship was a social, not a "natural" relationship, it could not only be artificially established but also artificially annulled. He gives an example of the "cutting ekar" ritual among the Fanti of the Gold Coast:

> *Cutting ekar* is a particular mode of disowning any one's blood relation. When a man desires to disown a blood relative, he brings him before the elders of his town or village, and in their presence, as well as in the presence of the other members of his family, an ekar is cut in twain, and saying clearly, "We are now divided," he takes one-half and the disowned the other half. As soon as this ceremony is completed, the two persons have no more share or portion in the property of the other. Where a man is disowned, it affects him alone; but in the case of a woman, her issue is included, for the saying is, "the children follow the mother's condition." (*Society and Nature,* pp. 30-31)

The decline of the old blood covenant proceeded side by side with the breakdown of the parallel blood brotherhood. The process was speeded up with the rise of the family and private property. One example can be found in Evans-Pritchard's description of the Azande in modern times. He writes, "It is well known to Azande that blood-brotherhood counts little with princes when it clashes with their personal and political aims, and there are illustrative cases which tell how they have killed persons to whom they stood as blood-brothers, i.e. people belonging to clans with members of which a prince or some of his relatives have made a covenant of blood." And he adds:

> There can be no doubt of the general truth of the Zande contention that blood-brotherhood is no longer respected today as it used to be before European occupation of their country. All Azande with whom I have spoken about blood-brotherhood were unanimous in deploring the decay of the institution. They said that exchange of blood in the old days created a pact which was held as sacred by the two participants and their kin, while today people no longer regard their obligations seriously. . . . As in other departments of their life, custom has crumbled and blood-brotherhood is slowly losing its moral force. . . . Zande culture is adapting itself. (*Essays in Social Anthropology,* pp. 136, 155)

A reduction of the old group covenant can be found in the "bond" friendship pact made between individual men, which no longer had any connection with forging clan kinship ties. Ralph Piddington describes such a bond friendship in Tikopia:

> In Tikopia a somewhat similar kind of relationship exists [as blood brotherhood] but it is not interpreted in terms of kinship, nor is one partner assimilated to the clan of the other. The Tikopia relationship is therefore best called "bond friendship" — in fact the native term for it is *tau soa,* that is, people linked together as friends, or *soa.* Bond friendship is established voluntarily by two young men who ritually chew betel together. . . . Bond friends exchange gifts and visits from time to time, they assist each other in economic affairs and give mutual protection in situations of danger. (*Introduction to Social Anthropology,* p. 214)

In sum, to understand how the fratriarchy evolved from the primal horde to the tribe it is necessary to begin with the "parallel brothers" as the first expansion of fraternal ties from one group to another. These linkages of men from alien groups into brother-clans did not extinguish the separate identity of each clan. Although the members of the affiliated clans called one another "brother," indigenous brothers could always distinguish themselves from parallel brothers.

First, indigenous brothers were born in the same community, of the same group of mothers. Parallel brothers were born of a different set of mothers — called mothers' sisters — in a separate though neighboring community. Second, through various totemic markings and insignia, parallel kin could readily be distinguished from indigenous kin. Thirdly, no blood covenant was made between indigenous brothers; the covenant applied only to men who without the blood rite would be strangers.

However, as we have seen, the deficiency of the parallel brothership was its one-sided character. It represented an expansion of kinship in one direction only, sometimes referred to as a "straight" direction. While it produced more brothers and sisters, it did so under the same taboo that prevented them from mating with one another.

To achieve a fully rounded tribe, it was necessary to effect a new kind of alliance that would bring mating partners for the brothers and sisters into the maternal clan system of organization. This came about with the cross-cousin alliance —

an alliance in a "cross" rather than a "straight" direction. This brought about not more brothers but something new in kinship, brothers-in-law.

Cross-Cousins and Brothers-in-Law

The cross-cousin relationship, the third major building block in the construction of the fratriarchy, is usually presented as a marriage relationship between men and women rather than as a fraternal relationship between men and former stranger-men. Yet it was the fraternal relationship between the men that paved the road toward the regularized mating relationship between men and women.

The cross-cousin mating relationship was not marriage in our sense of the term. However, nineteenth-century anthropologists, in part bending to the puritanical standards of their day, called the primitive system of mating "marriage." Morgan used the term "group marriage" and Tylor the term "cross-cousin marriage." Since the term "marriage" is now imprinted in the literature, it should be understood that, where this term is used prematurely, it actually signifies no more than mating.

Morgan's term "group marriage" refers to a system of mating by which the brothers and sisters of one group mated with the sisters and brothers of another group. The term led to certain misunderstandings. It was construed by some to mean that a man had a "group" of wives in the manner of a polygamous setup. The term "sexual communism" used by Rivers did not improve matters in this respect; it was thought to mean that a group of women were the communal property of a man.

The system called "group marriage" was simply an intermating agreement or alliance made between two groups, i.e., two clans, to effect a new kind of fraternal relationship between them, one that included the interchange of sisters and brothers as mates. Within this collective agreement every match was made on a voluntary, individual basis. Far from monopolizing or controlling the sexual activities of any woman, a man had to wait until the desired partner gave him the signal that she was available as a mate. As this is often put, "the initiative in marriage came from the woman, not the man."

E. B. Tylor coined the useful term "cross-cousin" to signify an egalitarian connubial agreement between two matrilineal groups for a regularized, peaceful exchange of mates. As we have seen, a man could not marry his parallel or ortho-cousin since she was classified as his sister. But he could mate with a woman from his cross-cousin group since that was his officially recognized mating group. As Frazer writes:

> The distinction between cross-cousins and ortho-cousins is ignored by civilized nations, but is regarded as of fundamental importance by many peoples of the lower cultures, who, while they strictly forbid the marriage of ortho-cousins, allow, favor, or even enjoin the marriage of cross-cousins. (*Totemism and Exogamy,* vol. IV, pp. 119-20)

Although cross-cousin mating represented a group-to-group mating system, certain restrictions were enforced with respect to the age level of the women sought as wives. A man was denied access to any women in the generations older or younger than himself; he was permitted to mate only with a woman of his generation — his "marriage class" or "marriage division."

According to Tylor, the development of cross-cousin marriage "must be the direct result of the simplest form of exogamy," namely, the exogamy associated with matrilineal communities. A man is forbidden to marry a sister or a parallel cousin. He may mate with a cross-cousin or some other woman, the preferred union being with a cross-cousin.

The cross-cousin mating alliance is associated with the phenomenon called the "dual organization" of society. Each side in this alliance is described as a "moiety," derived from the French word meaning "one-half." The two moieties or halves constitute a whole; the reciprocal exchange of mates takes place between them. In the beginning the two moieties may have been two clans. At the end of the evolution of the dual organization they were two phratries of a tribe standing opposite each other.

Tylor, citing Codrington's data, showed how each side or moiety was a *veve,* a Melanesian term that means "mother" or "motherhood." This, he wrote, "implies that descent·follows the mother's side and a man must marry a wife of the other mother from himself, or as they say, not on his own side of the house but on the other" ("On a Method . . ." in *Source Book in Anthropology,* p. 469). Thus both the cross-cousin intermating alliance and the dual organization of society were developments within the matriarchal system of social organization. The two moieties were matrilineal.

At the same time cross-cousin mating can be regarded as the

starting point of the marriage institution. It would be a great mistake, however, to view the end of this process as identical with its beginning. Originally, cross-cousin mating between a man and a woman did not involve any common menage or change of residence on the part of either the woman or the man. The partners continued to live in their separate matrilineal divisions together with their mothers, brothers, and sisters. They met as they wished for sexual intercourse, which may or may not have involved any continuous association. Only in the last stage of the evolution of cross-cousin mating did cohabitation become prevalent and lead to the pairing couple.

From this standpoint the use of the terms "husband" and "wife" for cross-cousin mates is misleading. Aboriginal terms for spouses were applied not simply to the individual pair but to all the members of the specific mating-class in which a man or woman found their sexual partners, as A. M. Hocart points out:

> In all systems with two or more divisions the same term is applied by a man to the woman he marries and other women whom he does not marry, but might lawfully have married. Thus a Lauan calls his wife *wati,* her sister *wati,* her sister's ortho-cousins *wati.* He has innumerable *wati* whom he may never meet in all his lifetime. They are simply his female cross-cousins, the women of the same generation as his own in those groups with whom his group has the *jus connubii.* Conversely she calls all her male cross-cousins *wati.* Unfortunately the term is commonly translated wife or husband, and thus Morgan was led to suppose that these women were once actually wives, and that all the men they called *wati* were once really their husbands. In other words, there was once community of wives, all the men of one side had all the women on the other side in common. This theory confuses mating with marriage. There is no evidence that group *marriage* was ever practised in that manner. (*The Progress of Man,* p. 257)

Thus the classificatory term *wati* — and its equivalent in other languages — does not mean "husband" or "wife" in our sense of the term. Rather it means a man or woman of the eligible mating-class in the opposite moiety or division with whom a woman or man can have lawful sexual relations. Here too, since the terms have been imprinted into the record, and since we lack adequate substitutes, the terms "husband" and "wife," like the term "marriage," will continue to be used for the sake of convenience.

Another correction that should be made with respect to cross-cousin mating is the frequent use of the phrase, "a man marries his mother's brother's daughter." This makes it appear that systematic first-cousin marriages were the rule, with the son of a mother marrying the daughter of her genetic brother. This is just as incorrect as the notion of genetic brother-sister marriages. In both instances classificatory mothers and brothers are involved, not family relatives. Therefore the best way to express the reciprocal connubial agreement is to say, as Tylor did, that a man marries a daughter of a mother in the opposite maternal division or *veve*. Similarly, the extremely clumsy formula, "a man may only marry a mother's mother's brother's daughter's daughter" can be better expressed by saying that a man may only marry a woman of his own mating-class on the opposite side, namely, a woman of his own generation.

The basis for cross-cousin mating has perplexed many anthropologists, especially those who believe marriage and the family have always existed. As Hoebel formulated this riddle: "Why cross-cousin marriage? . . . It is a *bete noir* of anthropology but it refuses to yield a satisfactory answer" (*Man in the Primitive World*, p. 202).

It was understandable to most anthropologists that under the law of exogamy a man would be obliged to "marry out," particularly since this was interpreted as an avoidance of incest. But why was the man obliged to "marry in" to another group where, in our kinship terms, the women appeared to be first cousins — only one step removed from sister-brother "incestuous" marriage? The fact is that they were no more first cousins in a genetic sense than were the sisters and brothers. Rather they were cross-cousins under the classificatory system, which signified that they were eligible as mating partners. Here again errors have been made by not recognizing the vast distinction between primitive classified kinship and our family kinship.

However, even an understanding of the classificatory system does not by itself explain the riddle of cross-cousin mating. As this problem usually appears, why was a tribe "divided into" two halves, with each side providing the mates for the other? While the law of exogamy seemed to be explicable, what was the meaning of the law of endogamy that arose with the cross-cousin mating system? Why didn't the men and women find their mates wherever they pleased rather than being directed toward a specific group?

This question cannot be answered so long as the cross-cousin relationship is regarded as simply a marriage arrangement between men and women. More fundamentally, it was a new kind of fraternal relationship between men. So long as the men with whom the women mated remained outsiders and strangers to the brothers of these women, they were real or potential enemies, feared and distrusted by the women's brothers. An accidental encounter between a woman's brother and her lover could trigger a fight and result in death.

Tylor's statement that a man must "marry out" or be "killed out" has often been quoted but without sufficient explanation. If he married out at random he could very well be killed out by the woman's kinsmen as a stranger-enemy. As a cross-cousin, however, he was no longer an enemy but a friend, a brother-in-law.

This is the fundamental reason for the cross-cousin relationship; it was necessary to bring former foemen together in a fraternal alliance that would permit peaceful mating relations between the groups. This provides the answer to the question: Why the law of endogamy? It was made necessary by the earlier rule of exogamy and conditions of life in the epoch of cannibalism. Briffault notes this situation as follows:

By virtue of the rule of exogamy sexual association between members of the same group is almost everywhere strictly prohibited. A man or a woman must obtain his or her sexual partners from another group. But that is by no means an easy matter in primitive conditions. . . . The members of one's own group are in primitive society "our people," all other individuals are "strangers," which is synonymous with "enemies." . . . A member of one group cannot, in any primitive society, visit another group without observing elaborate ceremonial precautions designed to satisfy the members of the group which he is visiting that no hostile or treacherous purpose is contemplated. In Australia, remarks Mr. Mathew, "when a blackfellow crosses the boundary line of his own territory, he takes his life in his hands. . . ." For a lover to pay a stealthy visit in the night to a female of a strange group is thus almost impracticable;

and unless there exists some friendly understanding between the two groups, it is equally impossible in the daytime. (*The Mothers*, vol. I, pp. 560-61)

This accounts for the secrecy that in the earlier period surrounded the sexual relations between men and women. It is sometimes erroneously ascribed to "modesty" or "delicacy," according to our attitudes toward sex. Crawley writes on this subject:

> The savage is far more secretive in this function than is civilised man; what Riedel states of the Ceramese, is true of the generality of savage and barbarous peoples. In Ceram, he says, all natural functions, especially that of coition, are performed in secret, by preference in the forest. Similarly in the Aru Islands and in Wetar. . . . In Fiji, from motives of delicacy, "*rendezvous* between husband and wife are arranged in the depths of the forest, unknown to any but the two." (*The Mystic Rose*, vol. I, p. 216)

With the advent of the cross-cousin relationship, men who had formerly confronted each other as actual or potential enemies were now assured of safe conduct in the land of their cross-cousins, who, through the alliance, were obliged to furnish each other mutual protection. This removed the earlier perils of the random hunt for mates. It instituted a regulated system of mating exchange. Julius Lippert, who calls these intermarrying moieties "connubial leagues," writes that "the need of acquiring wives peacefully . . . contributed materially toward the establishment of peaceful intercourse between alien groups" (*Evolution of Culture*, pp. 334-35).

In some regions women say, "We marry our enemies." Elsewhere they say, "We marry our cross-cousins." Both are statements of historical fact; the mating exchange system converted former enemies into cross-cousins.

Both types of fraternal relationships, the parallel brotherhood and the cross-cousin alliance, enlarged the groups of men who could trust one another as friends. It did not put an end to all hostilities, since both types of pacts were subject to breakdowns under certain conditions. However, the "in-fighting" among affiliated or allied men was subject to restrictions that did not prevail among total strangers.

One example of this distinction can be seen in the reference by Rafael Karsten to the head-hunting Jíbaros:

> The Jibaros never make trophies of the heads of such
> enemies as belong to their own tribe; that is, with whom
> they reckon blood relationship. An Indian who did this
> would run the risk of being himself killed by his tribes-
> men, even by those neutral before. On the other hand, it is
> the rule that when a victory has been attained over a for-
> eign tribe, the heads of the slain enemies are taken. (*Primi-
> tive Heritage*, pp. 520-21)

The following account by Chapple and Coon shows the different treatment accorded cousins as contrasted with complete
strangers:

> The Bedouin, as we have seen, distinguish between tribes
> which they call "cousins" (Beni el 'am) and those which
> they do not, and treat them accordingly. They will not
> attack a camp of "cousins" before daybreak, and when
> they capture a "cousin" they will not kill him or tie him
> up, but simply tag him with a piece of cloth and leave
> him sitting on the sidelines on parole not to rejoin his
> own side until he is ransomed. They do not show this
> deference to outsiders. (*Principles of Anthropology*, p. 629)

Driberg points out that men can count on the protection of
allied men even in the midst of hostilities:

> Certain qualities of behavior are demanded in battle in
> addition to manliness. . . . If he finds that there is a rela-
> tive-in-law or a blood-friend on the opposite side, not only
> must he refrain from attacking them, but at the risk of his
> own life he must protect them from his own party. (*At
> Home with the Savage*, p. 99)

The terms of address used by cross-cousins often indicate
their relationship to each other by way of the woman who is
the sister of one and the wife of the other. W. I. Thomas remarks that "a man may refer to his wife's brother as his wife,
and he in turn is called husband by his wife's brother." He
gives the following illustration:

> This mode of address is used on the battlefield. If a wound-
> ed man catches sight of his sister's husband, he will say,
> "husband, I am getting killed." Then his brother-in-law,

if a brave man, will give help or even die with his wife's brother. (*Primitive Behavior,* p. 112)

Some anthropologists have noted the intense desire of primitive men to acquire brothers-in-law and, after acquiring them, to give public manifestations of their "love" for each other. Thomas writes:

Brothers-in-law love each other. A man will present his sister's husband with a gun and horses, and on the other hand receives game from his wife's brother, as well as horses captured on a war expedition. When a man recites his coups, he will say, "I captured a horse and gave it to my brother-in-law." (ibid., p. 112)

Claude Levi-Strauss notes that in New Guinea, as the natives put it, "the real purpose of getting married is not so much to obtain a wife but to secure brothers-in-law" ("The Family," in *Man, Culture and Society,* p. 270). But neither he nor others who have observed the same phenomenon explain the reasons for it.

Margaret Mead also came upon the desire for brothers-in-law in the primitive regions she was investigating. Although she was searching for cases of incest among the Arapesh, she found that the natives were not only disinterested in the subject but unable to furnish any examples. Instead, they kept returning again and again to the subject of brothers-in-law. To her insistent questions, they answered, "No, we don't sleep with our sisters, we give our sisters to other men and other men give us their sisters." Mead comments, "Obviously. It was as simple as that. Why did I press the point?"

Nevertheless, she did press the point, asking what would the old men say in the event that a young man wished to take his own sister to wife. Nobody knew, she reports, since nobody had ever discussed such a matter. She thereupon asked the young men to question the old men, one at a time, and then reports that all their answers came down to this:

What, you would like to marry your sister! What is the matter with you anyway? Don't you want a brother-in-law? Don't you realize that if you marry another man's sister and another man marries your sister, you will have

at least two brothers-in-law, while if you marry your own
sister you will have none? With whom will you hunt, with
whom will you garden, whom will you go to visit? (*Sex
and Temperament,* p. 84)

Thus, Mead concludes, "Incest is regarded among the Arapesh not with horror and repulsion toward a temptation that
they feel their flesh is heir to, but as a stupid negation of the
joys of increasing, through marriage, the number of people
one can love and trust." Indeed, the essence of the intense desire for brothers-in-law is to multiply the number of trusted
friends and collaborators in social life and labor.

As Mead learned from the Arapesh aborigines, both types
of alliances, brother affiliations and cross-cousin linkages, produced an outreach of fraternal relations that covered many
miles. She writes:

> Each man plants not one garden, but several, each one
> in cooperation with a different group of his relatives. In
> one of these gardens he is host, in the others he is
> guest. . . . each year a man's food-stakes lie not in one
> plot directly under his control but scattered about . . . on
> the land of his relatives, three miles in one direction, five
> miles in another. . . . The same lack of individualism ob-
> tains in the planting of coconut-trees. . . . In hunting, too,
> a man does not hunt alone, but with a companion, some-
> times a brother, as often a cousin or a brother-in-law. . . .
> It is the same also with house-building. (ibid., pp. 19-21)

The expansion of kinship ties in two directions, one creating
parallel brothers and the other cross-cousins, laid the foundation for the network of clans comprising a tribe. This makes
it possible to reconstruct the main steps in the evolution of
the primal horde into the full-fledged tribe.

8

From Primal Horde to Tribe

Few studies have been made of the evolution of savage society from its earliest unit, the primal horde, to the full-fledged tribe at the height of its development. This has created problems in trying to analyze the various units or segments that comprise a tribe and explain how they are marked off from one another.

Morgan and other pioneers describe a tribe as composed of two phratries, each composed of a number of clans. Since Morgan's time a tribe has usually been described as "divided into" various segments, with no uniform agreement even on the names of these segments. What some call a "clan" might be referred to by others as a "sib," a "lineage," or some other term.

The first question is: How did the tribe come into existence? According to one view, it arose through a process of segmentation or "fission." According to another view, the tribe was produced through a process of affiliation or "fusion" of alien groups for mutual services and protection. In fact, both views are correct. The tribe was formed through processes of both fission and fusion.

In the earliest period split-offs from the mother-horde moved away in search of new feeding grounds. Each split-off carried with it the internal structure of the mother-horde as defined by totemism and taboo. Some segments moving to neighboring territories may have retained for a time their kinship ties to the mother-group. But others, wandering far afield, did not. In general, given the absence of historical memory in primeval times, these dispersed segments became alienated from one another, as Lippert suggests with respect to Australian and New Zealand tribes:

> . . . there can be no doubt that all these tribes . . . can
> only have originated by fission from older ones. . . . As
> long as a group remembered that a neighboring tribe,
> which had perhaps broken away to secure a better food
> supply, was related to itself by blood through its mothers,
> the latter was not an alien tribe. . . . But when this memory
> faded, there was no longer any conceivable connection or
> tie between them; the other tribe were strangers. . . . In
> view of the absence of artificial aids as well as of a his-
> torical sense, the memory of common blood must naturally
> have faded easily and often. (*Evolution of Culture,* p. 89)

In the epoch Lippert speaks of, these groups were not yet
tribes but primal hordes. He shows that they were still immersed
in the cannibalistic practices that stemmed from regarding
strangers as no more than animals. In time, however, these
separate hordes acquired the "artificial aids" they needed for
peaceful social relations in the form of covenanted affiliations
and alliances.

This process is sometimes described as a series of "progressive
combinations" leading from small separate units to the network
of units comprising a tribe. From this standpoint, the first
progressive combination brought about the parallel brothers,
and the second the cross-cousins or brothers-in-law. The first
produced the affiliated clans; the second produced the two
phratries standing opposite each other as intermating moieties.

Lewis Morgan found the maternal gens or clan to be the
basic unit of the tribe. This raised the question of what had
preceded the clan. Morgan called it the "consanguine family." He
thought this was a "blood-related" group in our sense of the
term and that these consanguine relatives married one another.
As he put it, the earliest sexual relations featured the "intermarriage of brothers and sisters, own and collateral, in a group"
(*Ancient Society,* p. 393).

This was wrong on two counts. First, the existence of a "consanguine family" or any other kind of family at the beginning
of human life was in direct conflict with Morgan's insistence that
the maternal clan was the original social unit and the family a
latecomer in history, along with the patriarchy and private
property (ibid., pp. 477-78). Secondly, he thought that the
earliest "intermarriage of brothers and sisters" occurred within
the same group, when in fact such intermarriages took place
only after two alien groups had entered into an alliance for
this purpose, i.e., into a cross-cousin relationship.

Both Morgan's term "consanguine family" and Howitt's term "undivided commune" fell into disuse, the latter also implying brother-sister marriages. Since their time the best term that has come into use to designate the earliest social group is "primal horde." To be more accurate, it could be called a "maternal primal horde."

The horde was not a father-family. It was a maternal grouping of mothers, their brothers, and the children of the mothers. The maternal horde was the predecessor of the maternal gens or clan. The difference is that the horde stood alone, unaffiliated with other hordes. The clan, on the other hand, is one of a number of affiliated clans that form a larger organization, the tribe. This important point is perceived by Moret and Davy, who write, "When the horde becomes a social segment instead of being the entire society, it changes its name and is called the clan, but it preserves all its constituent features" (*From Tribe to Empire,* p. 55).

Foremost among these constituent features are the totemic divisions, with the members classified by sex, age, and occupation, as well as the taboos placed on the food and sex hunt. Contrary to Morgan's view of the "intermarriage of brothers and sisters," the first commandment in history was to "hunt out," whether for food or for mates. In-horde or in-clan "marriage" or mating was impossible; both the horde and the clan were exogamous.

The first form of "intermarriage" came about with the connubial agreement between two exogamous clans for the interchange of mating partners. Only then did the brothers and sisters of one side intermarry with the sisters and brothers of the other side. This clan-to-clan mating alliance appears in its most highly developed form in the two tribal phratries which stand opposite each other as the intermating sides of the tribe.

This represents the "dual organization" at its peak of development. Each phratry is composed of a number of clans that are parallel brother-clans to each other. But the two phratries are cross-cousins to each other in that the brothers and sisters of the clans in one phratry find their mates among the sisters and brothers of the clans in the opposite phratry. Through this dual organization the deficiencies of the earlier one-sided law of exogamy were amended by the two-sided law of endogamy, which brought former alien groups together in an intermating alliance. Those who had formerly been commanded to "marry out" were now provided with a new and safer means for mating. They could "marry in" to the opposite side of the tribe.

In tracing the evolution from the primal horde to the tribe, the following are the principal units involved:

1. *The Primal Horde:* This is a maternal unit composed of sisters and brothers who may not mate — it is *exogamous*.

2. *The Clan:* This is the maternal unit that Morgan called the gens. It was formed when isolated hordes joined together; as linked or affiliated units of a larger network they are known as clans. Whether it is a parallel clan or a cross clan, it is an *exogamous* unit.

3. *The Phratry:* This large group incorporated a number of brother-clans and is itself a "brotherhood." The phratry is also called "moiety," "division," or "side," because it always stands opposite another phratry, the two comprising the tribe. The phratry is *exogamous*.

4. *The Tribe:* This is the *"endogamous commune."* It is composed of two phratries (divisions, moieties, sides). Each side is composed of brothers and sisters or parallel brothers and sisters. They must find their mates in the opposite side or phratry, i.e., among their cross-cousins.

With the tribe we come upon the dual organization in its full development, featuring both the law of exogamy and the law of endogamy. Although reference has been made to a smaller, less important "third phratry," its existence has been rejected as highly dubious. The tribe was composed of two phratries standing in a reciprocal fraternal-sexual relationship to each other. Each phratry was exogamous; together they were endogamous.

The discovery of the dual organization came about slowly and posed as many problems as the cross-cousin relationship. Lewis Morgan did not use the term "dual organization," but his term "phratric organization" amounts to the same thing. He wrote with respect to the Iroquois and other tribes:

> Each phratry (De-a-non-da-yoh) is a brotherhood as this term imports. The gentes in the same phratry are brother gentes to each other and cousin gentes to those of the other phratry. (*Ancient Society,* p. 90)

W. H. R. Rivers, who used the term "dual organization" and made the most significant contributions on the subject, was at first convinced that it was invariably matrilineal, although later he wavered somewhat on this question. He wrote:

In the dual organization the whole population consists of two exogamous groups which I call moieties, a man of one moiety having to marry a woman of the other. Further, in every case where this form of social organization is known to exist, descent is in the female line so that a man belongs to the moiety of his mother. (*History of Melanesian Society,* vol. I, p. 17)

A. W. Howitt found the same fundamental divisions in Australia: "It may be laid down as a general rule that all Australian tribes are divided into two moieties, which intermarry, but each of which is forbidden to marry within itself" (*Native Tribes of South-East Australia,* pp. 88-89).

One problem connected with the discovery of the dual organization was that the two sides seemed to be mirror-images of each other, having no separate names or identities. In Melanesia each side called itself a *veve* (motherhood). Rivers notes that in the northeastern part of the Gazelle Peninsula in Melanesia "the moieties have no definite names, but the people think of their own and the other moiety as 'we' and 'they' or as 'our stock' and 'their stock'" (*History of Melanesian Society,* vol. II, p. 500). These were vague terms to investigators.

However, the aborigines had their own means for making the necessary distinctions between different segments of the tribe, among them totemic insignia. Goldenweiser describes the dual organization of the Haida and Tlingit peoples of the northwest Pacific Coast as follows:

There are two main social divisions or phratries among the Tlingit known as the Raven and Wolf. The principal function of these phratric groups is to control intermarriage, no marriage being permitted within a phratry. Descent is maternal, the children belonging to the phratry of the mother. (*Anthropology,* pp. 330-31)

A. P. Elkin notes that the objective of the Australian divisions is to distinguish between brothers and sisters and their cross-cousins. He writes:

Moiety means half, and over quite a large area of Australia, each tribe is divided into two halves or moieties. This division, known as the dual organization, is a definite social and ceremonial grouping. Moreover, it is . . . totemic in

> nature. . . . each moiety has in some regions an animal
> or bird for its totem and name, such as eagle-hawk and
> crow, white cockatoo and black cockatoo, plains kangaroo
> and the hill kangaroo. . . . if it be matrilineal, I belong
> to my mother's moiety and my father belongs to the other
> one. In any case, the dual division separates brothers
> and sisters on the one hand from cross-cousins, and neces-
> sitates the use of distinct terms for these two groups of
> relations. (*The Australian Aborigines*, pp. 95-96)

Some discussions have taken place on whether or not the dual
organization had any connection with cross-cousin marriage.
To most anthropologists it seemed that the tribe for some
unaccountable reason had "divided itself in half" and then
commanded the members of the one side to marry the members of the other. As Crawley expresses this mystery:

> The tribe is divided into two exogamous sections or
> phratries; marriage outside the tribe is forbidden, and also
> within the phratry, but is commanded between the two
> phratries. . . . This interesting arrangement is now well
> known. How is its origin to be explained? (*The Mystic
> Rose*, vol. II, p. 213)

Here again, as in the case of cross-cousin marriage, the
answer cannot be found if the dual organization is viewed
as simply an intermarriage agreement between the two moieties,
while overlooking the fraternal relations it produced between
the men of both sides. Of the various hypotheses presented on
this subject the only correct one was that which took into account this aspect of the matter.

Why the Dual Organization?

One attempt to answer this question was made by A. L.
Kroeber. He viewed the dual organization as a "plan" for the
arbitrary division of the tribe, with each individual (and indeed
everything on earth) assigned to one or the other moiety.
"Related to the plan," he wrote, "is the fact that all human
beings with whom one has dealings are considered kin — are
made into kin, if necessary — and put into one or the other
moiety."

What was the reason for this peculiar plan? He gives the following psychological explanation:

> There may well be in the nature of the human mind a deeply implanted tendency to construe and organize its world in terms of duality, bipolarity, and dichotomization, and this inclination may lie at the root of all moieties in Australia and elsewhere. But if there exists such a tendency, it is a psychological fact. (*The Nature of Culture*, pp. 91-92)

This psychological approach has been taken over by Levi-Strauss and his disciples.

Another widespread theory regarded the dual organization as designed to prevent incest. Indeed, Frazer hailed the division of the community into two intermarrying sides as a great "moral reformation" and turning point in history:

> . . . the evidence points to the conclusion that the dual organization, or division of a community into two exogamous and intermarrying classes, was introduced for the purpose of preventing the marriage of brothers and sisters. . . . That organization, which may be described as the first great moral reformation of which we have any record, absolutely prevented these objectionable unions. . . . Henceforth instead of marrying their own sisters . . . they now exchanged them in marriage for the sisters of men who belonged to the other exogamous class. . . .
>
> Thus the exchange of sisters . . . appears to have been the very pivot on which turned the great reform initiated by the dual organization of society. (*Folklore in the Old Testament*, vol. II, pp. 233-34)

As we have discussed, Frazer attributed this great moral reformation to "the minds of a few men of a sagacity and practical ability above the ordinary" who thought up the scheme of "sister exchange." This "sister exchange" thesis has contributed to the erroneous impression that the men of the matriarchy controlled the lives and activities of their sisters and sisters' daughters much as fathers today control their wives and daughters. In fact, the primitive system of cross-cousin mating involved just as much "brother exchange" as it did "sister exchange," since it was cross-mating for both sexes. It is therefore more accurate and less biased to say that the sisters and brothers of one moiety found their mates among the brothers and sisters of the other moiety.

Moreover, since the dual organization was invariably matrilineal, it was not the creation of a few "men of sagacity." The evidence indicates that it was instituted by the women at a certain stage in the evolution of the matriarchy. In Melanesia, for example, the intermating alliance was brought about by the women of two *veves* (motherhoods), and the same is true wherever the dual organization existed.

Morgan perceived this female starting point of the cross-alliance when he wrote that the Kamilaroi tribes of Australia derived themselves from "two supposed female ancestors, which laid the foundation for two original gentes." He concludes, "With the two gentes started into being simultaneously the whole result would have been attained since the males and females of one gens would marry the females and males of the other . . ." (*Ancient Society*, pp. 53-68). In short, matrimony has its roots in an alliance between the mothers in one *veve* and the mothers-in-law in another *veve* for the peaceful pursuit of mates by their sons and daughters.

Moreover, contrary to Frazer's thesis, the dual organization did not arise out of any need to preserve sexual morality or prevent incest. It arose out of the need to bring hostile groups of men into a fraternal alliance that would make possible peaceful mating relations between the men and women of both sides.

This was precisely the point that Tylor perceived. He was one of the few scholars to avoid the trap of the incest theory and focus his attention upon the fighting relations between groups of men. His hypothesis for explaining the dual organization is the correct one because he saw the overriding need to curb the strife and bloodshed among men in the most ancient epoch of human life. He also noted the important part played by women in controlling men, in their dual capacity as sisters of the men on one side and wives on the other. He wrote:

> Exogamy lies far back in the history of man, and perhaps no observer has ever seen it come into existence, nor have the precise conditions of its origin yet been clearly inferred. . . . But as to the law of exogamy itself, the evidence shows it in operation over a great part of the human race as a factor of political prosperity. It cannot be claimed as absolutely preventing strife and bloodshed, indeed . . . the

intermarrying clans do nevertheless quarrel and fight. Still by binding together a whole community with ties of kinship and affinity, and especially by the peace-making of the women who hold to one clan as sisters and to another as wives, it tends to keep down feuds and to heal them when they arise. . . . Exogamy thus shows itself as an institution which resists the tendency of uncultured populations to disintegrate, cementing them into nations capable of living together in peace and holding together in war till they reach the period of higher military and political organization. ("On a Method . . . ," in *Source Book in Anthropology*, pp. 470-71)

Despite his penetrating insight into the phenomenon of the dual organization, Tylor erred in making *exogamy* the tie that bound the two sides together. In reality it was *endogamy* that furnished the basis for this union between the two exogamous moieties or phratries.

Tylor was not alone in making this mistake. Most scholars have failed to see the actual historical development from exogamy to endogamy. They have taken the opposite point of view — that society began with an "endogamous commune."

Since this is one of the central errors in anthropology, it must be examined in more detail.

Exogamy, Endogamy, and Cannibalism

The pioneer scholars set forth the thesis that the earliest human horde was an "endogamous commune." In the beginning, they reasoned, "promiscuous" sexual relations prevailed. Intermarriage of brothers and sisters added incest to injury. Later, a great "moral reformation" divided this "undivided commune" and put an end to endogamy and promiscuity within the basic social unit.

The anthropologists of the Victorian era were aware that their theory of the endogamous commune would arouse great moral indignation. This is indicated in a letter from Reverend Lorimer Fison to his collaborator, Lewis Morgan, cited by George Thomson:

"In my own mind I accept it [the Undivided Commune, i.e., the endogamous horde] as sufficiently proved but I do not positively assert it for these two reasons; (1) I expect violent opposition and therefore resolved to narrow as far as possible the ground of controversy; (2) the Undivided Commune means nothing more or less than 'promiscuity' and this would be terribly shocking to many of my best friends among the ministers. . . . In short, I do not doubt the former existence of the Undivided Commune, but I do not consider it necessary for my purpose to assert it. . . . Life is thorny, and whispering tongues can poison truth." (*Studies in Ancient Greek Society,* p. 84)

Although, to his credit, Fison adhered to his position, his anxiety was misplaced. The sequence of evolution was not from endogamy to exogamy but exactly the opposite. The primal horde was an exogamous commune which, after it made affiliations with other hordes, became part of a larger unit, which was an endogamous commune.

The primal horde was indeed an undivided commune and had no affiliations to other hordes. But this did not make it an endogamous commune with brothers marrying their own sisters. On the contrary, the most conspicuous feature of the primal horde was the sex taboo that made all the women in the horde forbidden females. But the matter goes deeper than this, because the taboo was a double prohibition, governing food as well as sex.

The rule of exogamy, which is the corollary of the double taboo, likewise has two clauses. In both cases the most important clause is connected with food, i.e., with cannibalism. Under the double law of exogamy the hordesmen were commanded to "hunt out"—whether for food or for mates. In other words, not only were brothers forbidden to mate with sisters; they were also forbidden to hunt, kill, or eat their brothers. The primal horde was thus in a double sense an *exogamous* commune. Within it all possibility of cannibalism had been banished. By the same token, though this was not the motive for instituting taboo and exogamy, there was no possibility of incest.

The early scholars made their mistake because of their one-sided view that the rule of exogamy was solely a sexual prohibition. But the first task that confronted primeval humanity was to institute the prohibitions required to reconcile the new male occupation of hunting and meat eating with the beginnings of social organization.

The essential characteristic of exogamy is that it is a law of *exclusion.* Endogamy, on the other hand, is a rule of *in-*

clusion. The latter came about through the one-sidedness of the former, a deficiency that was unavoidable from the historical standpoint. Cannibalism could only be conquered one step at a time, beginning with its total exclusion from the primal horde. But this earliest achievement was too restricted.

Under the rule of exogamy the hordesmen were obliged to hunt outside their own territory. But this made them predatory intruders into the territories of other hordes. The problem was magnified in the earliest period by the notion that those who were non-kin were non-human. This resulted in raids and counter-raids between separate hordes, with men killing and eating other men. Thus the one-sidedness of the law of exogamy only intensified problems of cannibalism in the relations between separate hordes.

These problems were overcome through the interchange of totemic kinship ties between hordes, joining them first as linked brother clans and then adding allied cross-cousin clans. As we have seen, food and blood unions joined men as parallel brothers while food and sex unions joined them as brothers-in-law. This is the essence of the endogamic relationship — the interchange of kinship ties through the interchange of food, sex, and other necessities of life.

Endogamy, the rule of *inclusion,* came about with these affiliations and alliances, which reached their apex with the dual organization and its fraternal intermating alliance between two phratries of the tribe. In other words, the endogamous commune arose with the dual organization and not before. In evolutionary sequence the exogamous commune, the primal horde, came first, while the divided endogamous commune came afterwards.

The pioneer scholars made their error through the misinterpretation of certain statements made by the aborigines, particularly in Australia where totemism existed until recent times. The natives said that formerly there had been no taboos on their totems, and they had freely mated with them. Significantly enough, they said that formerly they had also eaten their totems without restriction. Both practices, they pointed out, had been a functional necessity. In effect, what they were saying is that men need food and mates, and in the beginning they ate and mated with their own kin. But after a time, their ancestors, realizing the "awful consequences" of these practices, had put a stop to them.

The investigators, focusing upon the sex clause, interpreted this to mean that the "awful consequences" referred to incest. They drew the conclusion that even the most primitive peoples had discovered in some empirical way that incest could lead to the degeneration and annihilation of the human species and out of this came a universal abomination of it. In the absence of an understanding of the hazards of cannibalism, which posed the real threat of annihilation of the species, this seemed to be a plausible explanation.

This resulted in overlooking some very important clues to the method by which separate hordes affected fraternal alliances through the interchange relationship and pushed the boundaries of cannibalism farther and farther afield. Certain rituals performed at totemic centers indicate this mechanism. One of the most ancient, preserved in Australia, is "Intichiuma." It has been studied in considerable detail by Spencer and Gillen as well as Frazer.

Intichiuma, sometimes described as an "increase ceremony" or a "multiplication rite," is essentially a system of food and labor interchange. Each totem group or clan is in charge of certain animals and plants that the members of the group nurture and protect, not for their own use, but to hand over to other groups. This is said to increase the total food supply of the region for the benefit of all. As Frazer describes it:

> In other words, the *intichiuma* ceremonies are performed by each totem group, not on its own behoof, but on behoof of all the others, the general effect of all the ceremonies being supposed to be an increase of the total supply of food available for the whole tribe, which, it is needful to bear in mind, includes a large number of totem clans. The system is, in fact, one of cooperative magic — each group works its spells for the good of all the rest and benefits in its turn through the enchantments practised by the others. (*Totemism and Exogamy,* vol. I, p. 109)

Frazer subsequently decided that there was nothing mystical about Intichiuma; it was a "thoroughly practical system designed to meet the everyday wants of the ordinary man in a clear and straightforward way." Thus, "if I am a Kangaroo man, then I provide flesh for Emu men and in return I expect them to provide me with a supply of emu flesh and eggs, and so on right through all the totems" (ibid., p. 185).

Intichiuma therefore represents a system of food interchange. One group of men gives food to other groups of men, receiving food in turn from the other groups. But there were certain puzzling features about this curious system.

According to the aborigines, before Intichiuma came into existence, the men ate the animals and plants they later inter-changed with other groups. But with the advent of Intichiuma they began to "deny themselves" the food on which they had formerly subsisted and instead handed it over to others. They even gave testimony that the self-denial process was not quite completed; they still "ate a morsel" of the food in the ceremonial that preceded handing it over.

In other words, with the advent of Intichiuma the food they had formerly eaten without restriction was placed under a taboo. However, it took time to effect a total taboo. Even today during the Intichiuma ceremony, each group of men "eat sparingly" of the tabooed food before handing it over. As Spencer and Gillen put it, "at the present day the totemic animal or plant, as the case may be, is almost, but not quite tabu . . ." (*Native Tribes of Central Australia,* p. 206).

This raised the question: Why did men deny themselves food upon which they had formerly subsisted and come to protect and nurture it for others? As Frazer puts it, "Why should they trouble themselves to multiply animals or plants which, by their rules, they are almost wholly debarred from eating?" He surmises that this might represent the origin of totemism. "Have we not in these *Intichiuma* ceremonies the key to the original meaning and purpose of Totemism among the Central Australian tribes, perhaps even of Totemism in general?" (*Totemism and Exogamy,* vol. I, pp. 108, 113).

Frazer's questions circle around the main point of the totemic taboo, which is cannibalism. As we have seen (Chapter 2), totemism arose as the earliest protectorate of humans and their food supplies. Those who were totem-kin were under the taboo not to kill or eat other totem-kin. In the first stage this self-denial applied only to the men in the primal horde, the indigenous "milk-and-blood brothers." But in the second stage, with the extension of totem-kin ties to parallel brothers, the self-denial was extended to the linked clans. And in the third stage it applied as well to the allied or cross-cousin clans.

Frazer discerned this in his own way when he ventured the hypothesis that aborigines had observed that "animals as a rule and plants universally, do not feed upon their own kind." Hence, he said, "Grub men refused to feed upon grubs, Grass Seed men upon grass seed, and so on through all the other animal and vegetable totems" (ibid., vol. I, p. 121). This shot in the dark hit close to the mark, the struggle against cannibalism.

The self-denial covered plant as well as flesh foods. The main objective was to closely restrict the killing and eating of animals and, by the same token, of non-kin humans. The net effect of the restrictions was to place protective taboos upon food of all kinds. This not only helped men to distinguish edible flesh from totemized flesh but prevented any plundering of plant foods before they had matured and permission had been given for eating them. Thus the totemic protection of human food supplies moved side by side with the protection of humans from cannibalism.

From this standpoint the food interchange system called Intichiuma was indeed an "increase" or "multiplication" ritual. It permitted the increase of humans and the multiplication of their food supplies. This was the essence of the totemic protectorate that began within the solitary primal horde and was then extended to other hordes through the mechanism of interchange.

Although few studies have been made of the totemic interchange system as such, its results have been seen by many anthropologists. Margaret Mead, writing about the unselfish and highly cooperative Arapesh of New Guinea, writes that "each man hunts that others may eat." She adds:

> The ideal distribution of food is for each person to eat food grown by another, eat game killed by another, eat pork from pigs that not only are not his own but have been fed by people at such a distance that their very names are unknown. Under the guidance of this ideal, an Arapesh man hunts only to send most of his kill to his mother's brother, his cousin, or his father-in-law. The lowest man in the community, the man who is believed to be so far outside the moral pale that there is no use reasoning with him, is the man who eats his own kill — even though that kill be a tiny bird, hardly a mouthful in all. (*Sex and Temperament,* pp. 28-29)

Thus the food interchange system which arose out of the struggle against cannibalism impressed upon men the most fundamental lesson of social life. They learned that they could not live as humans through the appropriation of the necessities of life as animals do, each for himself alone. They learned that humans are above everything else social beings who can survive only through cooperation with other groups of human beings.

The same system of interchange that produced such effective results in increasing food supplies was then extended to the realm of mates. The food interchanges that brought hostile groups of men together in fraternal, cooperative relations paved the way for the peaceful mating relations that arose with the cross-cousin alliance and the exchange of mates between cooperating groups.

Margaret Mead, in her study of the Arapesh, reports a statement made by the aborigines which she calls "a series of rather esoteric aphorisms" (*Sex and Temperament,* p. 83). A closer examination, however, shows that the statement is not so esoteric; it is a description of the primitive food and sex interchange system.

Here is the statement:

> Your own mother,
> Your own sister,
> Your own pigs,
> Your own yams that you have piled up,
> You may not eat.
> Other people's mothers,
> Other people's sisters,
> Other people's pigs,
> Other people's yams that have piled up,
> You may eat.

The main reason that this may appear unintelligible to us is that they used the term "to eat" for both eating and mating. This is not unusual. There are other primitive languages where the same term is applied to both eating and mating, indicating that originally little distinction was made between these two hungers. Cora Du Bois writes that "sex and food are inextricably associated in the minds of the Atimelangers. . . . the male genitals are associated with his digestive system and . . . an orgasm is described with a food adjective" (*The People of Alor,* p. 101). W. I. Thomas, citing Schapera's African studies, notes that the term "to eat" is used in the sense of "to copulate" (*Primitive Behavior,* p. 247).

The Arapesh statement, as Mead says, expresses the unselfish, cooperative spirit of these aborigines. But it does more than that; it is an expression of the primitive interchange system by which this cooperation was brought about. In fact, Mead sees the results of this mechanism for cooperation when she explains the aphorisms as follows:

> This sums up the Arapesh attitude towards selfishness, their feeling that there is an intimate connexion between a man and his yam-crop that would make his eating from it rather like incest, and similarly that to appropriate for one's own purposes one's mother or sister would be of the nature of antisocial and repellent hoarding. . . . The native line of thought is that you teach people how to behave about yams and pigs by referring to the way that they behave about their female relatives. (*Sex and Temperament*, pp. 83-84)

The extension of kinship ties from one horde to another through the interchange of food and mates enabled the separate hordes to join together in the larger and stronger network of clans required for survival. Marshall Sahlins writes on this point:

> The kin ties thereby created become social pathways of mutual aid and solidarity connecting band to band. It does not seem unwarranted to assert that the human capacity to extend kinship was a necessary social condition for the deployment of early man over the great expanses of the planet. (*Scientific American*, vol. 203, no. 3, p. 81)

Once it was born, the savage interchange system passed through a very long evolution. It not only brought about the fraternal linkages of men from the primal horde to the tribe, but even went beyond this to link tribes together in a league of tribes — before the system was destroyed and supplanted by the commodity exchange system of civilization.

9

The Interchange System

Gift Reciprocity

One of the most conspicuous features of primitive society is its systematic "gift-giving" or "gift-exchange." To some anthropologists this signifies a strong sense of social reciprocity. E. Adamson Hoebel writes:

> The fundamental key to gift giving is the reciprocity underlying all social relations. Each social action on behalf of others evokes, or is taken in expectation of, a reciprocal action. The passing of a gift is a beneficence that brings a return in expectancy. "Do unto others as you would have others do unto you," has positive as well as negative connotations. (*Man in the Primitive World*, p. 346)

This mutual courtesy does not adequately bring out the unique characteristics of the primitive system of reciprocity. Fundamentally it was a system of interchange that had passed beyond its earliest totemic form to reach its matured form.

This primitive relationship stands out in sharp contrast both to the animal conditions of life that preceded it and to the civilized social relations which succeeded it. Animals cannot create a system of interchange since they lack a social structure based upon cooperative life and labor. Civilized society, on the other hand, created a totally different system. Today people give gifts on certain occasions, such as Christmas, birthdays, and anniversaries. But gift-giving is not basic to modern socioeconomic relations, which are based on commodities, articles produced for exchange on the market. Gift-giving, incidental in our society, was fundamental in primitive society.

211

J. H. Driberg makes the point that gift-exchange of this type differs radically even from barter, which preceded commodity exchange as the most elementary form of exchanging use values. Barter, he says, "requires an accepted standard of values, an agreement as to the rates of exchange, whereas in the gift-exchange there is no bargaining or haggling of any kind" (*At Home with the Savage,* p. 212). In the Trobriand Islands, where barter was beginning to coexist with the more ancient gift-exchange system, Malinowski tells us that the natives looked with contempt upon those who mixed their gift-giving ceremonies with any trace of the commercialism that accompanies barter (*Argonauts of the Western Pacific,* pp. 189-90).

Some anthropologists are reluctant to recognize the noncommercial essence of the primitive interchange system, which provides such glaring confirmation of the communal character of primitive society. This is the case with the economic anthropologist Melville J. Herskovits, who writes, "The concepts 'private property' and 'communism' are too general, too heavily charged with emotional content to be anything but liabilities where scientific objectivity is sought" (*Economic Anthropology,* p. 330).

Other anthropologists are not so hesitant in arriving at an objective evaluation after a scientific investigation of the subject. Radcliffe-Brown, describing the gift-exchange system of the Andaman Islanders, says "the Andamanese have customs which result in an approach to communism." He writes:

One of these is the custom of constantly exchanging presents with one another. When two friends meet who have not seen each other for some time, one of the first things they do is to exchange presents with one another. Even in the ordinary everyday life of the village there is a constant giving and receiving of presents. . . .

It is considered a breach of good manners ever to refuse the request of another. Thus if a man be asked by another to give him anything that he may possess, he will immediately do so. If the two men are equals a return of about the same value will have to be made.

Almost every object that the Andamanese possess is thus constantly changing hands. Even canoes may be given away, but it is more usual for these to be lent by the owner to his friends.

> It has been stated above that all food is private property and belongs to the man or woman who has obtained it. Every one who has food is expected, however, to give it to those who have none. . . . Generosity is esteemed by the Andaman Islanders one of the highest of virtues and is unremittingly practised by the majority of them. (*The Andaman Islanders*, pp. 42-43)

Some observers have noted with surprise that a refusal to either give or to accept gifts was treated as an antisocial act. This is understandable in a society where the act of interchange represents the essential medium of social intercourse. The refusal to give or to receive would place a person outside the pale of communication within a tribal community. The social character of the interchange system is pointed out by Richard Thurnwald in writing about the Banaro society:

> The exchange system maintains a great socializing influence, for by its means all members of the tribe are connected with, and dependent on, each other. This appears in the different ceremonials where persons are assigned special functions, as well as in the marriage system, which has spread a network of all kinds of relationships, not only over the gens, but over the tribe itself. (*Source Book in Anthropology*, p. 294)

Marcel Mauss has made the best contribution to an understanding of the primitive gift-giving system. He calls it a system of "total prestations" which encompassed everything from such tangibles as food and products of labor to intangibles like rituals and ceremonies, and even included people themselves. He writes:

> In the systems of the past we do not find simple exchange of goods, wealth and produce through markets established among individuals. For it is groups, and not individuals, which carry on exchange, make contracts, and are bound by obligations; . . . the groups, or the chiefs as intermediaries for the groups, confront and oppose each other. Further, what they exchange is not exclusively goods and wealth, real and personal property, and things of economic value. They exchange rather courtesies, entertainments, rituals, military assistance, women, children, dances, and

feasts. . . . Finally, although the prestations and counter-prestations take place under a voluntary guise they are in essence strictly obligatory, and their sanction is private or open warfare. (*The Gift,* p. 3)

Despite this insight into the gift-exchange system, certain of its features remain puzzling. Wherever it has survived in full-fledged form there is an almost frenzied preoccupation with it. Gift-giving and receiving seems to be the central activity of all the communities. This is especially pronounced in the great "pot-latches" of the northwest Pacific Coast, a region where cannibal-ism has persisted up to recent times. Mauss writes about them:

> The tribes have a two-fold structure: at the end of spring they disperse and go hunting, collect berries from the hill-sides and fish the river for salmon, while in winter they concentrate in what are known as towns. During this period of concentration they are in a perpetual state of effervescence. The social life becomes intense in the extreme, even more so than in the concentration of tribes that manage to form in the summer. There are constant visits of whole tribes to others, of clans to clans and families to families. There is feast upon feast, some of long duration. On the occasion of a marriage, on various ritual occasions, and on social advancement, there is reckless consumption of everything which has been amassed with great industry from some of the richest coasts of the world during the course of summer and autumn. Even private life passes in this manner; clansmen are invited when a seal is killed or a box of roots or berries opened; you invite everyone when a whale runs aground. (ibid., pp. 32-33)

This is not all. The gift-giving festivals include a curious rit-ual: the destruction of a portion of the things given and re-ceived, which are burned, thrown into the sea, or broken up. Mauss tells us:

> Consumption and destruction are virtually unlimited. In some potlatch systems one is constrained to expend every-thing one possesses and to keep nothing. . . . The principles of rivalry and antagonism are basic. . . . everything is con-ceived as if it were a war of wealth. . . . Whole cases of candle-fish or whale oil, houses, and blankets by the thou-sand are burnt; the most valuable coppers are broken and

thrown into the sea to level and crush a rival. . . . Thus
in a system of this kind much wealth is continually being
consumed and transferred. (ibid., pp. 35-36)

Many anthropologists have described this destructive practice
that accompanies the lavish gift-giving festivals, although few
have given any satisfactory explanation of it. As Moret and
Davy observe, the potlatch is not only "distinguished by its
markedly sumptuary character" but also "by the competitive
character of this opposition of the clans, which appear to be
engaging in a mortal struggle as much as in a series of peaceful collective contracts" (*From Tribe to Empire*, p. 91).

What was the meaning of a system of interchange so sweeping
in scope that virtually nothing was excluded, not even men,
women, and children? (This inclusion of everything from the
necessities of life to human beings themselves discloses what
can be called a system of "life-exchange.") On the other hand,
what is the origin of the destructive practice sometimes called
"killing" property, which carries the connotation of "death-exchange"?

Why do these opposite forms of interchange—life-exchange
and death-exchange—emerge so prominently in what appears
to be simply a system of gift-exchange? The starting point for
an investigation of this two-sided system of reciprocity must
begin with the primitive system of institutionalized fighting
usually called "blood revenge."

The Origin of Blood Revenge

Although the primitive system of fighting is usually called
"warfare" and the fighters "warriors," it has little in common
with modern wars and armies. Many anthropologists have
pointed out that warfare in the true sense of the term is a
late development in history. It implies territorial conquest or
other forms of subjugation by which one nation seeks to control
and exploit the resources and population of another nation.

The Australian aborigines, says Radcliffe-Brown, "have no
conception of the possibility of territorial conquest by armed
force" (*Structure and Function,* p. 34). Hocart makes the same
point. "Wars to acquire territory are unknown to many peoples.
It never enters a Solomon Islander's head to annex territory.
Still more unknown are commercial wars." He says "The Australian Blacks are described as most peaceful. They occasion-

ally go on the warpath to avenge the death of one of their own number whom they believe to have been killed" (*The Progress of Man*, p. 269).

Some primitive groups surviving to the present day are still unacquainted with war. Marshall Sahlins writes:

> Warfare is limited among hunters and gatherers. Indeed, many are reported to find the idea of war incomprehensible. . . . war is even further inhibited by the spread of a social relation — kinship — which in primitive society is often a synonym for "peace." (The Origin of Society," *Scientific American,* vol. 203, no. 3, p. 81)

Similarly, Ruth Benedict reported: "I, myself, tried to talk of warfare to the Mission Indians of California, but it was impossible. Their misunderstanding of war was abysmal. They did not have the basis in their own culture upon which the idea could exist . . . " (*Patterns of Culture*, p. 41). According to Ashley Montagu, "It is difficult to convince an Australian aborigine that there exist peoples who make organized attacks upon other peoples in order to kill and maim as many of them as possible as quickly as possible" (*Anthropology and Human Nature*, p. 59).

Nevertheless, as the record shows, an organized institution of fighting did exist in primitive society. In its most developed form, it was a prearranged combat between two opposing sides; they met periodically for the purpose of settling grievances between them which had accumulated over the preceding period. These combats are variously called the "regulated fight," the "standup fight," the "vengeance fight," the "expiatory combat," the "pitched battle," and "cyclical warfare." In some regions these fights occurred on call; in others they were an annual event; in still others they occurred every five years or more.

The fights were conducted according to specific rules understood by both sides, with the proceedings carefully supervised by headmen or chiefs. These umpires called a halt to the bloodletting as soon as the grievances were settled. Far from being wars of extermination, they ended with the warriors of both sides joining together after the battle to exchange gifts and restore peace and fraternal relations.

Apart from the deaths that occur in the course of the battle, the regulated fight looks more like a systematized game than a combat. Indeed, some anthropologists include the regulated fight in their reports on sports and games. In a chapter entitled "Games and Warfare— Symbols and Techniques of Competition," Chapple and Coon cite Camilla Wedgewood's report of the regulated fight in New Caledonia:

> Wedgewood states that in northern New Caledonia, the villages are divided up into two divisions, much like the Red and White moieties of the Creek, or the two sides involved in the dart game in Tikopia. These two sides have a formal battlefield, on which they always fight, and they meet there in battle once every five years. When the time for the battle approaches, the leaders of the two sides send heralds, whose persons are inviolable, to make arrangements. By this means a day is set, and the warriors of the two sides meet at the battlefields, where they first work together clearing the undergrowth which has grown up since the last combat. When the field is ready, they line up facing each other, and start off with oratorical contests, followed by single combats between chiefs, in which as a rule no blood is shed. Then the armies start hurling spears or shooting arrows at each other, and after this, close in and fight hand to hand combats with clubs.
>
> When the first victim has been killed, they stop for the day to hold a funeral, and begin again the next day, until enough people have been killed or until the point has been reached beyond which the combat would become too serious for the maintenance of equilibrium, when they grow tired of it and agree to stop. After this, they have a formal peace-making ceremony in which they pay each other in pigs or some other commodity for each man killed, and have a feast together. (*Principles of Anthropology*, p. 630)

What is the meaning of an organized combat in which blood is shed and a certain number of deaths exacted and yet neither side conquers any territory or gains any other property advantages? And why, apart from the bloodletting, does the fight resemble a formalized sport or game?

To get at the answers to these questions we must trace back from the highly developed stage of the regulated fight to its origin in a form of fighting known as the "blood revenge" institution. Here we find a reason for what can be called "reciprocity" in bloodshed. The fight between two communities of men is designed to punish those who have killed or shed the blood of a member of the kin-group.

Blood revenge therefore represents a system of punishment and counter-punishment between two communities but one that is regulated to prevent a total rupture between them. Hence, after the punishment, peace and fraternity are restored through the exchange of feasts and gifts.

From this standpoint, primitive blood revenge is also called "vengeance retribution," the "principle of retaliation," and the "reprisal system." It is an integral part of the primitive blood kinship system and cannot be separated from it. All those who regard themselves as the blood-kin are bound to participate in exacting punishment of those who shed the blood of their kin. As Robertson Smith puts it, this obligation to avenge the death of a kinsman "affords a sure practical test of what kindred meant and how it was counted" (*Kinship and Marriage in Early Arabia,* p. 26).

Since primitive blood kinship was established on a communal basis, blood revenge was likewise communal. The whole community was held responsible for the actions of each individual member. It was not necessary that any specific culprit be found and killed in reprisal for the death of a kinsman — any member of his community would suffice to satisfy the claims of blood. "The whole kin is answerable for the life of its members," says Robertson Smith. "If my kinsman is slain by an outsider I and every other member of my kin are bound to avenge his death by killing the manslayer or some member of his kin" (*The Religion of the Semites,* p. 272). Only in the last stage of its evolution, when it was in process of breaking up, did blood revenge become transformed into the "blood feud" — a system of fighting between individuals or families.

The community character of the original blood revenge system is pointed out by Hartland:

When society is organized by clans the members of a clan are considered between themselves as brothers and sisters. Their duty to one another is one of mutual defence and support. An offence against one is an offence against all, and immediately unites the clan against the offender and his clan. For, conversely, the offence of one member is the offence of all. If a member of the clan be killed, by so much is the strength of the clan reduced. . . . revenge by the slaughter of one of the offending clan is the rule. . . . It is the duty of every member of the clan offended to exact revenge; and the responsibility of the injury rests not merely on the actual individual offender but, by virtue of the solidarity of the clan as the social unit, on every member of his clan. (*Primitive Law,* pp. 52-53)

Blood revenge was not only a communal system of punishment, it was originally exclusively matrilineal, following the mother-line. By this criterion neither cross-cousins nor, later, husbands and wives, nor fathers and mothers, stood on the same side of the blood revenge line. Married partners stood on opposite sides, each with his or her matrilineal blood kin. As Hartland writes, "When a man is slain his avengers are his brothers and mother's brothers; when a woman is killed they are her sons, brothers and maternal uncles" (*Primitive Society,* p. 74).

It is significant that even after the family came into existence blood revenge continued to follow the mother-line. E. N. Fallaize writes in a summary article on "Family" that the blood feud "follows the blood, i.e. the duty of vengeance falls first upon those who belong to the mother's kin and not upon those whose connexion has been brought into existence by marriage" (*Encyclopedia of Religion and Ethics,* vol. V, p. 719).

This explains why, even after the family was formed, the mother's brother carried out the obligations of blood revenge in connection with his sister and sister's children. Hartland writes about many African peoples, "The mother's brother has greater rights over a child than the father, and the duty of blood revenge falls to him even against the father" (*Primitive Paternity,* p. 281).

According to Tylor, "In most Australian tribes the children belong to the mother's clan, not the father's; so that in native wars father and son constantly meet as natural enemies" (*Anthropology,* p. 247). Raymond Firth reports a Polynesian legend to this effect:

In an ancient tale, the killing of Pu Kefu, a lad sides with his mother's brother against his father and so brings about his father's death. The Tikopia display no horror at this indirect parricide; the boy's action seems to them an obvious corollary of his close association with the mother's brother. (*We, the Tikopia,* p. 203)

Some anthropologists conclude from this that a "hereditary enmity" exists between fathers and sons. More accurately, the blood revenge institution existed long before the father-family came into existence. In its origin, blood revenge was a part of the maternal clan system of blood kinship which had produced the matriarchal brotherhood. Thus the primitive system of community solidarity could not escape the defects inherent in its virtues.

Nonetheless, certain questions arise in connection with this primitive system of crime and punishment. Why did it assume the form of blood revenge? Why, in a communal society, did so many men regularly kill others when they knew that this would bring about blood reprisals upon themselves? How did this killing and counter-killing, a reciprocity in death, wind up as the regulated vengeance combat closely resembling a sport or game?

There is little agreement among scholars who have studied the blood revenge system as to why primitive punishment took this form. Edward Westermarck tended to view revenge as no more than an emotional reaction that is normal among humans in conflict. This assumes that revenge in the modern sense of the term is an unchanging universal characteristic. W. H. R. Rivers took exception to this psychological approach because it ignored the sociological factors that led to the primitive system of blood revenge and the changes that occurred in it in the course of its evolution. (*Psychology and Ethnology*, pp. 8-12)

William Graham Sumner combined a sociological with a psychological explanation. He stated: "The custom of blood revenge was a protection to all who were in a group of kinsmen. It knit them all together and served their common interest against all outsiders. Therefore it was a societalizing custom and institution." At the same time he said, "Blood revenge was nothing but an exercise of revenge and it had all the limitations of revenge. . . . It was entirely irrational" (*Folkways*, pp. 499, 505-06).

In fact, the primitive system of blood revenge was far from irrational. It was the logical outcome of the ignorance of natural death. To the savage mind all deaths came about through acts of killing, visible or invisible, on the part of strangers and enemies. This made it mandatory for kinsmen to band together to punish those who had inflicted these losses upon their community.

It may seem incomprehensible to us that grownups in the past did not understand that people can die of old age, disease, or other causes and that everyone who lives must die. But, as Lippert observes, "There must have been a time when primitive man did not know that he must die. Does the animal know anything of the kind?" Among savage peoples, he writes, the idea is prevalent that "death is not natural and can not occur in the undisturbed course of things" (*Evolution of Culture*, pp. 104-05).

Even if no one saw the presumed "killing," it was thought that the killer performed his evil act through some form of magic or sorcery. "Amongst the Central Australian natives," write Spencer and Gillen, "there is no such thing as belief in natural death; however old or decrepit a man or woman may be when this takes place it is at once supposed that it has been brought about by the magic influence of some enemy" (*Native Tribes of Central Australia*, p. 476). This evil magic in turn produced counter-magic and counter-magicians or sorcerers to determine the group to which the killer belonged.

Survivals of this ancient ignorance of the biological fact of death have been found in many primitive regions. The following is a portion of Crawley's documentation on the subject:

> In British Guiana blood-revenge is closely connected with the system of sorcery. If a man dies and it is supposed that an enemy has killed him by means of an evil spirit they employ a sorcerer to find him. . . .
> . . . In Tongareva, death is attributed to witchcraft. . . . Amongst the Dieri and cognate tribes of Australia, "no person dies a natural death. . . ." Amongst the Murray River natives, at the funeral of a dead person, a relative generally attempted to spear some one, till it was explained that the deceased did not die by sorcery. . . .
> Amongst most Congo tribes death is seldom regarded in the light of a natural event. . . . Amongst the Bongos, old women are especially suspected of alliance with wicked spirits, and are accused if sudden death occurs. . . . In the tribes of East Central Africa, disease and sudden death are attributed to witchcraft. (*The Mystic Rose*, vol. I, pp. 97-104)

In view of the savage ignorance of natural death, the avenger of blood was, as Tylor points out, only "doing his part toward saving his people from perishing by deeds of blood." He adds:

Therefore, when a man dies, his kinsmen set themselves to find out by divination what malignant sorcerer did him to death, and when they have fixed on some one as the secret enemy the avenger sets out to find and slay him; then of course there is retaliation from the other side, and an hereditary feud sets in. This is one great cause of the rancorous hatred between neighbouring tribes which keeps savages in ceaseless fear and trouble. (*Anthropology,* p. 257)

Although some distinctions were subsequently made between different kinds of deaths, natural death remained poorly understood for a long time. Malinowski writes that "the Trobrianders, in common with all races at their culture level, regard every death without exception as an act of sorcery, unless it is caused by suicide or by a visible accident, such as poisoning or a spear thrust" (*The Sexual Life of Savages,* p. 161).

Ignorance of death, then, is at the bottom of blood revenge. This institution goes very far back in history and passed through many changes in the course of its evolution. As society advanced to a higher economic level and culture, compensation in the form of goods or money took the place of death reprisals. Tylor writes, "The old fierce cry for vengeance sinks into a claim for compensation. . . . so they take the blood-money and loose the feud" (*Anthropology,* pp. 257-58). Eventually civilized laws on crime and punishment replaced the blood revenge customs.

The tenacity of the ancient blood revenge institution can be seen in its survivals in ancient Greek civilization and in the Old Testament. Sumner cites the matriarchal Eumenides of Aeschylus: "Not all the wealth of the great earth can do away with blood guilt." The same theme was propagated by the early Biblical patriarchs: "The law of Israel was, 'Ye shall take no ransom for the life of a man-slayer, which is guilty of death; but he shall surely be put to death'" (*Folkways,* pp. 501-02).

Blood revenge is sometimes called the "principle of retribution." According to Hans Kelsen, it manifests the great value placed upon human life, which "to primitive man is the most precious, if not perhaps the only good." From this he concludes:

The institution of blood revenge, which can be traced back to the beginnings of social development, indicates clearly that death is not only the oldest crime but also the oldest socially organized punishment. . . . Blood revenge applies the most ancient social norm; he who kills must be killed. It is the most obvious manifestation of the principle of retribution. (*Society and Nature*, pp. 53-54)

We are familiar with this concept of retaliation—the *lex talionus*—in the saying: "An eye for an eye, a tooth for a tooth, a death for a death." In historical sequence the death talio came first.

However, since the objective was not to take lives but to preserve them, savage peoples worked out the means for overcoming their death-exchange system—despite their ignorance of natural death. The mechanism by which they accomplished this transformation from death- to life-exchange was through the gift-interchange system.

The Principle of Equivalence

The primitive exchange system is usually analyzed in purely economic terms as the barter of products with different use values. Closer examination discloses that this was not the original form of the savage interchange system. Its most curious feature was the fact that the things given and received as gifts were often exactly the same kinds of things. They did not have different use values as do articles involved in bartering.

This extraordinary feature was uncovered by Malinowski in his studies of the Trobriand Islanders. He noted that the gifts given and received were so equal in type, quantity, and quality that the transaction clearly did not have a utilitarian or economic motive. When food was exchanged for food—and this was the most fundamental interchange—it was on the basis of exact equivalence. Yams given were of the same size and quantity as yams received; the same was true of pigs. Sometimes the very same items were given back later to the giver. Malinowski writes:

And it is important to realise that in almost all forms of exchange in the Trobriands, there is not even a trace of gain, nor is there any reason for looking at it from the purely utilitarian and economic standpoint, since there is no enhancement of mutual utility through the exchange.

Thus, it is quite a usual thing in the Trobriands for a type of transaction to take place in which A gives twenty baskets of yams to B, receiving for it a small polished blade, only to have the whole transaction reversed in a few weeks' time. Again, at a certain stage of mortuary ritual, a present of valuables is given, and on the same day later on, the identical articles are returned to the giver. (*Argonauts of the Western Pacific*, p. 175)

It is not difficult to see where the phrase "Indian giver," frequently and thoughtlessly used today, comes from; it implies a gift that is not really a gift since it is later taken back. In savage society, both sides gave and both sides took back what they gave. What was the meaning of this? Malinowski, puzzled by the phenomenon, writes:

Again, since in savage communities, whether bountifully or badly provided for by nature, everyone has the same free access to all the necessities, is there any need to exchange them? Why give a basketful of fruit or vegetables, if everybody has practically the same quantity and the same means of procuring it? Why make a present of it, if it cannot be returned except in the same form? (ibid., p. 168)

Malinowski offered both a psychological and a sociological hypothesis. In native psychology there is "the love of give and take for its own sake; the active enjoyment in possession of wealth, through handing it over" (ibid., p. 173). From the sociological standpoint, he observes "the deep tendency to create social ties through exchange of gifts." To this he adds:

Apart from any consideration as to whether the gifts are necessary or even useful, giving for the sake of giving is one of the most important features of Trobriand sociology, and, from its very general and fundamental nature, I submit that it is a universal feature of all primitive societies. (ibid., p. 175)

If gift interchange on the basis of exact equivalence was once universal and not restricted to the Trobrianders, it becomes all the more imperative to find out why.

Here it is necessary to turn back to the blood revenge institution where, in the demand of a death for a death, such a principle would have manifested its crucial importance. And this is precisely what we find. The principle of exact equivalence originated in death-exchange and then was carried over into the first stage of gift-exchange — or life-exchange.

Hans Kelsen points out that "among the Orokaiva, blood revenge is described by a word which means 'exchange of death souls'" (*Society and Nature,* p. 60). But under the principle of equivalence one side could exact from the other side only a death for a death — and not one death more. This would have furnished an effective means for holding the reprisal system down to a minimum. If more lives were taken, more would be demanded in retribution. Under such circumstances the whole system could escalate in ever more deaths and counter-deaths.

To avoid this, there had to be an exact accounting of such deaths. John Layard gives an example of this in Malekula which he describes as "Equalizing the Number of Dead on Both Sides." He writes:

> This process of equalizing out by revenging one death by another is called *simbaten.* Thus if A has killed B, then the clansmen of B will attempt to avenge him by killing a clansman of A, and, if successful, the avenger will call out as he kills him *"Simbaten A,"* meaning "Equivalent for the death of A." (*Stone Men of Malekula,* p. 599)

The interlocking relationship between the death talio and gift-giving has survived in primitive regions where the regulated fight still prevails. First the men fight; after the required number have been killed, they make peace through the interchange of food and gifts. Rivers summarizes the practice in Melanesia as follows:

> The people fight till one or more men have been killed on either side; in some islands it is necessary that an equal number shall have been killed on each side. As soon as it is seen that each side has lost a man or men, the fight comes to an end automatically; there is no parleying or arrangement of terms. Some time after, the two opponent peoples exchange presents which are of equal value on both sides. There is no question of the offenders giving a larger amount in compensation for the injury which was the pri-

mary cause of the quarrel. Moreover, in the island of Eddystone in the Solomons, the party which takes the initiative
in the exchange is not that of the offenders, but the order
of giving depends on the drawing of the first blood in the
fight. The side which first kills first gives. (*Psychology and
Ethnology*, p. 9)

In regions where the regulated fight was held only at certain
times, such as annually, some kind of accounting system was
required to maintain a tally of the number of deaths suffered
by a community in the interval between the fights. It seems that
one of the earliest of such tallies took the form of cut-off heads.
The function of the earliest "headman" was to be the keeper
of these tallies. According to William Graham Sumner, "The
Dyaks keep an account current of the number of lives which
one tribe 'owes' to another. The Hill Dyaks, whose wars are
constant and bloody, are very scrupulous about this account
of heads due" (*Folkways*, p. 501).

This practice may also explain the drying and shrinking
of heads. W. I. Thomas cites the practice of the Sarawaks:

 . . . the ostensible object . . . is that their balance of heads
may be settled; for these people keep a regular account
of the numbers slain on each side on every occasion; these
memorandums have now, perhaps, become confused
amongst the sea tribes, but amongst those of the hills, where
fewer people are killed and fighting is less frequent, the
number to which each tribe is indebted to the other is regularly preserved. . . . baskets full of them may be seen
at any house in the villages of the sea tribes. . . . they
are . . . the most valuable property and an accident which
destroys them is considered the most lamentable calamity.
(*Primitive Behavior*, pp. 377-78)

It is quite understandable why the loss of such "memorandums" would be regarded as a disaster, for without them how
could an accurate death score be maintained? And without
such a tally there could be needless destruction of life.

Some tallies are not easily recognizable because they are
in the form of carved wooden heads and assumed to be only
ornaments or decorations. Such were the "necklaces" of carved
heads described by Leo Frobenius in a chapter entitled "Personal Adornment." Their real meaning however peeps out from
his description:

A Walonga native of the Mongala district wore suspended from a thong three heads, carved in wood, in memory of his three murdered brothers. The pendant was to keep him constantly in mind that he had still to avenge his brothers' deaths. Such is the custom in the Walonga village. Each of such wooden heads demands an expiation, the death of a man belonging to the tribe that killed his relatives. When the victim is slain, a great feast is held in the Walonga village. The murdered man is eaten, and his wooden head burnt. In this way such an apparently harmless necklace may be the witness of a long and very sad family record. (*Childhood of Man,* p. 28)

As blood revenge began to fade away, death-necklaces became changed — first into necklaces symbolizing fraternity among men, and ultimately into ornaments for women.

The principle of equivalence was a major achievement for ancient humanity when the hazardous conditions of life and the ignorance of natural death are considered. It held down reprisals to a rigid minimum: one for one and no more. Kelsen remarks that a Jibaro Indian never takes more than one life "even if he has the opportunity of killing more" (*Society and Nature,* p. 59).

In the course of time even this one-to-one ratio was reduced. The savages broke their principle of equivalence to give more scope to life-exchange over death-exchange. With the further development of gift-giving, baskets loaded with food more and more displaced the baskets of decapitated heads. Finally, a solitary individual sufficed as retaliation for all the deaths that had occurred over a period of time.

It should be noted here that modern methods of warfare introduced into primitive regions when the European conquerors began their invasions pushed the principle of equivalence in an opposite direction and destroyed it. Savages were unaccustomed to weapons more lethal than clubs, boomerangs, bows and arrows, etc., and even these were used in a restricted manner. But the introduction of guns and the massacres they produced soon shattered the old rule of equivalence.

John Layard gives an example from Malekula. In the 350-year period of orally transmitted history on Vao there is no record of indiscriminate massacres — until the introduction of muskets. Here is how he describes the tragic results of using such deadly weapons to settle accounts:

These, lacking the means to defend themselves against this unknown and deadly form of attack, were in this way slaughtered in such numbers that it was impossible any more to equalize the number of dead. Whereas in the old days the number of dead in any given war was rarely more than two or three on either side, and if the victors wanted peace, the discrepancy in numbers seldom demanded more than the sacrifice of one victim on their part, once muskets had been introduced the discrepancy became so great that all the rules of warfare were abandoned, and wholesale massacres took place.

In this way, during the latter part of the nineteenth century the Small Islanders practically wiped out the whole population of what was once a flourishing district containing innumerable villages. . . . The same tragedy occurred even in warfare between the two Sides of each individual Small Island. . . . The more farseeing of the Small Islanders now bitterly regret these suicidal ravages which have so seriously reduced their numbers in face of the growing menace of the whites. . . . (*Stone Men of Malekula*, p. 603)

Once the aborigines were set to fighting each other on this unrestricted scale, they became easy prey for the white conquerors who coveted their lands and natural resources.

Chapple and Coon make the point that Europeans, up to recent times at least, made formal declarations of war and abided by certain rules for the treatment of prisoners and for protecting civilians — that is, in their wars against other Europeans:

However, they were seldom concerned about formalized rules when fighting non-Europeans; in South Africa, white colonists have been known to go out on shooting expeditions to exterminate the Bushmen without declaring war or taking prisoners or sparing women and children, and to leave poisoned meat lying around for them to eat; other such hunts have been known in Australia, and in Tasmania the settlers fought a war of deliberate extermination against the blacks. In Tierra del Fuego, it used to be a common practice for sheep ranchers to go out shooting Onas in general after some of them had killed their sheep. In all of these wars against bothersome primitives, no holds were barred. (*Principles of Anthropology*, p. 629)

These predatory wars of conquest stand in stark contrast to the savages' system of settling death grievances on a minimum basis. Despite their ignorance about natural death they found other ways to settle these grievances than the reprisal system that demanded a death for a death. In the course of this effort they transformed the regulated pitched battle into regulated sports and games.

From Sham Fights to Sports and the Arts

While much has been written about the blood feud and the obligation to avenge the blood of a "slain" kinsman, the connection is seldom made between this and the primitive ignorance of natural death. Consequently, serious misinterpretations have been made of the savage system of fighting and regulated infighting. Many reports make it appear to be a senseless occupation, stemming from some kind of psychological aberration. The reality is quite otherwise.

Survivals in primitive regions of the various substitutes found to expiate deaths without inflicting more deaths show how savages solved this crucial problem despite their biological ignorance. Elkin remarks of some tribes in Australia:

> Incidentally, this should enhance our appreciation of his intelligence. When confronted with the problem of the magical causation of death, the necessity of dealing with the personal agent and at the same time, appreciating tribal and social facts and the task of preserving the cohesion of the tribe, he is able to find a solution, even though it means some inconsistency and the escape from an inexorable logic. For, after all, intelligence is shown by recognizing and solving the problems of life. (*Australian Aborigines,* pp. 328-29)

Solving the problems of life and death was a trial-and-error process in which numerous substitutes were found for the extreme penalty, death. These ranged from physical tortures and partial mutilations to satirical recitations and songs.

The regulated fight in which accounts were settled by inflicting reprisal killings gradually gave way to what is called the "mock fight" or "sham fight." In these, physical punishments were supposed to take the place of deaths, although occasionally, by design or accident, one individual was killed, at which point the fight ended.

The sham fight was conducted according to the same rules as a pitched battle. The declaration of war was framed as an invitation from one community to another to "come and settle things." Chiefs from both sides acted as umpires, calling a halt to the fighting when enough punishment had been inflicted on the side held responsible for the deaths. In some of these fights no weapons more deadly than whips could be used. The following example is given by Driberg:

> Among the Lango should two factions of the tribe be involved in a dispute, the elders are hastily summoned, a tall tree is felled and one of its branches lopped off. A dozen men are chosen from each body of disputants, and armed with long hide whips. . . . No spears may be carried and should anyone produce a weapon more lethal than a whip, it is confiscated and destroyed, and his house is burnt to the ground. . . . At a given signal the combatants lash at one another, and when the umpire thinks that enough punishment has been inflicted, he tells them to stop fighting, and a completely satisfactory peace is restored. (*At Home with the Savage,* p. 171)

Sometimes the fights are called "reconciliation" fights, although they follow the customary pattern. First the opponents exchange blows; afterwards they exchange food and gifts and become reconciled. The following is an example from Spencer and Gillen:

> In this instance the group which is supposed to have suffered the injury sends a messenger to the old men of the offending group, who says, "Our people want you to come and have a friendly fight." This peculiar form of meeting is called *Umbirna ilirima,* which means "seeing and settling (things)." If the offending group be willing, which they are almost sure to be, then the meeting is held . . . and a more or less sham fight takes place with boomerangs, no one being any the worse. (*Native Tribes of Central Australia,* p. 462)

In the transitional period from death-reprisal to the sham fight, the passions aroused in the sham fight might spill over to convert it into a real fight. Tylor, writing about the Botocudos of Brazil, states that a quarrel "might be settled by a solemn cudgelling match, where pairs of warriors belaboured one another with heavy stakes." But if "the beaten party take to their bows and arrows, the scene may change into a real battle" (*Anthropology*, p. 111).

Another example given by Tylor from Australia conveys a hint of how duelling first came into existence. He writes:

> . . . one tribe sends another a bunch of emu-feathers tied to the end of a spear, as a challenge to fight next day. Then the two sides meet in battle array, their naked bodies terrific with painted patterns, brandishing their spears and clubs, and clamouring with taunts and yells. Each warrior is paired with an opponent, so that the fight is really a set of duels, where spear after spear is hurled and dodged or parried with wonderful dexterity, till at last perhaps a man is killed, which generally brings the fray to an end.
> (*Anthropology*, p. 111)

One of the most misunderstood forms of savage fighting is the practice of taking scalps by the American aborigines. The small piece of flesh taken from the head of a man was a substitute for killing the man or decapitating him. Thomas, taking vigorous exception to the misleading statements made on this subject, says that "most people are untrustworthy observers and draw inferences from their preconceived notions, rather than from what actually takes place." He adds:

> Among the Plains tribes a scalp was . . . regarded as an emblem of victory and was a good thing to carry back to the village to rejoice and dance over. . . . Usually the scalps taken were small, a little larger than a silver dollar, but like any other piece of fresh skin they stretched greatly.
> (*Primitive Behavior*, p. 503)

There was ample reason for rejoicing when the scalp of a solitary victim sufficed to retaliate for all the deaths suffered by a community over a period of time. Moreover, the scalp was treated with the same respect as a human being; it was honored and "adopted" into the community as a testimonial that, with death accounts settled, hostilities were at an end.

Ruth Benedict describes the Zuni "war dance," which could also be called a "peace and adoption" dance:

> The scalp throughout the long and elaborate ceremonial of the war dance is the symbol of the man who has been

killed. . . . It must be honored by the dance and must be
adopted into the pueblo by the usual adoption rites. . . .
The scalp-dance prayers are very explicit. They describe
the transformation of the valueless enemy into a sacred
fetish of the people and the joy with which the people
acknowledge the new blessing. (*Patterns of Culture,* p. 107)

The practice of the American aborigines called "counting
coups" represents another stage in the evolution of reprisals.
In this battle the man who won the highest admiration from
his fellows was the one who did *not* scalp or in any other
way injure his opponent even when he had the weapons to
do so. An illustration of this changing code of ethics can be
seen in a report by G. B. Grinnell, cited by Thomas:

The chief applause was won by the man who first could
touch the fallen enemy. In Indian estimation the bravest
act that could be performed was to count coup — to touch
or strike — a living unhurt man and to leave him alive,
and this was frequently done. Cases are often told of where,
when the men of two opposing tribes faced each other in
battle, some brave man ran out in front of his people,
charged upon the enemy, ran through the line, struck one
of them, and then, turning and riding back, returned to his
own party. If, however, the man was knocked off his horse,
or his horse was killed, all of his party made a headlong
charge to rescue and bring him off. . . .
It was regarded as an evidence of bravery for a man
to go into battle carrying no weapon that would do any
harm at a distance. It was more creditable to carry a
lance than a bow and arrow; more creditable to carry
a hatchet or war club than a lance; and the bravest thing
of all was to go into a fight with nothing more than a
whip, or a long twig — sometimes called a coup stick. I
have never heard a stone-headed war club called coup
stick. . . . (*Primitive Behavior,* pp. 499-500)

The Japanese jujitsu method of offense and defense depends
upon bodily techniques for overthrowing an opponent; Brasch
describes it as "essentially combat without a weapon." The
same is true of the term "karate" which means "empty hand."
Brasch writes that "its name highlights its principal feature;
the hand holds no weapon, not even a stone" (*How Did Sports
Begin?,* pp. 238, 247).

It is not difficult to see how primitive fighting exchanges, becoming more and more "sportsmanlike," would lead in the course of time to actual sports and games. Physical encounters such as cudgeling and whipping would, minus the use of staves or whips, become wrestling and boxing. The American Indian game of lacrosse, which, according to Brasch, was on some occasions a "bloody encounter" between hostile groups, turned into a sport.

According to Brasch and others, the severed heads of enemies were once used as footballs. In time this could have led to using balls made out of pigskin or other leather.

Chapple and Coon, despite their doubts about any evolutionary sequence from primitive fighting exchanges to modern sports and games, nevertheless give examples that point to such a development. Among these they cite the following report by Mary P. Haas on "Creek Intertown Relations":

> The towns of the Creek confederacy were divided into "fires" or moieties, called reciprocally "my friend" and "my opponent." In English they call the sides Red, or War, and White, or Peace. The towns on the same side were friendly; those on the other side hostile, or at least distrustful. This opposition came to a climax in the lacrosse game, described earlier. Once a year a town of one moiety would challenge a rival of the other moiety. Each town had some particular rival on the other side, but would play anyone who challenged. . . .
>
> As Miss Haas points out, the symbolism of the game is that of war, since the terms used to describe the negotiations and plays are taken from the context of war. Furthermore, the adoption of a defeated village by its conquerors is exactly what happened when the Creeks won a military victory; there was much adoption of prisoners, as well as ritual torture and killing of some of them. It is quite possible that the Creek system of ball games may have supplanted internecine warfare at the time of the formation of the confederacy, although this is a purely speculative historical deduction. (*Principles of Anthropology*, p. 627)

Primitive spear throwing evolved into the dart game that was popular in both Polynesia and North America. Nowadays the dart game can be played by a solitary individual, but it was originally played between opponent teams. As Chapple and

Coon describe this game in Tikopia, it is not only reminiscent of the old combat involving killing the opponent but goes even farther back to the time when those who were killed were also eaten. The teams are composed of twelve to twenty men on each side and the object is for each team to get its darts ahead of those of its rival. When a side scores, it is said to have "eaten" its opponents (ibid., p. 621).

The evolution from primitive fighting to sports and games can also be seen in the fact that the earliest sports took place at the time of mortuary ceremonies. Along with the reciprocal burial of the dead by the opponents, various contests took place between them. Frazer gives some examples in his section called "Funeral Games":

> . . . when the Southern Nicobarese dig up the bones of their dead, clean them, and bury them again, they hold a feast at which sham-fights with quarter-staves take place "to gratify the departed spirit." . . . In Laos, a province of Siam, boxers are similarly engaged to bruise each other at the festival which takes place when the remains of a chief or other important person are cremated. The festival lasts three days, but it is while the pyre is actually blazing that the combatants are expected to batter each other's heads with the utmost vigour. . . . The Bashkirs, a Tartar people of mixed extraction, bury their dead and always end the obsequies with horse-races. Among some of the North American Indians contests in running, shooting, and so forth formed part of the funeral celebration.
>
> The Bedouins of the Sinaitic peninsula observe a great annual festival at the grave of the prophet Salih, and camel-races are included in the ceremonies. . . . The custom of holding funeral games in honour of the dead appears to be common among the people of the Caucasus. (*The Golden Bough,* Part III, *The Dying God,* pp. 96-98)

The Olympic contests of ancient Greek history have their origin in these funeral festivals. According to Frazer, "Some of the ancients held that all the great games of Greece — the Olympic, the Nemean, the Isthmian, and the Pythian — were funeral games celebrated in honour of the dead." He adds:

> These Greek traditions as to the funeral origin of the great games are strongly confirmed by Greek practice in historical times. Thus in the Homeric age funeral games, including

chariot-races, foot-races, wrestling, boxing, spear-throwing, quoit-throwing and archery, were celebrated in honour of dead kings and heroes at their barrows. . . .

Nor were the Greeks in the habit of instituting games in honour only of a few distinguished individuals; they sometimes established them to perpetuate the memory or to appease the ghosts of large numbers of men who had perished on the field of battle or been massacred in cold blood. . . . At Athens funeral games were held in the Academy to commemorate the men slain in war who were buried in the neighboring Ceramicus, and sacrifices were offered to them at a pit; the games were superintended and the sacrifices offered by the Polemarch or minister of war. (ibid., pp. 92-96)

Perhaps even more curious than sports and games is the origin of drama and the dance in the same process of transcending blood revenge. In these arts in their earlier forms the regulated combat is "acted out" with astonishing realism. In his remarkable study of Australian and other corroborees, or community dances, Ernst Grosse quotes from Mundy's example from New South Wales. The dancers painted white streaks on their heads and bodies so that in the moonlight they resembled skeletons. Brandishing their weapons, he writes, "one would think the dancers were about to break one another's skulls," yet at the end no one is injured or killed. He describes the dance as follows:

The dancers performed first a series of complicated and wild movements in which clubs, spears, boomerangs, and shields were brandished. Then "all at once the mass divided into groups, and with deafening shrieks and passionate cries they sprang upon one another in a hand-to-hand fight. One side was speedily driven out of the field and pursued into the darkness, whence howls, groans, and the strokes of clubs could be heard, producing the perfect illusion of a terrible massacre. . . ." (*The Beginnings of Art*, p. 219)

In our concepts a dance performed by mock skeletons might be called a "dance of death." But in savage society, where it represented a victory over death through a mock representation in dance-and-drama form, it was really a "dance of life."

Radcliffe-Brown describes a stylized dance in the Andaman

Islands which he calls a peace-making ceremony, but which is rather another illustration of the substitute found for killing in the form of dance and drama. He writes:

> The dancers are divided into two parties. The actions of the one party throughout are expressions of their aggressive feelings towards the other. This is clear enough in the shouting, the threatening gestures, and the way in which each member of the "attacking" party gives a good shaking to each member of the other party. On the other side what is expressed may be described as complete passivity; the performers stand quite still throughout the whole dance, taking care to show neither fear nor resentment at the treatment to which they have to submit. Thus those of the one side give collective expression to their collective anger, which is thereby appeased. The others, by passively submitting to this, humbling themselves before the just wrath of their enemies, expiate their wrongs. Anger appeased dies down; wrongs expiated are forgiven and forgotten; the enmity is at an end. (*The Andaman Islanders*, p. 238)

Radcliffe-Brown tells us that after the dance the men exchange weapons, "which is simply a special form of the rite of exchanging presents as an expression of good-will." He adds, "The special form is particularly appropriate as it would seem to ensure at least some months of friendship, for you cannot go out to fight a man with his weapons while he has yours."

The dance as one of the great social unifiers in primitive society has impressed a number of scholars. W. I. Thomas reiterates the data collected by Ernst Grosse on the subject:

> The dances of the hunting peoples are, as a rule, mass dances. Generally the men of the tribe, not rarely the members of several tribes, join in the exercises, and the whole assemblage then moves according to one law in one time. All who have described the dances have referred again and again to this "wonderful" unison of the movements. In the heat of the dance the several participants are fused together as into a single being, which is stirred and moved as by one feeling. During the dance they are in a condition of complete social unification, and the dancing group feels and acts like a single organism. *The social significance of the primitive dance lies precisely in this effect of social*

unification. It brings and accustoms a number of men who, in their loose and precarious conditions of life, are driven irregularly hither and thither . . . to act under one impulse with one feeling for one object. It introduces order and connection, at least occasionally, into the rambling, fluctuating life of the hunting tribes. . . . It would be hard to overestimate the importance of the primitive dance in the culture development of mankind. . . . In Australia the corroborry at least serves "as an assurance of peace between single tribes. Two tribes, desiring to confirm mutual good feeling, dance it together." (*Source Book for Social Origins,* pp. 591-92; emphasis in the original)

Along with the dance and drama, other art forms made their appearance as substitutes to satisfy the claims of blood. Among these are songs, oratory, poetry, satires and jokes. These are called "song-combats" or "oratorical contests" or "satirical recitations." Each side was supposed to take the verbal humiliation with good grace, awaiting its turn to give back equivalent punishment. They provided a nonlethal method by which each side could "flatten" its opponents, and they are sometimes called "slanging matches" or "drumming matches."

These contests or performances were conducted like other sham fights, reconciliation fights, and games. The people assembled on both sides and watched the performance closely, judged the merits of the oratory, songs, or slanging, and at the end decided the winner. Such contests have survived up to recent times among the Eskimos. Johan Huizinga gives a picturesque example:

When an Eskimo has a complaint to make against another he challenges him to a drumming contest. . . . The clan or tribe thereupon gathers at a festal meeting, all in their finest attire and in joyful mood. The two contestants then attack one another in turn with opprobrious songs to the accompaniment of a drum, each reproaching the other with his misdemeanours. No distinction is made between well-founded accusations, satirical remarks calculated to tickle the audience, and pure slander. For instance one singer enumerated all the people who had been eaten by his opponent's wife and mother-in-law during a famine, which caused the assembled company to burst into tears. This offensive chanting is accompanied throughout by all kinds of physical indignities directed against your opponent, such as breathing and snorting into his face, bumping him with your forehead, prizing his jaws open, tying him to a tent-pole — all of which the "accused" has to bear with equanimity and a mocking laugh. Most of the spectators join in the refrains of the song, applauding and egging the parties on. Others just sit there and go to sleep. During the pauses the contestants converse in friendly terms. . . . Finally the spectators decide who the winner is. (*Homo Ludens*, p. 85)

We sometimes say, "If looks could kill . . . ". Thomas cites a report by Swanton on the Tlingit Indians which shows that under certain circumstances looks apparently could "kill" an opponent:

Great rivalry was always exhibited by the two parties . . . and their endeavors to outdo each other sometimes almost resulted in bloodshed. Each side attended carefully to the slightest remark made by an opponent, especially by the two song leaders with which each was provided, and the least slight, though couched in the most metaphorical language, was at once seized upon and might precipitate a riot. The actions of each dancer were also scrutinized with great care, and any little mistake noted and remembered. The strain upon a dancer was consequently so great that, if a fine dancer died soon after the feast, it was said, "The people's looks have killed him." (*Primitive Behavior*, p. 384)

Huizinga notes that the slanging match persisted in Greece up to the historical period. He writes:

Greek tradition has numerous traces of ceremonial and festal slanging-matches. The word *iambos* is held by some to have meant originally "derision," with particular reference to the public skits and scurrilous songs which formed part of the feasts of Demeter and Dionysus. The biting satire of Archilochus is supposed to have developed out of this slating in public. . . . Further, at the feasts of Demeter and Apollo, men and women chanted songs of mutual derision, which may have given rise to the literary theme of the diatribe against womankind. (*Homo Ludens*, p. 68)

The "diatribe against womankind" is clearly an innovation of patriarchal society. Originally the mutual insults and hostility were expressed between men and represented one of the means by which they freed themselves from death reprisals.

Another substitute for death exchange can be found in the enigmatic institution called the "joking relationship." It is intelligible only within the framework of the effort to find substitutes for blood vengeance. This practice of men joking with one another instead of fighting or even slanging each other is sometimes called "privileged familiarity" or "permitted disrespect." As Radcliffe-Brown describes it:

> The joking relationship is a peculiar combination of friendliness and antagonism. The behavior is such that in any other social context it would express and arouse hostility; but it is not meant seriously and must not be taken seriously. There is a pretence of hostility and a real friendliness. To put it another way, the relationship is one of permitted disrespect. (*Structure and Function,* p. 91)

The joking relationship is most prominent in the relations of male cross-cousins, allies on opposite sides of the marriage divide. Radcliffe-Brown writes:

> To quote one instance of these, the following is recorded for the Ojibwa. "When cross-cousins meet they must try to embarrass one another. They 'joke' one another, making the most vulgar allegations, by their standards as well as ours. But being 'kind' relations, no one can take offence. Cross-cousins who do not joke in this way are considered boorish, as not playing the social game."
> . . . in East Africa, as we learn from Mr. Pedler's note, the Zigua and Zaramu do not joke with one another because a yet closer bond exists between them since they are *ndugu* (brothers). But beyond the field within which social relations are thus defined there lie other groups with which, since they are outsiders to the individual's own group, the relation involves possible or actual hostility. . . . It is precisely this separateness which is not merely recognised but emphasised when a joking relationship is established. The show of hostility, the perpetual disrespect, is a continual expression of that social disjunction which is an essential part of the whole structural situation, but

over which, without destroying or even weakening it, there is provided the social conjunction of friendliness and mutual aid. (ibid., pp. 93-95)

In other words, the joking relationship was mandatory, for if those who had formerly been enemies failed to see the joke when they encountered each other, they would not only be regarded as boorish but might even be suspected of spoiling for a fight.

The general effect of these various substitutes for the blood revenge fight was to bring men together in economic and social cooperation and set up standards of excellence other than bravery on the battlefield. Instead of spearing or scalping, the new spirit of competition brought a striving to be the best in productive activities. A commingling of the new spirit with the old can be seen in the following by Chapple and Coon:

In Africa we have a record of the clearing activities performed by the Bemba in Northern Rhodesia. Here a number of men will clear all the fields belonging to them in turn. The men climb the trees and chop off the limbs with small axes, leaving the trunks standing. The work is strenuous, exciting and dangerous. It offers an opportunity for rivalry; the men shout as they hack at the limbs, pretending that they are dismembering enemies. As each limb falls, they shout special cries. . . . their conversation when they are on the ground is largely concerned with tree-cutting, even in non-cutting seasons. (*Principles of Anthropology*, pp. 181-82)

Lucy Mair, writing about the Ibo of eastern Nigeria, states that "the most important duty of the age-grade of young active men is not fighting but communal labour. . . . When some public work had to be done — for example the clearing of a road — portions would be allotted to the two moieties, who were expected to compete in speed and efficiency" (*Introduction to Social Anthropology*, pp. 58-59).

Thus the blood revenge institution became increasingly undermined as substitutes were found for death reprisals and as even the substitutes, from physical beatings to reciprocal insults, became more and more corroded. The arts, sports, and games took off on their own independent paths of development.

In some primitive regions it became increasingly difficult to muster the headmen, the forces, or even the spirit of rivalry and competition to 'put up a good show in a sham fight, let alone a real fight. In Margaret Mead's report on the Arapesh, for example, she describes how they had lost all interest in maintaining these old traditions:

> And the problem of social engineering is conceived by the Arapesh not as the need to limit aggression and curb acquisitiveness, but as the need to force a few of the more capable and gifted men into taking, against their will, enough responsibility and leadership so that occasionally, every three or four years or at even rarer intervals, a really exciting ceremonial may be organized. No one, it is assumed, really wants to be a leader, a "big man." "Big men" have to plan, have to initiate exchanges, have to strut and swagger and talk in loud voices, have to boast of what they have done in the past and are going to do in the future. All of this the Arapesh regard as most uncongenial, difficult behaviour, the kind of behaviour in which no normal man would indulge if he could possibly avoid it. (*Sex and Temperament,* p. 27)

In addition to the entertainments and games that served as substitutes for blood reprisals, certain other practices cannot be explained except as part of the same struggle of ancient humanity to liberate itself from endless feuding and fighting. One of these was to transfer the blame for deaths and injuries from men to things, and to punish the things instead of the men.

Frazer illustrates this form of retaliation as it was practiced by the Kukis of Chittagong in northeastern India. He writes, "If a man should happen to be killed by an accidental fall from a tree, all his relations assemble and cut it down; and however large it may be, they reduce it to chips, which they scatter in the winds, for having, as they say, been the cause of the death of their brother." The same practice, he says, prevails among the Ainos (or Ainus) of Japan, who take this kind of vengeance on a tree from which a person has fallen and been killed. (*Folklore in the Old Testament,* abr. ed., p. 398). The same practice can be found in ancient Greek civilization, according to Frazer:

At Athens, the very heart of ancient civilization in its finest efflorescence, there was a court specially set apart for the trial of animals and of lifeless objects which had injured or killed human beings. The court sat in the town-hall (*prytaneum*), and the judges were no less than the titular king of all Attica and the four titular kings of the separate Attic tribes. . . . The offenders who were here placed at the bar were not men and women, but animals and implements or missiles of stone, wood, or iron which had fallen upon and cracked somebody's crown, when the hand which had hurled them was unknown. What was done to the animals which were found guilty, we do not know; but we are told that lifeless objects, which had killed anybody by falling on him or her, were banished by the tribal kings beyond the boundaries. Every year the axe or the knife which had been used to slaughter an ox at a festival of Zeus on the Acropolis was solemnly tried for murder before the judges seated on the bench of justice; every year it was solemnly found guilty, condemned, and cast into the sea. (ibid., p. 401)

It is not clear just when humans became aware of the fact that deaths occurred through natural causes as well as hostile acts. From the evidence, however, the death reprisal system was overcome even before this. The diminution of death exchange moved side by side with the acceleration of gift exchange which, in the final analysis, was the exchange of life and hospitality for hostility and death.

From Hostility to Hospitality

While the transformation of the enemy into the cross-cousin is fairly well documented, this is not the case with the transformation of the enemy into the host and the guest. The term "host" derives from the Latin *hostis,* which originally meant "stranger" or "enemy." And in an article on "Strangers" by P. J. Hamilton-Grierson we learn: "That the good treatment of the stranger was an innovation on the previous practice is shown by the fact that one word in several languages is used to express the conception of "enemy" and that of "guest" (*Encyclopedia of Religion and Ethics,* vol. XI, p. 891).

In primitive society, get-togethers were on a formalized community basis. These are called by various names — "feasts," "festivals," "potlatches," "peace ceremonials," "corroborees." They all have the same objective — to confirm in a ceremonial festival the fraternal relations that have been established between the communities. Some are small clan-to-clan get-togethers between neighboring groups; others are massive regional festivals calling together phratries and even whole tribes.

These festivals are sponsored on an alternating basis; first by one of the opposing sides, then by the other. Although lavish hospitality is their keynote, there is also an undercurrent of hostility carried over from the days when hosts and guests were enemies. In friendly rivalry each tries to outdo the other in hospitality. The more massive the food- and gift-giving, the greater is the prestige for the host.

In some regions the origin of this custom is evident in the fighting stance with which such occasions begin. According to Franz Boas, writing about the Kwakiutl, "The invitation to a potlatch in which host and guests rival in prodigality is likened to war. The messengers who carry the invitation are called warriors . . . and the arriving guests sing war songs . . ." (*Race, Language and Culture*, p. 234).

A picturesque description by F. E. Williams of such a festival among the Orokaiva peoples of New Guinea is cited by Thomas:

> Food will have been gathered from the gardens and bountifully displayed on platforms. The guests, arriving in their several parties, come striding single file into the village, each party headed by its man of first importance, befeathered club on shoulder. No smile adorns his face, but rather an expression of fierceness, which, however unsuited it may seem to the hospitable occasion, is nevertheless Orokaiva good form. Tempestuous shouts of welcome greet the visitors, which they accept without a flicker of weak-minded gratification. . . . and so they file majestically through the village until they reach the place allotted them, when they seat themselves somewhat abruptly and relax into a more sociable attitude. Meanwhile, the women have been busy at peeling and chopping the taro, and the pots are cooking in rows. If it be an occasion of any importance the pigs are slaughtered and, having been dismembered, lie in reeking heaps on the high platform where the butchering is performed in rather studied publicity. The stench may soon be nauseating to a European, though to Orokaiva nostrils it has no doubt a pleasant and promising savor. An onlooker

who would appreciate the gaiety and charm of the scene must not be too fastidious.

Towards the end of the day comes the formal distribution of food. The master of the feast, conferring anxiously with his friends, has been setting out the taro in heaps, making them correspond by laborious arithmetic with the number of his principal guests. Now that the tally appears satisfactory, he turns with an enthusiasm bordering on violence, to the distribution. With loud shouts he and his assistants rush back and forth depositing, or often rather hurling down, bunches of taro before the guests, who accept them with a fitting appearance of indifference. In the same way the pig flesh — legs, quarters, chines, and entrails — are bestowed on top of the taro heaps, and the guests are ready to depart. They have been sufficiently regaled throughout the day; the food thus distributed is to be carried home. The women pack it into their string bags and prepare to move off. Men and children will bear their part. One remembers the spectacle of a diminutive child bearing away the blood-spattered head of a huge pig, balanced with difficulty and pride upon his own small crown. Thus laden with proofs of friendship the guests depart to await the time when, in a year or so, they will make a similar return of hospitality. (*Primitive Behavior,* pp. 186-87)

Here the laborious arithmetic involves not a count of decapitated human heads but bunches of taro and other food. The food the hosts hurl at their guests is testimony that spears are not being hurled. The "studied publicity" surrounding the butchering of the pigs is a public demonstration that animals, not humans, are being slaughtered. In this manner the old hostility stemming from ignorance of the causes of death and the demand for blood retaliation is now buried under an avalanche of hospitality — "fighting with food," as it is sometimes called. In a report on the Trukese, Thomas Gladwin and Seymour B. Sarason write:

While in the old days lineage often fought lineage in very real fights, nowadays they fight with food. One lineage will challenge another to a food fight, and the members of each lineage will work desperately for days and weeks to produce more food than the other. This culminates in a great feast in which each lineage tries to consume the output of the other, although only after each item has been carefully counted, and a victor determined. . . .

The people of Romonum, in recounting their life histories, always remembered to mention the food that was brought out and eaten at the resolution of every crisis. This, it appears, healed the breach caused by whatever issue or episode was involved at the time. (*Truk: Man in Paradise,* pp. 53, 57)

The central place occupied by food in the hospitality festival has been noted by many writers. The food is usually piled up in great public displays. It is the first thing to greet the eyes of the arriving guests. Alexander Goldenweiser cites Firth's report of the spectacular displays put on by the New Zealand Maori tribes. An immense amount of labor went into the construction of the huge stages or scaffolds upon which the baskets of provisions were loaded; these were eighty to ninety feet high and twenty or thirty feet square at the base. They were built up in pyramidal form "so as to present to the eye, when completed, one solid mass of food!" Considering their primitive tools, he writes, the mere organization of men and materials "was an economic feat of no mean kind." He adds:

> The manifest purpose of building such structures was to impress the guests and to give scope for the display of the food to the best advantage. . . . The distribution and partaking of the food on such occasions was accompanied by much ceremony, magical rites, and the singing of songs. . . . Considerable importance was attached to the ceremony of apportioning the food, and every effort was made by the donors of it to make the presentation as effective as possible. (*Anthropology,* pp. 158-59)

According to Mauss, among the Maori, food is personified and is "identical with Rongo, the symbol of plants and of peace. The association of ideas becomes clearer; hospitality, food, communion, peace, exchange, law" (*The Gift,* p. 87).

Along with the practice of fighting with food we find its corollary, fighting with gifts; that is, the interchange of various things on a generous scale and the destruction of a portion of them. The destructive practice is usually explained as a contest between rival chiefs for prestige and power. A familiar example is cited by Thomas. Among the Kwakiutl tribes, "a chief will burn blankets, a canoe, or break a copper" to show that "his mind is stronger, his power greater, than that of his rival. If the latter is not able to destroy an equal amount of property without much delay, his name is 'broken.' He is vanquished by his rival" (*Primitive Behavior,* p. 387).

However, as Mauss points out, such interchanges are not made between individuals but between groups, with the chiefs acting as intermediaries. Their objective is to achieve social solidarity; as Mauss puts it, "The Tlingit and Haida of North-West America give a good expression of the nature of these practices when they say that they 'show respect to each other'" (*The Gift,* p. 4).

A similar misinterpretation is to see the interchanges as motivated by the desire for economic or propertied advantages. An example is Boas's view of the potlatch: "the underlying principle is that of the interest-bearing investment of property" ("Ceremony and Economics," in *Primitive Heritage,* p. 330). Melville Herskovits wavers on the matter. He writes that in gift and ceremonial exchange "their non-economic aspects are most apparent," but he accepts reports from those who seek to portray the practice in commercial terms, e.g. Tueting's statement that, in Malekula, "a gift is at most a venture, a hopeful speculation." The native looks to receive "an advantage at least equal to the value of his yam." His conclusion: "The idea that anything may be freely given is unknown" (*Economic Anthropology,* pp. 155, 160).

In fact, the interchange system, despite its "fighting stance," was not based upon speculations or investment in property holdings; it was an exchange of gifts designed to establish and maintain fraternal relations among men. To "kill" things instead of men was a marked advance over blood vengeance. As Thomas observes of the Tlingit, "They say that formerly they were rivals in feats of bravery in war, but now they "fight only with property'" (*Primitive Behavior,* p. 385). For the sake of accuracy this should be amended: now they 'fight only with gifts."

Some anthropologists have lamented the wasteful practice of burning valuable things like oil and blankets in these interchanges. "The waste of both consumable and capital goods entailed by a wholesale destruction of private property is obvious," says Hutton Webster. "It keeps many a primitive community sunk in direst poverty" (*Taboo,* pp. 183-84). However, all human progress is bought at a price, and the periodic destruction of some useful articles was not an exorbitant price to pay for converting death-exchange into life-exchange.

In its most literal form this life-exchange was an exchange of living individuals to take the place of those who had died. This is often called "adoption," a term that can be misleading. Since it included adults as well as children some anthropologists prefer the term "kinship equivalents." Thomas writes, "The practice of adoption or the creation of social equivalents has had wide variations, ranging from the friendly interchange of children in small communities to the adoption of whole tribes by other tribes" (*Primitive Behavior*, p. 140).

The widespread interchange of children in primitive regions has been recognized as a means of preserving fraternal relations and peace between communities. No doubt it operated on the principle: if you have our children and we have your children, there is less likelihood of fighting and more of exchanges. In a sense the interchanged children play the part of hostages for keeping the peace.

Some investigators prefer the term "incorporations" to the term "wholesale adoptions." Julius Lippert uses the term "artificial fraternization" (*Evolution of Culture*, p. 284). Fraternization is probably the best term for expressing the underlying objective of the interchange of people as well as food and other gifts.

Individual adoptions were generally to replace members of a community who had been killed or had died. Hans Kelsen writes on this point:

> Since the individual is nothing but a member of his group, he can be replaced by another one. . . . Hence the institution of adoption, widespread among primitive peoples, especially the Indians. Its function is to replace the deceased member of the group by a living individual. (*Society and Nature*, p. 13)

The interchange of children, which is also called "fosterage," was not permanent and did not change their natal kinship ties. Where adoption was permanent, a ritual was required to make the individual a member of the blood-kin group. In an article by Hartland on "Adoption" we are told:

> Artificial kinship is a well-recognized and widely practised mode of strengthening societies founded, as savage and barbarous societies are, on real or pretended community of blood. By means of artificial kinship, strangers are adopted into a clan or kindred. Various methods are em-

ployed for this purpose, of which the most celebrated is the Blood Covenant. (*Encyclopedia of Religion and Ethics,* vol. I, p. 105)

The practice of "adopting" the enemy captured alive on the battlefield represents a signal departure from the earlier practice of killing him. According to Morgan, "Captives when adopted were often assigned in the family the places of deceased persons slain in battle, in order to fill up the broken ranks of relatives" (*Ancient Society,* p. 80). After the rise of patriarchal class society, captives were no longer adopted as kinship equivalents; they were seized as slaves. To the matriarchal savages, however, "adoption" furnished the ultimate means for converting death exchange into life exchange.

In the end, after all the travail and struggle to find a road out of the blood vengeance obligation, even the psychology and behavior of men changed radically. The practice of hosts hurling bunches of taro and other food at their guests, or of guests arriving in war regalia singing war songs, fell into disuse. Similarly, the blustering, swaggering, insulting attitudes struck in the song, dance, and drama combats gave way to politeness, courtesy, and self-deprecation. Herskovits gives one example of this:

> When a man visited his relatives living in another village, he was honored by a feast and a dance, the most important feature of which was the exchange of complimentary remarks between the principals and the enumeration of the gifts each was about to make the other. Here deprecation of one's own contribution and extravagant praise for what was received were the order of the day. (*Economic Anthropology,* p. 164)

In other regions, most notably old China, self-deprecation took the form of a "contest" in courtesy. Huizinga writes:

> Competition for honour may also take, as in China, an inverted form by turning into a contest in politeness. The special word for this — *jang* — means literally "to yield to another"; hence one demolishes one's adversary by superior manners, making way for him or giving him precedence. The courtesy-match is nowhere as formalized, perhaps, as in China, but it is to be met with all over the world.

He adds, "We might call it an inverted boasting-match, since the reason for this display of civility to others lies in an intense regard for one's own honour" (*Homo Ludens,* p. 66). Even so, it is quite an advance if a man's honor is satisfied with a courtesy bow, when formerly it could only be satisfied when he raised his bow to shoot.

However, the gift-giving system had other aspects than these courtesies. Before it passed out of history it led to human sacrifice, on the principle that to sacrifice a portion would preserve the whole.

From Punishment to Self-Punishment

Under the code of the blood brotherhood in its early form, those who were held responsible for the death of a kinsman must suffer the punishment of death to one of their members. Subsequently this blood reprisal was reduced; a portion of the man's body became a surrogate for killing the man. Finally, savages found another device — self-mutilation and self-punishment.

When the death of a man was the price of peace, a community would offer up one of its own members as the scapegoat or sacrificial victim to avert a revenge expedition and its bloody consequences. John Layard gives an illustration from Malekula, a region where cannibalistic practices prevailed up to recent times. He writes that the men seize one of their own members, "truss him up like a pig, decorate him for sacrifice, and send him to the enemy, those who deliver him bearing a cycas leaf, emblem of peace." He adds:

> As a rule, the victim is sent, if possible, alive, and it is said that the enemy thus appeased force him to dig a pit for the fire in which he is to be roasted, and then sacrifice him with all the ritual due to an enemy captured in battle, and then eat him. Sometimes, however, he may be killed first. . . . The process may not seem very pretty from our point of view, but it at least prevents further bloodshed. . . . (*Stone Men of Malekula,* pp. 599-600)

Other reports show it was not always necessary to seize someone to serve as the victim; very often a man would voluntarily deliver himself, thereby paying with his life to redeem the other members of his community from blood reprisal. In the course of time a substitute was found for the human victim in the form of an animal, usually a pig. In Malekula the tusked boar was the preeminent sacrificial animal, and the aborigines explicitly state that the pig is the substitute for the former sacrifice of human beings.

This practice has left innumerable survivals. On every occasion that required such a ritual, not only at deaths but also at marriages and general peace ceremonies, an animal or fowl was sacrificed to commemorate the occasion. Driberg, writing about some African tribes, gives an example of a peace pact:

> An animal is sacrificed between the two armies, and selected portions publicly eaten by the representatives. Its carcass may be buried and with it several articles symbolizing the new peace. A hatchet may thus be buried, or a spear after it has been broken in two to emphasize the pacific intentions of the combatants. Solemn curses are then pronounced on any who break the peace. (*At Home with the Savage,* p. 169)

Cutting off finger joints was a common form of self-punishment. Evidently this practice has a very long history. Stenciled hands on the rock face of European caves date back to the upper paleolithic period, perhaps thirty thousand years ago; according to Grahame Clark, "Upwards of 200 hands are outlined by coloring matter on the rock face, and many show fingers apparently cut short at the tip or middle joint."

He says that among the numerous primitive peoples who practice analogous mutilations different reasons are given, but often it represents "a sacrifice to avert further deaths." Among some tribes of northwest Canada, the little finger is commonly sacrificed, as they say, "to cut off the deaths" (*From Savagery to Civilization,* p. 60).

Hocart likewise refers to the "prints of hands with joints missing" that have been found in paleolithic caves. "So many joints are missing in these prints that many archaeologists refuse to believe they were really amputated," he writes, indicating his own doubts on the matter. Nevertheless he notes that the same practice occurs in Fiji and that the idea seems to be "that the joints are sacrificed in lieu of the whole person" (*The Progress of Man,* pp. 157-58). In fact, similar practices have been found in primitive regions all over the globe.

Thomas cites Williams on the Friendly Islanders who frequently cut off one or more of the bones of their little fingers. "This was so common that scarcely an adult could be found who had not in this way mutilated his hands." He gives the following poignant example:

> On one occasion, the daughter of a chief, a fine young woman about eighteen years of age, was standing by my side, and as I saw by the state of the wound that she had recently performed the ceremony, I took her hand, and asked her why she had cut off her finger. Her affecting reply was, that her mother was ill, and that, fearful lest her mother should die, she had done this to induce the gods to save her. "Well," I said, "how did you do it?" "Oh," she replied, "I took a sharp shell, and worked it about until the joint was separated, and then I allowed the blood to stream from it. This was my offering to persuade the gods to restore my mother." When, at a future period, another offering is required, they sever the second joint of the same finger; and when a third or a fourth is demanded, they amputate the same bones of the other little finger; and when they have no more joints which they can conveniently spare, they rub the stumps of their mutilated fingers with rough stones, until the blood again streams from the wound. (*Primitive Behavior*, pp. 302-03)

Self-inflicted lacerations served the same purpose as the cutting off of finger joints and other parts of the body. These are often called "mourning rites" and are sometimes found in combination with funerary sports and games. Frazer says, "In Fortuna, an island of the South Pacific, when a death has taken place friends express their grief by cutting their faces, breast, and arms with shells, and at the funeral festival which follows pairs of boxers commonly engage in combats by way of honouring the deceased" (*The Golden Bough*, Part III, *The Dying God*, p. 97).

The practice persisted in the Olympic games and even into Roman times, according to Frazer:

> Thus the Olympic games were supposed to have been founded in honour of Pelops, the great legendary hero, who had a sacred precinct at Olympia, where he was honoured above all the other heroes and received annually

the sacrifice of a black ram. Once a year, too, all the lads of Peloponnese are said to have lashed themselves on his grave at Olympia, till the blood streamed down their backs, as a libation to the departed hero. Similarly at Roman funerals the women scratched their faces till they bled. . . . (*The Golden Bough*, Part III, *The Dying God*, p. 92)

Gradually the mutilations, gashes, and bloodlettings were replaced by milder forms of self-punishment in atoning for deaths, such as weeping, wailing, keening, etc., with only an occasional scratching of one's face or tearing of one's hair. The weeping ritual was often accompanied by an embracing ritual. Radcliffe-Brown writes that among the Andamanese "the weeping is obligatory, a matter of duty," and it takes place not only upon a death but also at marriages and initiations.

The weeping on the occasions enumerated is therefore not a spontaneous expression of individual emotion but is an example of what I have called ceremonial customs. In certain circumstances men and women are required by custom to embrace one another and weep, and if they neglected to do so it would be an offence condemned by all right-thinking persons. (*The Andaman Islanders*, pp. 244, 240)

These weeping and embracing rituals had the same object as self-mutilation — to avert the reopening of hostilities when deaths occurred. In the end they left a relic in the form of "mourning rites."

One of the numerous relics of hostility-hospitality reciprocity is the way Central Eskimos welcome strangers. As the guest slowly approaches, "one of his hosts gives him a severe blow and awaits a blow in return, and an exchange of blows continues until one of the combatants yields." After this the stranger is welcomed with a feast. Among the Eskimos of Cumberland Inlet, "after having exchanged blows, they kiss one another, and the stranger is hospitably received by all" (*Encyclopedia of Religion and Ethics*, vol. XI, p. 888).

With the expansion of food and gift interchange, the fraternal relations established on a local scale moved outward in a widening circle. Interchange began as the connective tissue uniting separate hordes into the network of clans and phratries comprising the tribe. The system then passed beyond the relatively narrow limits of the dual organization, converting more distant strangers from enemies to friends.

For an understanding of this aspect of the interchange system we are largely indebted to Malinowski and his study of the Kula exchange system in the Trobriand Islands.

The Kula "Ring" — Intertribal Interchange

Bronislaw Malinowski's study of the kula exchange system, described in *Argonauts of the Western Pacific*, has been acclaimed as a major contribution to anthropology. Although he did not draw some of the most significant conclusions from his findings, his data shows the interchange system at its peak of development.

Within a tribe, interchange took place between segments: between parallel clans and between the two opposite moieties or phratries that formed the dual organization. But once the interchange system broke out of these boundaries, it came to embrace other tribes, taking the form of a "ring" encompassing the "four quarters" of their known world.

Malinowski defines the kula as "a form of exchange, of extensive, inter-tribal character; it is carried on by communities inhabiting a wide ring of islands, which form a closed circuit" (p. 81). Two types of articles are passed around from one group to another in this circuit; one consists of red shell necklaces and the other of white shell armbands or bracelets. Both are standardized, easily made articles.

Among the features of the kula that have puzzled anthopologists is the fact that the articles are not permanently owned by any individual or group; they are merely held for a time and then passed on to other individuals and groups in the circuit. They are in continuous circulation, passing from hand to hand, from group to group, around the ring with the one article going in a clockwise direction, the other crossing it in a counter-clockwise direction.

Another seeming oddity is the worthlessness of these articles from a commercial standpoint. Malinowski describes them as "ugly, useless, ungainly, even tawdry." Through constant handling they are "worn-out . . . clumsy to sight and greasy to touch" (pp. 88-89). Yet they are valued, even "reverenced," above everything else. It seems that without the circulation of these articles life itself would come to a halt.

... this simple action—this passing from hand to hand of two meaningless and quite useless objects—has somehow succeeded in becoming the foundation of a big intertribal institution, in being associated with ever so many other activities. Myth, magic and tradition have built up around it definite ritual and ceremonial forms, have given it a halo of romance and value in the minds of the natives, have indeed created a passion in their hearts for this simple exchange. (p. 86)

Malinowski is torn by conflicting considerations on how to analyze the phenomenon. Can it be called a trading network? The objects are worthless and in any case never pass into private ownership. On the other hand, Malinowski thinks it may be a "form of trade" in the widest sense of the term (pp. 84-85). In the end he draws a somewhat tortured analogy between these worthless, ugly objects and the British crown jewels, which embody in themselves vast wealth. Malinowski decides that both are revered for their "historic sentimentalism" as heirlooms (p. 89).

In fact, the kula is not a trade relation, not even in the most elementary form, barter. Malinowski himself admits that, while barter exists in the Trobriand Islands, the aborigines make a clear distinction between it and the kula. While in barter haggling occurs, kula gifts are "never discussed, bargained about and computed." He writes:

> The natives sharply distinguish it from barter, which they practise extensively, of which they have a clear idea, and for which they have a settled term—in Kiriwinian: *gimwali.* Often, when criticising an incorrect, too hasty, or indecorous procedure of Kula, they will say, "He conducts his Kula as if it were *gimwali.*" (p. 96)

How, then, should the kula be analyzed? Mauss calls it a kind of "grand potlatch" based on "a vast system of prestations and counter-prestations." It seems, he says, "as if all these tribes, the economic, ritual and sexual services, the men and the women, were caught in a ring around which they kept up a regular movement in time and space" (*The Gift*, pp. 25, 20). The kula ring is the most extensive form of the interchange system, embracing tribes hundreds of miles apart. The necklaces and bracelets are the symbols of fraternity and peace that maintain the unity and solidarity of "the ring." Malinowski himself describes the kula in this sense:

> We see that all around the ring of Kula there is a network of relationships, and that naturally the whole forms one interwoven fabric. Men living at hundreds of miles' sailing distance from one another are bound together by direct or intermediate partnership, exchange with each other, know of each other, and on certain occasions meet in a large inter-tribal gathering. . . . It is a vast, inter-tribal net of relationships, a big institution, consisting of thousands of men, all bound together by one common passion for Kula exchange, and secondarily by many minor ties and interests. (*Argonauts of the Western Pacific*, p. 92)

Thus the kula represents the symbolical or ritualistic act of interchange, in which the necklaces and bracelets are passed from group to group to reaffirm peace, friendship, and cooperation among them. This ritual was the sanction for the visits and counter-visits that were periodically made between the groups and for the actual gift-exchanges that followed in their wake. The result was a continuous line of gift-giving and receiving, of exchange and counter-exchange of food, products, magic, marriages, and everything necessary to sustain life on a fraternal basis.

Generosity was the keynote of the social relationships built up through the interchange system. Malinowski takes exception to the idea that savages are motivated by the spirit of "grab and never let go," which is the characteristic spirit of our society. With them "quite the reverse is the case," he writes; "with them to possess is to give — and here the natives differ from us notably." He concludes: "Meanness, indeed, is the most despised vice, and the only thing about which the natives have strong moral views, while generosity is the essence of goodness" (ibid., pp. 96-97).

There was no other way for savage men to liberate themselves from the fears and insecurities of their times than through such a system of generosity and hospitality. The intertribal interchange system was in effect a "lifeline" of social solidarity between masses of men who had formerly distrusted, feared, and fought one another.

Malinowski's description of the great overseas expeditions

to "kula" with the feared foreigners, and the solemn and careful preparations made for them, discloses the danger and heroism involved. The most spectacular featured as many as a hundred big war-canoes and covered distances of a hundred miles or more over shark-infested seas. It is difficult to say which dangers the savages feared the most — sharks, shipwreck, or the foreign men with whom they were preparing to kula. Malinowski describes their ambivalent attitude on this score. The greater the distance involved in an expedition, the more elaborate were the magical rituals and precautions taken to ward off dangers.

The same apprehension was manifested by the men who played host. Two generations ago, says Malinowski, an observer watching the landing of such a huge fleet and noting the atmosphere charged with anxiety, dread, awe, and magical incantations, might have concluded that he was about to see "one of those big onslaughts in which the existence of whole villages and tribes were wiped out" (ibid., p. 44).

Now, however, these were not war-canoes but gift-canoes, and the sailors were not invaders but invited guests. All these seagoing expeditions and counter-expeditions were conducted on a well-regulated basis, known in advance to the host tribe and in due course reciprocated by them. What, then, accounts for their extreme apprehension upon the arrival of a fleet of men armed with nothing more lethal than some worn-out necklaces and bracelets? As Malinowski puts it:

> It seems absurd, from the rational point of view, that the natives, who know that they are expected, indeed, who have been invited to come, should yet feel uncertain about the good will of their partners, with whom they have so often traded, whom they have received in visit, and themselves visited and re-visited again and again. Coming on a customary and peaceful errand, why should they have any apprehensions of danger, and develop a special magical apparatus to meet the natives of Dobu? (ibid., p. 345)

The natives explained to Malinowski the reasons for their trepidation, which he duly reports without grasping the implications:

> As I sat there, looking towards the Southern mountains, so clearly visible, yet so inaccessible, I realize what must be the feelings of the Trobrianders. . . . For there, to the

west of the Amphletts, they see the big bay of Gabu, where once the crews of a whole fleet of Trobriand canoes were killed and eaten by the inhabitants of unknown villages, in attempting to *kula* with them. And stories are also told of single canoes, drifted apart from the fleet and cast against the northern shore of Fergusson Island, of which all the crew perished at the hands of the cannibals. . . .

Sailing has to be done, so to speak, on straight lines across the sea. . . . Not only that, but they must sail between fixed points on the land. For, and this of course refers to the olden days, if they had to go ashore anywhere but in the district of a friendly tribe, the perils which met them were almost as bad as those of reefs and sharks. If the sailors missed the friendly villages of the Amphletts and of Dobu, everywhere else they would meet with extermination. (ibid., pp. 221-22)

The dangers therefore consisted, first in trying to establish kula interchange relations with distant strangers and enemies, and then in reaffirming these relations through periodical visits and counter-visits. Both cannibalism and death reprisals faced these culture-heroes as they sailed forth on their mission to expand the ring of fraternity.

By the time Malinowski arrived to study the aborigines, the worst dangers were behind them. But in a region recently emerged from cannibalism and death reprisals, a few generations were not sufficient to remove all the remaining distrust between tribes situated at great distances from one another. Hence the elaborate precautions and magical preparations that preceded every big overseas expedition, and from the other side the equally careful rituals performed by the hosts when the huge fleets of men landed on their shores as guests.

Commenting on one such expedition to Dobu, a native explained to Malinowski:

"The Dobu man is not good as we are. He is fierce, he is a man-eater! When we come to Dobu, we fear him, we might kill us. But see! I spit the charmed ginger root, and their mind turns. They lay down their spears, they receive us well." (ibid., p. 346)

Notwithstanding the magic of the ginger, it is apparent that gingerly behavior was considered good form after the men landed to allay any suspicion as to the object of their visit:

It is the customary rule that the Trobrianders should be received first with a show of hostility and fierceness; treated almost as intruders. But this attitude entirely subsides after the visitors have ritually spat over the village on their arrival. (ibid.)

The final practical step is carried out by the Dobu women, who "take the spears away" from their men, after which tensions subside and everyone relaxes.

Along with the food and gift interchanges, sex interchange was one of the rewards for the men who had braved the hazards of a kula expedition. These sexual relations are often called "marriages." According to Malinowski, the armshells or bracelets were conceived as a female principle and the necklaces as a male principle. "When two of the opposite valuables meet in the Kula and are exchanged, it is said these two have married" (ibid., p. 356). But Mauss reports the more pungent expression of the aborigines, who say, "We have given armshells and necklaces and they will come and they will meet, like dogs which come to sniff" (*The Gift,* p. 24).

How little these "marriages" resemble our own can be seen in an interesting legend told to Malinowski by the Trobrianders. According to this report, some men from Boyowa were blown off course on a kula expedition and stranded on the coast of Kaytalugi. "There, having survived the first reception, they were apportioned individually and married." After a time, the guests repaired their canoes and set sail for their home shores.

According to Malinowski, these sailors already had "wives" in their own localities. When they arrived back home "they found their women married to other men." Happily, says Malinowski, "Such things never end tragically in the Trobriands. As soon as their rightful lords reappeared their women came back to them" (*Argonauts of the Western Pacific,* pp. 223-24). If some did not return we may surmise that the deprived "lords" soon found replacements, just as the "wives" they had left behind them did.

It is a common mistake to view the casual sex relations among primitive peoples as though they were all "marriages." Sex interchange was part and parcel of the social interchange system, and this remained the case even after the first more permanent pair-matrimonies came into existence. As we have seen, pair-cohabitation could not begin until fraternal relations had been firmly established between the men of the intermarrying communities.

Malinowski's report shows how, before a man visiting a distant community could "marry" a woman there, he first had to submit to what might be called a period of "probation" under the surveillance of her male kinsmen. During this period he was confined to the male sector or clubhouse of the community:

> It is quite customary for men from the Trobriands to remain for a long time in the Amphletts, that is, from one expedition to another. For some weeks or even months, they lived in the house of their partner, friend or relative, careful to keep to the customs of the country. They will sit about with the men of the village and talk. They will help in the work and go out on fishing expeditions. (ibid., p. 272)

According to Malinowski, the Trobriander would probably find his sojourn in the Amphletts "uncongenial." Accustomed to "easy intrigues" in his own country, "here he has completely to abstain not only from sexual relations with women married or unmarried, but even from moving with them socially." He is "entirely debarred from any intercourse with women" (ibid., p. 272). The natives explain why they abide by these restrictions; they fear the *bowo'u,* the local sorcerers, who might give them a sound thrashing.

Gradually, through continuous good behavior on the part of the suitor, the rules of avoidance were relaxed. Once the male kinsmen were satisfied that the suitor had no hostile intentions toward any members of the community, he was free to approach women. Even then, as Malinowski points out, some men never succeeded in securing a "wife" in the distant region.

In the Trobriands as elsewhere, when a woman agreed to a proposal, she signified this by accepting a token gift from the man. This might be a piece of betel, a tobacco leaf, a shell, or some other symbolic item. Malinowski misunderstood this act of interchange between the pair; he viewed these tokens of peace and friendship as "luxuries" secured by the woman through the sale of her sexual favors:

> Disinterested love is quite unknown among these people of great sexual laxity. Every time a girl favours her lover, some small gift has to be given immediately. This is the case in the normal intrigues, going on every night in the village between unmarried girls and boys, and also in

> more ceremonial cases of indulgence, like the *katuyausi*
> custom, or the mortuary consolations. . . . A few areca-
> nuts, some betel pepper, a bit of tobacco, some turtle-shell
> rings, or spondylus discs, such are the small tokens of
> gratitude and appreciation never omitted by the youth. An
> attractive girl need never go unprovided with the small
> luxuries of life. (ibid., p. 182)

The fact is that such commonplace items as betel nut, tobacco,
shells, etc., are not luxuries to the woman. She does not have
to be attractive to a man to receive things that are in plentiful
supply and at her own disposal. It is her *act of receiving*
these things, not the things, which is of crucial importance.
When a woman accepts the token she is accepting the proposal
of sexual intercourse from the man, while he in turn is signifying by the same token that his intentions toward her kinsmen
are of the friendliest.

The man, far from "providing" the woman with luxuries, is
himself "provided for" in the critical matter of protection. For
once a woman has accepted the man as her lover she will
see to it that he is not harassed or injured by her brothers
in the event of a momentary flareup of hostility.

The kula of the Trobriand Islands is not the only example
of intertribal interchange; it is simply the one that has received
the most intensive study. On the North American continent,
the Iroquois designated their League of Tribes as the "Great
Peace" and spread their fraternal relations over tremendous
distances. Here, too, the interchange of shells furnished the symbol for the social intercourse between the tribes, and periodic
festivals were held to affirm these peace pacts.

Relics of this fraternal "ring-making" have survived to the
present day, although they are often almost unrecognizable
in their decayed forms. Margaret Mead tells of Arapesh men
"walking about to find rings." She writes that a "mountain
man" will walk a whole day inland to receive a gift from a
"plainsman" and then walk two days back in the opposite
direction toward the sea to present the gift to a "beach friend."
She, too, takes this to be some kind of peculiar trading for
the purpose of making a "profit," even though this contradicts
her statement that their whole system is founded upon "voluntary gift-giving" (*Sex and Temperament,* pp. 10-11).

Today the little gold circlet or wedding ring is exclusively
associated with marriage. But this may be a vestige of its more
ancient symbolism. Among the Arapesh, Mead tells us, peace

is restored after a fight through the exchange of rings, each man giving a ring to the man he has wounded (*Sex and Temperament,* p. 24).

Now let us examine the part played by women in the interchange system.

Women's Role in Peace-Exchange

Bachofen wrote that "matriarchal states were particularly famed for their freedom from intestine strife and conflict." He pointed in particular to the "great festivals" at which many different peoples joined together and "delighted in a sense of brotherhood" (*Myth, Religion and Mother Right,* p. 80). However, few anthropologists have detailed the part played by women in creating this peace interchange and brothership among men.

There are innumerable reports about what the men do at the corroborees, festivals, or peace pacts. They slaughter pigs or other animals (or humans); they engage in regulated or sham fights; they compete in games and perform magic rituals; they count out gifts and hurl or give them to their guests; they burn or destroy a portion of the gifts; and they bury the hatchet or smoke the peace pipe together ceremonially. But how many reports tell that women made the gifts and gave them to the men to give to other men in return for peace and friendship? And how many anthropologists have written about the influence of the women at these momentous celebrations?

This deficiency can be seen in Malinowski's study of the Trobriand kula. He writes:

> . . . the position of women among them is by no means characterised by oppression or social insignificance. They have their own sphere of influence, which, in certain cases and in certain tribes, is of great importance. The Kula, however, is essentially a man's type of activity. . . . women do not sail on the big expeditions. From Kiriwina young, unmarried girls would sail East to Kitava, Iwa, and Gawa, and from these Islands even old, married women, indeed whole families come to Kiriwina. But they do not carry on overseas Kula exchange, neither among themselves, nor with men. (*Argonauts of the Western Pacific,* p. 280)

This and other brief statements tell us little or nothing about women's role in the kula. It is reported that a man sends his "wife" with a kula gift to another man, but the reason for this female intermediary is left obscure. Again, Malinowski writes that old women he calls "chief's wives" sometimes "interpolate" themselves into the kula transaction. In one instance it was to transmit the item from a chief to his son. "This interpolation gives the women much pleasure, and is highly valued by them," he writes. "In fact, at that time I heard more about that than about all the rest of the exchanges associated with this overseas trip" (ibid., p. 281). But Malinowski does not tell us what he heard.

It is not difficult to understand why the kula was a man's activity. Women were not the hunters and warriors. Women were not suspicious and fearful of other women, even those who were not of their own kin, despite their ignorance of natural death. There is no indication that women had any difficulty communicating with stranger-women even in the most remote epoch of social evolution. From the record it appears that women always had the capacity to band together for mutual cooperation and protection. To the present day the characteristic picture of primitive women shows them working together in amiability and enjoying one another's company.

An example of the cooperative, sisterly relations among women in New Guinea is given by Margaret Mead in *Sex and Temperament in Three Primitive Societies:*

> Tchambuli women work in blocks, a dozen of them together, plaiting the great mosquito-bags from the sale of which most of the *talibun* and *kina* are obtained. They cook together for a feast, their clay fireplaces (circular pots with terraced tops, which can be moved from place to place) set side by side. Each dwelling-house contains some dozen to two dozen fire-places, so that no woman need cook in a corner alone. The whole emphasis is upon comradeship, efficient, happy work enlivened by continuous brisk banter and chatter. (p. 252)

She contrasts this behavior of the women with that of men, where "there is always strain, watchfulness, a catty remark here, a *double entendre* there"; in short, where suspicion and hostility lurk under the surface of fraternal relations. She adds:

And whereas the lives of the men are one mass of petty bickering, misunderstanding, reconciliation, avowals, disclaimers, and protestations accompanied by gifts, the lives of the women are singularly unclouded with personalities or with quarrelling. For fifty quarrels among the men, there is hardly one among the women. Solid, preoccupied, powerful, with shaven unadorned heads, they sit in groups and laugh together, or occasionally stage a night dance at which, without a man present, each woman dances vigorously all by herself the dance-step that she has found to be most exciting. Here again the solidarity of women, the inessentialness of men, is demonstrated. (p. 257)

It is the women who do the work and make the things that the men interchange with one another. Mead writes, "The minor war-and-peace that goes on all the time among the men, the feelings that are hurt and must be assuaged, are supported by the labour and contributions of the women." At the festivals which repair the easily-ruptured relations among men, the women do the work while the men play the games.

Mead writes, "These festivals are a break in the vigorous workaday life of the women. Swift-footed, skilful-fingered, efficient, they pass back and forth from their fish-traps to their basket-plaiting, from their cooking to their fish-traps, brisk, good-natured, impersonal. Jolly comradeship, rough, very broad jesting and comment, are the order of the day" (p. 257). About the men's performances and games she writes, "The women's attitude towards the men is one of kindly tolerance and appreciation. They enjoy the games that the men play, they particularly enjoy the theatricals that the men put on for their benefit. A big masked show is the occasion for much pleasure" (p. 255).

It is not surprising, then, that the men, who are so dependent upon the women for food and other necessities of life, should be so concerned with how women look upon them. As Mead puts it, "What the women will think, what the women will say, what the women will do, lies at the back of each man's mind as he weaves his tenuous and uncertain web of insubstantial relations with other men. Each man stands alone, playing his multiplicity of parts, sometimes allied with one man, sometimes with another; but the women are a solid group, confused by no rivalries, brisk, patronizing, and jovial" (pp. 263-64).

Mead's report is significant because it is one of the few to show the maturity and power of primitive women in guiding the affairs of the community. Women played the key role in making men into brothers and teaching them how to make brothers and brothers-in-law out of other men. It was the women who labored to amass the food and boiled it in huge pots for the feasts, and who toiled to accumulate the baskets, blankets, pots, shell ornaments, and other things to be interchanged at the festivals. In short, it was the women's labor that created the gifts that converted enemies into friends.

The women played a role in peace alliances not only through the food and gift interchange but also through the interchange of sexual partners. In the period of the dual organization, the women of one side made connubial agreements with the women of the other side for the intermating of their daughters and sons when they grew up. D. D. Kosambi, writing about the survival of this practice in India, calls it "exchange-intercourse in 'bread and daughters'" (*Ancient India*, p. 50).

The ritual by which such an intermating agreement was sealed has survived in some parts of India. Briffault describes it:

> The collective connubial relations of Nayar women, though attended with little or no formality, were preceded by a ceremony, the tying of the "tali," which was performed on Nayar girls before the age of eleven. The "tali" is a small gold leaf through which a hole is bored with the finger, and which is tied round the neck of the girl. The rite is not peculiar to the Nayars, but is general among Dravidian races in India. Very similar customs are observed by other peoples. (*The Mothers*, vol. I, p. 707)

The part played by sex interchange is a little-known aspect of the primitive interchange system. This is largely due to the modern puritanical outlook on female sexuality, and to the reluctance of men in patriarchal society to acknowledge the independence and freedom of primitive women in sexual intercourse. That this independence existed cannot be doubted if one reads the reports of settlers and missionaries; they were quite offended by it.

One example can be found in the complaints of Father Jacob Baegert, who reported on the Southern California Indians about two hundred years ago:

They met without any formalities, and their vocabulary did not even contain the words "to marry," which is expressed at the present day in the Waicuri language by the paraphrase *tikere undiri*—that is, "to bring the arms or hands together." They had, and still use, a substitute for the word "husband," but the etymological meaning of that expression implies an intercourse with women in general. ("An Account . . . ," in *Reader in General Anthropology*, p. 73)

The good padre complained that the women were independent and "not much inclined to obey their lords," and that after the wedding ceremony at the mission "the new married couple start off in different directions . . . as if they were not more to each other to-day than they were yesterday. . . ." Worst of all, they failed to suffer from shame, fear, jealousy, or guilt about their sexual freedom:

They lived, in fact, before the establishment of the missions in their country, in utter licentiousness, and adultery was daily committed by every one without shame and without any fear, the feeling of jealousy being unknown to them. Neighbouring tribes visited each other very often only for the purpose of spending some days in open debauchery, and during such times a general prostitution prevailed. (ibid., p. 73)

It is a common misconception of men trained in patriarchal attitudes and concepts to mistake the free sexual relations of primitive peoples with the prostitution or "paid relations" that arose only after patriarchal class society came into existence. Thus we find references to "orgies," "debaucheries," "Saturnalia," "abandonment to vile passions," and the like. As a result, in reports of intergroup festivals, there are many descriptions of the men's simulated battles and massacres but few accounts of the "love dances" between men and women that followed.

Ernst Grosse gives a description of an Australian corroboree. In essence it is a dramatic representation of the history of the interchange system—how it began with the death talio between men and wound up with the intermating alliance of men and women.

In the simulated battle, the male dancers brandish weapons and clubs and appear to be breaking one another's skulls.

The women participate as sideliners, singing loud and soft and beating time with their hands. However, while there are no reservations in detailing the war dance and its simulated massacre, the same is not true of the love dance, as Grosse notes:

> The love dances of the Australians are passed over in most accounts with a few suggestive references. They are hardly suitable for exhaustive descriptions. . . . "I have seen dances," writes Hodgkinson, "which consist of the most repulsive of obscene motions that any one can imagine, and although I was alone in the darkness, and nobody observed my presence, I was ashamed to be a witness of such abomination." (*The Beginnings of Art,* pp. 219-20)

Radcliffe-Brown reports the ceremony in the Andaman Islands in which two hostile groups made peace with each other. He describes a picturesque pantomime-dance of mild punishment and reconciliation:

> When the two groups have agreed to make friends and bring their quarrel to an end, arrangements are made for this ceremony. The arrangements are made through the women of the two parties. . . . The women of the camp keep a look-out for the approach of the visitors. When they are known to be near the camp, the women sit down on one side of the dancing ground, and the men take up positions in front of the decorated cane. Each man stands with his back against the *koro-cop,* with his arms stretched out sideways along the top of it. None of them has any weapons.
>
> The visitors, who are, if we may so put it, the forgiving party, while the home party are those who have committed the last act of hostility, advance into the camp dancing. . . . The women of the home party mark the time of the dance by clapping their hands on their thighs. . . . The visitors dance forward in front of the men standing at the *koro-cop,* and then, still dancing all the time, pass backwards and forwards between the standing men, bending their heads as they pass beneath the suspended cane. The dancers make threatening gestures at the men standing at the *koro-cop* . . . [who] stand silent and motionless, and are expected to show no sign of fear.
>
> After they have been dancing thus for a little time, the

leader of the dancers approaches the man at the end of the *koro* and, taking him by the shoulders from the front, leaps vigorously up and down to the time of the dance, thus giving the man he holds a good shaking. The leader then passes on to the next man in the row while another of the dancers goes through the same performance with the first man. This is continued until each of the dancers has "shaken" each of the standing men. The dancers then pass under the *koro* and shake their enemies in the same manner from the back. After a little more dancing the dancers retire, and the women of the visiting group come forward and dance in much the same way that the men have done, each woman giving each of the men of the other group a good shaking.

When the women have been through their dance the two parties of men and women sit down and weep together.

The two groups remain camped together for a few days, spending the time in hunting and dancing together. Presents are exchanged, as at the ordinary meetings of different groups. The men of the two groups exchange bows with one another. (*The Andaman Islanders,* pp. 134-35)

The "good shaking" performed as a dance is a substitute for more lethal methods of settling grievances in the past. But this report is especially significant because it does not overlook the part played by the women in effecting the peace-pact through the artistic device of a peace dance. As Radcliffe-Brown writes, "All peace negotiations were conducted through the women. One or two of the women of the one group would be sent to interview the women of the other group to see if they were willing to forget the past and make friends" (ibid., p. 85).

Earlier anthropologists, such as A. W. Howitt, referred to the women peace negotiators as "ambassadors." Writing about the Australian tribes, Howitt says that on ordinary occasions the messenger sent to call together a tribal council is an old man. "But in any other matter which might be attended by danger, or where treachery is feared, it is not men but women who are sent." He then describes the various measures taken by the female ambassadors to restore peace:

On such occasions, it is thoroughly understood that the women are to use every influence in their power to obtain a successful issue for their mission, and are therefore free

of their favors. . . . If the mission is successful, there is
a time of license between its members and the tribe, or
part of a tribe, to which it has been sent. . . . The license
is not regarded with any jealousy by the women of the
tribe to which the mission is sent. It is taken as a matter
of course. They know of it, but do not see it, as it occurs
in a place apart from the camp.

The members of such a mission are treated as distinguished guests. Food is provided for them, and on their
return home, after about a week's stay, they are loaded
with presents. . . . In cases where such a mission has been
successful, women of the other tribe usually accompanied it
back, to testify its approval by their tribe. . . . Agreements
so made are probably observed as faithfully as are many
treaties more formally made by civilized people. (*Native
Tribes of South-East Australia,* pp. 682-83)

Howitt's report differs from the usual accounts of peace negotiations where, if women are mentioned at all, it is in an
incidental or even derogatory manner. In describing the peace
negotiations of the Ona of Tierra del Fuego, Chapple and
Coon say that the side suing for peace "sends an old woman,
not worth capturing, to the hostile camp" to transmit the
message (*Principles of Anthropology,* pp. 619-20). In fact, the
woman goes to make peace not because she is worthless but
because of the high esteem in which she is held by men. There
is a further practical reason for sending women on dangerous
missions; whereas a man might be killed on sight, a woman
was immune. There are not a few reports of women traveling
back and forth from their own community to that of a hostile
group with no fear of being molested. This is notably different
from civilized society, where an unescorted woman is often
regarded as sexual prey by men.

Another interesting fact about savage society is that a woman
was the best protectress of a stranger who might otherwise be
attacked by the men. Both aspects of this immunity of women
are given in an article on "Strangers" in *The Encyclopedia
of Religion and Ethics:*

In some parts of Morocco the stranger must have the escort
of some saint or woman of the country; and among the
Indians of the Goajira Peninsula women are so much
respected that a stranger protected by them may travel in

perfect security. . . . The women of the Ghils protect the stranger against the cruelty or license of the men. . . .

In New Caledonia a chief who wishes to sue for peace sends a woman with a man who has friends in the enemy's tribe to carry his proposals. The Dieri send women as ambassadors or messengers. . . . In many instances women act as envoys to hostile tribes without fear of molestation . . . and in some countries a traveler escorted by a woman and an outcast who takes refuge with a woman are treated as inviolable. (vol. XI, pp. 891-94)

Puzzled by this power of unarmed women in primitive society, the writer wonders: "Is it her office or her sex?" His answer is somewhat mystical: "It seems as if it were the mysterious sanctity attributed universally by uncultured man to womankind that operates as a protective agency." In fact, as we have seen, there were solid reasons for this enormous respect for women by "uncultured man."

Travelers, missionaries, and others, unaware of this power of primitive women to furnish safe-conduct for them, and misunderstanding their sexual invitations, have lost their lives because of it. Briffault writes that "in Madagascar a missionary closely escaped being murdered because he refused the proffered hospitality. I have heard of similar perils incurred by missionaries in New Zealand, in the early days, from the same cause" (*The Mothers,* vol. I, p. 636).

Indeed, as recently as 1955, five young American missionaries were killed in the jungles of Ecuador, which are inhabited by Stone-Age Aucas. According to the missionaries' diary, they had dropped gifts from their airplane, establishing the first contact with the aboriginal men. But they failed to understand or could not accept contact with a woman who subsequently appeared with her daughter, whom they called "Delilah," with the result that during the night they were speared to death. One of the widows later went to the same region, taking her young daughter with her, and settled there without incident. As females they were inviolable.

Long after the interchange system was displaced by the commodity-exchange system, certain holidays preserved the part played by women in peace-exchange. One of these is a ceremony called "Carrying Out the Death and Bringing in the Summer, Spring, or Life." This medieval custom still survives in some regions of Europe and elsewhere. It has been described by Frazer (*The Golden Bough,* Part III, *The Dying God,* pp.

233-40) and by George Thomson (*Aeschylus and Athens,* p. 135).

A puppet in human form called Death is pelted with stones, drowned, or torn to pieces. The actors in "Carrying Out the Death," a party of young girls and boys, take the puppet out of the village into the woods. They spend the night in the woods in "sexual license." Returning the following day, they bring back "Summer, Spring, or Life" in the form of boughs of a tree, or they set up a whole tree, in the manner of a maypole, around which they dance.

In seeking to explain its enigmatic features, some thought that the ceremony represented the death and resurrection of the god of vegetation who returns each year with a new bountiful crop. Another view has it that Death was the public scapegoat upon whom all the evils of the past year were laid and that these were expelled from the community along with Death itself. In our view the drama commemorates the victory over death-exchange through the interchange of food and gifts, the night in the forest being a relic of the former sexual interchange. Bringing in the summer, spring, and life in the form of a tree — which from time immemorial has been one of the prime symbols of womankind — is implicit recognition of the part played by women in the peacemaking interchange.

Relics of the interchange of sex continued, on an individual basis, even after marriage became a well-entrenched institution. Completely misunderstood, these have been dubbed "hospitality prostitution," "wife-exchange" or "wife-trading." In fact, at times of danger a wife would interpose herself between her husband and a stranger who otherwise might have killed each other. Briffault writes on this point:

> The participation of the guest in his host's wife is a necessary token of his friendship. . . . This practice, very inaptly called "hospitality prostitution," is not a matter of misguided benevolence, but a necessary pledge that the guest is a friend and not an enemy. For the guest to refuse is equivalent to repudiating the assumed brotherhood, and is thus tantamount to a declaration of war. (*The Mothers,* vol. I, p. 636)

In some regions woman's powers to bring about peace between men has been projected onto a different level in an attempt to mollify the angry forces of nature. Among some Eskimos, when the harsh conditions of life threaten famine, sex interchange may be invoked as a magical way of negotiating peace with nature. This aspect is described by Peter Freuchen:

> As a means of persuading nature to greater generosity, wife-trading was — in earlier days — often ordered by the *anga-kok,* the local conjurer. When the hunting had been bad, and starvation followed, the absence of game was thought to be caused by certain evil spirits, and it was up to the wise man to find out why they were offended and to try to appease them. Often he ordered a common exchange of wives. . . . If thus all the men in the village had visited all the women, and it had not improved the hunting luck, the *angakok* had to find other means of persuading the great woman who lies at the bottom of the sea and who sends out the animals to be taken for food. (*Book of the Eskimos,* p. 91)

The reputation of woman as peacemaker survived among the North American Indians up to the very last stage, the leagues of tribes. Lippert writes:

> When they wished to relate that they had intrusted the functions of peace in their confederation to the Delawares, they said that they had appointed that tribe as their wife. "We will take her into our midst; the other warring nations, however, shall be the husbands and dwell around the wife. . . . And the men shall listen to the woman and obey her." And they said to the Delawares, symbolizing the economic sphere of the women: "We herewith present you with a maize stalk and a hoe." (*Evolution of Culture,* p. 236)

The same interchange system that linked masses of men in fraternity also paved the road toward matrimonial relations between individual men and women, producing the "pairing couple."

10

The Beginnings of Marriage

When did pair-marriage begin and why did it make such a late appearance in history? This question is not asked by those who believe that marriage has always existed. But it preoccupied a number of scholars who drew a clear distinction between sex as a natural need, shared by humans and animals, and marriage as a social institution exclusive to humans.

The first step toward marriage was the cross-cousin inter-mating alliance between two communities. This was not yet marriage since the pair did not change residence or live together under one roof. The man remained a member of his clan and phratry, the woman of hers. The men of both sides received rights of passage into the territory of the other side to peacefully seek their mates.

At this stage the "hereditary enmity," as it is usually called, between the men of the two sides was at least as pronounced as the sexual association between the men and women of the two sides. Rivers, for example, tells us that the hostility between the men of the two *veves* (matrilineal moieties) in the Banks Islands and northern New Hebrides was not extinct up to our times. It was said that formerly "a man who left his own part of the house, and went over to that occupied by the other *veve* was in danger of being killed" (*History of Melanesian Society,* vol. II, p. 95). John Layard describes this same situation in Malekula:

> In the Small Islands by far the most important aspects of kinship as regards the influence on warfare is the division of each island, both geographically and socially, into two Sides mutually dependent on one another but permanently hostile. . . . These Sides in all cases have the profoundest suspicion of one another, a suspicion which is at any time liable to break out into open hostility. . . . When we con-

273

sider that at least half the population of one Side of each Island takes its wives from the other Side of the same Island the hostility may seem to us very curious. (*Stone Men of Malekula,* pp. 590-91)

Frazer was of the opinion that the totemic system contained the clues to the problem of what he saw as the "perils" surrounding sex and marriage relations. He expressed the hope that a more exact acquaintance with savage modes of thought would in time clear up this "central mystery" and disclose not only the meaning of totemism but the origin of the marriage system (*The Golden Bough,* Part VII, *Balder the Beautiful,* vol. II, p. 278).

In a way he was right. A further probing of totemism will disclose why marriage was so long delayed in coming into existence. The perils involved in this central mystery of anthropology, however, were not connected with sex as such but with a subject we have already touched upon — cannibalism.

The Strange Combination of Sex and Cannibalism

It is understandable that the members of the earliest groups, still subhuman or hominid, would be unable to understand the distinctions between themselves and other animals. Some savage groups in modern times still fail to make the distinction. Just as they conceive of non-kin humans as "animals," they attribute to animals the capacity to create for themselves a social organization the way humans do.

Lucien Levy-Bruhl observes that "the Cherokees believe that fishes live in companies like human beings, that they have their villages, their regular paths through the waters, and that they conduct themselves like beings endowed with reason" ("How Natives Think," in *The Making of Man,* p. 775). Animals were also supposed to behave like humans. Frazer quotes Mooney as follows:

. . . "in Cherokee mythology, as in that of Indian tribes generally, there is no essential difference between men and animals. . . . The animals, like the people, are organized into tribes and have like them their chiefs and townhouses, their councils and ballplays. . . . Man is still the paramount power, and hunts and slaughters the others as his own necessities compel, but is obliged to satisfy the animal tribes in every instance. . . ." (*The Golden Bough,* Part V, *Spirits of the Corn and of the Wild,* vol. II, pp. 204-05)

There are many illustrations of hunters who apologize to the animals they have killed and go through purification and expiation rituals just as they do in the case of humans killed on the battlefield. Hans Kelsen sums this up:

> Primitive man frequently regards the killing of an animal in the same way as the murder of a man. Since the exigencies of life compel him to kill animals, he tries his best to avoid the menacing retribution. In the works of Tylor, Frazer and Levy-Bruhl many examples can be found which show hunters begging the animal's pardon or trying in every way to placate the animal. After a hunting expedition, the participants, as after war against another tribe, undergo purification and expiation ceremonies. Those parts of the slain animals which have not been eaten are buried like a human body, and the same mourning ensues as for a deceased relative. (*Society and Nature,* p. 80)

Totemic alliances were made with animals as with humans. In some instances this resulted in a "tamed" animal, in others it did not. If it did not, this was proof that the "animal tribe" had broken the pledge of brotherhood and committed misdeeds which called for blood vengeance. Kelsen cites the report of the missionary, John Heckewelder, who wrote about the dialogue between an Indian and a member of a bear tribe, at which he happened to be present:

> I have already observed that the Indian includes all savage beasts within the number of his enemies. . . . A Delaware hunter once shot a huge bear and broke its backbone. The animal fell, and set up a most plaintive cry, something like that of the panther when he is hungry. The hunter, instead of giving him another shot, stood up close to him and addressed him in these words:
> "Hark ye! You are a coward, and no warrior, as you pretend to be. Were you a warrior, you would show it by your firmness and not cry and whimper like an old woman. You know, Bear, that our tribes are at war with each other, and that yours was the aggressor. You have found the Indians too powerful for you, and you have gone sneaking about in the woods, stealing their hogs; perhaps by this time you have hog's flesh in your belly. Had you conquered me, I would have borne it with courage

and died like a brave warrior; but you, Bear, sit here and cry, and disgrace your tribe by your cowardly conduct."

I was present at the delivery of this curious invective. When the hunter had dispatched the bear, I asked him how he thought that poor animal could understand what he said to it. "Oh," he said in answer, "the Bear understood me very well. Did you not observe how *ashamed* he looked while I was upbraiding him?" (*Society and Nature,* p. 27)

Frazer gives other examples of blood revenge taken by humans on animals. Among the Kukis of India, "Blood must always be shed for blood; if a tiger even kills any of them near a village, the whole tribe is up in arms and goes in pursuit of the animal." Again, among the Toradjas of Central Celebes, "blood-revenge extends to animals; a buffalo that has killed a man must be put to death." On the other hand, the rights of blood revenge exercised by humans are reciprocally extended to the animal "tribe." Frazer writes:

If a crocodile kills somebody, the family of the victim may thereupon kill a crocodile, that is to say, the murderer or some member of his family; but if more crocodiles than men are killed, then the right of revenge reverts to the crocodiles, and they are sure to exercise their right on somebody or other. (*Folklore in the Old Testament,* abr. ed., pp. 398-99)

Under circumstances where some animals are thought to be like humans, it is not surprising that some humans are thought to be like animals. This was the case in the relationship between kin and non-kin before the non-kin acquired totemic status. Under the one-sided law of exogamy, a man did not hunt, kill, or eat totem-kin, and under the same law he could not mate with his totem-kin. Andrew Lang summarizes this double taboo:

The creature from which each tribe claims descent is called "of the same flesh," while persons of another stock are "fresh flesh." A native may not marry a woman of "his own flesh"; it is only a woman of "fresh" or "strange" flesh he may marry. A man may not eat an animal of "his own flesh"; he may only eat "strange flesh." (*Myth, Ritual and Religion,* vol. I, p. 63)

This produced a paradoxical situation. One group of men killed and ate men of another group who were "strange flesh." At the same time these men, as "strange flesh," were eligible as mates for their sisters. This was the peculiar relationship that existed before the two sides of men were totemized and cross-cousin mating came into existence.

It is fortunate that at least one survival of this ancient state of affairs was studied by investigators and is now part of the anthropological record. In Alfred Metraux's book *La Religion des Tupinamba* (1928), the reports of early travelers and investigators among these Brazilian tribes since the sixteenth century are summarized in the chapter titled "The Cannibalistic Rituals of the Tupinamba."

In essence, this is a description of a regulated combat in which the men who went to battle had the objective of taking prisoners alive. For this purpose they carried ropes rolled around their bodies with which to tie them up. It is clear from the description that the engagement between the two sides was conducted according to the customary rules, with elder men acting as umpires.

After fighting at a distance for a while, the men closed in, each trying to disarm and capture an opponent. The captive belonged to the man who touched him first; a practice that is similar to "coup." In the melee some men were killed, no doubt on the basis of equivalence, after which the fight ended. Before leaving the battlefield, the dead were roasted and eaten, and the blood of the wounded captives was drunk. Some of the cooked flesh was taken back to the camp along with the captives.

For the return trip the victors tied up their captives with the ropes they had brought, saying to each one, "You are my chained-up animal." Before the heroes and their "animals" were permitted back into the community of women and children, they were placed in the usual retreat or quarantine on the outskirts, to become purified of their defilement. After this they all entered their homeground for the victory celebration.

At these ceremonies a formal speech and counter-speech took place between the captives and the victors. The captives said, "We came out as brave men should to take you and eat you — you are our enemies. The truly brave die in the country of their enemies. Our people will revenge us upon you." In return the victors replied: "You have killed many of our people, and we will exact vengeance."

After this the captives were released. They were in no way

hampered in their movements. They knew perfectly well there was no place to which they could escape even if they wanted to. Their own people, far from welcoming them, might even have killed any who attempted to escape their obligations. The men themselves felt that to be killed and eaten ceremonially was the most honorable fate for a brave, once he had been captured. Such, apparently, was the ancient spirit of reciprocity.

During the period that the captives remained alive they were, so to speak, adopted into the community. They became members in good standing, enjoying the rights and freedom accorded to honored guests. Nothing distinguished a captive from members of the community except the cord around his neck. Reports differ on the length of captivity; in some cases it was said to be many months, in others years.

Now we come to the peculiar matrimonial aspect of the affair. These captive "animals" were not only permitted but encouraged to mate with the unmarried women of the community. A request for a sister or a daughter in marriage, says Metraux, was always well received and considered very honorable. The marriage was celebrated five days after the captive's arrival.

This may shed light on a cryptic reference made by Metraux. He says that on the return trip from the battlefield to the victors' homeground, if the captives met with any women on the road they would cry out, "I, your food, am arriving." But if the word "food" is translated as "flesh," it would correspond to the double meaning inherent in the primitive term, which applied to both eating and mating. Both meanings were applicable on this occasion.

Matrimony did not save the captives from the day of reckoning, at least not all of them. The village council chose the time of execution and sent invitations to friendly communities to come and participate. Elaborate preparations were made for the festival, which lasted a number of days. At the appointed time a fire was lit and the ceremonial club shown to the captive, who even handled it for a while. Afterward the club was used to shatter his skull. We are told that morsels from the cannibal feast were shared by all, including the bereaved wife. We are also told that the same rites were practiced if, instead of a man, a jaguar was killed.

There are conflicting reports on what happened to a male child born of the union of the captive and a woman of the victorious group. Some say he was regarded as a child of the enemy and killed, sometimes on the same day as his father. Others say he was given over to the mother's brother to be reared. But daughters were thought to be of the same nature as their mothers and were usually spared.

This report spells out in detail what others only fleetingly refer to — the cannibalism that accompanied blood revenge. It appears that reciprocity in cannibalism preceded reciprocity in death exchange, and for a time the two may have coexisted. The above example indicates a combination of both. This leads to the hypothesis that the regulated combat was not only a punishment for death, but also a punishment for eating forbidden food.

The earliest totemic rule can be spelled out, as Lippert suggests, in the venerable saying of the Garden of Eden: "Ye shall not eat of it, neither shall ye touch it, lest ye die" (*Evolution of Culture,* p. 123). This first commandment was a taboo against cannibalism.

This is the answer to Frazer's "central mystery," the perils surrounding sex. It explains not only the fundamental meaning of the totemic institution, but also the origin of the marriage institution. So long as scholarly attention was focused upon sex, the more fundamental perils of food — cannibalism — could not be seen.

Totemizing the "animals" was the first step toward creating the cross-cousin relationship between men, which paved the way for the cross-cousin mating relationship between men and women. Frazer cites a myth from Australia that expresses this process:

> The Dieri tribe has a legend that mankind married promiscuously till Muramura (Good Spirit) ordered that the tribe should be divided into branches . . . the members of each division being forbidden to intermarry. The tribes of Western Victoria . . . had to introduce "fresh flesh" which could only be done by marriage with strangers; so they got their wives from a distance and hence the introduction of the pelican, snake and quail totems. (*Totemism and Exogamy*, vol. I, pp. 64-65)

This raises certain questions: If ancient hunters regarded non-kin men as "animals," was this the case also with non-kin women? Did the men kill and eat females as "strange flesh," as they did in the case of men? Despite the absence of comprehensive studies on the subject, there is sufficient direct and indirect data to suggest a negative answer.

Women and Animals

In the massacres that followed the introduction of guns and modern methods of warfare into primitive regions, there is evidence that women and children were killed, in some instances even eaten. But these were aberrations that came with the decay of the tribal system.

Among the totemic taboos placed upon young men at the time they were initiated into hunting, the most stringent were the prohibitions on "anything female." This included not only human females but animal females and the offspring of both. Along with this we have evidence that the cannibal repast was for men only, and female flesh was "abhorred as poisonous."

These facts indicate that the "tabooed woman" was all women. As the mothers, the sustainers of life, females could not be killed or eaten. This principle was inculcated first by the "milk-and-blood" mothers, then by the parallel mothers (mothers' sisters) and finally by the cross-cousin mothers (mothers-in-law). Men were surrounded by a trinity of mothers — the "Three Fates," the "Three Sisters."

Among the North American Indians the totemic names for the Three Sisters are Maize, Beans, and Squash. But whatever their names, and these are myriad, these three categories of women fashioned the building of the fratriarchy. By the same token, in the eyes of savage men women were always "human." Men on the other hand were human only through their blood kinship to the mothers; this made them brothers. But non-kin men were "animals." That was the original status of the husbands and fathers.

This hypothesis is borne out by the data. The close identity between men and animals in the eyes of savages has long been recognized and documented.

There is no equivalent documentation, however, on women having ever been conceived as "animals." On the contrary, origin myths portray women as having always been human, and where men appear they are invariably brothers or mothers' brothers. They are human because they are the blood kin of women. Husbands and fathers either do not appear at all in these origin myths or are portrayed as "animals" or "totem animals."

This theme comes forward in innumerable tales of women "married to an animal," who also give birth to "animals." These are often called "origin myths," but they are distinctly different from the earlier origin myths which tell of a sister and a brother coming up out of the ground as the maternal clan pair who created the world. The tales of the "woman married to an animal" are not origin myths as such but rather myths of the origin of marriage and the family.

The list of animals "married" to women covers the whole range of totemic animals. The most common is the dog—that easily domesticated animal which led all the rest in fulfilling obligations in totemic alliances with humans.

The following is a portion of Briffault's data on the subject:

> The clan or tribe is commonly regarded as having sprung from the union of the totem, or some other animal, with a woman. Thus, for example, the Iroquois tribes of New Netherlands regarded themselves as derived from the intercourse of women with bears, deers, or wolves. . . . The Eskimo of Smith Sound trace some of their clans to the union of a woman with a bear; other Eskimo tribes believe themselves to be descended from a woman and a dog. The Tlinkit of Alaska say that some clans sprang from the union of women with sharks. The Dene regard themselves as issued from the union of the first woman with a dog. The Ainu of Japan also believe that they are the progeny of women who had intercourse with dogs. . . . The kings of Kandy traced their origin to the union of a woman with a lion. The rajahs of Chuta Nagpur claimed to be sprung from the union of a woman with a serpent, a genealogy which is found the world over. The house of Cleves traced its descent from a woman with a swan. (*The Mothers*, vol. III, pp. 187-88)

Frazer reports the Ainu legend of the woman who had a son by a bear, "and many of them who dwell in the mountains pride themselves on being descended from a bear" (*The Golden Bough*, Part V, *Spirits of the Corn and of the Wild*, vol. II, p. 182). Franz Boas writes:

> In the tale of the origin of the cannibal society of the Bella Bella, it is told how a woman gave birth to a number of dogs, who attained the secrets of the cannibal society. This tale is found over the whole of the northwestern portion

of North America, among all the Athapascan tribes, among the Eskimo, and all along the North Pacific Coast. (*Race, Language and Culture*, p. 381)

Robertson Smith says about the Arabs that down to recent times the members of a "dog tribe" called themselves "dogs," or "brothers of dogs," or "sons of dogs" (*Kinship and Marriage*, p. 222).

As marriage evolved, the woman married to a subhuman later became a woman married to a god, a superhuman. In both instances the woman retains her human status. There are many tales of the woman married to both a dog and a god at the same time, which would indicate a transition from one to the other. Briffault observes that "in Egypt where the gods of a highly developed religion preserved to the last much of their primitive totemic animal characteristic, unions of women with the animal god were a prominent feature" (*The Mothers*, vol. III, pp. 189, 250). A final relic may be the fairy tale of Beauty and the Beast, in which the beast attains human form by marrying the woman.

In real life, however, the "animal" achieved his human form before marriage by passing through a ritual called "initiation" that gave him cross-cousin status, the first step in the development of the husband.

Rites of Passage and "Making Men"

Arnold van Gennep coined the useful term "rites of passage" to describe the primitive rituals performed on the occasion of "life crises" such as birth, initiation, marriage, and death. He divided the process into three main phases: separation, transition, and incorporation (*The Rites of Passage*, p. vii). These ceremonies involve actual "passage" from one age-group to another, from one occupation or social function to another, or from one territory to another.

The one called "initiation" is apparently the oldest of all these rites and presents the greatest enigma. It is usually thought of as a "puberty rite" marking the passage of a boy from childhood to adulthood, the primitive equivalent of the contemporary "confirmation" ceremony, which is explicitly a puberty rite. There seems to be little room for doubt that our modern ceremony is a survival in changed form of the ancient rite, but this is inadequate to explain the origin or meaning of the ancient rite.

To begin with, the primitive ritual is not limited to one occasion, the time of life when a youth reaches puberty. The farther back we go, the more the ceremony becomes a long-drawn-out series of rites which begins when a boy is only five years old and proceeds over many years before the cycle is completed. Van Gennep, among others, rejects the idea that the savage initiation ritual was only a puberty rite and says that "physical puberty cannot be the chief cause of such lengthy ceremonies extending through several stages." He concludes that "it would be better to stop calling initiation rites 'puberty rites'" (ibid., pp. 65, 68-69). How, then, shall the ceremony be analyzed?

It is sometimes called "initiation into manhood," and at other times "initiation into sex and marriage." But a closer look shows that it had very little to do with sex or marriage as such; it was almost totally concerned with "manhood." John Layard's studies of initiation in Malekula divide the ritual into two parts: "initiation into manhood" and "initiation into sex." Yet virtually all the data he gives centers upon the manhood aspect, which was a mass communal ceremony performed on every generation of young men without exception. On the other hand, initiation into sex was no more than the permission boys received, once they had become men, to seek a mate.

As Layard describes the difference between the two aspects of initiation, the hunt for sexual mates is left entirely to the individual men "according to their own desire and at a time that suits their own individual taste" (*Stone Men of Malekula,* p. 496). Thus while sex or marriage was optional for each individual man, the rite of passage into manhood was mandatory for all young men, who collectively passed through it. But the question persists: What was its meaning and purpose?

According to the customary view, the "manhood" rite marks the point when a youth leaves off being a child and becomes a man, assuming adult responsibilities. A. W. Howitt expresses this:

> The intention of the ceremonies is evidently to make the youths of the tribe worthy members of the community

according to their lights. Certain principles are impressed upon them for their guidance through life — for instance, to listen to and obey the old men; to generously share the fruits of the chase with others, especially their kindred; not to interfere with the women of the tribe, particularly those who are related to them, nor to injure their kindred in its widest sense by means of evil magic. Before the novice is permitted to take his place in the community, marry, and join in its councils, he must possess those qualifications which will enable him to act for the common welfare. (*Native Tribes of South-East Australia,* p. 638)

A similar view is taken by A. P. Elkin:

From the point of view of the tribe, the novice is being made, through a system of discipline and teaching, a worthy member of society and a future custodian of its sacred mythology and ritual. Moreover, the social sentiments on which the unity of society depends are being inculcated in his mind, and at the same time are being strengthened in the minds of all present at the ceremonies. (*Australian Aborigines,* p. 176)

According to Mircea Eliade, initiation was also a basic history class where the young men learned about the great accomplishments of the Ancestors, who laid down customs and traditions for all succeeding generations:

. . . initiation is equivalent to introducing the novice to the mythical history of the tribe; in other words, the initiand learns the deeds of the Supernatural Beings, who, in the dream times, established the present human condition and all the religious, social, and cultural institutions of the tribe. All in all, to know this traditional lore means to know the adventures of the Ancestors and the other Supernatural Beings when they lived on earth. In Australia these adventures amount to little more than long wanderings during which the Beings of the dream times are believed to have performed a certain number of acts. . . . the novices are obliged to retrace these mythical journeys during their initiation. They thus relive the events of the dream times. . . . the mythical Ancestors do not create the world, but transform it, thereby giving it its present form; they do not create man, they civilize him. . . . What is communicated to the novices is, then, a quite eventful mythical history — and less and less the revelation of the creative acts of the Supreme Beings. . . . To be initiated is equivalent to learning what *happened* in the primordial Time. . . . (*Rites and Symbols of Initiation,* pp. 39-40)

Setting aside the mystical framework of this approach, the question is: What did happen in primordial time to so transform the world that it has to be commemorated by every generation of youth? And why, at the same time that the youth were instructed by the old men through lectures and homilies, were they obliged to go through some very peculiar ordeals, punishments, and frightening experiences, apparently designed to engrave these lessons on their minds?

Spencer and Gillen venture the hypothesis that the incidents acted out in initiation "may be commemorative of a reformatory movement which must at one time have taken place in the tribe in regard to cannibalism." They add:

Traces of this still linger on, but only traces. . . . The natives say that the idea of attacking another party, as represented in the first incident, is connected with eating the men who were killed. This, taken in conjunction with the fact that the second incident indicates a taming of the wild men whose natures are thereby made less fierce, may perhaps point back to a time when some powerful man, or group of men, introduced a reformation in regard to the habit of cannibalism. (*Native Tribes of Central Australia,* p. 368)

In other words, initiation represents both an "acting out" and a commemoration of the victory over animalism and cannibalism; and this was the great achievement of the Ancestors of the Alcheringa — the most remote or "dream" period for the aborigines.

From this standpoint the history lesson is not mythical but real; the participants were not Supernatural Beings but humans — or at least hominids on their way to becoming full-fledged *Homo sapiens.* The ritual called "initiation into manhood" originated when men learned how to make "animals" into other men. And in some primitive regions this is precisely the term applied to the ritual: it is called "making man."

This corresponds to the savage notion that nothing exists that has not been "made" by humans, including themselves. Hans Kelsen observes that "the customary characterization of primitive man as a 'man in a state of nature,' or a 'natural man' is inept," and he explains why:

> Nothing appears "natural" to him because everything, as soon as he seeks to explain it, is "artificial" or "made," not necessarily by himself but by his fellow-men. . . . Primitive man is not a "natural man" because he is a "social man" in the strictest sense of the word. . . . Since he knows no nature, he cannot imagine a supernature. (*Society and Nature*, p. 48)

Thus savages not only made tools and weapons, masks and magic, gifts and rituals, songs and dances — they also "made" animals into men. They did this through their system of reciprocity or interchange. Man did not, as the saying goes, "lift himself by his bootstraps." Two opposing communities of men each worked at elevating the "animals" of the opposite side to their own human status.

Spencer and Gillen report Australian legends of the Alcheringa Ancestors in which both women and men participated in the transformation of rudimentary beings into humans at various totemic centers. They write that one tradition is "a crude attempt to describe the origin of human beings out of non-human creatures who were of various forms; some of them were representatives of animals, others of plants, but in all cases they are to be regarded as intermediate stages in the transition of an animal or plant ancestor into a human individual who bore its name as that of his or her totem" (*Native Tribes of Central Australia,* p. 392).

These legends, which are difficult to interpret because they are so heavily framed in totemic disguises, are in keeping with the initiation rituals that continued long after totemism began to fade away. Initiation was a reciprocal ceremony, conducted between the men of the two intermarrying sides. The older men of both sides were in charge of the proceedings, giving instructions, watching over the youth as they passed through their ordeals or "tests of endurance," and guiding them through their mimic acts and performances. In the end the youth emerged from the ordeals bearing all the required "marks" upon their bodies testifying to their newly acquired manhood. Among these, the most universal was the "mark" of circumcision.

The rite of passage called "initiation," therefore, did not originally mark the passage of a youth from childhood to adulthood. It commemorated the passage of a community of "animals" into humans who, as humans, could no longer be killed or eaten. Survivals in some regions of a single sacrificial human offering made at the time of initiation indicates the transition away from cannibalism. Briffault gives examples of such an offering made at the time of the *barbung* or initiation ceremony in Australia:

> "Before cannibalism ceased to be practised by the tribes dealt with in this paper," says Mr. Mathews, "it was the custom to kill and eat a man during the barbung ceremonies. The victim was an initiated man of the tribe, and his flesh and blood were consumed by the men and the novices." "The tribe in whose territory the meeting is held," we are told elsewhere, "are required to give up one of their men to be killed and eaten by the visitors." At the succeeding ceremony held in the latter's territory, they in turn provide the victim. (*The Mothers,* vol. II, p. 697)

Hutton Webster writes:

> It is most likely that in many cases what we regard as merely tests of courage and endurance were once of deeper significance. . . . Thus cannibalism, formerly an initiatory rite among some Australian tribes, may have been retained as a magical practice . . . long after it had been abandoned as a general custom. (*Primitive Secret Societies,* p. 350)

In addition to being a ritual reflection of the epoch of cannibalism, the initiation ceremony is a commemoration of the rise from animalism. Its central feature is a pantomime called "death and rebirth." As this is usually described, all the novices undergoing initiation "die" and then are "reborn" into a wholly new life. Webster writes:

> Almost universally initiation rites include a mimic representation of the death and resurrection of the novice. The new life to which he awakes after initiation is one utterly

forgetful of the old; a new name, a new language, and new
privileges are its natural accompaniments. (ibid., p. 38)

On the same point Chapple and Coon write:

In many societies, this is dramatically acted out. The initiate is regarded as "new-born," and in the ceremony he is
born, fed in child fashion, taught to walk and eat and
is reintroduced to the other personnel of his system, including the members of his own family. (*Principles of
Anthropology,* p. 485)

Here again, the usual assumption is that the child dies and
a man is born. But the drama that is acted out in the ceremony, especially in its more primitive forms, is clearly a story
of cannibalism and animalism. The novices are killed and
eaten by a "devouring monster," a "demonic being," a "mythical animal," or some other terrible figure. In oceanic regions
the devouring animals are not lions or tigers but carnivorous
fish. Layard tells us that in Malekula the circumcision operation "is likened to the biting of a shark, the chief devouring
monster in this part of the Pacific," and the term used by the
aborigines to indicate circumcision means "the shark bites"
(*Stone Men of Malekula,* p. 485).
Sometimes the boys are boiled, baked, steamed, or roasted
before they are devoured. And when they are resurrected, it
is from the belly of the monster. Briffault describes one of the
more literal forms of this drama, in northern Papua:

Among the Yabim, for instance, an enormous hut is built
in a secluded spot in the bush, which represents a monster
whose huge mouth, richly furnished with teeth, forms the
front of the hut, while a palm forms its backbone, which
tapers to a long tail. Bull-roarers are swung by men inside the body of the animal. The initiates are swallowed
through the mouth of the monster and remain secluded
in its belly for three or four months. When they are restored
to the world they appear stupefied, their eyes are sealed
with plastered chalk, and it is only by degrees that they
awake and recover their senses. (*The Mothers,* vol. II,
p. 688)

Eliade also describes some elaborate "stage effects": "Often the cabin represents the body or the open maw of a water monster, a crocodile, for example, or of a snake," he writes. "Being shut up in the cabin is equivalent to being imprisoned in the monster's belly" (*Rites and Symbols of Initiation*, p. 35). It is not difficult to discern in these man-eating animals the origin of the fire-snorting dragons in the fairy tales of a later period.

The evolution of the blood revenge system can be charted through these death and rebirth ceremonies. In the earliest and crudest versions the pantomime is cannibalistic. In later versions we find the equivalent of a blood revenge combat and a mock massacre. The boys are obliged to "run for their lives" while being pursued by masked men in devilish outfits. Terrified and shrieking, they race into the forest where the mock massacre takes place. Afterwards the boys return safe and sound to the camp. Occasionally, when one boy does not return, he is said to have been devoured by the monster.

In a still more refined version, the massacre is abandoned and the boys are merely obliged to lie down on the ground and "play dead" for a time. Sometimes special effects are achieved by heaping upon their inert bodies the bloody entrails of animals which, to all appearances, are their own guts. After the rebirth, the boys rise up, go to the stream, and wash themselves.

In the most advanced version, all the violent expressions of death and rebirth are abandoned, and the boys merely "go to sleep" for a time in what is referred to as a "dream world." When they awaken they are supposed to have completely forgotten their past.

This "cutting off" of the past is the most important part of the initiation ceremony at every stage of its evolution. All the ordeals, devourings, frightening experiences, are only preliminary to the supreme lesson in this "history class"— the total rejection of the past. Howitt observes that "the intention of all that is done at this ceremony is to make a momentous change in the boy's life; the past is to be cut off from him by a gulf which he can never re-pass" (*Native Tribes of South-East Australia*, pp. 638-39).

This feature is misunderstood by those who view initiation as a mere puberty rite. They think it means that the boys have reached the age of manhood, and therefore may never again return to their childhood days and close association with their mothers and sisters. It is often said that between them now there has been erected an "impassible barrier."

But this does not correspond to the facts about the matrilineal kinship system. Apart from the sex taboo, which was established at birth, there was never any barrier between kinsmen and kinswomen, before or after initiation. On the contrary, a man's matrikin represented his "closest kin," his "blood kin," and he retained that kinship for life, even if he married or left his own community. The cutting off of the past, therefore, cannot be taken as a rupture of this relationship.

It is more likely that the "cutting off" refers to the gulf between men and their past created by the conquest of cannibalism. As Eliade perceives it, "It is through initiation that men attain the status of human beings; before initiation they do not yet fully share in the human condition" (*Rites and Symbols of Initiation,* p. 3). Once the novices have been initiated and elevated into human status, they are reminded through the ritual that they are forever cut off by an impassible barrier from animalism and cannibalism . . . lest they forget.

It has been said that ritual in general is the collective expression of unforgettable experience. Nowhere is this more true than in the struggle against cannibalism. First came the deed, then the enactment and reenactment of the deed, and finally the commemoration of a deed whose origin was unknown with an invented rationale to explain it.

The rite of passage called initiation gave the young men the "right of passage" into the territory of former enemies who were now cross-cousins, obliged to receive them with hospitality. It has been pointed out that while savages did not "own" their land according to our concepts of private ownership, they were careful not to trespass upon one another's territory. As Radcliffe-Brown says of the Australian aborigines:

> The rights of the horde over its territory can be briefly indicated by saying that no person who is not a member of the horde has the right to any animal, vegetable, or mineral product from the territory except by invitation or consent of members of the horde. Acts of trespass . . . seem to have been very rare in the social life of the aborigines but it appears to have been generally held that anyone committing such a trespass could justifiably be killed. This . . . is modified by obligations of hospitality whereby, when there is an abundance of some kind of food at a certain time, members of friendly neighbouring hordes are

invited to come in and share it. (*Structure and Function in Primitive Society,* pp. 33-34)

Elkin writes on the same point:

> . . . Aborigines do not wander anywhere and everywhere in search of food, contesting the rights of others who may forestall them, but in visiting the countries of other local groups, even of the same tribe, they must observe relationship and visiting rules. Such rules, incidentally, prevent clashes and preserve social cohesion. (*Australian Aborigines,* p. 18)

Precautions against trespass are wholly understandable at a time when an unidentified or "unmarked" man could be mistaken for a predator or enemy. Rights of passage were essential not simply in the quest for food but also in the search for mates who, under the law of exogamy, were to be found in alien territory. Thus initiation was in effect a "matrimonial passport" giving the "marked" men access to one another's territory.

"A tribe ceases to regard or treat a stranger as an enemy if he has married into it," we are told in the article on "Strangers" in *The Encyclopedia of Religion and Ethics.* At the same time, since "intermarriage does not always produce peace," special concessions are made for these individuals in the event of the outbreak of hostilities:

> In the Marquesas a man who has married a woman of a neighboring tribe may pass to and fro between it and his own tribe in time of war and without fear of molestation . . . and among the tribes of the Napa hills a native who has married a girl of another village and resides with her there is regarded as a neutral and may safely go from her village to his own even during hostilities. (ibid., vol. XI, p. 889)

The various incisions and other marks made on the bodies of the young men during initiation ranged from temporary painting to permanent tattooing and scarring. They served as visible evidence of the youth's new status as an initiated man with the right to enter the territory of his cross-cousins.

Radcliffe-Brown cites a legend of the Andaman Islanders about the first man to become tattooed. Although Radcliffe-Brown fails to make explicit the underlying meaning of the act, the ditty sung by the man is clearly connected with self-preservation:

> What can now strike me?
> I am tattooed, I am tattooed!
> (*The Andaman Islanders,* p. 219)

Of all the marks signifying an initiated man, circumcision is one of the longest preserved. While today circumcision is performed upon a male child after its birth and not at puberty, it remains a mark of both manhood and matrimony in some ethnic groups, and a woman will not accept an uncircumcised man as a husband.

Circumcision is often practiced today as a hygienic measure. Historically, however, the custom can be traced back to the totemic era when non-kin "animals" were made into men and a major conquest was achieved over cannibalism.

In some primitive languages the term for circumcision means "to kill" and also often has the sense of "to devour." Eliade gives an interesting example:

> . . . circumcision is equivalent to death, and the operators are dressed in lion skins and leopard skins; they incarnate the divinities in animal form who in mythical times first performed initiatory murder. The operators wear the claws of beasts of prey and their knives are barbed. They attack the novices' genital organs, which shows that the intention is to kill them. . . . circumcision is expressed by the verb "to kill." But soon afterward the novices are themselves dressed in leopard or lion skins; that is, they assimilate the divine essence of the initiatory animal and hence are restored to life in it. (*Rites and Symbols of Initiation,* p. 23)

According to Eliade, an origin myth "tells of a primordial Animal who killed human beings in order to resuscitate them; in the end the Animal was itself killed, and this event, which took place in the beginning, is ritually reiterated by the circumcision of the novices" (ibid., p. 24). In short, the mark of manhood commemorates the most important event of prehistory — the conquest of animalism and cannibalism.

Women, Initiation, and Secret Societies

It is a common mistake to say that girls as well as boys are initiated in primitive society. Female "confirmation" began only after initiation dwindled to a puberty rite, and even then it was a pale copy of the male ritual. Moreover, it is found only among some peoples; others have no ceremony at all when girls reach puberty. In its original form initiation was an all-male ritual, performed by the older men upon the young men.

In ethnographic data there are no pantomimes of females being swallowed up and disgorged by cannibalistic ogres; there are no mimic acts of combat, flight, and pursuit, and no mock massacres of women; there are no female death and resurrection scenarios. Only the male sex passes through rituals in which initiates die as animals, to be reborn as humans. As Elkin says bluntly, "a girl is not initiated" (*Australian Aborigines,* p. 189).

It is sometimes thought that certain practices at the time of a girl's first menstruation represent female initiation. She is marked with certain taboo insignia and is segregated from men at these times, associating only with other females. As we have seen however (Chapter 4), these customs are followed not simply at the time of a woman's first menstruation but at all her periods and during childbirth. The "marks" a woman displays at these times indicate whether or not she is in a tabooed or inaccessible condition.

The "marks" a man receives at the time of his initiation are of a different type and order. These are usually associated with his eligibility for marriage; without them he would not be acceptable as a husband. They are received in various ordeals or tests of endurance that he passes through in a ritual signifying "manhood." Briffault writes:

> . . . there is one social function for which the successful performance of initiation rites is indispensable; marriage is absolutely forbidden to a youth before he has been duly certified as having attained to the status of hunter or warrior, and no woman or girl would entertain the unheard-of notion of marrying a youth that has not undergone those tests. The marks which constitute the certificate of having successfully passed through them are an indispensable condition of marriage. Where these consist in circumcision a

woman would scorn to have anything to do with the un-circumcised; where they consist in having teeth knocked out, no woman will look at a man who possesses a complete denture; where they consist in various tatu marks, paintings, or scars, these are the necessary passport to feminine favour. Ceremonies of initiation are the portal to one social institution and function only, namely, marriage. (*The Mothers,* vol. II, p. 199)

This is one side of the matter. But it leaves out the even more fundamental aspect: that the matrimonial passport is also a fraternal passport. The "marks" the initiated man receives in the ordeals signify not simply his eligibility as a husband to a woman in an alien community; they also signify that a former enemy is now acceptable to the woman's male kin as a cross-cousin, a brother-in-law, a friend.

It is sometimes thought that the clitoris operations performed upon young women in some primitive regions are both evidence of female initiation and an expression of eternal male domination over women. This is not the case. Such brutalities against women did not occur until men began to practice barbarities against other men. Along with the clitoris operations upon females came the operations on men called "subincision" or the "terrible rite," from which many men died. Spencer and Gillen describe this cruel mutilation of the male sexual organs, and so far as is known the clitoris operation takes place only in those regions where subincision of men is practiced.

These and other barbaric rites signify the decay of the tribal organization. As Hartland writes, "Barbarous cruelty is not an accompaniment of the lowest savagery. The Ashanti and the people of Dahomey whose bloody rites were a byword were far above the lowest savagery. The Aztecs were a comparatively civilized people" (*Memoirs of American Anthropological Association,* 1917, vol. IV, p. 69).

Another common error on the subject of women and initiation is the theory that women were "strictly debarred" from the male ceremony. It is often said that men regarded their ritual as "sacred" and that the presence of women at such times would be "contaminating" to men; thus any women found in the vicinity at the time of the ceremony could be killed. This flows from an unhistorical approach.

Spencer and Gillen give considerable material on the part

played by women in the Australian initiation ceremonies, showing a high degree not only of participation but of guidance
and control over the proceedings, especially by the old women.
Far from being debarred, women were both visible and vocal.

Elkin refers to "sisters" present at the operation of circumcision, "processing around the mass of men who completely
hide the candidate." He concludes:

> To sum up. Women play a part in all important sacred
> rituals. It may consist of observing prescribed taboos while
> the men are in the secret places; chanting, answering ritual
> calls; being present as observers or as minor participants
> in final scenes just off the secret ground or at the general
> camp; and preparing food. The older women know the
> sequence of rites as well as their own roles, and direct
> the younger women in their duties and observances. One
> or two old women may hold official authority over the
> rest, although an old man is usually left in the camp to
> see that all rules are kept. (*Australian Aborigines*, pp.
> 190-91)

Primitive legends bear out this guiding and controlling role
of the women. "According to the myths of some tribes," says
Elkin, "women originally owned the ceremonies, but let the men
take them and henceforth act on their behalf. They are also
credited with introducing the stone circumcision knife in some
regions to replace the crude fire-stick 'surgical instrument' which
the men had been using" (ibid.). Howitt and others report the
same legend. Spencer and Gillen describe it as follows:

> One day the men were, as usual, circumcising a boy with
> a fire-stick when an old woman rushed up, and telling the
> men that they were killing all the boys because they were
> using a fire-stick, showed them how to use a sharp stone,
> and ever afterwards the fire-stick was discarded. (*Native
> Tribes of Central Australia*, p. 402)

It was only with the rise of male secret societies that women
were debarred from participation in these rituals, and even
threatened with death should they be found in the vicinity.
However, this represents a radical change in initiation, and
it corresponds to changes taking place in society. Where formerly all the male youth of a tribe passed through initiation

on an equal basis, the practice gradually became reserved for specially selected men of rank or wealth.

As Hutton Webster writes, the original initiation ceremonies, which were tribal and communal, had "a definite and reasonable purpose; the young men growing into manhood must learn their duties as members of the community. . . ." But this changed:

> Tribal secret societies, such as those of Melanesia and Africa, arise, as we have seen, through what has been described as a process of gradual shrinkage of the original puberty institution in which, after initiation, all men of the tribe are members. But with the gradual limitation of membership and especially with the reservation of the upper ranks in these associations to the more powerful members of the tribe, such as the heads of totems, the shamans, and the richer and more prominent men generally, secret societies of the familiar type emerge. (*Primitive Secret Societies*, pp. 74, 135)

Like all great social changes, the secret society is at first hardly discernible. It makes its appearance as a kind of parallel development with the former tribal initiation ceremony. Elkin gives a hint of this when he describes the rituals "proceeding simultaneously at two levels; the men's secret level; and the camp level, the province of the women." The two "meet from time to time" in the performance (*Australian Aborigines,* p. 191).

Gradually the secret, elitist, male-only ritual displaced the community-wide public ritual. Originally designed to join men together in fraternal relations by eradicating the kin versus non-kin division between them, initiation now became an opposite kind of ritual. It expressed new divisions between men, this time based upon distinctions of rank and wealth.

Along with this, the brutality of men against other men gained ascendancy. As secret societies arose, the hierarchy of men began to make their own rules, subverting the former tribal and communal rules. Heavy floggings, smokings, burnings, and skewerings all but killed the initiates; and many did die of their tortures. Lord Raglan remarks of this "diversity" of punishment, "We find communities in which it is harmless and others which have almost exterminated themselves by means of it" (*Jocasta's Crime,* p. 54).

Eliade points out that the men claimed sanction for their brutalities against other men by contending it was the will of some superhuman being or sky god.

> There is no need of multiplying examples to show, on the one hand, the continuity between puberty rites and initiations into secret societies, and, on the other hand, the constant increase in the severity of the ordeals. Initiatory torture is characteristic of the Melanesian secret societies and of some North American confraternities. The ordeals through which the Mandan novices had to pass, for example, are famous for their cruelty. To understand the meaning of initiatory torture, we must bear in mind that suffering has a ritual value; the torture is supposed to be inflicted by superhuman beings. . . . (*Rites and Symbols of Initiation,* p. 76)

Secret societies are sometimes called "societies of masks" because the men concealed their identities behind devilish masks when they ran wild during initiations or plundering expeditions. Leo Frobenius describes their ravages: "On their approach, men, women, children and old people all take to flight, that is, take refuge in their houses, and should anyone be found in the fields, on the highway, or in any other place, he is either killed or carried off and no more is ever heard of him" (*Childhood of Man,* p. 210).

There is considerable evidence that women fought against these assaults upon the matriarchal commune by setting up counter-rituals, customs, and institutions that are sometimes called "women's mysteries." Eliade writes:

> Just as the men's secret societies terrorize women, the women insult, threaten, and even strike the men whom they encounter in the course of their frenzied processions. Such behavior is ritually justified; these are women's mysteries, whose results might be endangered by the presence of men. This is confirmed by the fact that while they are gardening — an activity which is reserved for them alone — Trobriand women have the right to attack and knock down any man who comes too close to their gardens. (*Rites and Symbols of Initiation,* pp. 79-80)

At the most critical juncture, the passage from matriarchy to patriarchy, the Amazons make their appearance in history. According to Emanuel Kanter, these legendary female warriors who fought with arms in hand "do not appear until barbarism is firmly established," and society is becoming "patriarchal in character" (*The Amazons,* p. 28). Despite their militancy, these heroic women were no match for the rising social forces of male supremacy, founded upon the private ownership of wealth.

Subsequently, as Webster observes, "The secret societies then pass out of existence or decline into purely social clubs" (*Primitive Secret Societies,* p. 135). The final relics can be found in the initiation rites of college fraternities and lodges. Even these sometimes feature "horseplay" or brutality that can bring death or permanent injury to an initiate. But these modern survivals of the barbaric secret society form of initiation are a far cry from the primitive communal initiatory rite.

In its original form, once the candidates were initiated as "men" they could seek mates, who would make them husbands. To prepare them for their entry into the community of their wives, the initiation ceremony included lectures on their proper behavior in the presence of their wives' relatives. Webster sums this up:

> . . . the actual initiation of the youth is in charge of the totemic moiety of the tribe from which, as an initiated man, he will be allowed to choose his wife. In other words, at the *Boras* those in charge of the lads are their real or potential brothers-in-law. The care of the novice during the ceremonies rests always with men of the moiety opposite to his own. The reason for this arrangement becomes evident when it is remembered that the principal purpose of the initiatory rites among the Australian natives is to prepare the lads for marriage. The strict regulations under which marriage is permitted, and especially the careful assignment of the limits within which the novices may choose their future wives, are impressed upon the novices at the great inaugural meetings, in this clear and unequivocal fashion. (*Primitive Secret Societies,* p. 139)

What were the "strict regulations" and limits imposed upon the initiated men who, armed with matrimonial passports, exercised the right of passage into the community of their wives?

Visiting Husbands and In-Law Avoidance

To speak of savage initiation as "initiation into sex" can be highly misleading. It suggests that only after a youth reached adulthood did he become acquainted with sexual intercourse. In actuality, apart from the taboo which prevented sexual intercourse between matrikin, both females and males were acquainted with sexuality from the time they were children.

This point is made by Malinowski about the Trobrianders, where children go off in the bush to play *kayta* (sexual intercourse). He writes that this "infantile sexual act, or its substitute, is regarded as an innocent amusement," and his comments on the subject can be applied to primitive peoples in general:

> There are plenty of opportunities for both boys and girls to receive instruction in erotic matters from their companions. The children initiate each other into the mysteries of sexual life in a directly practical manner at a very early age. A premature amorous existence begins among them long before they are able really to carry out the act of sex. They indulge in plays and pastimes in which they satisfy their curiosity concerning the appearance and function of the organs of generation. . . . The attitude of the grown-ups and even of the parents towards such infantile indulgence is either that of complete indifference or that of complacency — they find it natural, and do not see why they should scold or interfere. (*Sexual Life of Savages,* pp. 55-56)

Initiation, therefore, was not designed to initiate the young man into the mysteries of sex. Rather, it was designed to instruct him as to his proper social behavior in the community of his future wife. Certain strict rules were followed by young hunters and warriors when they were visiting a territory not their own: at all times tread with care, speak softly, submit to surveillance by the future wife's male kin, and, above all, avoid the wife's mothers.

By far the most prominent of all such rules is the one known as "mother-in-law avoidance." The anthropological record is filled with examples, of which the following by Frazer are typical:

In the Banks Islands these rules of avoidance and reserve
are very strict and minute. A man will not come near his
wife's mother and she will not come near him. If the two
chance to meet in a path, the woman will step out of it
and stand with her back turned till he has gone by, or
perhaps, if it be more convenient, he will move out of the
way. At Vanua Lava, in Port Patterson, a man would not
even follow his mother-in-law along the beach until the
rising tide had washed her footprints from the sand. (*Totemism and Exogamy,* vol. II, p. 76)

Among the Navahos, says Briffault, the name for mother-
in-law, *doyishini,* means "she whom I may not see." Today
mothers-in-law are a popular subject of humor. But, as Briffault writes:

The well-known attitude of the savage towards his mother-
in-law is to him anything but a laughing matter. It is one
of the most constant rules in savage society that a man
may not speak to, and generally may not even look upon
the mother of his wife, and the breach of this rule is regarded with as much horror as the breach of the rules against
incestuous union. . . .
 In Australia . . . a man is warned of the approach of
his mother-in-law by the sound of a bull-roarer; and a native is said to have nearly died of fright because the shadow
of his mother-in-law fell on his legs while he lay asleep. It
was formerly death for a man to speak to his mother-in-
law; however, in later times, the wretch who had committed
this heinous crime was suffered to live, but he was severely
reprimanded and banished from the camp. (*The Mothers,*
vol. I, pp. 259-60)

To European settlers, this fear of old, unarmed women on the
part of men noted for exploits as warriors, was not only incomprehensible but ludicrous. Briffault cites an illustration involving a warlike Apache:

"One of the funniest incidents I can remember," says Captain
Bourke, "was seeing a very desperate Chiricahua Apache,
named Ka-a-tenny, who was regarded as one of the boldest
and bravest men in the whole nation, trying to avoid running face to face against his mother-in-law. He hung to

stones from which, had he fallen, he would have been dashed to pieces, or certainly would have broken several of his limbs." (ibid., p. 26)

A similar illustration is given by Hoebel:

> The Zulu warrior, spear in hand, is a paragon of ferocity, but when he meets his mother-in-law on the bypath, he ducks for the bushes and hides until she has passed. (*Man in the Primitive World,* p. 243)

What was the meaning of this peculiar mother-in-law taboo, which has been so often described but seldom analyzed? At most, certain inferences are made which, under closer scrutiny, are patently groundless.

According to one hypothesis, it was instituted to prevent sexual rivalry and conflict between mother and daughter for the husband's sexual favors. Even such an eminent scholar as Elkin falls into this trap. He writes: "The severest taboo is that which is observed all over Australia between a man and his wife's mother. . . . son-in-law and mother-in-law must neither see nor speak to one another; this, at least, prevents the possibility of competition between a girl and her mother for the affection of the same man . . ." (*Australian Aborigines,* pp. 123-24).

It would seem from this remark that the whole aboriginal population of Australia would be in a continuous uproar between mothers and daughters for access to the same son-in-law were it not for the rule of avoidance. This explanation becomes even more unlikely when we learn from Elkin that "this avoidance rule is extended to wife's mother's mother." Are we to assume from this that all the grandmothers were also in competition with their granddaughters for the same youth?

Even this does not end the absurdity of the hypothesis. We also learn from Elkin that the rule of avoidance applied not only to old women but also to old men on the wife's side. The same taboo, although somewhat modified, is extended to "the wife's mother's brother," the *ramba:*

> The avoidance of wife's "uncle" is not a mere form. He is usually called by a term signifying tabooed, and often it is the term which is used for mother-in-law. . . . the

whole male membership of the tribe is divided by this avoidance relationship. No man will go near or talk face to face with his *ramba, wolmingi, dalu,* or whatever be the term, with the result that this avoidance is often the first thing observed on entering a native camp, even at a mission. . . . A man swerves aside from the track to avoid meeting his *ramba* face to face, as I have seen happen with my own carrier. . . . The avoidance is not so complete as in the case of mother-in-law for the *ramba* men do see, and may sometimes speak to, one another from a distance. (*Australian Aborigines,* p. 125)

Since this avoidance of the wife's mother's brother cannot be explained in the same terms as that of the wife's mother — namely, as sexual competition between two females — Elkin is obliged to amend his explanation:

. . . the wife's mother's brother is brought within the range of the same taboo, no doubt because he belongs to the same local clan and country as the mother-in-law and therefore has the same "spiritual" history as she, and also because he was incarnated through the womb of the same mother as herself. He is therefore equivalent to her, a male mother-in-law — one of the tabooed group. (ibid., p. 124)

Here at last we come to the main point. Not only the wife's mothers but her mothers' brothers — indeed, all the older and younger kin of the wife — were members of the "tabooed group," and the rule of avoidance applied to all of them. This is entirely understandable when we remember the origin of the young hunter and warrior who is a visiting husband in his wife's community. He came from a former group of enemies. Although they are now cross-cousins and friends, the old distrust is not entirely eradicated. Prudence requires that his movements be restricted — to protect not only the wife's kin, but the visiting husband himself.

This was necessary under conditions where all deaths were attributed to a hostile act. Should a death or serious injury occur, suspicion might fall upon the former stranger visiting in his wife's community. This could lead to an outbreak of hostilities between the groups and a rupture of the intermarrying alliance. Avoidance rules were not aimed at preventing sexual jealousy between mothers and daughters. What was involved was *social intercourse* between former enemies converted into intermarrying groups.

The prominence of the mother-in-law avoidance, which endured even after others broke down, can only be attributed to the fact that the supervision, care, and protection of the community's children were in their hands. The area occupied by these women and children can be called the "citadel of maximum security." This area in particular would be the best guarded by the mothers' brothers and the least accessible to visiting strangers in search of wives.

Rivers perceived some of the factors involved when he concluded that the rules of avoidance were connected with "a condition of hostility between members of the two moieties of the community." He noted the ambivalent relations of mutual suspicion and mutual helpfulness that prevailed between the two sides, and that, as helpfulness increased and suspicions were allayed, the avoidances began to disappear (*History of Melanesian Society,* vol. II, p. 170).

Some reports from primitive regions in recent times hint at the perils formerly involved in love-making. One of the most picturesque is Fortune's description of the state of affairs in Dobu, a region not long removed from its cannibalistic past:

> One marries into a village of enemies, witches, and sorcerers, some of whom are known to have killed or to be the children of those known to have killed members of one's own village. The night divides the villages — apart from love-making, a hundred yards is as far as a thousand or ten thousand for all practical purposes. Even roaming for love-making should be done while the night is still young. In the dark spaces between the villages the agents of death roam — the death-dealing spirits of the women and men of all other villages, witches and sorcerers all. . . .
>
> The boys who go out for love-making then, go out with great boldness into a night filled with terrors. They are usually supported by a good conscience in that they have not given offence to the adults of other villages, a fact not so true of their parents. Nevertheless, they go into dangerous territory, for it is well known that in matters of sorcery and witch-craft native vengeance may visit the sins of the fathers, mothers, and mothers' brothers upon the children down the generations. (*Sorcerers of Dobu,* pp. 23-24)

Of all the fearsome beings classified as witches and sorcerers, the worst were the old women in the wife's community — none other than the mothers-in-law. Far from engaging in any amorous dalliance, any intelligent son-in-law would avoid them like the plague.

Malinowski, writing about the Dobuans from the Trobrianders' point of view, says that "the main instrument for wielding power and inflicting penalties in these lands, sorcery, is to a great extent in the hands of women. The flying witches, so characteristic of the Eastern New Guinea type of culture, here have one of their strongholds" (*Argonauts of the Western Pacific*, p. 41). In a further description he writes:

> Of all the dangerous and frightful beings met with on a sailing expedition, the most unpleasant, the best known, and most dreaded are the flying witches. . . . Dangerous as they always are, at sea they become infinitely more dreaded. For the belief is deep that in case of shipwreck or mishap at sea, no real evil can befall the crews except by the agency of the dreaded women. (ibid., p. 236)

Thus considerable courage was required on the part of young sailors setting out on kula expeditions to distant lands. They faced not only the dangers of sharks and shipwreck but the storms and tempests kicked up by these fearsome old women — their future mothers-in-law.

All this sheds light on the beginnings of marriage. Far from being eternal, pair-unions developed slowly and precariously over a long period of time. The right of safe passage into the community of cross-cousins was a signal advance over earlier fleeting encounters between the sexes in the forest. But there were still many hesitations, suspicions, and fears between the men of the two moieties, and these were reflected in the relations between the young men and old women.

This precarious situation can be seen more clearly in what is sometimes called the "institution of the visiting husband." In the earliest stage of matrimony the husband was little more than a visitor to his wife's community. He did not start out by occupying a separate house or hut with his wife; he was given accommodations in the male clubhouse reserved for strangers and visiting husbands. There under the surveillance of his wife's male kin he slept and took his meals. A survival of this ancient practice is noted by Webster:

In Samoa . . . the young men slept by themselves and received the visitors to the community. In the Fiji Islands at least two *Bures-ni-sa,* or strangers' houses, were found in every village. In them all the male population passed the night. "The women and girls sleep at home; and it is quite against Fijian etiquette for a husband to take his night's repose anywhere except at one of the public *bures* of his town or village, though he will go to his family soon after dawn." (*Primitive Secret Societies,* pp. 11-12)

According to some reports, when a visiting husband arrived at the village of his wife, he parked his weapons outside before entering. Others say that he did not immediately walk into the wife's community; he sat down at the outskirts and waited until one of his wife's kinsmen summoned him to the male clubhouse where he was given accommodations.

Thus before men achieved the status of full-fledged husbands, living and sleeping under the same roof with their wives, they passed through an interim period of history in which they were only part-time visitors. Briffault refers to them as "surreptitious" husbands, and to matrimony at this stage of its evolution as "clandestine marriage":

Even more extraordinary in the light of our notions than the position of the husband as a stranger, guest or visitor within the group to which his wife belongs is the fact that he is commonly a clandestine and surreptitious visitor. One of the Japanese words for marriage is "Home-iri," which may be interpreted "to slip by night into the house," and the expression accurately describes the mode of connubial intercourse among a large proportion of primitive peoples.

Among the Khasis "the husband came to his mother-in-law's home after dark only. . . . The Tipperah husband gains access to his wife's room like a burglar, and leaves it before dawn. Among the Yakut, the husband visits his wife in a similar manner after dark. . . . The Kuril never visit their wives publicly, "but steal to them privately in the night." Among the Tartars, the bride-groom likewise slips into the bride's house surreptitiously, and he is particularly careful not to be seen leaving it, for her male relatives are waiting, ready to administer a sound drubbing if they should happen to catch sight of him. (*The Mothers,* vol. I, pp. 513-14)

This indicates a certain advance on the part of the stranger seeking a bride; he has breached the "citadel," that is, the sector so carefully guarded because it is occupied by the older women and the children. He is now cohabiting with his wife, in the same sector and even under the same roof as that dangerous old witch, his mother-in-law. His chief concern now is to escape detection by his wife's male kinsmen. We learn from Briffault that often the mother-in-law herself acts as a "go-between" in the cause of love:

> The Kirghis bridegroom is secretly introduced into the bride's chamber by the "go-between," and he must depart before dawn. . . . In Khorassan, it was the rule for the mother of the bride to introduce the bridegroom secretly into the house by the back door; the male relatives were not supposed to know anything of his visits, and he had to depart before dawn. (ibid., p. 514)

The fearsome old witch gradually became transformed into a proper mother-in-law, although she still remained a formidable figure, to be treated with great circumspection. This explains the curious remark made by an Australian aborigine which Radcliffe-Brown reports as follows:

> In its most extreme form there is complete avoidance of any social contact between a man and his mother-in-law.
> This avoidance must not be mistaken for a sign of hostility. One does, of course, if one is wise, avoid having too much to do with one's enemies, but that is quite a different matter. I once asked an Australian native why he had to avoid his mother-in-law, and his reply was, "Because she is my best friend in the world; she has given me my wife." (*Structure and Function in Primitive Society*, p. 92)

With the development of the gift-giving institution and the increasing breakdown of the hereditary enmity between the intermarrying sides, the mothers' brothers took over the functions of go-betweens for their sisters' daughters and young suitors. Individual pair-matrimony developed on the basis of the community gift-interchange system, which was as much an expression of fraternal relations between the men of the two sides as it was of matrimony.

Van Gennep gives an example from among the Bhotiya of southern Tibet and Sikkim: "Uncles of the girl and the boy act as go-betweens and receive presents of money. They meet in the boy's house and then go with gifts to the girl's, to ask for her in marriage. If the gifts they have brought are accepted (ceremony of *nangchang*) the matter is concluded . . ." (*Rites of Passage,* pp. 121-22).

This part the mother's brother plays in the marriage of his sister's son or daughter has been much misunderstood. Sometimes the old man is thought to be the "husband" of the young girl instead of the go-between. A more common error is made with respect to the gifts he receives at the marriage of his sister's daughter. This is often seen as proof that, just as fathers in our society dominate their wives and daughters, in primitive society the brothers dominated their sisters' daughters.

The fact is that primitive brothers and mothers' brothers had no direct say in the marriages of either their sisters or sisters' daughters. Their sole concern was with the relations that existed between them and the men who came as suitors of their kinswomen. The act of interchanging gifts with these former strangers was their assurance that fraternal relations had superseded enmity.

The original match-makers in both peace and matrimony were women. Briffault writes about a survival in old China:

> That strange institution of go-betweens, or "Mei-jin," is looked upon as of a fundamental moral and quasi-sacred character quite unintelligible to us. Go-betweens were instituted by Niu-Kua, the mythical first female ruler who, with her brother, Fu-Hi, instituted marriage, and she was herself the "great" or "first" go-between. The emperor offered sacrifices to "The First Go-Between." (*The Mothers,* vol. I, p. 526)

Now let us turn to the part played by the female go-betweens in elevating the surreptitious visitors who slip by night into the house into husbands who can walk around in broad daylight.

Marriage by Mother-in-Law

Bachofen points out that the archaic Latin-based term for marriage indicates its matriarchal origin:

Indeed, the very word matrimony (literally mother-marriage) is based on the fundamental idea of mother right. One said *matrimonium*, not *patrimonium* (father-marriage, paternal inheritance), just as one originally spoke of a *materfamilias*. *Paterfamilias* is unquestionably a later term. (*Myth, Religion and Mother Right*, pp. 132-33)

Even the term "mother-marriage," however, would be more appropriate as "marriage by mother-in-law." In the first stage of pair-unions it was the man who entered the community of his wife. "The arrangement that a woman should, even after her marriage, continue to reside with her mother's family, and that her husband should take up his abode in his mother-in-law's house, is strange to our notions," Briffault writes. But he gives abundant documentation, of which the following from A. L. Kroeber on the Zuni is typical:

"The house," says Dr. Kroeber, "belongs to the women born of the family. There they come into the world, pass their lives, and within the walls they die. As they grow up, their brothers leave them, each to abide in the house of his wife. Each woman, too, has her husband, or succession of husbands, sharing her blankets. So generation succeeds generation, the slow stream of mothers and daughters forming a current that carried with it husbands, sons, and grandsons." (*The Mothers,* vol. I, p. 273)

At what point in this historical development did mere sexual intercourse leave off and actual matrimony begin? In our society the distinction is clearly established by law, and a legal or clerical certificate is issued to a married couple to signify that they have complied. But in primitive society, before law courts, churches, or monogamous marriage came into existence, it is more difficult to see a dividing line between mere sexual union and matrimonial union.

Some analysts draw the line at the point of cohabitation, that is, when a couple begins to live together under one roof. According to A. S. Diamond, "It is the fact of cohabitation that constitutes the marriage," that distinguishes it from "mere sexual intercourse" (*Primitive Law*, p. 220). But this is still an inadequate guide when we consider the primitive phenomenon called the "bachelor house" where males and females "cohabited" before they joined together as a cohabiting married pair.

These bachelor houses — or pairing houses — were established for unmarried girls as well as boys. Seligman writes that among the Wagawaga, "Certain houses are dedicated to the use of unmarried girls above the age of puberty who habitually pass the night in them. These, like the local man-houses, are called *potuma*." After dark, the young men proceed to the girls' *potuma*, squat down outside to indicate their eligibility as partners, and the girls select from among them (*The Melanesians of British New Guinea*, p. 500).

Malinowski, writing about the *bukumatula*, the bachelor house in the Trobriands, says that at the time of his studies there were five in one village and four in an adjoining village. Previously there had been many more in both villages, but their numbers had greatly diminished "owing to missionary influence." The missionaries' disapproval could not have been due to any unseemly behavior on the part of the couples having sexual intercourse, for, as Malinowski writes:

> Within the *bukumatula* a strict decorum obtains. The inmates never indulge in orgiastic pastimes, and it is considered bad form to watch another couple during their love-making. . . . I could find no trace of any "voyeur" interest taken by the average boy, nor any tendency to exhibitionism. Indeed, when I was discussing the positions and technique of the sexual act, the statement was volunteered that there are specially unobtrusive ways of doing it "so as not to wake up the other people in the *bukumatula*." (*Sexual Life of Savages*, p. 73)

According to Malinowski, a *bukumatula* affair was not marriage, although if such an affair turned out well it could lead to marriage. He writes:

> Another important point is that the pair's community of interest is limited to the sexual relation only. The couple share a bed and nothing else. In the case of a permanent liaison about to lead to marriage, they share it regularly; but they never have meals together; there are no services to be mutually rendered, they have no obligation to help each other in any way, there is, in short, nothing which would constitute a common menage. (ibid., p. 74)

Sexual cohabitation, therefore, did not furnish the basis for marriage so long as it remained simply sexual intercourse, confined to cohabitation in a bachelor house, and without involving any other rights or duties between the pair. To pass from such a liaison to the more substantial union of marriage it was necessary for the young woman to invite the young man to her mother's house.

The following is a portion of Briffault's documentation on the woman's role in proposing marriage:

> Among many peoples it has been noted that the initiative in individual marriage does not come from the men, but from the women. Thus among the tribes of Queensland, according to Mr. Thorne, "it is never usual, it appears, for the young man to make the first advances. . . . The 'gin' has the acknowledged right of showing her partiality for a particular person. We could not learn that the poor fellow has any right to refuse." Much the same thing has been noted by Dr. Howitt as regards the Kurnai at the other extremity of the Australian continent. In the northern Melanesian groups . . . the initiative in marriage comes from the young women, and in New Britain, New Hanover, New Ireland it is the women who select their husbands. Throughout southern Papua and in the adjacent islands of Torres Straits it is a rule, to which there appears to be no exceptions, that all advances and propositions of marriage must come from the woman and not from the man. . . . So important, indeed, is the rule . . . that, in Torres Straits, it has acquired the force of a moral law, and forms part of the kind of ethical catechism which is taught to young men at their initiation ceremonies. They are lectured on the impropriety of proposing marriage to a girl. It is the woman who proposes marriage, even when the man has other wives. (*The Mothers,* vol. II, pp. 168-69)

As Briffault points out, this custom changed where a patriarchal social order had been established along with male domination. But in Egypt, which retained its matriarchal customs for a very long time, "The courting was usually done by the women. The love-poems and love-letters which we possess are mostly addressed from women to men. . . . In fact, Egyptian ladies seem to have regarded it as their privilege to do all the courting" (ibid., p. 174).

In preliterate society however, a young woman made a marriage proposal not in a letter but by inviting the man to stay the night with her in her mother's house. The objective was to have the girl's mother take him as her son-in-law, establishing him as the daughter's official husband.

Investigators have often reported that in primitive society the mother-in-law "adopts" her son-in-law. This use of the term "adoption" can be confusing if it is conceived in terms of modern parents adopting children. In savage society such adoptions were connected with matrimony in its elementary stage of development. Before a man could be promoted from the status of lover to husband he must be accepted, that is, "adopted," by his mother-in-law.

Thus when a youth accepted the proposal for marriage from a girl it meant that he was now to be brought into close contact with the witch he had taken such great precautions to avoid. Fortune gives a picturesque description of such a confrontation between mother-in-law and son-in-law in Dobu. The young man begins by slipping surreptitiously into the woman's home in the night. If he does not secretly leave before dawn but remains until morning so that his mother-in-law would see him there, he is making his application to be her son-in-law. As Fortune puts it, the lad deliberately oversleeps. The mother-in-law, getting up before the couple, steps out onto the house platform where "she sits calmly blocking up the exit with her body." The youth, says Fortune, "feels respect and fear for the powerful old witch, his mother-in-law, as she sits blocking the exit of her house where he has lain with her daughter." The die is cast and his matrimonial application accepted.

The mother-in-law seated on the platform is as well understood a public announcement of a betrothal as any notice in a newspaper:

> The village see an unusual event has occurred. They gather, curious to see what youth will emerge. They send word to neighbouring villages and people from the environs gather. Everyone circles around and stares. Into this glare of curious publicity the youth and the girl descend at last from the house, and sit side by side on a mat on the ground. The spectators remain and do nothing but stare for half an hour or so. This staring ceremony makes the engagement. It is aggressive publicity directed towards a relationship which was before as aggressively private. (*Sorcerers of Dobu,* p. 22)

So long as the young man remained a roamer, visiting

young women on an occasional basis in the bachelor house
or elsewhere, he was not a candidate for marriage. He becomes
a husband when he has passed through the ordeal and is
ready to accept the work of husbandry — for, after the villagers
disperse, the girl's mother turns to the young man, thrusts a
digging-stick into his hands, and says, "Go, make a garden."
The power of this formidable old witch is such that, as Fortune
remarks, "When his mother-in-law gives him the digging-stick
he goes off most obediently to dig a garden" (ibid., p. 24).

Ruth Benedict, describing the same Dobuan betrothal ceremony, says, "From this time forward the young man has to
reckon with the village of his wife. Its first demand is upon
his labour. Immediately his mother-in-law gives him a digging-
stick with the command, 'Now, work!'" (*Patterns of Culture*,
p. 124).

Gardening work, formerly in the hands of women, was now
readily accepted by the young men. According to some reports
the men vied with one another to be the best gardener.
Malinowski writes of the Trobrianders:

> A good garden worker in the Trobriands derives a direct
> prestige from the amount of labour he can do, and the
> size of garden he can till. The title *tokwaybagula*, which
> means "good" or "efficient gardener," is bestowed with dis-
> crimination, and borne with pride. Several of my friends,
> renowned as *tokwaybagula*, would boast to me how long
> they worked, how much ground they tilled, and would
> compare their efforts with those of less efficient men. . . .
> Men vie with one another in their speed, in their thorough-
> ness, and in the weights they can lift, when bringing big
> poles to the garden, or in carrying away the harvested
> yams. (*Argonauts of the Western Pacific*, pp. 60-61)

Summing up their attitude, Malinowski says, "He wants, if
he is a *man*, to achieve social distinction as *a good gardener*
and a good worker in general" (p. 62, emphasis in the
original).

One meaning of "husband" is "a man who has a wife." But
a "husbandman" is a farmer, a tiller of the ground. Thus the
husband makes his appearance in history as a gardener working for his wife's kin.

From gardening it was a short step toward the care and
domestication of farm animals, and these were the two elements

required for a higher economy. Thus marriage developed side by side with the development of husbandry, a new occupation of men which more and more displaced their former occupation of hunting, and which laid the foundations for the higher culture of barbarism.

Gardening was only one of the productive skills mastered by the young husbands under the tutelage of their mothers-in-law. W. I. Thomas notes that among the Zuni a suitor not only worked in the fields of his prospective mother-in-law, but also collected fuel and made buckskin moccasins, skin and textile clothes, and a shell or silver necklace for the bride (*Sex and Society*, p. 78). Husbands became skilled in all that was formerly considered "woman's work."

Thus marriage from its inception did not hinge upon the sexual relations between a man and woman; it was centered entirely on economic and social relations. The young man accepted as a son-in-law could henceforth associate with the women and children in his wife's community. In fact, as some investigators report, the fearsome old mother-in-law began to display a special fondness for the young man whom she had adopted and who was now "cohabiting" with her and her daughter.

However, the term "cohabitation," like "adoption," has been seriously misunderstood. When the "cohabitation" of the youth with his mother-in-law is interpreted as a sexual relation, it leads to the misconception that he was married to both mother and daughter. Even Briffault fell into this error. He thought the mother-in-law avoidance created "constant embarrassments," and to elude these a "simple expedient" was adopted — for the son-in-law to marry the mother-in-law "pro forma" before marrying her daughter. As illustrations he gives the Navahos, the Cherokees, the Caribs, and other tribes (*The Mothers*, vol. I, p. 264).

This is not only absurd; it contradicts all the evidence on the stringent mother-in-law taboo which Briffault himself has documented in profuse detail. To be sure, the son-in-law did "cohabit" with his mother-in-law once she "adopted" him. But this was neither adoption nor cohabitation in our sense of the terms. It meant that the youth had the right of *social* association with those he formerly had to avoid.

Some investigators point to a period of betrothal by mother-in-law preceding marriage by mother-in-law. This betrothal, sometimes lasting as long as a year, is also called a period of "probation" preliminary to marriage. In that period the youth was on his best behavior, performing all the tasks required of him to demonstrate his desirability.

Although the dividing line between betrothal and marriage is often difficult to see in a given situation, there is one acid test. Marriage begins when the pair eat together.

This food union shows how little sex had to do with marriage in the formative stage of its evolution. In modern society sexual intercourse, theoretically at least, is frowned upon until a man and a woman have been officially married. This was not the case in primitive society. What Ruth Benedict writes with respect to the Zuni can be applied to other primitive peoples:

> The Puritan attitude toward sex flows from its identification as sin, and the Zuni have no sense of sin. . . . They do not suffer from guilt complexes, and they do not consider sex as a series of temptations to be resisted with painful efforts of the will. Chastity as a way of life is regarded with great disfavour. . . . Pleasant relations between the sexes are merely one aspect of pleasant relations with human beings. . . . Sex is an incident in the happy life. (*Patterns of Culture*, pp. 116-17)

This easy, informal attitude toward sexual intercourse, however, is not duplicated in the sphere of what may be called "food intercourse" between the sexes. The most scandalous behavior of a couple prior to matrimony would be their eating together. As Malinowski writes:

> In the Trobriands two people about to be married must never have a meal in common. Such an act would greatly shock the moral susceptibility of a native, as well as his sense of propriety. To take a girl out to dinner without having previously married her — a thing permitted in Europe — would be to disgrace her in the eyes of a Trobriander. We object to an unmarried girl sharing a man's bed — the Trobriander would object just as strongly to her sharing his meal. (*The Sexual Life of Savages*, p. 75)

This can only be interpreted as having originated in the ancient food segregation of the sexes and former cannibalistic practices between kin and non-kin. The food barrier was the last to fall. Although a man was now accepted as a husband working in his wife's community, during the period of betrothal or probation he could not eat food in the presence of his wife and her kin. Fortune gives another description of this situation in Dobu:

> The unfortunate future son-in-law cannot eat or drink in the presence of his future parents-in-law. He goes on working, hungry and tired. Let the anthropologist speak to a parent-in-law while the affair is still at this stage, and the old man guffaws most merrily at the miserable predicament of his future son-in-law. He is so very hungry — guffaw — but he cannot eat — guffaw — he digs and digs and digs most earnestly and strongly — guffaw. To the Dobuan father-in-law it is a most humorous and highly appreciated situation. But the young man gets away about noon, hungry, hot, and weary, and escapes to his own village to satisfy his needs. (*Sorcerers of Dobu*, p. 25)

This illustrates why in some primitive languages the term for the opposite moiety also means "food division." Crawley writes that "amongst the Damaras the word for 'marriage division' is *Oruzo*, which refers to food. . . . the clans of the Damaras are distinguished by food-taboos" (*The Mystic Rose*, vol. II, p. 227). The same principle prevailed even after the dual organization broke down and matrimonies were effected on a clan-to-clan or village-to-village basis.

However, even this most stringent of taboos was finally breached when betrothal by mother-in-law was advanced to marriage by mother-in-law. The ritual by which the couple was united in their first joint meal, or what we might call a "wedding breakfast," was performed by the two mothers-in-law, the wife's mother and the husband's mother. Here is Fortune's description of the Dobuan ceremony:

> When he is not working for his parents-in-law to be, the youth is working with his own kin to accumulate the food and gifts that must be exchanged between the villages against the marriage. Then when, after a year's betrothal or longer all is prepared, the marriage takes place. The groom's relatives take a gift of ornamental valuables, arm rings of white shell and necklaces of red shell, to the bride's relatives. The bride's mother receives the gift and distributes it to her kin. She and her female relatives then go to the

groom's village and formally sweep it throughout. At the same time they take a big gift of uncooked food, and after they have swept the village and given away most of this uncooked food, they cook some of the food which they retained for the purpose in the groom's village, give it to the groom's kin and receive a smaller gift of cooked food from the groom's kin.

Next day the groom's kin carry a big gift of uncooked food to the bride's village, give it to the bride's kin, cook a small part of it in the bride's village and give it to the bride's kin, and receive a smaller gift of cooked food from the bride's kin. (*Sorcerers of Dobu*, p. 25)

The wedding meal itself is quite simple and could be called "weaning by mothers-in-law." The bride's mother stuffs some of her cooked food in the groom's mouth and the groom's mother does the same with the bride. "The pair are now married," says Fortune, "the groom eating food in the presence of his mother-in-law in her village for the first time, and the bride eating food in the presence of her mother-in-law in her mother-in-law's village for the first time" (ibid., pp. 25-26).

It is noticeable that in this marriage ceremony everything is reciprocal except the sweeping ritual. Only the groom's village is "formally swept throughout." Since this represents a purification rite of some kind, the question arises: Why does it occur only in the village of the man, not the woman? Fortune does not deal with this problem. Nevertheless in another section he provides a clue to the answer when he tells us that the same "symbolic sweeping" occurs in connection with cannibalism and deaths.

He writes, "When the men returned victorious from war bringing home corpses for a cannibal feast, the women formally swept the villages throughout." From this he draws the remarkable conclusion that "it is the response of the women's group to good behaviour by the men's group, for when the men returned defeated and empty-handed the sweeping out was not done" (ibid., pp. 77-78).

According to Fortune, the male cannibal feast represents "good behavior." But the sweeping by the women shows it to be quite the reverse: the presence of corpses and cannibalism made a purification ritual necessary. This explains why in marriage, which brought about food intercourse between the sexes, the sweeping ritual occurred only in the groom's village, not the bride's. That was a ceremonial cleansing out of the former bloody relationship between men of the intermarrying communities and an affirmation of the new relationship.

Significantly, even at this stage of the evolution of marriage, the food barrier was not easily or rapidly broken. According to Briffault, "The eating of food together by the bride and bridegroom is among many peoples the essence of the marriage ceremony, and in many instances the only occasion in which they partake of a meal together."

In fact, in one of Briffault's illustrations, not the couple but the kin on both sides eat the food that joins the pair in matrimony:

> Among the Yakut the bride and bridegroom do not take part in the wedding banquet, but sit in a corner behind the door with their faces towards the wall, while their relatives partake of the wedding meal. "In front of each guest, on a horsehide which serves as a tablecloth, is placed a large piece of boiled meat with the bones attached. The relatives of the young couple exchange these pieces of meat, and this performance is the principal part of the Yakut marriage ceremony, symbolising the union between the families, which henceforth are to forget all enmity, and for the future be 'flesh of one flesh and bone of one bone.'"
> (*The Mothers*, vol. I, p. 557)

Food intercourse, the act that signified marriage, began slowly and precariously. For a long time it continued on a partial and limited basis with the pair returning to their former segregated practices after the wedding ritual. Even after the patriarchy took over, there were survivals of the ancient segregation of the sexes with respect to meat and meat eating. Julius Lippert tells us that after the Carians of Miletus had lost their matriarchal structure, the Carian women continued to follow the principle that "none should ever sit at meat with her husband." He further points out the clear-cut food division between the married couple, with men in charge of meat and slaughtering and women in charge of cereals and breadstuffs. He writes about Roman marriages:

> The bride entered the house of her husband bringing not only distaff and spindle but also a basket of cereals as her share of the common food, the German *Musteil*. Even

though the Romans had early made the fortunate advance
of transferring the cultivation of cereals to the hands of the
man, all traces of the old division of labor by sex had
nevertheless not disappeared. Rossbach says that grain
might very properly have been called the food supply
of the married woman, "for the principal business of the
materfamilias consists, according to the ancient law of
Romulus, in the preparation of the breadstuffs for the meals
and private sacrifice, while the rest of the *cena*,
the slaughtering of the animal and the preparation of the
meat, was left to the man." Even in the matter of sacrifices,
the offering of meat was always the affair of the man,
while the Vestalia, a feast which only the matrons celebrated, was called the feast of breads. (*Evolution of Culture*, pp. 267, 343)

The most important feature of marriage from its very inception has gone largely unobserved: it was a new kind of union
composed of husband and wife, distinctly different from the
former clan union of sisters and brothers. The two were in
fundamental antagonism to each other. Thus, although marriage was introduced by the mothers within the framework
of the maternal clan structure, in the end marriage would
undermine the matriarchy.

The Clash of Marriage and Matriarchy

With the advance toward an agricultural economy, tribal
society had reached its peak. Thereafter it began to decay.
The interlocking network of clans and phratries started to
break up into separate clans, each forming a village community. Side by side with this, matrimonial arrangements began
to be made on a clan-to-clan, village-to-village, and ultimately
family-to-family basis.

Under matrilocal marriage, the first form of matrimony,
the husband left his own clan or village to take up residence
in that of his wife. Although no longer surreptitious, he was
still in a sense a "visitor" to his wife's community, an "outsider" in a matrilineal community not his own. Kinship remained basically matrilineal, and the first clan-families, narrowed down from the tribe, retained many of their matriarchal
features.

The matrilineal exclusivity of the clan-family is well documented. Frazer's description of the peoples of Assam, in India, furnishes one example:

> Amongst the Garos, as amongst the Khasis, the system of mother-kin prevails. The wife is the head of the family, and through her all the family property descends. The tribe is divided into a great many family groups or "motherhoods," called *machongs*. All the members of a "motherhood" claim to be descended from a common ancestress; and all the children of a family belong to their mother's "motherhood," not to that of their father, whose family is barely recognized. Inheritance also follows the same course and is restricted to the female line. . . . The daughter must therefore inherit, and her daughter after her, or, failing issue, another woman of the clan appointed by some of its members. (*Folklore in the Old Testament*, abr. ed., p. 193)

Reports on primitive marriages stress the fact that they were unstable, subject to repeated interruptions and frequently ending in separation. But the underlying source of this instability has not been adequately analyzed.

So long as kinship remained matrilineal it was fratrilineal as well, with the mothers' brothers serving as guardians of their sisters and sisters' children. Unavoidably, however, matrimony planted a seed of conflict with this matrilineal arrangement.

It can be seen in the brittle relations, frictions, and tensions between intermarrying clan-families, as well as between the married couple. Fortune, writing about the situation in Dobu, calls it a "clash of incompatible solidarities" and a "conflict between the *susu* and the marital grouping" (*Sorcerers of Dobu*, p. 43). Ruth Benedict likewise, referring to the Zuni Indians, writes that "marriage, instead of being the social form behind which all the forces of tradition are massed, as in our culture, cuts directly across the most strongly institutionalized social bond in Zuni." That bond is the matrilineal blood bond which is shared not by man and wife but by the woman and her kin (*Patterns of Culture*, p. 76).

It is the men who are most affected by the conflict between matrilineality and matrimony. The man who leaves his own community for that of his wife has divided interests and loyalties. All his basic rights, responsibilities, and al-

legiances are with his sisters and other matrikin. This inhibits
the fuller development of his ties with his wife and her children.
The wife, on the other hand, is not torn by these conflicts so
long as marriage remains matrilocal. As a resident of her
own community she is surrounded and supported by her matrikin. As Ruth Benedict puts it, "For women there is no conflict.
They have no allegiance of any kind to their husbands' groups.
But for all men there is a double allegiance. They are husbands
in one group and brothers in another." She describes the situation among the Zuni as follows:

> To the women of the household, the grandmother and her
> sisters, her daughters and their daughters, belong the house
> and the corn that is stored in it. No matter what may hap-
> pen to marriages, the women of the household remain
> with the house for life. They present a solid front. They
> care for and feed the sacred objects that belong to them.
> They keep their secrets together. Their husbands are out-
> siders, and it is their brothers, married now into the houses
> of other clans, who are united with the household in all
> affairs of moment. It is they who return for all the retreats
> when the sacred objects of the house are set out before
> the altar. It is they, not the women, who learn the word-
> perfect ritual of their sacred bundle and perpetuate it. A
> man goes always, for all important occasions, to his
> mother's house, which, when she dies, becomes his sister's
> house, and if his marriage breaks up, he returns to the
> same stronghold. (*Patterns of Culture*, pp. 76-77)

Fred Eggan gives essentially the same picture with regard
to the matrilineal Hopi Indians:

> The central core or axis of the household is composed
> of a line of women—a segment of a lineage. All the mem-
> bers of the segment, male and female, are born in the
> household and consider it their home, but only the women
> normally reside there after marriage. The men of the lineage
> leave at marriage to reside in the households of their wives,
> returning to their natal home on various ritual and
> ceremonial occasions, or in case of separation or divorce,
> which is frequent. Into the household in turn come other
> men through marriage. . . .

We may view them as lines of women looking alternately to their brothers and to their husbands. On ritual occasions when men return to their natal household, the household group becomes a lineage, or a lineage segment; on ordinary occasions the household is composed of the same women plus their husbands and children. The household revolves about a central and continuing core of women; the men are peripheral with divided residences and loyalties. ("The Hopi and the Lineage Principle," in *Social Structure*, pp. 131-32)

A. I. Richards, who labels the shifting life and allegiance of men as the "institution of the visiting husband or the visiting brother," writes that marriages are easily broken. "A man who cannot stand the situation in his wife's village leaves and goes elsewhere. This might be described as the solution of the detachable husband" ("Some Types of Family Structure Amongst the Central Bantu," in *African Systems of Kinship and Marriage*, pp. 246-48).

Unlike the husband, the brother was not detachable. Whether or not he had a wife in another community, he was the male pillar in his own matrilineal community. Similarly, no matter how many husbands came and went as sexual consorts of a man's sisters, he remained their economic and social "consort." And the children looked to their mother's brother, not their mother's husband, as their guardian. Eggan writes of the Hopi:

A mother's brother has important relations with his sister's children. As male head of his sister's lineage and household his position is one of authority and control; he is the chief disciplinarian and is both respected and obeyed. The mother's brother has primary responsibility for transmitting the ritual heritage of the lineage or clan; he usually selects the most capable nephew as his successor and trains him in the duties of whatever ceremonial position he may control. (*Social Structure*, p. 135)

Thus, although the husband came to live with his wife in her community, he had few rights as a husband and none as a father to his wife's children, who were already provided for and protected by their mother and mother's brother. The husband remained an outsider and a visitor, and as such was obliged to be careful and submissive toward his wife's kinsmen. David M. Schneider, writing about the Trukese, states that "a wife's brother may make almost any demands on the sister's husband and these must be fulfilled. Failure to meet the demands of a wife's brother are grounds for terminating the marriage, and the brother will tell his sister to request the husband to leave" (*Matrilineal Kinship,* p. 231). The same situation prevailed in innumerable other primitive regions.

This is often interpreted as evidence that the brother has a power over the sister comparable to the domination of men over women in our society. In fact, it expresses only the brother's power over the outsider-husband if the latter is held responsible for some misdeed in the wife's community.

Ignorance of the causes of natural deaths and accidental injuries was at the bottom of the frictions and antagonism between brothers and husbands. Since the mothers' brothers were the guardians, they were obliged to take action against those suspected of having brought about, directly or indirectly, such evil happenings.

This fear and suspicion of outsiders created tensions not only between brothers and husbands but also between husbands and wives. Hoebel writes, "Husband and wife, coming as they do from different susus, are hostile at marriage and all their days thereafter. Each believes the other is trying to destroy him by foul magic" (*Man in the Primitive World,* p. 224). Even if a marriage managed to survive for any length of time while the pair were alive, no trace of it remained after the death of one or the other spouse. Hartland describes what happened to a husband on Rotuma, an island north of Fiji, when the wife died:

> The husband only remains in his wife's *hoag* during her life; on her death he is pushed out of one doorway of the house as the corpse is carried out through the other, signifying that he has now no right in it. (*Primitive Society,* pp. 57-58)

The problem was augmented with the breakdown of the cross-cousin alliance in which all the men on both sides were brothers who had no fear of one another when they mated with the sisters in the opposite moiety. But with the advent of pair-unions a heterogeneous group of men were thrown together in the same village through their marriages to the women of the village. In the absence of any alliance between some villages, the men were suspicious and fearful of one another. They could never be sure that they might not be secretly attacked or killed through evil sorcery. Fortune writes:

> Village solidarity further is expressed in the belief that disease and death among its constituent *susu* are not caused by its various *susu* members but by persons of other village allegiance, particularly persons with whom the village is connected by marriage—strangers introduced into the village or their kin in other villages. Village members are friends. Other villages are not to be trusted, although they must be married into. (*Sorcerers of Dobu*, p. 43)

Matrimony thus produced a deep division in the life of every married man. In his own matrilocality, with his sisters and other kin, he was an honored member of the community, a brother or mother's brother, with authority and prestige. In his wife's community he was a nobody, an outsider, subject to various humiliations, if not worse.

This inessential position of the husband can be seen in some of the terms used to describe him. In Dobu, according to Fortune, he was a "Resultant from Marriage" (ibid., p. 43). Kathleen Gough cites even more picturesque designations. In Yao, a husband "is always an outsider in his wife's village—a 'billy goat,' a 'chicken rooster,' or a 'beggar,' who merely followed his wife." She writes about the Minangkabau, "Traditionally, husband and wife did not normally co-reside: a husband visited his wife, chiefly for sexual purposes. He was a 'borrowed man' and a 'rooster'; he had no rights in his wife's lineage's property, nor she in his" (*Matrilineal Kinship*, pp. 581, 588).

Even where a man did reside with his wife, as among the Nayars, Gough writes: "Whatever the circumstances of residence, moreover, a man should place his duties to mother and sisters above those of wife and children" (ibid., p. 397). Max Gluckman remarks on the same situation in Africa:

> Divorce is frequent; women are liable to side with their brothers against their husbands. A man trusts his sister, and not his wife. "Your sister is always your sister, tomorrow your wife may be another man's wife." (*Custom and Conflict in Africa*, p. 74)

The growing antagonism between marriage and matrilineality led to a curious development, the individualization of the clan sister-brother relationship. As against the husband-wife pair joined in marriage, there arises what may be called a counter-institution, the sister-brother pair united in matrilineality. This has been noted in a partial and limited way by some anthropologists, although they do not see it as an evolutionary development stemming from the narrowing down of the clan system into a family system.

For example, Malinowski describes the situation in the Trobriand Islands as follows: "Within the matrilineal order, the brother and the sister are the naturally linked representatives of the male and female principle respectively in all legal and customary matters. In the myths concerning the origin of families, the brother and sister emerge together from underground, through the original hole in the earth. In family matters, the brother is the natural guardian and head of his sister's household and of her children." At the same time he notes that he must as often place the husband and wife side by side as the brother and sister (*Sexual Life of Savages*, p. 35). Lucy Mair, writing on the same subject, is more explicit:

> Although anthropologists habitually write of *the* mother's brother and *the* sister's son, most uncles have many nephews and most nephews many uncles. Occasionally, however, as in parts of Southern Africa, it is the rule that every brother is paired with a particular sister, and so is *the* mother's brother to her children. (*Introduction to Social Anthropology*, p. 91)

The antagonistic coexistence of sister-brother and husband-wife can be viewed as the harbinger of fundamental changes taking place in the matriarchal structure. The composition of the matriclan was changing; the community of sisters and brothers was becoming a community of individual pairs with opposing interests. So long as the matrikin relationship was indissoluble, the matrimonial tie was easily and repeatedly torn apart. Although muted at first, these contradictions were bound to grow and affect every aspect of life.

This can be graphically seen in the changes that came about in the interchange system. Gift-exchanges under the communal mode of life had resulted in joining masses of men in peace pacts. With the reduction of the large communities into individual villages, the interchange system was reduced to an exchange between individual men, husbands and brothers.

The peculiarities of these individual exchanges have been observed by some investigators. They have noted how the husband went to elaborate lengths to transport yams and other garden produce to his wife's brother, while he in turn was the recipient of similar foodstuffs from his sister's husband. Hoebel gives one example:

> Susu practices in Melanesia require that a man raise his crops on his sister's behalf. Since his sister's household is not his own household, he must in effect transfer the yams from his garden to the storehouses of his sister's husband. His storehouses in turn are filled in part by his wife's brother. (*Man in the Primitive World*, p. 344)

Malinowski points out the excessive time and work required to make these now meaningless exchanges:

> At harvest time all the roads are full of big parties of men carrying food, or returning with empty baskets. From the far North of Kiriwina a party will have to run for some twelve miles to the creek of Tikwa'ukwa, get into canoes, punt for miles along the shallow Lagoon, and have another good walk inland from Sinaketa; and all this is in order to fill the yam house of a man who could do it quite well for himself, if it were not that he is under obligation to give all the harvest to his sister's husband! (*Argonauts of the Western Pacific*, p. 174)

In another book Malinowski refers to the same phenomenon, the "general economic *chasse-croise* all over the district" when harvest-time displays and exchanges of food are being made which clearly serve no economic purpose. He writes:

> What could be more economically absurd than this oblique distribution of garden produce, where every man works for his sister and has to rely in turn on his wife's brother, where more time and energy is apparently wasted on display, on show, on the shifting of the goods, than on real work? (*Crime and Custom in Savage Society*, p. 37)

This represents the old interchange system at the point of *reductio ad absurdum*. It lost its meaning and purpose when it was reduced to exchanges between an individual brother and husband. Instead of creating fraternal relations, the burden of this outworn custom could only increase the frictions and tensions between men.

Not only the old exchanges but the divided duties of labor became burdensome. Where formerly tribal brothers and mothers' brothers represented the male pillar of support in a matriarchal-fratriarchal community, now an individual brother was required to provide for an individual sister. At the same time he was still expected to perform labor services for his wife and her kin while residing in their community. The following is an illustration from Briffault's data:

> In the Mortlock Islands the husband has his field in one part of the reef and passes backwards and forwards across the lagoon, to and from his wife's home in another part, lending a hand to the cultivation of her patch.
>
> Similarly, in the western islands of Torres Straits, where matrilocal marriage is the rule, it is common for men to marry in another island and to divide their time between their own plantation and that of their wife, crossing backwards and forwards at different seasons of the year between the two islands. If the husband, in later life, settles down in a more permanent manner, it is usually in the home of his wife. (*The Mothers*, vol. I, p. 292)

In actuality there was very little permanent settling down for a man in the period of matrilocal marriage. No matter how hard he tried to become integrated into his wife's community, there were regular interruptions of the marriage during his life and a permanent dissolution of it after death.

This antagonism between matrimony and matriarchy did not lessen with the advent of what is called "patrilocal" marriage. On the contrary, it grew worse, for now women too were drawn into the divided life and affected by the frictions, tensions, and conflicts that had afflicted men in matrilocal marriage. This requires a closer examination of the term "patrilocal marriage," about which some serious misconceptions have arisen.

The origin of matrilocal marriage can be clearly traced back to the cross-cousin mating alliance between two matrilineal moieties. It required only the further step of the "visiting husband" to bring about the cohabitation of the man with his wife in her community. But there is a conspicuous paucity of material on the origin of "patrilocal marriage." At what point did the wife depart from the age-old custom of remaining in her own community to begin living, at least part of the time, in her husband's community?

The term "patrilocal" hinders the search for an answer. In evolutionary sequence the husband made his appearance in history before the father. According to the accepted definitions, matrilocal marriage means that the husband goes to live in his wife's community, while in patrilocal marriage the wife goes to live in her husband's locality. Nothing in this definition indicates that when the wife goes to live with her husband, she is going to a community of "fathers." She is simply going to a community of possible husbands, one of which has become her actual spouse.

To be sure, after the husband acquired paternal functions in connection with his wife's child, we can speak of fathers and of "patrilocal marriage." But prior to that development we can only speak of the wife going to a "husband-locality" and not to a "patri-locality."

The term "patrilocal marriage" is misleading in still another way. It is usually conceived to be marriage in a male-structured community along the lines of a father-family. This is not the case. Both patrilocal and matrilocal marriage occur in exactly the same kind of clan and village, with a matrilineal structure. The husband comes from his matrilocality, the wife from hers. And whether they live together in the husband's or the wife's community, they are living in one spouse's *matrilocality*.

From this standpoint the use of the term "patrilocal marriage" is premature in a study of origins. However, in the absence of a better term and because this one has become standard, we will continue to use "patrilocal marriage" while understanding that we are really speaking of "husbandlocal marriage."

The evolution from matrilocal to patrilocal marriage is clear enough; what is missing is the original reason for the departure from the age-old practice of a wife remaining in her own community for life. Possibly it began on the basis of the simple principle of parity between matrilineal communities, with the married pair spending time in both. But the removal of the woman from her own locality was a long, slow, and precarious process, which was never fully achieved so long as matrilineal principles prevailed.

Survivals in some regions confirm this. According to Kathleen Gough, writing about the Nayars, "In some cases the wife might occasionally move for a few weeks to live in the husband's natal home if circumstances made this particularly desirable. Such an arrangement was however very modern in Central Kerala; it was much disliked by women and was seldom resorted to." She also writes:

> A woman's contacts with her husband's kin were obviously less regular than those of a man. A woman never went to her husband's taravad to visit him for personal reasons but only to pay polite social calls on his kinswomen. . . . Neither husband nor wife did any tasks at all in each other's homes. Each remained always an outsider to whom polite behavior was due. (*Matrilineal Kinship,* pp. 395, 368)

A similar situation exists among the Mapillas. Gough writes that "in all classes a woman's relations with her spouse's kin are slighter than those of a man. She seldom lives with them and her visits are a matter of ceremonial obligation. Mutual politeness characterizes her relations with her husband's kinswomen . . ." (ibid., p. 439). And among the Mayombe, she writes, there is a saying to the effect that "marriage dies, but relationship (i.e., matrilineal kinship) does not die" (ibid., p. 586).

Briffault gives illustrations of the uncertainties and hesitations that characterized the transition from matrilocal to patrilocal marriage:

> Thus in some parts of Dutch New Guinea a man may take his wife to his home for a year, after which she returns to hers, where he visits her. . . . Among the Massim tribes of eastern New Guinea all degrees of transitions and, as it were, hesitations between matrilocal and patrilocal marriage customs occur; it is incumbent on the men to spend some time in the wife's family and to make a garden there, but they also cultivate a patch round their own homes, and they spend the first years of their married life in a semi-migratory existence between the two homes. . . .
>
> Among all the peoples of northern and of central Asia no custom is more persistently and strictly observed than that which requires the bridegroom to reside for a more or less prolonged period in the wife's family, or that the bride, after a short residence with her husband, shall return for a prolonged period to her own home. Those customs, which are similar to the practices now observed in some parts of New Guinea and Africa which, to our knowl-

edge, are in a state of transition from recent matrilocal to patrilocal usages, suggest that they are survivals of a time when marriage throughout those parts of Asia was also permanently matrilocal. (*The Mothers*, vol. I, pp. 293-96)

Under these circumstances it would be more accurate to speak of patrilocal marriage as "migratory marriage" since the pair shift their residence back and forth between the matri-locality of the wife and the matrilocality of the husband. This is sometimes called "alternate residence" or "virilocal" or "duo-local" residence. Fortune gives an example of an equitable arrangement in Dobu, with the couple spending alternate years in the two localities:

Each marital grouping possesses two house sites, each site with a house built upon it. The woman has her house in her village, the man has his house in his village. The couple with their children live alternately in the woman's house in the village of the woman's matrilineal kin, and in the man's house in the village of the man's matrilineal kin. The change in residence usually takes place each gardening year, so that the one spouse spends alternate years in the other's place and alternate years in own place; but some couples move more frequently to and fro. (*Sorcerers of Dobu*, pp. 4-5)

Even this arrangement did little to dispel the underlying conflicts between matrimony and matrilineality. Each spouse was an "outsider" to the other spouse's kin. As Ruth Benedict describes the Dobuan arrangement:

If an inviolably private house and garden are provided for the married pair, on whose home ground and under whose hostile eyes shall they lie — the susu of the wife or the susu of the husband? The problem is solved logically enough, but in a way that is understandably uncommon. From marriage until death the couple live in alternate years in the village of the husband and the village of the wife.

Each alternate year one spouse has the backing of his own group and commands the situation. The alternate year the same spouse is a tolerated alien who must efface himself before the owners of his spouse's village. Dobuan

> villagers are divided by this rift into two groups which stand always over against each other. . . . (*Patterns of Culture*, p. 126)

Benedict writes that "it is easy for the spouse who is on home ground to turn to his susu, especially to the mother's brother, for support in the marital quarrels that recur constantly in Dobu. The mother's brother is usually only too willing to lecture the outsider publicly or send him or her packing from the village with obscene abuse" (ibid., p. 127).

Unaware of the underlying source of this suspicion and friction between spouses, Benedict attributes it to the "unfaithfulness" of the wife. This conflicts with her own statement that "faithfulness is not expected between husband and wife, and no Dobuan will admit that a man and woman are ever together even for the shortest interval except for sexual purposes" (p. 127). It is far more likely that the friction results from "unfaithfulness" of a wholly different type. Should an injury or death take place in the husband's community while the wife was residing there, it could be attributed to a hostile act by her male kinsmen, practicing their sorcery from afar. This could bring the wife under suspicion for her faithfulness to her own kin and betrayal of her husband's kin.

Thus patrilocal marriage (or migratory marriage, as we have called it) did not alleviate the conflicts between marriage and matriarchy. Even apart from the permanent ruptures that a death in the community could produce, there were periodic separations of the pair on a whole series of occasions: at times of menstruation, for extended intervals at the time of birth, on ritual occasions, and sometimes for no discernible reason. Briffault cites the lament of an early missionary named Hurel, writing about the Bakerewe peoples:

> "A custom which is very injurious to good understanding and to stability in marriage is the habit which the women have of going back to their family on the least occasion. If she is indisposed, the woman says: 'I am going home.' If a feast is held by her people, she says: 'I am going home.' And those residences, often very prolonged, demoralise the poor husband, who is left alone. But he is powerless to alter things; it is the fashion." (*The Mothers*, vol. I, p. 304)

Meyer Fortes writes about the Ashanti in a similar vein:

After marriage the ideal is for a man to have his own home and to have his wife and children living with him. But this ideal is less often realized than Ashanti believe. Even though it is nowadays buttressed by Christian teaching, which has a wide influence, the ideal of the "patrilocal" family as the normal domestic group has not wholly asserted itself. The bonds of matrilineal kinship work too strongly against it. (*Social Structure,* p. 65)

Of all the occasions that a woman living in her husband's community might go back home, the most universal was when she gave birth to her child, which accorded with the principle that every child should be born among its own matrikin. These were protracted stays, sometimes for a period of several months; they could even become permanent separations.

Patrilocal marriage did not give the husband any rights to his wife's children. If she severed the marriage, the children followed their mother back to her matrilocality.

At this early stage of its development, marriage represented as much a dislocated sister and brother as it did a relocated husband and wife. For just as the wife had her closest interests and ties with her own matrikin, the husband's primary place was with his sister and sister's children, not with his wife and her children. One of the most graphic descriptions of this divided life is provided in Fortune's account of a Dobuan marriage ceremony:

The distaff kin of the groom or bride who are the visitors bringing gifts sit at the end of the village nearest their own village. A wide space in between separates the two parties. There is no casual intermingling between the two parties. Every woman present is with her brother. Every man present is with his sister and sister's children. No group of man, wife, and child is to be seen in either of the exchanging parties. Fathers-in-law are out of it, as are all of Those-resulting-from-marriage in either village. It is strange to a European to look on a marriage ceremonial which is celebrated with an entire absence of anyone in a family-by-marriage group. All marriage ceremonial, at its inception and later, however, is marked by a complete disappearance of the marital grouping. After dusk, when the day's ceremonial is ended, husbands come back to their wives and children. All day they were with their sisters and sisters' children, if they belonged to either of the contracting villages. If they did not belong to the contracting villages they either visited their sisters afield, or else formed male parties with other purely masculine business in view. (*Sorcerers of Dobu,* p. 26)

As in life, so in death. A man's burial ground was with his sisters and other matrikin. The remains of the wife and her children were buried with her matrikin. Fortune writes:

> Here below the soil within their stone set circular enclosure lie the mothers, and mothers' brothers, the grandmothers on the distaff side and their brothers, and so, for many a generation back, the ancestors of the villagers on the distaff side. . . . On the paternal side the ancestors of the village owners lie utterly dispersed in the villages of many stranger clans, the villages of their respective mothers and female ancestors. (ibid., pp. 1-2)

Symbolically enough, however, apart from these graveyards of the sister-brother matrilineal kin, husband-wife marriage ties were growing in strength as each married couple came to possess its own house. The need for private dwellings was created when men of different villages were thrown together through marriage to women of one village. Although by this time women too were thrown together by marriages to men of a village, the situation was not quite the same; it was among strange men that suspicions, fears, and hostilities were rife.

This is made clear by Fortune, who writes that "each Dobuan village shelters a heterogeneous collection of men of different village allegiance who distrust one another thoroughly. Suspicion of sorcery and poisoning tactics *within* the village runs very high at times." He contrasts this with villages where "all resultants-from-marriage are women and suspicion of foul tactics within the village is not found" (ibid., p. 9).

Private houses were constructed for married couples to hold down the tensions and animosities that might otherwise arise between strange men. This valid consideration gradually led to the invalidation of the communal property of the matriarchal period, which had been transmitted from mothers to daughters, with brothers sharing in this maternal inheritance. Privacy for personal security was a small step toward the private ownership of property.

Layard makes this point in his studies of Malekula:

Within the village each married man possesses an enclosure, fenced round with stones usually surmounted by a high screen of interwoven reeds. . . . No man ever enters the enclosure of another without invitation. Indeed, the general communism and publicity of life is counterbalanced by a very great sense of possessiveness about a man's actual home. (*Stone Men of Malekula*, pp. 40-41)

In this way, subtly and inexorably, the matriarchal commune was gradually undermined. In the most literal sense the maternal clan's last refuge was the graveyard. As Fortune perceived in Dobu, the huts above ground contained married pairs. But "the *susu* has no common house for its exclusive use. Its only exclusive communal resting place is in the graveyard" (*Sorcerers of Dobu*, p. 4). The end was near for the matriarchs; soon even this ultimate refuge would disappear and be replaced by family burial plots.

A social system comes into existence out of the specific needs of humanity at a given stage of history, and corresponds with the level of humanity's economic development. After these needs have been fulfilled the organization itself becomes outworn; it can only be a fetter upon further development. This was the case with the matriarchy.

The matriarchy was born in the struggle to elevate humanity above animalism and cannibalism. Once this mission had been accomplished, it gave way to new forms that responded to compelling new needs. Such were the reasons that the husband-wife partnership, combining sexual union with socioeconomic union, had to prevail over segregation of the sexes and sister-brother partnership. In addition, the dichotomy between kin and stranger had to go; the time had come for the recognition of the father and of patrilineal kinship.

However, society progresses through protracted and painful struggles. The antagonism between marriage and matriarchy grew into an irreconcilable conflict between the father-family and the fratriarchy. Nothing less than a colossal social revolution could resolve it.

Part III
The Patriarchy

11

The Matrilineal Family

The basic factors that brought humanity to a higher economic
level and closed the long epoch of savagery have been pointed
out by many historians and economists. Most important was
the advance from food gathering and hunting to food production, beginning around 8,000 years ago. Simple horticulture
or garden culture, which had developed in the higher phase
of savagery, led to the larger-scale agriculture that marks the
epoch of barbarism. This provided more abundant and dependable supplies of food for humans; by supplying fodder for
animals, it also promoted stock-raising.

Agriculture and stock-raising mark the dividing line between
savagery (also called the paleolithic period) and barbarism
(the neolithic period). The permanent surpluses of food gave
rise to larger concentrations of population, new and more
complex divisions of labor, and the development of specialized
crafts. With further advances — metallurgy, the wheel, the calen-
dar, and writing — barbarism gave way to civilization within
a few thousand years.

According to Benjamin Farrington, "The vital period in which
the new techniques were developed is roughly the two millennia
from 6,000 to 4,000 B. C." He adds:

> When history is really taught as it ought to be taught,
> so that everybody is made to understand, as the founda-
> tion of his intellectual life, the true story of human society,
> one of the most fundamental lessons will be the concrete
> and detailed exposition of the nature of this great revolu-

tion in man's control over his environment. The film, the museum, the workshop, the lecture, the library, will combine to make the significance of these vital two thousand years sink into the historical consciousness of mankind. This technical revolution constitutes the material basis of ancient civilization. No comparable change in human destinies took place between it and the industrial revolution of the eighteenth century. The cultures of the ancient empires of the Near East, of Greece and Rome, and of Mediaeval Europe, all rest on the technical achievements of the neolithic age. (*Greek Science*, vol. I, p. 18)

One of the significant changes that attended this neolithic technical-economic revolution is left unmentioned. This was the dying out of cannibalism. In the previous period garden culture and the interchange of garden produce and other gifts had made steady encroachments upon it. But its definitive end was brought about through agriculture. The grain belts of wheat, oats, barley, and rice, and the introduction of bread as the "staff of life," delivered the final blow to this ancient scourge in the more advanced regions.

The abolition of cannibalism is recorded in the myth-history of Egypt, located in the "fertile crescent," the cradle of civilization. According to the Greek historian Diodorus, the Egyptian goddess Isis learned how to make bread and, together with her brother, Osiris, put an end to cannibalism. E. A. Wallis Budge writes:

> . . . Osiris forbade men to eat each other. Isis had found out how to make bread from wheat and barley, which had hitherto grown wild with the other herbs of the field, and men, having learned the arts of agriculture, adopted the use of the new food willingly, and were thereby enabled to cease from the habit they had of killing and eating one another. Every student of African customs, ancient and modern, knows that the tradition recorded by Diodorus rests on fact. . . . (*Osiris*, p. 167)

The family makes its appearance at the turning point from savagery to barbarism. Its emergence is reflected in the legends of Isis, the barbarian goddess, who is described in seemingly contradictory terms as both the sister of Osiris and the wife of Osiris. It would be incorrect to view this as a sister-brother marriage; rather, it represents a telescoped version of the historical changeover from the sister-brother clan partnership to the husband-wife family partnership.

The Isis cult was widespread; it originated in Egypt around 2000 B. C. and spread to ancient Greece and Rome. Isis, the original Earth Mother or Universal Mother, was the prototype of the Greek Demeter and the Roman Hera. More than any of her successors, Isis personified the full transition from maternal clan to father-family and from the social mother to the family mother.

Isis begins as the sister of Osiris, as the bread-maker who assists him in the suppression of cannibalism. Subsequently she evolves into his wife. With the birth of her child she becomes a family mother. In her final form she is pictured holding up her child, Horus, prefiguring the sacred mother and son that emerged with the father-family.

The father-family, however, was not the first family to appear in history. Morgan, in his pioneering studies, gave the name "pairing family" to the earliest family unit, placing its emergence on the boundary line between savagery and barbarism. Morgan was acutely aware of the problem involved in finding a suitable name for this unit. He wrote, "Among savage and barbarous tribes there is no name for the family. . . . The family name is no older than civilization." He concluded that "if any name was given to the anterior family it is not now ascertainable" (*Ancient Society*, pp. 77-78, 478).

This problem is implicitly recognized by many later anthropologists, including those who insist that there has always been a father-family. Although they have abandoned Morgan's "pairing family," they use terms that amount to the same thing; namely, a family in which the father is recognized but does not play the role he does in the fully developed father-family. Among these terms are: the "elementary" family, the "primitive" family, the "mother" family, the "conjugal" family, the "marital grouping," and the "matrilineal family."

In this book we propose to use "matrilineal family" or "matrifamily" in place of Morgan's term. "Matrifamily" is more descriptive of the kind of unit that preceded the father-family. It was a family still embedded in the matriclan, inheriting its maternal and fraternal structure, customs, and traditions. Matrilineality still overshadowed the paternal relationship taking root within the matrifamily.

The numerous changes the family has passed through in the course of its evolution have tended to obscure the qualitative turning point in the transition from matrifamily to father-family. The matrifamily stands on the side of the last stage of the matriarchal order, the father-family on the side of the victorious patriarchy.

Morgan's sequence of family development must be reexamined and amended from this standpoint. He saw the following five stages: 1. the consanguine family; 2. the punaluan family; 3. the syndyasmian or pairing family; 4. the patriarchal family; and 5. the monogamian family (ibid., pp. 393-94). The first two are incorrectly called "family" since they belong to the pre-family epoch. The "consanguine family," as we have seen (Chapter 8), is more accurately named the maternal primal horde, predecessor of the maternal clan. The "punaluan family" is also misnamed since it was only a cross-cousin mating relationship between men and women. The Hawaiian term *punalua* is translated as "intimate companion" or "spouse," indicating that it was a pairing couple but not yet a pairing family.

Thus the "pairing family" that Morgan placed third in his sequence of stages was in fact the first family, a matrifamily still undetached from the matriclan and not yet a father-family. By contrast Morgan's last two forms, the patriarchal and monogamian families, are father-families in the full sense of the term. Both belong to the patriarchal era.

The chief difference between them is that in Morgan's patriarchal family a man can have multiple wives, while in the monogamic family only one woman can be the lawful wife. However, both are patriarchal; the father is the central figure, controlling the lives and destinies of wife (or wives) and children. And both are "monogamic" in that the wife or wives belong exclusively to one man, the husband, the father of their children.

The matrifamily is the starting point for an exposition of the origin of the father-family. In the course of this investigation we will see how the growing collision between the mothers' brothers and the fathers shattered the fratriarchy and ushered in the patriarchy.

Couvade: "Making" the Father

In our day a man is not a father unless he is the genitor of a child; paternity is based upon an ascertainable biological relationship between a man and his offspring. But in savage and barbaric societies the biological facts about paternity were

unknown. It is therefore pointless to begin the search for the
origin of fatherhood by trying to locate the biological father.
Paternity began as a social relationship between a woman's
husband and her child.

Before the idea of biological paternity can be grasped, it is
necessary to understand that sexual intercourse between a man
and a woman is the indispensable first step toward conception.
But primitive people did not know this simple fact about the
birth process. They attributed conception to various causes,
not one of which was connected with sexual intercourse. They
thought women gave birth spontaneously through their magical
powers, or through something that entered their womb, or
through something they ate or were given to eat, perhaps
by a man. If a man was involved at all, it was through food
intercourse, not sex intercourse.

This naive notion that a woman could conceive by eating
something persisted well into the historic period. Briffault notes
that "the Manchus were descended from a girl who conceived
through eating a red fruit. . . . Attis was conceived by his
mother eating almonds, or, according to another version, a
pomegranate. Hera conceived Hephaistos by eating a flower,
and Hebe by eating lettuce" (*The Mothers*, vol. II, p. 453).
Lord Raglan gives further illustrations:

> Rachel conceived Joseph by eating mandrakes. Zoroaster
> was conceived through his mother's eating milk mixed
> with "homa," and the Irish hero Cuchulain through his
> mother's eating a worm. Pliny, Virgil, and St. Augustine
> believed that mares could be fertilized by the wind, and
> a modern Moorish proverb expresses the same belief with
> regard to baboons. (*Jocasta's Crime*, p. 15)

The primitive ignorance of biological paternity is well documented. Raglan writes that "this ignorance is reported from
many parts of Australia, and from New Guinea, New Caledonia, the Trobriand Islands, and Central Borneo." It was
once universal. Hartland points out that

> the truth that a child is only born in consequence of an
> act of sexual union, and that the birth of a child is the
> natural consequence of such an act performed in favouring
> circumstances, and that every child must be the result of
> such an act and of no other cause, was not realized by
> mankind; that down to the present day it is imperfectly

realized by some peoples and that there are still others among whom it is unknown. (*Primitive Paternity*, vol. II, p. 250)

There are reports that, even when the facts about conception and birth were made known to primitive peoples, they refused to accept them as true. Some were inclined to view the information as a defect in the intelligence of the white man. Malinowski relates how the Trobrianders went to great pains to explain to him that sexual intercourse had nothing to do with the birth of a child.

Their attitude to their own children also bears witness to their ignorance of any causal relation between congress and the ensuing pregnancy. A man whose wife has conceived during his absence will cheerfully accept the fact and the child, and he will see no reason at all for suspecting her of adultery. One of my informants told me that after over a year's absence he returned to find a newly born child at home. He volunteered this statement as an illustration and final proof of the truth that sexual intercourse has nothing to do with conception. . . .

My friend Layseta, a great sailor and magician of Sinaketa, spent a long time in his later youth in the Amphlett Islands. On his return he found two children, borne by his wife during his absence. He is very fond of them and of his wife; and when I discussed the matter with others, suggesting that one at least of these children could not be his, my interlocutors did not understand what I meant. (*Sexual Life of Savages,* pp. 193-94)

Frazer points out that the biological facts of life we take for granted could not have been known to primitive peoples. While the part played by the mother in the birth process is obvious, he wrote, how could people in the pre-scientific era "perceive that the child which comes forth from the womb is the fruit of the seed which was sowed there nine months before?" (*Totemism and Exogamy*, vol. IV, pp. 61-62).

Margaret Mead makes the even more important point that to the primitive mind children were not the fruit of a momentary act of sexual congress but of years of patient nurture and care:

The Arapesh have no idea that after the initial act which establishes physiological paternity, the father can go away and return nine months later to find his wife safely delivered of a child. Such a form of parenthood they would consider impossible, and furthermore, repellent. For the child is not the product of a moment's passion, but is made by both father and mother, carefully, over time. (*Sex and Temperament in Three Primitive Societies*, p. 31)

Mead here puts a finger on the most essential characteristic that made the husband the father of a woman's child, namely, that he now had the right to assist his wife in the care and protection of her child. From this standpoint, a new "male mother" makes his appearance in history — the "husband-mother" — as against the former male mother, the mother's brother. Thus fatherhood as a social institution did not begin on the basis of sexual intercourse between a man and woman but as a set of maternal functions performed by the man for his wife's child.

The husband's right to perform these maternal functions was established socially, that is, ritually, by what is called "couvade." The subject of couvade gripped the attention of such early scholars as Bachofen, Tylor, and Frazer, but has since received little serious attention. Yet it holds the key to explaining the origin of the father and the patrilineal relationship.

The ritual was first noticed during the voyages of Columbus when his crew landed in the Caribbean Islands, but it was only in the last century that Tylor applied the term "couvade" to the practice. He took the term from the Basque work *couver*, meaning "to sit on eggs." The practice is not limited to this area; it is found in many regions of the globe. As Lowie puts it, "The couvade thrives in bleak Fuegia no less than in the South American tropics" (*Introduction to Cultural Anthropology*, p. 357).

Couvade, also called a "father rite," resembles the initiation ritual by which a man was "made" into an eligible husband, and may even be an extension of it. But it has its own specific characteristics; it made the man first into a "male mother" or, as some have called him, a "second mother."

The central feature of couvade is the imitation by the man of a woman in childbed; the ritual is therefore sometimes called "male childbed." As it is usually described, the wife, directly after giving birth, goes about her daily activities without further ado. But the husband takes to his hammock or bed, "lying in" for a time. He is treated as an invalid and subjected to strict taboos and rules of avoidance. He is expressly forbidden to do work of any kind, must not engage in violent activities such as hunting, and may not touch any weapons. He is especially forbidden to eat flesh foods. He undergoes a period of complete fasting from which he is gradually released by being fed weak gruel or mash, normally given to infants. Old women minister to his needs, supervise his observance of the taboos, and assist his recovery.

The early anthropologists were baffled by this curious custom. The various hypotheses they presented to explain it hardly seem to refer to the same subject. The Jesuit priest Josef F. Lafitau thought couvade was motivated by a dim consciousness of original sin. Max Mueller thought the prospective father was so harassed and henpecked by a bunch of women that he imagined himself to be a martyr, felt ill, and took to bed. Frazer's theory was based upon his concept of "sympathetic magic," while Ernest Crawley thought it was a device to fend off evil influences. Lippert stood alone in the view that couvade was a form of redemption sacrifice by the father in lieu of the sacrifice of his firstborn son. (A summary of this subject appears in Lippert's book *The Evolution of Culture,* Appendix E, pp. 672-73.)

One thread of agreement ran through these conflicting interpretations; the phenomenon was believed to be connected with the transition from a matrilineal to a patrilineal basis of society. According to Bachofen, couvade was an indicator of the relationship between father and child in the transition from mother right to father right. This view was supported by others, including Tylor, who decided that couvade was nothing less than "the very sign and record of that vast change." He also noted that, through the ritual, the husband became a "second mother."

Couvade, then, is to be regarded as the last of the rites of passage "making men" out of former strangers and enemies. Initiation gave a man the right to be a husband in the community of his wife. Couvade allowed him to have close association with his wife's child, to hold it in his arms, nurture and care for it. It appears that this right was at first restricted to male children. Thus two males who had formerly belonged to different and hostile communities, separated by their "hereditary enmity," were joined together as father and son — or, more accurately, as husband-mother and son.

This would explain the restrictions and taboos placed upon a man in the process of becoming a father. Forbidding work or violent activities meant that the former foeman could not hunt or kill any living creature while he was being made into a father. Chapple and Coon, citing Beatrice Blackwood, describe the couvade among the Buka peoples in the Solomon Islands: "During this period he must on no account carry or lift a heavy object, or touch a knife, ax, or any sharp instrument. It is believed that if he did so, the child would be injured" (*Principles of Anthropology,* p. 489).

Lippert gives other examples of such precautions. "In South America, when a child dies, the father is usually blamed for not having scrupulously adhered to this usage. After a Carib of Guiana has become a father, he may not shoot any large game for a time" (*Evolution of Culture,* p. 455).

The strict prohibition against cutting even applied to gardening work. W.I. Thomas cites a report on the Uduk of the Sudan: "During pregnancy for seven months, and for two months after birth, the husband must do as little work as possible and must under no circumstances cut anything—crops, grass, or wood" (*Primitive Behavior,* p. 22).

The reasons the Orokaiva and other aborigines give for this abstention from work are illuminating. "If he were to strike at a young sapling with his axe, it would be as if he struck at his baby's neck," says Thomas. "The 'blood would come up' and the child would choke and die." One man stated that he could not fell a tree until his child was two years old, for "it would be the same as cutting his baby's throat" (ibid., p. 22).

The man who is not working is giving a public demonstration that he is not cutting anything down—animal, vegetable, or human. He is therefore not liable to blood reprisal. If an unforeseen accident or death should occur during the couvade, how could the father be suspected of any evil intent? Was he not "lying in," lying inert in his bed?

Couvade testifies that the father does not enter history as the biological male parent of a child but through a ritual giving him social recognition as the father. As Rivers puts it, "The family to which a child belongs is not determined by the physiological act of birth, but depends on the performance of some social act." In parts of Melanesia where the earlier elaborate ritual had dwindled to a perfunctory rite, "the father is the man who plants a leaf of the cycas-tree before the door of the house," while elsewhere "the man who pays the midwife becomes the father of the child" (*Social Organization,* p. 52).

Couvade rituals have survived in a number of primitive regions studied in this century, although they have not always been recognized as such. Margaret Mead's account of the birth of an Arapesh child contains features typical of couvade, however much other aspects of the ceremony have been altered. The father, as is typical, cannot be present at the birth, so the child is delivered away from home. When mother and child return from their retreat, the father goes through the performance of lying in bed having a baby. There are the usual food taboos and other restrictions. According to Mead, "A man who bears a first child is in as precarious a state as a newly initiated boy or a man who has killed for the first time in battle." After the ordeals and rituals are completed we learn that "the new father is become one of those who have successfully borne a child" (*Sex and Temperament,* pp. 33-36).

Fundamentally, then, the social act that makes a man into the father of a child consists of imitating the mother in bearing the child and then becoming a "second mother" in caring for and protecting the child. Even after the birth performance fades away, the male maternal functions remain. In *The Sexual Life of Savages,* Malinowski gives an illustration of this from his studies of the Trobriand Islanders:

> We have already seen that the husband fully shares in the care of the children. He will fondle and carry a baby, clean and wash it, and give it the mashed vegetable food which it receives in addition to the mother's milk almost from birth. In fact, nursing the baby in the arms or holding it on the knees, which is described by the native word *kopo'i,* is the special role and duty of the father (*tama*). . . . Again, if anyone inquires why children should have duties towards their father, who is a "stranger" to them, the answer is invariably: "because of the nursing (*pela kopo'i*)," "because his hands have been soiled with the child's excrement and urine". . . . (pp. 20-21)

Malinowski does not recognize this as an example of a "male mother," that is, a husband-becoming-a-father. Holding to the view that the father-family has always existed, he is troubled by findings which essentially refute that position. As he describes the Trobriand social structure:

> We find in the Trobriands a matrilineal society in which descent, kinship, and every social relationship are legally reckoned through the mother only, and in which women

have a considerable share in tribal life, even to the taking
of a leading part in economic, ceremonial, and magical
activities. . . . (p. 3)

In this matrilineal region, Malinowski tells us, "these natives
have a well-established institution of marriage, and yet are
quite ignorant of the man's share in the begetting of children."
The term "father" has "a clear, though exclusively social, definition: it signifies the man married to the mother, who lives
in the same house with her, and forms part of the household"
(p. 5).

Since no clearcut term for "father" exists in the Trobriand
language, Malinowski presents a somewhat tortured explanation for the two terms, *tomakava* and *tama,* that he trans-
lates as "father." He writes, "The father, in all discussions about
relationship, was pointedly described to me as *tomakava,* a
'stranger,' or, even more correctly, an 'outsider.'" At the same
time this outsider was also a *tama,* that is, the husband of the
mother living in the same household with her. He asks: "What
does the word *tama* (father) express to the native?" His answer
is: "'Husband of my mother' would be the answer first given
by an intelligent informant. He would go on to say that his
tama is the man in whose loving and protecting company
he has grown up" (p. 6).

A "husband of my mother" is not exactly the same as "my
father." To put the matter more accurately, after the "outsider"
became the husband of the mother, he was advanced to the
status of "male mother," or husband-mother—the first step
toward becoming the father of his wife's children. His functions
were to help feed, nurture, and protect his wife's children. But
this did not alter the clan and family structure, which remained
exclusively matrilineal and where, as Malinowski emphasizes,
"descent, kinship and every social relationship" were reckoned
through the mother line.

To translate native terms meaning "a man in transition to
becoming a father" as "father" in our patriarchal sense of the
term can only lead to confusion. Malinowski himself recognizes this, for he cautions us as follows:

It will be clear to the reader, therefore, that the term "father," as I use it here, must be taken, not as having the
various legal, moral, and biological implications that it
holds for us, but in a sense entirely specific to the society
with which we are dealing. It might seem better, in order

to avoid any chance of such misconception, not to have used our word "father" at all . . . but, in practice, this would have proved too unwieldy. The reader, therefore, when he meets the word "father" in these pages, should never forget that it must be defined, not as in the English dictionary, but in accordance with the facts of native life. I may add that this rule applies to all terms which carry special sociological implications, that is to all terms of relationship, and such words as "marriage," "divorce," "betrothal," "love," "courtship," and the like. (pp. 5-6)

This is good advice. All modern family and marriage terms have extremely limited usefulness in a study of the origin of the father-family. This applies not only to the father himself but also to the patrilineal relationship that grew up along with him.

The Father's Sister and Patrilineal Kinship

Another problem confronting those who believe in the eternal father-family is the phenomenon called "group fatherhood." The term was coined after it was discovered that a child would call not only his mother's husband his "male nurturer" or "father," but also many other men. As Rivers puts it, "A child of one group will give the same term to all the men of his father's group and generation which he applies to his own father, i.e. to all those who . . . would in some systems be called husbands . . ." (*Social Organization*, p. 184).

The term "group fatherhood" can be as misleading as "group marriage." The latter term does not mean that all the men are married to all the women of a group; it means that a fraternal-matrimonial alliance has been established between two groups for cross-cousin mating. "Group fatherhood" expresses the paternal or patrilineal relationship that grew up out of this cross-exchange mating. The men of one side were potential fathers of the children of the women of the other side, but the individual father was the man who was married to the mother and, through the prescribed ritual, became officially recognized as male mother of her child.

The patrilineal relationship came into existence in a later stage of the classificatory system of kinship, which had begun with matrilineal and fratrilineal relationships. It was the last "classified" relationship to appear in the matrilineal clan system before the turning point that created the father-family.

Although collective fatherhood may be puzzling to us, the aborigines had no difficulty distinguishing among men of the group. To a child, the man married to his mother was his "near" father, the others were his "far-away" fathers, his general patrilineal kin. Radcliffe-Brown gives an example:

> . . . the Kariera native uses his word *mama* (father), speaking of a large number of different related persons by the one name, but distinguishing in thought, though not in words, those of his "fathers" who are more nearly related to him from those who are more distantly related. In the modern blackfellow English he speaks of his "close-up" and "far-away" "fathers." The same is the case with every other term of relationship. With regard to the term for "father," a man's nearest relative of this kind is not necessarily the man who gave him birth but the man under whose care he lived as a child. ("Social Organization of the Kariera of Australia," in *Source Book in Anthropology*, p. 272)

The *mama* married to a child's mother was differentiated from all the other possible *mamas* who might have been the mother's husband. He was the child's "male mother" and in process of becoming the father.

Contrary to the widespread assumption among anthropologists that patrilineal kinship signifies a "paternal clan" along the lines of a father-family, the opposite is the case. Patrilineal kinship was born in the matrifamily, and it did not divest itself of the mark of this origin until the matrilineal system was completely crushed and replaced by the father-family.

The birth of patrikinship within the matrifamily can be seen in the figure of the "father's sister" who makes her appearance at this juncture. She is also called the "female father" as a counterpart of the male mother. This is correct providing we understand that in this instance the male mother is not the mother's brother but her husband.

Among those concerned with this curious figure was Rivers. Noting that she makes her appearance late in history along with patrilineality, he described her as follows:

> The relation between a woman and her brother's child is one of the utmost importance in the Banks Islands.

She is called *veve vus rawe* in Mota and corresponding terms in other islands, this name being due to a ceremony in which she takes a leading part. When a man is initiated into the division of *Avtagataga* in the *Sukwe* a number of women assist, who by this ceremony come to stand in the relation of *veve vus rawe* to the initiate. . . . In this ceremony the leading part is taken by the father's sister.

The father's sister may also be called *maranaga*, a name used for one of high rank and now adopted as the word for king or queen. She receives the greatest respect from her nephew who will not say her name, though he will take food from her and will eat with her from the same dish. (*History of Melanesian Society*, vol. I, pp. 38-39)

Behind the paternal disguise of this feared and respected figure of the father's sister can be detected the former mother-in-law—that is, all the older women in a wife's clan that a husband must avoid until he is permitted such association. Radcliffe-Brown writes concerning the Kariera:

A man applies the name *toa* to his father's sister and to the wife of any *kaga*, that is to any woman who might be his mother-in-law. He may not speak to any of these women, nor have any social dealing whatever with them. If for any reason he is obliged to be near one of his *toa* he must take care that he does not look at her. He will, if possible, interpose a hut or bush between himself and her, or else he will sit with his back to her. This rule breaks down when a man gets on in years and has been long married with children of his own. He then ceases to speak of these women as *toa*, calling them *yumani* instead, and he is permitted to speak to them if he wishes, although the old habit still shows itself, and he has very little to do with them. . . . A man must avoid all his *toa* . . . until the time comes when they can be regarded as *yumani*, and the necessity for avoidance ceases. (*Source Book in Anthropology*, pp. 278-79)

Elsewhere Radcliffe-Brown gives this series of examples:

Amongst the BaThonga the father's sister is called *rarana*, a term which Mr. Junod explains as meaning "female father." In some South African languages there is no special term for the father's sister; thus in Xosa, she is denoted by a descriptive term *udade bo bawo*, literally "father's sister." In Zulu she may be referred to by a similar descriptive term or she may be spoken of simply as *ubaba*, "father," just like the father's brothers. (*Structure and Function in Primitive Society*, p. 19)

The two occasions on which the father's sister is most visible are connected with the births and marriages of her brother's sons, usually referred to in studies as her "nephews." Rivers describes the ritual that takes place in Motlav at the time a man's wife gives birth. All the women of both villages, that is, the matrikin of both husband and wife, assemble at the house where the woman delivers her child and remain there for twenty days. After certain rituals with yam puddings and the "payment" of a gift by the husband to all the women, the final ritual takes place:

> . . . the women all sit down in a ring outside the house and the sister of the father of the child brings the baby out of the house and hands it to the first woman in the ring who passes it to the next and thus it goes round the whole circle, each woman holding the child for a time. When the father's sister again receives the child she carries it round the whole circle four times and then takes it to the mother who has remained in the house during the ceremony. (*History of Melanesian Society*, vol. I, p. 148)

The father's sister becomes deeply involved at the time her brother's sons get married, according to Rivers:

> It is in connection with marriage that the role of the father's sister becomes of the most importance. She arranges the marriage of her nephew in the ordinary course, and if the latter chooses for himself, she may forbid the match. A man would never marry against the will of his father's sister. It seemed also that if an unmarried woman wished to have sexual relations with a man she would first approach his father's sister, it being usual in Melanesia for such a proposal to come from the woman. (ibid., p. 39)

In fact, the father's sister played the central role not so much in connection with marriage as with the children born of a marriage. Unfortunately, in contrast to the abundant data on the mother-in-law, there is very little on the father's sister.

In part this is because the father's sister appears late in history, side by side with the father as the "male mother," and disappears soon after. It is also attributable to insufficient understanding of the vast distinction between the classificatory and family kinship systems.

The chief function of the father's sister was that of the "maker" of fathers or, more comprehensively, the maker of the paternal relationship between fathers and sons. Just as the two sets of mothers-in-law had "made" the marriage relationship between husbands and wives, creating a bond between former enemy groups, so the "father's sisters" or "female fathers" effected the relationship between husbands and their wives' children. They added the paternal or patrilineal relationship to the bonds between groups.

As Rivers interprets this, "The importance of the father's sister as a woman of the opposite and more or less hostile moiety of the community, I still believe to be an important element in the complex chain of causation through which the exceptional position of this relative has been produced" (ibid., vol. II, p. 164). It is also apparent from Rivers's probings that while the individual father's sister, like the individual father, is singled out from the group, this has not yet altered the classificatory system of kinship.

This is the most important point about the paternal relationship as it first appears — it is still within the basic structure of the matriclan, matrivillage, or matrifamily. In every instance kinship and descent are determined through the female line. The recognition of the husband, first as the male mother and then as the father of his wife's child, did not result in a father-family in our sense of the term. Nor did it result in a "patrilineal clan" in the sense of a structure that differed essentially from the matrilineal clan.

On the contrary, "patrilineal clan" is a contradiction in terms. Every clan was a matrilineal clan, featuring kinship and descent through the maternal line. Patrilineality began as no more than a patrilineal *relationship* between two matrilineal clans — the clan of the husband and the clan of the wife. Just as each matriclan recognized the men of the other matriclan as husbands of their women, so they now recognized these husbands as being the fathers of the women's children.

This paternal relationship, moreover, remained subordinate.

So long as the clan system remained in existence, the dominant relationship was matrilineal — and fratrilineal. It was precisely this dominance of the fratrilineal relationship that produced the antagonism within the matrifamily which eventually tore it apart. From the time that paternity was born, the matrifamily was divided.

12

The Matrifamily:
A Divided Family

"Life with Father," as portrayed in old-fashioned plays and motion pictures, shows an imposing gentleman who occupies the commanding position in the family, provides for its economic needs, endows it with his name, transmits his property to his sons, and expects his wife and children to cater to his needs and obey him. This roaring lion of a father is far removed from the paternal mouse who first enters history. At that point the father was last in the line of relatives — after the mothers, the sisters, and the brothers — and it took considerable time and turmoil before he moved all the way up to first place.

A picturesque description of the humble spot occupied by the nascent father is given by Rivers in reference to the Seri Indians of Baja California. "The male members sat under a rude shelter in order of precedence, the eldest brother nearest the fire, his brothers next to him in order of age, and then, often outside the shelter and exposed to the rain, the husbands of the women of the household" (*Social Organization,* p. 89).

Even after the male spouse came in out of the rain, occupied a house of his own with his wife, and was socially recognized as father of her child, life for father was hardly enviable. The mother's brother was the strong and permanent personage in his sister's life, while the father remained an incidental figure. This was true not only in the case of matrilocal marriage but also in patrilocal marriage. When the marriage broke up the woman went back to her own locality, taking her children with her. This ended not only the marriage but also the man's paternal relationship with his wife's children.

Even where a marriage survived for a long time, a father's relations with his wife's children were short-lived and limited. Malinowski, writing of the father in the Trobriand Islands where marriage is patrilocal, says that when the wife gives birth "the husband has then to protect and cherish the children, to 'receive them in his arms' when they are born, but they are not 'his' in the sense that he has had a share in their procreation." Although he is regarded as "a beloved, benevolent friend," he is not a "recognized kinsman of the children." Fundamentally he is a "stranger" to them. "The authority over the children is vested in the mother's brother," says Malinowski. He compares that kind of paternity to ours:

> In our own type of family we have the authoritative, powerful husband and father backed up by society. We have also the economic arrangement whereby he is the breadwinner, and can — nominally at least — withhold supplies or be generous with them at his will. In the Trobriands, on the other hand, we have the independent mother and her husband, who has nothing to do with the procreation of the children, and is not the bread-winner, who cannot leave his possessions to the children, and has socially no established authority over them. The mother's relatives, on the other hand, are endowed with very powerful influence, especially her brother, who is the authoritative person, the producer of supplies for the family, and whose possessions the sons will inherit at his death. Thus the pattern of social life and the constitution of the family are arranged on entirely different lines from those of our culture. (*Sex and Repression in Savage Society,* p. 25)

This does not tell the whole story about the father's relations with his wife's children at this stage. He was their father only during their infancy and early childhood, that is, while they were under the care of the mother and lived in the same household with their parents. As they grew older, they shifted away from their father and became closer to their maternal kin — the girls to their mothers, the boys to their mothers' brothers. Elizabeth Colson writes about the Plateau Tonga:

> If children live with their father there is usually a warm affectionate relation between them while the children are still small. As they grow older, this relation alters. The daughters are drawn into the activities of their mother

and older sisters almost as soon as they can walk. They eat with the women and begin to be trained for their future work. Discipline is usually left to the mother, who is in direct charge of their work, but despite this she becomes their confidant and mentor and a more formal relationship develops with the father. By the time they near puberty, the father will disavow any knowledge of their affairs. A man does not inquire directly into the sexual life of his daughter. If he suspects that she is pregnant, he must ask her mother or her mother's brother or some other relative to question her. He himself does not handle the resulting negotiations to collect damages. When his daughters marry, they go off to join their husbands. . . . (*Matrilineal Kinship,* p. 76)

She adds that "small boys remain longer in close association with their father, since by the age of four or five they are drawn into the eating group of the men." Within a few years, however, even this close association changes. As the boy grows older and "learns the difference between matrilineal and other kin, his attitude toward his father changes and there is a loosening of the tie between them." This "results in a more formal relationship which replaces the old familiarity." In due course the son moves away from the father altogether, and the father "has no power to prevent the move" (ibid., p. 76). According to Colson, "At about the age of ten, he moves from the family house to one of the boys' houses. Here he lives until he goes off to work or marries" (ibid., p. 79).

Where the mother lives in her husband's locality, when the time came for the boy to separate from his father he went back to his mother's village, there to be tutored by his mother's brothers. This divided residence is sometimes called "duolocal" or "virilocal," since the boy lived part of his life with his father and part with his mother's brother in his mother's village. Hoebel gives an example of this dual residence from the Haida of the northwestern coast of the United States:

At the age of ten a boy leaves his parental home and moves into the household of his maternal uncle to have his training completed. He serves as a page to his uncle in war and an apprentice in industry. The uncle cares for him and subjects him to a rigorous regimen, including swimming in the winter ocean. The boy ultimately acquires titles, supernatural power, and other property from his uncle as his due. Exactly the same practice is followed by the Trobriand Islanders, and for the same reasons. (*Man in the Primitive World,* p. 242)

Hoebel further points out that in tribes with matrilineal descent such as the Hopi, the Zuni, and the Iroquois, "the boy continues to live at home until marriage since that is already the seat of the ceremonial functions he is to acquire from his maternal uncle." Duolocal or virilocal residence occurs only when his mother's residence is patrilocal, which obliges him to leave his father's village to return to his maternal village.

In sum, the matrifamily is fundamentally a divided family in which two adult men take turns bringing up a woman's son. So long as the child is with his mother, requiring mother-care, his father assists the mother as the child's caretaker. But, as he grows older, he comes under the guardianship of his matrikinsman, his mother's brother.

Malinowski describes the situation this creates in the boy's life:

But as soon as the child begins to grow up . . . certain complications arise, and change the meaning of *tama* for him. He learns that he is not of the same clan as his *tama,* that his totemic appellation is different, and that it is identical with that of his mother. At the same time he learns that all sorts of duties, restrictions, and concerns for personal pride unite him to his mother and separate him from his father. Another man appears on the horizon, and is called by the child *kadagu* ("my mother's brother"). This man may live in the same locality, but he is just as likely to reside in another village. The child also learns that the place where his *kada* (mother's brother) resides is also his, the child's "own village"; that there he has his property and his other rights of citizenship, and there his future career awaits him; that there his natural allies and associates are to be found. He may even be taunted in the village of his birth with being an "outsider" (*tomakava*) while in the village he has to call "his own," in which his mother's brother lives, his father is a stranger and he a natural citizen. He also sees, as he grows up, that the mother's brother assumes a gradually increasing authority over him, requiring his services, helping him in some things, granting or withholding his permission to carry out certain actions, while the father's authority and counsel become less and less important. (*Sexual Life of Savages,* pp. 6-7)

Malinowski, like other anthropologists, searches for the tie that binds father and son together where the mother's brother occupies so dominant a position. This usually comes down to the affectionate relationship between the father and his infant son. The father fondles and carries the infant about with him; he feeds and cleans it. He looks upon the child, says Malinowski, "with eyes full of such love and pride as are seldom seen in those of a European father. And praise of the baby goes directly to his heart and he will never tire of talking about and exhibiting the virtues and achievements of his wife's offspring" (ibid., p. 21).

These emotional ties are disrupted as the boy grows older and must move away from his father to begin a new life with his mother's brother. This creates what Malinowski calls an ever-present "duality" in the boy's life:

> Thus the life of a Trobriander runs under a two-fold influence — a duality which must not be imagined as a mere surface play of custom. It enters deeply into the existence of every individual, it produces strange complications of usage, it creates frequent tensions and difficulties, and not seldom gives rise to violent breaks in the continuity of tribal life. For this dual influence of paternal love and the matrilineal principle, which penetrates so far into the framework of institutions and into the social ideas and sentiments of the native, is not, as a matter of fact, quite well adjusted in its working. (ibid., pp. 7-8)

To illustrate this duality, Malinowski tells the story of an acute upheaval that occurred while he was in the Trobriand Islands. He cites it as the most dramatic of such incidents, and indeed it reads like a Greek tragedy. The account deserves extended review since Malinowski himself found it significant enough to analyze in two separate studies: *The Sexual Life of Savages* (pp. 12-16) and *Crime and Custom in Savage Society* (pp. 101-05).

The crisis took place in Omarakana, the residence of a chief. The wife of the chief lived with him in his village. He became the father of her son, Namwana Guya'u, of whom he was very fond. However, the chief's matrilineal kinship ties were with his sisters and sisters' sons. One nephew, Mitakata, came into conflict with his son; this triggered the crisis. Underlying the immediate rupture was a "feud of long standing" between son and nephew, the origin and nature of which are obscure.

The feud came to a head when the nephew, Mitakata, was imprisoned by the white resident magistrate. The son was held to be the instigator of this injury; he accused the nephew of "adultery" which, in the primitive concept of the term, branded him as a thief. In retaliation the whole group of kinsmen banded together to banish the son from their village. Malinowski cites the expulsion proclamation delivered by the "eldest brother" (mother's brother) of the imprisoned nephew:

> "Namwana Guya'u, you are a cause of trouble. We, the Tabalu of Omarakana, allowed you to stay here, to live among us. You had plenty of food in Omarakana. You ate of our food. You partook of the pigs brought to us as a tribute, and of the flesh. You sailed in our canoe. You built a hut on our soil. Now you have done us harm. You have told lies. Mitakata is in prison. We do not want you to stay here. This is our village! You are a stranger here. Go away! We drive you away! We drive you out of Omarakana." (*Sexual Life of Savages,* p. 13)

These words, says Malinowski, were hurled "each, like an individual missile," across to the hut where the son sat brooding. The rupture was irreparable: "Before the night was over, Namwana Guya'u had left Omarakana for ever. He had gone over and settled a few miles away, in Osapola, his 'own' village, whence his mother came." He could never return to the village of his father.

Even though the father was a chief holding considerable influence, he could do nothing to help his son:

> His kinsmen had acted strictly within their rights, and, according to tribal law, he could not possibly dissociate himself from them. No power could change the decree of exile. Once the words "Go away" . . . had been pronounced, the man had to go. (ibid., p. 14)

The tragic results of this "feud" between two men, a son and a nephew, reverberated far beyond the two individuals. The chief "remained for three days in his hut, and when he came out he looked aged and broken by grief." For weeks the mother and sister wailed "with loud lamentations as for the dead." Within a year the mother, "who wailed and wailed and refused to eat," died of grief. The relations between the intermarrying villages were disrupted and "there was a deep rift in the whole social life of Kiriwina."

What was the source of this extreme reaction to the crime of "telling lies"? Malinowski ascribes the feud between nephew and son to the fact that the father seemed to favor his son and "gave him more than his share of wealth and privilege," which aroused the resentment of the nephew. This explanation may be partially valid; by the twentieth century this primitive region had been to some degree affected by such considerations of rank and property. But the matter goes deeper than this, as Malinowski himself recognizes. In his other study he writes:

> The two principles Mother-right and Father-love are focussed most sharply in the relation of a man to his sister's son and to his own son respectively. His matrilineal nephew is his nearest kinsman and the legal heir to all his dignities and offices. His own son on the other hand is not regarded as a kinsman; legally he is not related to his father, and the only bond is the sociological status of marriage with the mother. (*Crime and Custom in Savage Society*, p. 101)

As Malinowski's account shows, son and nephew, as non-kin, are hereditary enemies, carrying on a custom that began in the ancient past. Despite patrilocal marriage and the recognition of the woman's husband as the father of her son, the son remains an "outsider," a "stranger" in the village of his father, from which he can be banished if he is charged with a misdeed. His own village is that of his mother; there he has his permanent residence and kinship ties.

In other words, marriage and paternal ties counted for little compared to matrilineal "blood kinship" ties. Under the hereditary "blood bond" obligation, the kinsmen of the nephew who had been incarcerated had to avenge the injury done to him. In the old days this would have led to a blood revenge fight; at the time of Malinowski's observations it was reduced to banishing the outsider. In the divided family matrilineal obli-

gations took precedence over any affectionate ties formed between father and son.

Malinowski saw this "duality" so clearly that he was able to
point out the difficulty of teaching a patriarchal religion to
aborigines whose true kinsmen were their mothers' brothers:

> We must realize that the cardinal dogma of God the Father
> and God the Son, the sacrifice of the only Son and the
> filial love of man to his Maker would completely miss
> fire in a matrilineal society, where the relation between
> father and son is decreed by tribal law to be that of two
> strangers, where all personal unity between them is de-
> nied, and where all family obligations are associated with
> mother-line. We cannot wonder that Paternity must be
> among the principal truths to be inculcated by proselytizing
> Christians. Otherwise the dogma of the Trinity would have
> to be translated into matrilineal terms, and we should have
> to speak of a God-*kadala* (mother's brother), a God-sister's-
> son, and a divine *baloma* (spirit). (*Sexual Life of Savages,*
> pp. 186-87)

Malinowski's description of the role of the mother's brother
in matrilineal communities is all the more important since he
firmly believed that the eternal human group was the biological
family consisting of a father, a mother, and their children.
His own evidence tends to refute this unhistorical view. The
Trobriand family, like similar survivals throughout the primitive world, was not a father-family but a matrifamily in which
the father played an insignificant and even ephemeral role in
relation to his wife's children.

This absence of a father-family in our sense of the term
has troubled some anthropologists, particularly in the light
of Malinowski's studies. Referring to this data, Ralph Piddington writes:

> A child, its mother and its mother's brother all belong
> to the same clan, while the father belongs to another owing
> the obligations which we have mentioned, not to his own
> children, but to those of his sister.
>
>   If, then, society excludes the father from this social scheme,
> where does he enter into family life? Stripped of the func-
> tions which we attribute to him, can the "father" be said
> to exist in such a community, and if so, in what sense?
> (*An Introduction to Social Anthropology,* vol. I, p. 155)

These are pertinent questions. From the evolutionary standpoint the father is not "stripped" of his functions; he is just
beginning to acquire them. However, the process was long
drawn out. For the father to acquire more rights and an enduring position in relation to his wife's children, he had to
encroach upon and eventually usurp the long-established primacy of the mother's brother. Rivers articulates this problem:

> It is only as the rights of the father increase that those
> of the mother's brother gradually become more obvious.
> In every community in which the rights of the father
> are gradually growing in strength and importance there
> must be occasions of conflict between the mother's brother
> and the father, and it will only be slowly that the respec-
> tive positions of the two will become defined. It is sig-
> nificant that in Southern Melanesia I record the clearest
> and most definite functions of the mother's brother in the
> Banks Islands, and the change in the direction of recog-
> nition of the rights of the father has probably made great-
> er progress here than anywhere else in that region. . . .
> . . . Let us assume that at one time the mother's brother
> was the sole guardian of his nephew, and that the father
> had no rights towards his son. Under such conditions
> there is no social need for any definition of functions. It
> is only when the rights of the father begin to be asserted
> that it becomes necessary to define these rights, and since
> the rights of the father are an encroachment on those of the
> uncle, a definition of the latter also becomes necessary.
> (*History of Melanesian Society,* vol. II, p. 157)

Logically it would seem that, once the father began to assert his rights in connection with his wife and her children,
the mother's brother would be ready and willing to relinquish
his rights since this would free him to become the father of
his own family. But such was not the case. On the contrary,
the resistance of the mother's brother to the encroachments
of the father can be seen in the emergence of the "avunculate,"
a counter-institution to the father-family unit.

The term "avunculate" is derived from the Roman "avuncu-
lus," meaning maternal uncle. It is a narrowed-down version
of the clan brotherhood in which all the mothers' brothers
were guardians of their sisters' sons. Now the individual maternal uncle performs these functions for an individual sister.

Lippert describes this phenomenon, which emerges in the transitional period between matrifamily and father-family: "From a combination of male protective power and matrilineal descent there arises the so-called 'avunculate,' which, in a peculiar way fills the hiatus between the organizations of mother-right and father-right" (*Evolution of Culture,* p. 248).

Many anthropologists have interpreted this peculiar institution as evidence of the everlasting domination of the male sex over the female sex: just as women today are under the domination of their husbands and fathers, so in primitive society they were subjugated by their brothers and mothers' brothers. But the avunculate came into existence out of a struggle between two categories of men. It represents the resistance of the men of the matriarchy, the mothers' brothers, against the encroachments of the incoming men of the patriarchy, the fathers.

This resistance sprang from the matrilineal blood bond that obligated men to protect their sisters and sisters' children from any harm that might be wrought by outsiders or strangers. That bond between sister and brother survived up to the historical period, as Lippert points out:

> Strabo reports as a curiosity that among the southern Arabians with their primitive form of the family the brother occupied a position of honor with reference to his sister's children. Earlier authors show us that this conception was likewise once current among both the Persians and the Greeks. The sister esteemed her brother higher than her husband because of the bond of blood and because of his relation of protection over her children. Herodotus has illustrated this in the anecdote of the wife of Intaphernes. Of her kinsmen who were condemned to death, Darius promised to liberate the one of her choice. She chose neither her husband nor her child but her brother, because he alone could not be replaced. The tragic factor in the Antigone of Sophocles is based on this same idea of the intimacy of the fraternal bond, which alone warrants the supreme sacrifice. (ibid., p. 258)

Some anthropologists have drawn Freudian inferences from this close attachment of sister and brother; they assume that the brother harbored secret incestuous desires for his sister. In fact, the bond between them had nothing to do with sexual desire; it was connected with the blood revenge institution which made it mandatory upon the brother to avenge or punish the injury or death of his sister or a member of her family. As Lippert writes, "The husband is not the born avenger of the blood of his wife, for he is not of her blood. The obligation rests on her blood relatives. . . . The woman's uterine brother, on the other hand, is her nearest blood relative and therefore her natural protector" (ibid., p. 256).

As with sister and brother, so with maternal uncle and nephew. They too were obligated by their matrilineal blood tie to defend and protect one another. As Lippert puts it, "nephew-right" was the corollary of mother's brother right. "As long as no kinship is recognized between a child and its procreator, its maternal uncle is in fact its nearest male relative in the generation of 'fathers,'" he writes. Accordingly, "the nephew will succeed the uncle as his next of kin." And he adds, "A survey of the distribution of nephew-right shows that only a few civilized peoples have risen above this last remnant of mother-right, and many of them only within historical times" (ibid., pp. 257-58).

Evidence of this persistence of nephew-right can be found in the contests that arose over ancient kingships because the line of succession from father to son had not yet been consolidated. Briffault writes:

> . . . the rights of succession lay in the female line, and if a male of the royal family had a claim to the throne it was not through his father, but through his mother, and he did not succeed his father but his uncle. That this was the rule of succession in primitive Rome we are expressly told by Dionysius of Halicarnassus, who makes Tatia say, speaking of Tarquin to his nephew: "Not only his property, but also his kingdom belongs to you by hereditary right, since you are the eldest of his nephews." (*The Mothers,* vol. I, p. 423)

Moret and Davy point out, "It is remarkable that not one of the Roman kings was immediately succeeded by his son on the throne. Yet several left sons or grandsons behind them" (*From Tribe to Empire,* p. 36). Ancient Egypt provides other examples of succession from maternal uncle, based on kinship to the reigning queen mother or queen sister.

The voluminous evidence on the preeminence of the mother's

brother in the period before the father-family discloses a curious kind of blind spot in anthropologists. They do not see that *fratriliny* is the male corollary of *matriliny*.

Male Descent from the Mother's Brother

We are so accustomed to the system of descent from fathers to sons that it seems inconceivable there ever was any other kind. Yet the evidence shows that patriliny, which came into existence along with the father-family, was preceded not simply by matriliny but also by "fratriliny," that is, descent from mother's brother to sister's son.

It is strange to think of a line of descent through a man who could not, under the stringent sex taboo, be the father of his sister's child. Some anthropologists, trying to solve the puzzling phenomenon of a man looking upon a sister's son as his own, made the mistake of concluding that in these instances brothers married their own sisters. Others rejected this conclusion, among them J. J. Atkinson. He searched for a clue to explain "how a sister's son came also to be a brother's son without having recourse to the theory of incestuous union of brothers and sisters" (*Primal Law,* p. 283). But he could not find the answer.

The solution is simple enough once we remember that primitive peoples were ignorant of the fact that sexual intercourse between a man and a woman was necessary for conception. Any older man could perform the functions of fatherhood for a child and in that sense the child was "his." In the matriclan and continuing into the matrifamily, that older man was the mother's brother.

Paternal functions are social functions, whether or not they are performed by a woman's sexual mate. The older man provides for and protects the youth, oversees his education and occupational training, and transmits skills, customs, traditions, and personal possessions to him. Originally these tasks were performed collectively by all the older brothers for their younger brothers, or, put another way, by the mothers' brothers for their sisters' sons. But with the breakdown of the tribal commune into separate clans and matrifamilies, these were narrowed down to individual functions. Just as a brother was paired off with a sister, so an individual maternal uncle came to take charge of his nephew.

This continued as long as the matrifamily remained in existence. Even after the mother's husband became recognized as the father through a couvade ritual or some other social act, the mother's brother retained his preeminent position in regard to his sister's son. Despite the close association of the father with his wife's child during its early years, the basic line of descent, inheritance, and succession remained matrilineal — and thereby, so far as male children were concerned, fratrilineal.

Evidence on this has been presented even by those who insist that the father-family is eternal. Malinowski, for example, shows that in the Trobriand Islands every social relationship is reckoned through the mother-line.

> This attitude is also to be found embodied, in an even more telling manner, in the rules governing descent, inheritance, succession in rank, chieftainship, hereditary offices and magic — in every regulation, in fact, concerning transmission by kinship. Social position is handed on in the mother-line from a man to his sister's children, and this exclusively matrilineal conception of kinship is of paramount importance. . . . (*Sexual Life of Savages,* p. 4)

Meyer Fortes describes the situation among the Ashanti:

> Matrilineal descent has a compelling influence on conduct, because it is the basis of lineage and therefore determines political allegiance, rights of succession and inheritance, the regulation and validation of marriage, and corporate support in such crises as death, and nowadays, economic distress. A man is legally obliged to consider the interests of his sister's children because he is their legal guardian and they are his potential heirs. . . . They ensure the continuation of the lineage segment sprung from the mother. (*Social Structure,* p. 76)

David M. Schneider writes, concerning the "interdependence of brother and sister" in matrilineal communities, that, while the sister depends on her brother for protection and other functions, "the brother depends on his sister for the perpetuation of his descent line and the provision of an heir" (*Matrilineal Kinship,* p. 11). Thus, whether marriage was matrilocal or patrilocal, so long as the family remained matrilineal the male line of descent was from mother's brother to sister's son.

Consequently it is a great mistake to speak of a "male line

of descent" without clearly specifying whether it is from the mother's brother or from the father. Unfortunately, even the most perceptive scholars have failed to make the distinction. Robertson Smith writes that "originally there was no kinship except in the female line, and the introduction of male kinship was a kind of social revolution which modified society to its very roots" (*Kinship and Marriage in Early Arabia,* p. 213). In fact, it was the introduction of *father* kinship and descent through the *father-line* that represented the great social upheaval.

Marvin Harris falls into a similar mistake when he writes:

> The most bedeviled part of Morgan's kinship sequences was his insistence that the matriclan was chronologically prior to the patriclan. Here Morgan was a participant in one of the most heated and useless discussions in the history of the social sciences. . . . Furthermore, the idea that matrilineality is a result of confusion concerning paternity is wholly confounded by the numerous cases of primitive peoples who deny that the male is necessary for conception but who regard themselves as descended from a line of males, and by the universal recognition of some degree of kinship with both maternal and paternal relatives, regardless of the nature of the unilineal rule. (*The Rise of Anthropological Theory,* p. 187)

To be sure, as Harris says, primitive peoples denied that the male was required for conception. And it is also true that despite this ignorance they "regard themselves as descended from a line of males." What he fails to see is that these males were not the mothers' husbands but the mothers' brothers — a wholly logical line of male descent in a matrilineal (and fratrilineal) family.

Moreover, while it is true that with the advent of the father there was a "universal recognition of some degree of kinship with both maternal and paternal relatives," the question is: to *what* degree? It is only in patriarchal civilized nations that the father has achieved unchallenged recognition as the central figure in his family. In the father-family the line of descent is unambiguously traced through the father-line; it is fixed by law. But this is still not the case in numerous primitive regions which have not gone beyond the matrifamily. There we find only a slight degree of recognition of the father, and the line of descent flows through the mother-line from mother's brother to sister's son.

Contrary to Harris's opinion, the heated discussion has not been useless nor was Morgan wrong in his insistence on the priority of the matriclan. Like other anthropologists, Morgan made mistakes. But his evolutionary approach was certainly not one of them. His discovery of the maternal clan and the classificatory system of kinship laid the foundations for a scientific study of the origin and evolution of the father-family as well as other patriarchal institutions.

Morgan's use of the term "pairing family" flowed from his recognition of the fact that the original family was not a father-family. Subsequent data has given us clearer insight into the original family as a divided family in which two men per-formed paternal functions for a woman's child — with the decisive and permanent functions lodged in the mother's brother.

Survivals of this "divided family" have been found at virtually all stages of development, with the father at various levels of recognition and functions. But in all cases the father continues to remain subordinate to the mother's brother. A few reports should suffice to document this.

A good example of the role of the father at the lowest level of his development can be found in Kathleen Gough's studies of the Nayars of Central and North Kerala in *Matrilineal Kinship*. Despite the disintegration of the Nayar matriarchal structure over the past hundred or more years, these people have remained strongly matrilineal, with a matrifamily still embedded in a matriclan. In Central Kerala the husband has barely emerged from the status of "visiting husband," and the term *sambandham* (Sanskrit for "joining together") indicates pair-matrimonies or pairing couples.

Although Gough adheres to the theory of the eternal father-family, her descriptions of the Nayars show only a budding family unit and often none at all. The term "father," she writes, "refers to any husband of the mother in the *sambandham* relationship, and the term 'patrilateral kin' to the matrilineal kin of such a man" (p. 364). In this region of short-lived "joinings," the woman usually has a succession of husbands and the child a succession of "fathers." The functions of these "fathers" were extremely limited:

The most peculiar characteristic of the Central Nayars is that although a form of marriage existed they did not institutionalize the elementary family of one man, one woman, and their children. This group was in no sense a legal, residential, commensal, productive, or distributive unit. An individual man had no legal rights in a particular wife and her children. He did not reside with them, did not eat regularly with them, did not produce with or for them, and he did not customarily distribute goods to his children. (p. 363)

We are further told that the man would make small gifts to his wife's child, would play with him on visits, and offer him friendly counsel as he grew older. "However, a man had no right to interfere in any way in his child's training, and the child had no customary obligations to him. If he ended his relationship with the mother he had no further contact with the child" (p. 364).

Just as the mother had a succession of husbands, her children had a succession of "fathers." Gough writes:

Children addressed all their mothers' husbands as acchan, adding the caste title in the case of a father of higher caste. Both boys and girls stood in the father's presence and accorded him respect, but without the extreme submissiveness due to an older matrilineal kinsman. In spite of the Malayali adage "No Nayar knows his father," it seems probable that almost every Nayar regarded some particular man as his genitor, but his relationship with this man might be anything from a permanent, warm attachment to almost total lack of recognition. (p. 364)

The central male figure in the life of a Nayar child was the *karanavan,* the matrilineal kinsman or mother's brother. He was the legal guardian of his sister's children and responsible for his nephews' training in laws, customs, morality, and literacy, as well as in agricultural work and military skills. The sisters' sons owed him obedience, loyalty, and respect. Above all, maternal uncle and nephew stood on the same side in the event of a clash with enemies. "A man should show loyalty to his mother's brothers in relations with outsiders, if necessary defending them with his life," says Gough

(p. 349). Since the father was an "outsider," this means that a man stood against his father, if it came to that.

Corresponding to the weak status of the father, the relations between a child and its father's kin were flimsy. When a marriage was terminated the child's relations with them were also ended.

> No rights or obligations existed between the individual and his patrilateral kin. These relationships, when they existed, were a matter of individual friendliness or of polite etiquette. A person might visit his or her father's taravad [matriclan] as long as the father's marriage to the mother endured, especially if the father lived close by. However, although marriage has been monogamous for the past seventy to eighty years, I found in one Cochin village in 1949 that only 48 per cent of sibling groups containing children under fifteen had any contact with their father's matrilineal kin. (p. 364)

This report is especially significant in view of the invasion of patriarchal institutions and class and caste influences in this region from the time of the British conquest in 1792. Laws had been passed in both Central and North Kerala in the 1930s to make marriage monogamous. New property laws made it possible for the members of a taravad (matriclan) to "divide their matrilineal ancestral property on a per capita basis" (p. 394). Despite all this, Gough's data shows that marriage remained on the most elementary, easily dissolved basis, with the father barely more than a visiting husband.

As Gough admits in a special comment, "In general, the restricted use of reference terms for affines [marriage partners] and the lack of terms for patrilateral kin other than the father reflect the slenderness of the marriage tie and the lack of obligations to these kin" (p. 382).

In North Kerala we find a slight advance in the status and stability of the father:

> A man's children and all his wife's kinsfolk of junior generations treat him with affectionate respect. He is a "father" or "grandfather" to all of them. . . . As he grows older they, and especially his own children, become his allies in the house and stabilize his position. . . . The karanavan will be his brother-in-law and age mate, toward whom he has

learnt to accommodate himself through long association. If he has earned the loyalty of his wife's house he may spend happy hours in the downstairs rooms and the outer veranda, playing with the grandchildren, and his advice will be sought with genuine respect rather than merely ceremonious politeness. (p. 436)

However, even at this point, where a man has achieved a respected status as a father in his wife's household, he cannot relinquish his permanent ties and responsibilities as a mother's brother to his sister and her children. As Gough puts it, "Traditionally, of course, it is at this point that a man often becomes the karanavan [mother's brother] of his own natal house and must begin to loosen the ties with his conjugal family" (p. 436).

At what point in history did a husband cease to return to his sister and her children? When did men cease playing a double fatherhood role? In short, when did the divided family become the integral one-father family?

To answer this question we must first remove some serious misconceptions about "bilateral" kinship and "patrilineal" descent. It is frequently said or implied that, just as the father-family has always existed, so also has bilateral kinship, i.e., the reckoning of kinship through both mother- and father-lines. Further, it is said, descent through the father-line has not only been the norm throughout all history but exists even in many primitive matrilineal regions at the present day. The tremendous difficulties involved in achieving descent through the father-line have been obscured as a result of these misconceptions.

Errors Regarding Paternal Descent

There is a glaring absence of data on when or how the maternal (and fraternal) line of descent gave way to descent through the father. In part this is due to the insistence that the father-family has always existed, which implies that paternal descent is an equally permanent fixture. This proposition does not correspond to the voluminous evidence that descent through the father-line has not been achieved in many primitive regions to the present day. Lucy Mair sums this up:

Examples of societies with patrilineal descent are the classical Romans, the Chinese, and the pastoral peoples of eastern and southern Africa. Examples of societies with matrilineal descent are a large number of American Indian and Australian peoples, many indigenous peoples of Indonesia and Malaya, the Bantu peoples of central Africa and the Akan peoples of Ghana. (*Introduction to Social Anthropology*, p. 65)

In virtually all the regions mentioned by Mair, paternal kinship is recognized to a greater or lesser degree; nevertheless, as she says, matrilineal *descent* still prevails. It is therefore incorrect to assume, as many anthropologists do, that descent through the father-line automatically follows wherever recognition of the father is found. This overlooks the protracted period of evolution before descent through the mother's brother changed to descent through the father.

The difficulties in discerning this transition are connected with the changeover from the classificatory system of kinship to the family system. The breakup of tribal society into separate clans and villages, the emergence of the matrifamily within the clan, and the introduction of the father and patrilineal kin created problems for primitive peoples in finding suitable terms for new kinship categories.

Under the classificatory system the "older man" — originally the mother's brother — performed the functions of "father." Then a new older man appeared, the mother's husband, who also became a "father." The awkwardness of distinguishing between the two can be seen in the descriptions given of the term *tate*, a term for "father" in a number of primitive languages.

In Angola, according to Lippert, the father has no power over his son, who, in the event of the dissolution of the marriage, always follows his mother. "But the boy cannot escape the paternal authority of his mother's brother, whom he addresses as *tate* (father)" (*Evolution of Culture*, p. 259). On the same subject Hartland writes:

> In Loango the uncle is addressed as *Tate* (father). He exercises paternal authority over his nephew. . . . The father has no power; and if the husband and wife separate the children follow the mother as belonging to her brother. (*Primitive Paternity*, vol. I, p. 281)

The terms required for designating new kinds of kin acquired through marriage and recognition of the husband as father came into existence slowly, through a series of crude approximations. Lippert points to some effects of this process:

> . . . the more advanced kinship systems of the Indians seek to distinguish in name between the true father and the mother's brother and father's brother. . . . Of the eighteen systems compared by Lubbock, fourteen attempt to distinguish the mother's brother from the true father by restricting the old name to the latter and choosing a new one for the former. The Japanese call him the "second little father;" all the other thirteen systems use a word translated as "uncle." It must have seemed less important to differentiate the father's brother from him, and only eight of the systems attempted to do so. The Micmacs and Japanese choose the term "little father;" three systems add a word translated by the prefix "step-" and probably meaning little more than "strange;" the others use "uncle" for the father's brother also. (*Evolution of Culture*, p. 84)

These illustrations indicate that the increasing differentiation between the father and other members of the paternal kin did not alter the basic line of kinship in the matrifamily, which went through the maternal (and fraternal) line. Although the mother's husband gradually acquired increasing recognition and rights as the father of his wife's child, the line of descent remained as before.

Some errors have been made through a misinterpretation of the gifts given by the father to his wife's son, which are described as "inheritance" of the father's "property." As we have seen, gift-giving originated as a means of establishing peaceful relations between men of hostile communities. These also became "marriage gifts" signifying the intermarrying alliance between groups. With the recognition of the father, the same principle applied; the gifts testified to the paternal relationship between father and son. Such gift-giving cannot be called inheritance of property in our sense of the term.

In the early development of marriage and paternity, the former "outsider" gave regular tokens of peace and friendship to all the members of his wife's kin, not simply her son. These gifts were such standard items as betel and tobacco. Kathleen Gough writes that the Mapilla husband of North Kerala, "like the Nayar husband in Central Kerala, knows that tact is required. . . . A thoughtful husband never enters the house without bringing betel leaves, areca nuts, and tobacco for his mother-in-law and her sisters" (*Matrilineal Kinship,* p. 435).

Malinowski tries, without much success, to distinguish between the "free" gifts given by a father to a son and the inheritance of the father's possessions. He writes:

> . . . it is clear that in a matrilineal society, where the mother is the nearest of kin to her children in a sense quite different to that in our society, they share in and inherit from her all her possessions. It is more remarkable that the father, who, according to native belief and law, is only the mother's husband, and not the kinsman of the children, is the only relation from whom free gifts are expected. The father will give freely of his valuables to a son, and he will transmit to him his relationships in the Kula. . . . Also, one of the most valuable and valued possessions, the knowledge of magic, is handed over willingly, and free of any counter-gift, from father to son. . . . Also, any special luxuries in food, or such things as betel-nut or tobacco, he will share with his children as well as with his wife. (*Argonauts of the Western Pacific,* p. 178)

Once again, such easily acquired items as betel and tobacco leaves are not "luxuries" for children. It is simply that the *act of giving and receiving* these tokens affirms the man's status as a husband and father in the household. The act testifies to the changed status of a man who was formerly the "hereditary enemy" not only of his wife's brother but also of her son.

Even when the gifts made by a father to a son became more substantial, they still do not represent the inheritance of property. If the father plants a tree or makes a garden for his wife's child, these do not become the child's permanent possessions. The land and the produce from the tree or garden remain in the father's matrilineal line of inheritance and pass from mother's brother to sister's son. Malinowski himself writes, "The ownership of trees in the village grove and ownership in garden plots is ceded by the father to his son during the lifetime of the former. At his death, it often has to be returned to the man's rightful heirs, that is, his sister's children" (ibid., p. 178).

Similarly, Fortune alludes to the things a Dobuan father can and cannot give to his wife's offspring: "There are many things that he cannot provide for his children. His village land, his personal name, his skull, his status, his village palms, and fruit trees he cannot by any possibility alienate from his sister's child in favor of his own child" (*Sorcerers of Dobu,* p. 15).

Moreover, the man is "obliged by law and induced by his affection for his sister and her children to teach his sister's child his magical formulae." If he also shares his magic with his wife's child, the Dobuans regard it as "a very horrifying and subversive action" (ibid.). Even the limited inheritance that does pass from father to son is a new custom, disliked by the aborigines.

The reason for this distrust is not difficult to locate. It is through his magical formulae that a man can divine the "enemy" who has brought about a death or injury to a member of his kin group. Such magic should be retained in the matrilineal clan and family for their protection against outsiders, among whom the "enemy" will be found. How, then, can a man who must train his sister's son in the skills of magical divination also train the "outsider," the son of his wife and his former hereditary enemy? It is a clear case of the "subversion" that was penetrating and corroding the matrifamily.

This hereditary enmity, which trailed along the whole route of the evolution of the matriclan system down to the matrifamily, produced the abrasions and conflicts that repeatedly tore the divided family apart. Kathleen Gough writes with respect to the Central Kerala Nayars:

> Good men were men who devoted themselves first to the service of their feudal lords, and second to the welfare of their taravads. Weak and immoral men were men who became inveigled by their wives and children, so that they tried to make unnecessary gifts to their wives and neglected their taravads. An ideal karanavan was one who broke off his marital ties in old age and devoted his energies solely to his sisters' children. (*Matrilineal Kinship,* p. 361)

Under these circumstances, where inheritance remained basically matrilineal, the line of kinship descent remained unchanged;

it, too, was matrilineal, with the male line passing from mother's brother to sister's son. A graphic illustration of this in modern times is given by Briffault. "The son of a powerful chief at Bassam in French New Guinea, on being asked whether he would not be a rich man when his father died and he inherited some of his wealth, answered, 'Why should I? I am only his son'" (*The Mothers,* vol. I, p. 506). Thus it is a serious mistake to assume that a paternal relationship between a man and his wife's son automatically means inheritance and descent through the father-line.

A related error concerns the question of "bilateral" kinship and descent. As this is commonly described, a child traces its kinship and descent through both father and mother. Hoebel writes:

> The conjugal family is always bilateral. Since it takes two to make a conjugal family, and since each spouse already belongs to a preexisting family, the marriage union links two units into a new one. The child has its ties to both its father's and its mother's conjugal families as well as to the one into which it is born. (*Man in the Primitive World,* p. 221)

The "conjugal" family Hoebel refers to is by definition not a father-family but a matrifamily. The child traces its basic kinship ties through the mother and mother's brother, and descent through matriliny and fratriliny. Recognition of the father does not change this and is only incidental and episodic in the child's life.

Hoebel himself admits this when he writes that "the conjugal family is a temporary association. It begins and ends with the union of the pair and the dispersal of the children" (ibid., p. 222). (In actuality the children are not "dispersed" from their matrikin; they simply cut loose from their association with their father upon the termination of the marriage.) Hoebel also observes that "the instability of the conjugal family and its short time span also limit its usefulness as a means of inheritance of property and perquisites." Even in conjugal families that endure for a long time, the inheritance of property does not pass from father to son but from mother's brother to nephew. Hoebel more or less concedes this when he writes, "Since a boy in a matrilineal clan system belongs to his mother's clan and not to his father's, inheritance from father to son is ruled out for all clan-linked privileges" (ibid., p. 242).

These facts refute the widespread notion that the family is always bilateral, with kinship and descent traced through both father-line and mother-line. Patriliny did not begin until the father-family had won supremacy over the matrifamily.

Failure to detect the priority of male descent through the mother's brother has created great problems even for scholars who support the priority of the matriarchy. Some have resorted to the use of other terms to try to get around these difficulties. Rivers, for example, specified that he used the term "descent" only in the sense of "membership in a group" (*Social Organization*, p. 86).

A boy can be said to have "membership" in his father's as well as his mother's clan. But they are vastly different memberships. His association with his father's clan is incidental and limited, and ends when the marriage is dissolved. By contrast, his membership in his mother's clan is indissoluble. His line of descent, inheritance, and succession are maternal and fraternal. Without this clear distinction, it is all too easy to fall into the trap of believing in everlasting bilateral descent and an everlasting father-family.

This is not the only trap that awaits the unwary investigator. Perhaps the most ambiguous and misinterpreted term in anthropology is the term "patriclan." Too often it is used in the sense of an enlarged father-family or a clan in which the father stands at the head of the wife and children. In fact, so long as the clan system prevailed, only the mother-brother relationship was permanent, while the father-mother relationship was incidental and easily terminated.

The term "patriclan" expresses only a paternal or patrilineal relationship between two matriclans. It is true that to a child the clan of his father is his "patriclan." However, father and son belong to separate matriclans. The son belongs to the clan of his mother and mother's brothers. The father belongs to the clan of his sisters and sisters' sons. In short, *every "patriclan" is structurally a matriclan.* Failure to understand this maternal underpinning of the "patriclan" has produced gross distortions in ethnography.

Radcliffe-Brown, who was among the first to attempt to disqualify the evolutionary approach, provides a good illustration of the widespread misinterpretation of the "patriclan." He asserts that it is a "strange idea," an "absurd notion," to think that "matrilineal descent is more primitive, i.e. historically earlier, than patrilineal descent," and adds:

From the beginning of this century we have been acquainted with societies, such as the Herero, in which both matrilineal and patrilineal lineages are recognized; but these were dismissed as being "transitional" forms. This is another example of the way in which attachment to the method and hypotheses of conjectural history prevents us from seeing things as they are. (*Structure and Function in Primitive Society*, p. 82)

However, upon examining the illustrations given by Radcliffe-Brown, we find that his own attachment to the unhistorical approach produces "conjectural" history; it prevents him from "seeing things as they are" even in the light of some of his own statements. He writes about the OvaHerero of southwest Africa:

Through his mother a child derives membership in an *eanda,* a matrilineal clan; through his father he becomes a member of an *oruzo,* a patrilineal clan. There is thus a double system of clans crossing one another. (ibid., p. 39)

This even-handed disposition of a child's "membership" in both his father's and mother's clans is misleading. First, it leaves out the most basic fact about the *oruzo,* namely, that it is a patrilineal clan only to the child and his mother. To the father it is his *eanda,* that is, his matrilineal clan. Structurally both clans are matriclans, with an *oruzo* or patrilineal relationship linking them together. Secondly, the child's permanent kinship ties and line of descent are with the mother and mother's brother in their *eanda* and not with the father in his *eanda.*

Radcliffe-Brown admits this when he says that "a man cannot belong to the *eanda* of his father or to the *oruzo* of his mother." Since the *oruzo* of the mother is the same as that of the child, that is, the father's *eanda,* we are speaking here of two matriclans, the father's and the mother's. Thus a man cannot belong to his father's matriclan; he belongs to his mother's matriclan. This knocks out Radcliffe-Brown's contention that a child has "membership" in both his father's and mother's clans. At most the child has an episodic and easily terminated "membership" in his father's matriclan during the period that his mother's marriage endures.

Radcliffe-Brown's unhistorical approach is designed to fortify the thesis of the eternal father-family. In his view, "Everywhere in human society the status of an individual is very largely determined by birth as the child of a particular father and particular mother" (p. 38). But the evidence he gives does not sustain this thesis. A son's status is determined by the *matriclan* into which he is born. Since he cannot belong to his father's matriclan he must belong to his mother's matriclan. This is hardly proof of an everlasting father-family.

E. Sidney Hartland, a more historical anthropologist, gives a truer insight into the matriclan structure of the Herero:

> Every Herero was a member at once of his father's *oruzo* and his mother's *eanda*, for whether a married woman entered her husband's *oruzo* or no, she never quitted her native *eanda*. If she entered her husband's dwelling on marriage she returned to her mother's hut for the birth of her offspring; and her brother became the guardian of her children. (*Primitive Society*, p. 74)

A correct understanding of the clan structure of the Herero is important because they exemplify the highest and last stage in the development of the matriclan and matrifamily system. In this pastoral region the former interchanges of betel, tobacco, and other such items have advanced to the interchange of cattle. This is a signal of the potential advance to bride price and the firmer hold this gives the father upon his wife and children. However, while the Herero stand on the threshold, they fall short of making the transition to the father-family. They retain their matriclan and matrifamily structure.

What accounts for this remarkable tenacity of the matrifamily? What was the source of this stubborn adherence to a one-sided system of kinship and descent through the mother-line in the face of the growing claims of the father and of the irreversible development of patrilineal kinship? What caused the long delay in completing the transition from matrifamily to father-family — and still prevents some primitive peoples from effecting the change?

This brings us back to a reexamination of the "blood bond" that was an integral part of the matrilineal kinship system and the associated obligation to punish those who brought death or injury to any member of the "blood kin." The advent of the matrifamily did not eradicate this obligation of blood revenge; it merely narrowed it down to clan and family.

By virtue of this requirement every son was obliged to stand as a nephew on the side of his mother's brother when "blood debt" obligations were involved. Hartland writes concerning the Herero:

> The blood-feud is carried on only by the *eanda*. When a man is slain his avengers are his brothers and mothers' brothers; when a woman is killed they are her sons, brothers and maternal uncles. And the objects of their vengeance are the guilty person and his *eanda*; the *oruzo* in either case has nothing to do with the matter. (ibid.)

Oruzo ties, that is, patrilineal ties between father and son, were severed whenever a confrontation took place between the *eanda* of the father and the *eanda* of the mother's brother. As Robertson Smith puts it, "The duty of blood revenge is paramount and every other obligation is dissolved as soon as it comes into conflict with the claims of blood" (*Religion of the Semites*, p. 272).

Blood kinship, which was restricted to the maternal line alone, stood in the way of a rapid and easy development from the matrifamily to the father-family. This can be seen more fully when we examine its disruptive effects upon family unity.

The Cutting Edge of the Blood Line

As previously noted, the blood revenge institution came into existence out of the savage ignorance of the natural causes of death, which made it obligatory for male kinsmen to punish those who were adjudged to be guilty of slaying a member of the matrikin. This ignorance continued even after tribal society broke up into separate clans and matrifamilies. However, the punishments for death took different forms and had different results.

Blood vengeance was originally a community affair of men only, carried out through the regulated fight between moieties. Despite the intermarrying alliance the two sides remained "hereditary enemies." After the death scores were settled, peace was restored through feasts and the interchange of gifts between the opposing sides. These encounters did not disrupt family life because the family was not yet in existence.

This situation changed with the emergence of the matrifamily.

What had formerly been a community affair involving men only became a matriclan and matrifamily matter, drawing in women and children. The hereditary enemies, the father who belonged to his matriclan and the mother and children who belonged to her matriclan, were now living together in the same household.

The matrilineal "blood line" therefore sharply divided the members of the primitive family. Since deaths were attributed to sorcery on the part of "outsiders," suspicion fell upon the stranger who had married into the matrikin group. In the matrifamily, the mother and her children, backed up by her brothers, were lined up against the father and his kinsmen. Whichever group suffered the death, the usual result was the termination of the marriage. This severed the father's ties to the children.

Anthropologists have observed the prominent part played by sorcery in the frictions between spouses and in the consequent weakness and instability of the primitive family. Kathleen Gough, for example, writes that among the Nayars "the institution of sorcery provided a covert outlet for interpersonal hostilities between affines which could find no expression in open conflicts between their groups as a whole. The result of the hostilities was often termination of the particular marriage, for the spouses, unable to bear the machinations of their relatives, would often end their relationship" (*Matrilineal Kinship*, pp. 361-62).

Observations of this type, however, do not disclose the source of the fear of sorcery—ignorance of natural death. Nor do they take into account the evolution of the blood vengeance institution which originally demanded a death for a death. Although the regulated combat had been largely abandoned by the time of the matrifamily, there were other punishments—social, physical, and emotional—inflicted upon the family members whenever death intruded upon a household.

Among these is a curious ritual sometimes called a "plundering expedition," which took place when a child died or was seriously injured. The mother's kinsmen turned out to punish the presumed culprit—the father. This was a modified form of blood revenge; the main objective was to inflict reprisals upon a man's possessions rather than on the man himself. After the punishment, peace was restored through a feast given by the father.

Hartland sees this ritual as evidence of the "alien position" of the father in the primitive family. Among the Maori, he notes, when a child dies or even has a nonfatal accident, the mother's relatives headed by her brother turn out in full force against the father. "He must defend himself until he is wounded. Blood once drawn, the combat ceases, but the attacking party plunders his house and appropriates everything on which hands can be laid, finally sitting down to a feast provided by the bereaved father" (*Primitive Paternity*, vol. I, p. 279).

Later, this "laying hands on" was turned into its opposite — it became a benediction or blessing bestowed by one good or saintly person upon another. But in its origin, it was the old blood retribution reduced to matrifamily size.

Without this historical approach the ritual is sometimes misinterpreted as "robbing" a man of his "property." W. I. Thomas cites a report by Maning, a colonial judge in New Zealand, who confessed that "the offenses for which people were plundered were sometimes of a nature which, to a mere *pakeha* (white man) would seem curious." Among his illustrations was one in which a child fell into the fire and was almost burned to death. "The father was immediately plundered to an extent that almost left him without the means of subsistence; fishing nets, canoes, pigs, provisions — all went; his canoe upset, and he and all his family narrowly escaped drowning — some were, perhaps, drowned. He was immediately robbed, and well pummeled with a club into the bargain . . ." (*Primitive Behavior*, p. 572).

The judge could see that this was not a robbery in our sense of the term; he states explicitly that "personal property was an evanescent sort of thing altogether." But he was not aware of the consequences of the primitive ignorance of natural death and did not know that this ritual was a reduced version of the old blood vengeance institution. Thus he was flabbergasted by a code of ethics in which the man who was being "robbed" did not resist his punishment but on the contrary welcomed it. As the report states:

Indeed . . . it would have been felt as a slight, and even an insult, *not* to be robbed; the sacking of a man's establishment being often taken as a high compliment, especially if his head was broken into the bargain; and to resist the execution would not only have been looked upon as mean and disgraceful in the highest degree, *but it would*

> *have debarred the contemptible individual from the privilege*
> *of robbing his neighbors*; which was the compensating
> expedient I have alluded to. (ibid., emphasis in the original)

The father receiving the punishment would, in his turn, become a mother's brother punishing his sister's husband.

Many anthropologists have noted the instability of the primitive family, but they seldom relate these frequent breakups
of marriage ties to death. They fail to understand the plundering expeditions as a substitute form of punishment for death,
and they do not see that after a time such punishments gave
way to self-punishments in the unending effort of primitive
peoples to stay the hand of death and avert its consequences.

These self-punishments represent the earliest form of what
are usually called "mourning rites" or "death pollution" rituals,
which in some regions were extremely painful and bloody.
The following examples are taken from Frazer:

> Thus among the tribes of Western Victoria a widower
> mourned his wife for three moons. Every second night he
> wailed and recounted her good qualities, and lacerated
> his forehead with his nails till the blood flowed down his
> cheeks; also he covered his head and face with white clay.
> . . . he would burn himself across the waist in three lines
> with a red-hot piece of bark. A widow mourned for her
> husband for twelve moons. She cut her hair quite close, and
> burned her thighs with hot ashes pressed down on them
> with a piece of bark till she screamed with agony. Every
> second night she wailed and recounted his good qualities,
> and lacerated her forehead till the blood flowed down her
> cheeks. At the same time she covered her head and face
> with white clay. . . . Children in mourning for their parents
> lacerated their brows. Among the natives of Central Victoria
> the parents of the deceased were wont to lacerate them-
> selves fearfully, the father beating and cutting his head
> with a tomahawk, and the mother burning her breasts
> and belly with a firestick. This they did daily for hours
> until the period of mourning was over. Widows in these
> tribes not only burned their breasts, arms, legs, and thighs
> with firesticks, but rubbed ashes into their wounds and
> scratched their faces till the blood mingled with the ashes.

Among the Kurnai of South-eastern Victoria mourners cut and gashed themselves with sharp stones and toma- hawks until their heads and bodies streamed with blood. In the Mukjarawaint tribe of Western Victoria, when a man died, his relatives cried over him and cut themselves with tomahawks and other sharp instruments for a week.

Among the tribes of the Lower Murray and Lower Darling rivers mourners scored their backs and arms, sometimes even their faces, with red-hot brands, which raised hideous ulcers; afterwards they flung themselves prone on the grave, tore out their hair by handfuls, rubbed earth over their heads and bodies in great profusion, and ripped up their green ulcers till the mingled blood and grime presented a ghastly spectacle. . . .

In the Kabi and Wakka tribes of South-eastern Queens- land . . . mourning lasted approximately six weeks. "Every night a general, loud wailing was sustained for hours. and was accompanied by personal laceration with sharp flints or other cutting instruments. The men would be content with a few incisions on the back of the head, but the women would gash themselves from head to foot and allow the blood to dry upon the skin." (*Folklore in the Old Testa- ment*, pp. 390-91)

In the course of time the self-punishments became less severe. Applying grease, soot, or other substances on the body took the place of gashes and mutilations. The living spouse shut himself or herself up in a hut or other secluded place, under- going penance rituals until the period of mourning was over. The substances were then washed off and the penitent could return to normal life again.

The fact that women mourned for a longer period of time than men, and often gashed themselves more vigorously, can be attributed to their endless efforts to stay the hand of death and preserve the peace and unity of the clans and families. Even after mourning rituals dwindled to public lamentations and modified self-punishments, it was primarily the women who performed these rituals. To the present day among some ethnic groups, women wail, lament, tear their hair and scratch their faces in formalized mourning rituals whose origin and meaning has long vanished from history.

Mourning rites and death pollution rituals came into existence

side by side with the development of the father and patrilineal
kinship, with the husband-father living under the same roof
with his wife and children. Kathleen Gough writes that "death
pollution" is not observed by either husband or wife among
the Nayars or Tiyyars. The incidental position of the husband
in these strongly matrilineal clans can be seen in the following:

> Traditionally a woman left her husband's natal house
> after his death and before the funeral. Today, if the hus-
> band has built a private house for his wife and children,
> the wife remains in this house. She lives in it throughout
> the days of the funeral rites but takes no part in them.
> Traditionally a woman was buried in the garden of her
> natal house. Today her body may be either buried or cre-
> mated in the garden of the house which her husband has
> given to her. If the husband is living he may finance the
> funeral, but it is conducted by the woman's children and
> matrilineal kin, and the husband takes no part in the cere-
> monies. If the wife's funeral takes place in her natal home
> the husband usually attends it as a guest. (*Matrilineal Kin-
> ship,* p. 413)

In regions where paternal functions and patrikinship are
nonexistent or underdeveloped, the husband does not publicly
mourn the wife nor she her husband. The spouses who do not
live together as a family unit in life are separated after death,
each to be buried in a different graveyard by his or her matrikin.

This situation changes where father-right and patrilineal kinship are fairly well developed. Here the public displays of be-
reavement are performed by the "outsider" married into the
kin. However much grief is felt for the loss of one's own matrilineal kin, this is a personal and private affair. The public ritual is performed by the spouse; either by the husband for his
wife or the wife for her husband. These highly visible and exaggerated displays of grief are designed to demonstrate that
the living spouse and his or her kinsmen are not responsible
for the death through evil magic.

Malinowski describes such a mourning ritual in the Trobriands where, with few exceptions, every death is regarded
as the result of sorcery:

> The ostentation with which the widow and children have
> to display their grief, the thickness — literally and meta-

phorically speaking — with which they put on their mourning are indeed striking. . . . In the first place, it is a duty
towards the dead and towards his sub-clan, a duty strongly
enjoined by the code of morals and guarded by public
opinion, as well as by the kinsmen. "Our tears — they are
for the kinsmen of our father to see," as one of the mourners simply and directly told me. In the second place, it
demonstrates to the world at large that the wife and children were really good to the dead and that they took great
care of him in his illness. Lastly, and this is very important, it allays any suspicion of their complicity in his murder by black magic. To understand the last queer motive,
one has to realize the extreme fear, the ever-vigilant suspicion of sorcery, and the unusual lack of trust in anyone at all with reference to it. (*Sexual Life of Savages*,
pp. 160-61)

Although anthropologists are generally aware of the profound disturbances caused by death in primitive society, they
tend to underestimate it as the source of the repeated breakups of marriage and family ties. Searching for other causes,
they often fix upon "adultery" as causing the frictions and difficulties between husband and wife. The fear and anger dis-
played by a husband at his wife's association with a strange
man is interpreted as a reaction to her sexual unfaithfulness.

The concept of adultery, however, was a late development;
it did not exist in pre-propertied society. The husband's animosity was due to his fear that he might be killed by the sorcery of a strange man; if his wife was associating with such
a man, he might suspect her of complicity.

Death in the family was the most frequent and most implacable shatterer of ties not only between spouses but between father
and child. If the mother died, the father was banished from the
household where he had lived with his wife and children. And
if the father died, the son was banished from the household
where he had lived with his father. It was between father and
son that the edge of the matrilineal blood line was sharpest
and cut deepest.

Fortune gives a description of this in *Sorcerers of Dobu*,
involving a widower named Maiwortu. When his wife died,
this Resultant-from-Marriage was not permitted to see her corpse
or mourn her intimately. The bereaved man "had to hide himself within a house," his conduct resembling that of a guilty

murderer. For a year he had to submit to a grueling penance ritual under the surveillance of his dead wife's kin. Fortune observes:

In the village of his dead wife the widower has not sung, he has not smiled, he has not danced, he has not looked at another woman. The greater part of the time he has blackened his body over with charcoal from the fire. He has put away all his body ornaments, all sweet scented herbs. He has eaten the roughest and worst food. . . . Round his neck he wore the many looped, black, rope-like *mwagura,* the badge of mourning. For the earlier month or two of mourning he remained confined in the enclosure beneath the house of death seated on the ground. Later he emerged to do toilsome work for his dead wife's mother or sister, work of no recompense for him. (p. 12)

At the end of the year the widower is released from his penance and is about to be banished from his wife's village, his ties to his children permanently severed.

He has mourned all night before the day of the final gift of yams. After the gifts have been set up ceremonially in a wood fenced square and then distributed among the village kin of the dead, a sister's son of his deceased wife will cut the loop, the *mwagura,* that was about his neck. Tomorrow comes this final rite—the time of his mourning done. The sister's sons and brothers of his wife will lead him by the hand to Mwaniwara, the farthest eastern point of the island. There they will wash his body coat of charcoal from him in the sea (for the year he has not bathed in sea or in stream). They will cleanse him, anoint his body with oil, replace his body ornaments, and place fragrant herbs in his armlets. They will then lead him by the hand to his own village. *He will never enter their village again.* (pp. 12-13, emphasis in the original)

Whatever the emotional effects upon the children, they suffered no economic or social distress as a result of the banishment of their father. The children, says Fortune, "belong to the village of their dead mother. There they inherit village status and land, a girl from her mother's sister, a boy from his mother's brother" (p. 13). He emphasizes the fact that "Dobu practices the avunculate, inheritance from mother's brother to sister's son" (p. 62). Here mother's brother right prevailed over father right.

This was a husband who had been ritually "made" into a father. As Fortune writes, "While the mother lived the father was 'he who holds the infant in his arms.'" Indeed, he was clearly a model father, for he "played with and carried the young children everywhere." But with the death of his wife he was "unmade" as a father and thrown back to his former status as a stranger.

In another case Fortune describes how a son was banished from his father's village upon the father's death. While the father was alive the son, like his mother, was a Resultant-from-Marriage, and lived every alternate year in his father's village. But upon his death, the son might do no more than lurk around the outskirts of his father's village; he could never again enter it.

> The child of a dead father is called Boundary Man by the Owners of the Village of the deceased. The sister's son of the dead is Owner. Boundary Man is so called because he cannot enter his father's village boundary or eat a single nut or fruit of the trees of his father's village or any food grown on land that was his father's. (p. 14)

These examples provide striking evidence of the transient, even ephemeral, character of patrilineal ties compared to the basic matrilineal — and fratrilineal — bonds. Elizabeth Colson's description of the Plateau Tonga serves to sum up this widespread pattern:

> Links between matrilineal groups cut across clan boundaries and are tied to the life span of particular individuals. Every person is "an honorary member" of his father's matrilineal group. In all matters which concern him, his matrilineal kinsmen (*basimukowa*) are brought into contact with his father's matrilineal kinsmen (his *basyanausi*). The two groups continue their cooperation throughout his life, but on his death the tie which joins them vanishes. Each matrilineal group is thus associated with a large number of similar groups of other clans as it cooperates with the groups of the fathers of its members and with the

groups of the children of its male members. But these ties change with each death and with each marriage and do not form permanent linkages between groups. (*Matrilineal Kinship,* p. 41)

The child who became a "member" or "honorary member" of his father's community while his mother was married to a man in that community, lost both his father and his membership through death or divorce. The permanent guardian of a child remained the "matrilineal father," the mother's brother.

Although Kathleen Gough does not draw any historical inference from her investigations, she gives a clear picture of the power of the "matrilineal father" among the Mayombe. She writes that the children were "unequivocally under the authority of their descent-group head," which is her term for the mother's brother in charge of the youth. She adds:

The father had no right to discipline them, but sent a recalcitrant son to his mother's brother for correction. Conversely, a son whose father ill-treated him ran away to his mother's brothers, who returned him only if the father pleaded for pardon. Their descent-group head could if he wished command children to come and live with him, and boys usually left the father's village as early as the age of ten. If their mother died or was divorced, children were removed by their guardian. . . . The father's normal relationship with his children is described as affectionate and unauthoritative, their mother being the disciplinarian in their early childhood, and the mother's brothers, in later life. If a son's descent group became involved in feud with that of his father, however, the son was obliged to oppose him on behalf of his own matrilineal group. (*Matrilineal Kinship,* pp. 586-87)

In this reference to the blood feud — the inescapable obligation of the matrikin — we can see the full operation of the cutting edge of the blood line. So long as a one-sided matrilineal kinship system prevailed, with male descent passing from mother's brother to sister's son, fatherhood remained an incidental and repeatedly terminated relationship. By the same token the matrifamily remained a divided family, with a sword of Damocles always hanging over it.

Noting the "insecurity and impermanence" of marriage, Julius Lippert writes: "Compared with the indestructible bond of common blood, the marital tie was at first only a gossamer thread, and upon such the mother did not wish the fate of her children to depend" (*Evolution of Culture,* p. 262). This implies that the weakness of the marriage tie created the instability of the family unit. In reality it was the other way around. The flimsiness of marriage was caused by an inflexible, one-sided matrilineal blood kinship system which made the father a permanent outsider to his wife and children. Or, put another way, it made the son, whose basic allegiance was to his mother's brother, a permanent stranger to his father. This cleavage in the matrifamily could not be overcome so long as it remained divided between two "fathers."

Elizabeth Colson reports that the Plateau Tonga, despite the inroads of modern influences, have been unable to change the maternal line of descent even in our times: "Men say, 'How can we trust our sons? They trust only their own matrilineal group.'" And she adds:

> Yet today many are questioning a system of descent which affiliates a child with its mother's line, whereas formerly they accepted it without question. The old formulation was that the head and right arm belonged to the father; the body and left arm to the matrilineal group. This association is a common ritual motif. Nowadays men snort and argue that the whole of the child belongs to the father since he has paid bridewealth for the mother. Their carping, however, has not succeeded as yet in altering the descent system. (*Matrilineal Kinship,* p. 77)

This modern instance brings to the fore one of the most momentous problems to be solved in social history: When and how did the changes come about whereby the matrifamily, torn between two "fathers," gave way to the unified patriarchal family?

13
'Blood Price'
and the Father-Family

The matrifamily (Morgan's "pairing family") emerged at the beginning of barbarism, about eight thousand years ago. At the end of the barbaric period some five thousand years later, we find the full-fledged patriarchal one-father family. In civilized Greece and Rome the father is in total control of his wife and children, the line of descent is from father to son, and the mother's brother has vanished.

What took place in the middle period of barbarism to bring about this transition from the matrifamily to the father-family in the most advanced sector of the globe? This is a largely uninvestigated question. We have a clear picture only of the beginning and end of the process; in between our view is clouded. Thus it is necessary to break new ground in pursuit of a better understanding of this crucial turning point in history. Clarification of this subject will also shed light on the central mystery of anthropology — the transition from the matriarchal order to patriarchal, class-divided society.

The first point to be noted is that the advance made from the matrifamily to the father-family was not due to greater knowledge about physiological paternity. The earliest father-family was not based upon a father's known genitorship of a child but on ownership of it. The continuing ignorance about the facts of biological fatherhood in this period is obscured by the ambiguity of the term "to beget." To us it suggests an act of impregnation leading to the birth of a child. But originally it meant something quite different.

Lord Raglan, one of the few to investigate the history of fatherhood, poses the query: "What is a father?" This is not a witty remark but an essential historical question. He writes:

The obvious answer to this question is, as is often the case, the wrong one; the root word from which the word for father in all the Aryan languages is derived appears to mean nothing but "owner," and the same applies to the Semitic *ab, abu.* How has it come about that a word which meant "owner" now means "begetter"? The answer is that it has not; the word "father" had no necessary connexion with begetting. . . . He is their owner or father because he has performed a magical rite which . . . makes him their father whether he has begotten them or not. (*Jocasta's Crime,* p. 180)

Raglan is correct in saying that the term "to beget" was not originally connected with physiological paternity. However, he overlooks the fact that many terms have changed meaning in the course of social evolution, and this is the case with the term "to beget." In its archaic form, a father was a "begetter" in a different, more literal sense. To "beget" a child, a man must "get" it from his wife; he must "receive it in his arms" after performing the ritual that socially established him as its father.

But there is more to the matter than this. Raglan poses other penetrating questions: Why must a man beget a male child in order to become a father? Why should a man wish to be a father? He dismisses the notion that a man wants to become a father because of his "paternal instinct":

Those who hope to solve these problems by gazing earnestly into the fire instead of studying the facts will no doubt answer, "the paternal instinct," but why can this "instinct" only be satisfied by a son, never by daughters, and why in so many civilized communities is a man who has no son considered to be in a parlous state? Why must one invent an imaginary son when addressing a sonless Arab, and why in the mind of a Hindu are the ideas of paternity and immortality so closely connected? (ibid., p. 186)

In some patriarchal regions even at present a man is not regarded as a father unless he has begotten a son. Frequently when such a father alludes to his children he points only to his sons; daughters do not count. This may explain the remarkable prevalence of "barren" women in the Old Testament and other ancient archives. The woman who failed to give birth to a son was probably looked upon as "barren," no matter how many daughters she bore. Moreover, from its earliest pictorial representation to today, the invariable symbol of the father-family is the mother holding up a son — never a daughter.

So the question stares at us: Why should a man wish to be a father and why must he beget a son to achieve that status? Raglan's own answer is less than satisfactory.

> . . . a man is immortal only if he has a son. This belief has become modified both in language and ideas, but is still general, even among ourselves; a man wishes for a son to bury him and look after his grave; to keep his memory green; to succeed to his name or his title, and so keep it alive; to keep up the old place and the old family portraits. The Roman nobles kept their ancestors alive by means of portrait statues, and these bring us back to Egypt, and the portrait statues which were associated with mummification. (ibid., p. 187)

While this was true of the father-family once it came into existence, it sheds little light on its origin. Given the ignorance of physiological paternity, what was the compelling motive for a man to "beget" his wife's children as his own and to maintain this one-father family in perpetuity?

It was not enough for the father to beget his own son by "getting" it from his wife. Only when the mother's brother relinquished all claims to his sister's son could the father acquire it as his "own" or "own begotten" or "only begotten" son. This in turn required that the mother's brother abandon his sister and sister's children and "cleave" to his wife and wife's children.

How was this accomplished?

Betrayal and Fratricide

Fragments of historical data, including some myths and legends, indicate that strenuous efforts were made to resolve the difficulties of the divided family, torn by inexorable blood obligations. But these tell us more about the fratricidal strife that accompanied the changeover than they do about how the father-family was finally achieved.

Robertson Smith points out how blood kinship determined where a man stood in the event of an outbreak of hostilities:

> We have seen that an Arab tribe regarded itself as a group of kindred united by the tie of blood for purposes of offence and defence. In a society thus constructed no one, it is obvious, can belong to two groups; the commentator on the *Hamasa*, p. 124, says expressly that the same man cannot belong to more than one *hayy*. Before a man can enter a new *hayy* by adoption, he must "strip off" his old tribal connection (*khad'a*) or be expelled from it. (*Kinship and Marriage in Early Arabia,* p. 73)

For a man to "strip off" his blood bond to his maternal and fraternal kin was, in primitive terms, a betrayal of the first magnitude. It meant a reversal of the former situation where fathers and sons had confronted each other on opposite sides of the fighting line. Now it was matrilineal kin who would be in opposition to one another.

That this reversal took place cannot be doubted. For the first time in history we come upon strife and murder between men of the maternal brotherhood who from time immemorial had regarded one another's lives as sacred and inviolable.

Robertson Smith gives a historical fragment. Before the time of Mohammed, he writes, "the old notion of an absolute blood-bond binding the whole group together had been greatly relaxed. Family feeling was stronger than gentile or tribal feeling, and the mark of this is the numerous fratricidal wars that raged all over Arabia just before Islam. This decay of tribal feeling was, we cannot fail to see, connected with the rise of male kinship and paternity." Despite this, the old ties were still strong:

> Hodhaifa in attacking his mother's tribe in a matter of blood revenge deems it sufficient to direct that her house shall be spared . . . but on the other hand . . . 'Abd Manaf the Hodhalite bewails the death of his sister's son Dobayya, though he was sprung on the father's side from Solaim, the bitterest enemies of Hodhail, and had met his death while treacherously taking advantage of the friendship of his mother's kin to bring the Solaim upon them by surprise. "Though his father and he alike put on the garment of faith-

lessness to kindred bonds, though his perfidy admits of no defence, I would have saved the life of my sister's son." (ibid., pp. 186-87, 189)

Myth-histories likewise testify to the betrayals and treachery that mark the beginning of the transition from matriarchy to patriarchy. They cover the whole gamut of former matrilineal relations — brothers kill brothers, maternal uncles kill their sisters' sons, and nephews kill uncles.

Malinowski analyzes such legends in *Sex and Repression in Savage Society* (pp. 106-11). He arranges them in groups suggestive of their evolutionary sequence. The matriarchal character of the first group is unambiguous; it features a mother and brother but no father. The father figure is a cannibalistic ogre called Dokonikan, and the mother's son, Tudava, is the culture-hero who grows up to slay him.

Another group of myths deals with a sister who is abandoned by her brother as he goes off to become a husband and the father of his wife's children. Acts of cannibalism are also recited, along with tales of fratricidal strife.

Observing the "strange correspondence" between the mythical situations and the sociological reality, Malinowski writes:

> Thus in real life, as well as in myth, we see that the situation . . . is at cross variance with tribal law and conventional tribal ideals. According to law and morals, two brothers or a maternal uncle and his nephew are friends, allies, and have all feelings and interests in common. In real life to a certain degree and quite openly in myth, they are enemies, cheat each other, murder each other, and suspicion and hostility obtain rather than love and union. (*Sex and Repression in Savage Society*, p. 111)

These legends are not unique to the Trobrianders; their like can be found throughout the primitive world. Most widespread are the tales of two brothers who kill each other simultaneously and of the maternal uncle who "sacrifices" his sister's son. Both can be viewed as signaling the end of the fratriarchy; yet they tell us nothing about the beginning of the patriarchy. Where, then, can we find data on the full crossover from matriarchal to patriarchal society? The phenomenon called "blood redemption" provides the missing link in answering this question.

Blood Redemption of Fathers and Sons

Blood redemption, also called "sacrifice" or "redemptive sacrifice," is a ritual offering to redeem a blood debt. Its central feature is the killing of the firstborn son. The practice has left traces in both history and myth, but its meaning remains a mystery.

Robertson Smith points out: "Every one who reads the Old Testament with attention is struck with the fact that the origin and *rationale* of sacrifice are nowhere fully explained . . ." (*Religion of the Semites*, p. 3). Even he, who studied the question closely, could not believe these "grisly offerings" were a feature of a crucial period in human evolution. At the same time he confesses that "the consecration of first-born male children has always created a difficulty" (p. 464). Indeed, it seems incredible to us that there was ever a time when sons, the most prized children, were regularly slaughtered.

Blood sacrifice is as much a mark of the barbaric period as cannibalism is of the epoch of savagery. In fact, one grew up out of the other. According to Lippert, sacrifice is found "wherever cannibalism exists or has existed" (*Evolution of Culture*, p. 437). Survivals from all parts of the globe testify to the former universality of both. There are not a few examples where the two are combined and the sacrificial offering is also eaten.

William Graham Sumner points out that sacrifice, which has left such a deep imprint in human emotions, is not always connected with religion.

> Child sacrifice expresses the deepest horror and suffering produced by experience of the human lot. Men must do it. Their interests demanded it, however much it might pain them. Human sacrifices may be said to have been universal. They lasted down to the half-civilized stage of all nations and sporadically even later, and they have barely ceased amongst the present half-civilized peoples. They are not primarily religious. They are a reaction of men under the experience of the ills of life. . . . (*Folkways*, p. 553)

It is not sufficient to say that men "must" kill all the firstborn sons because "their interests demanded it." What were these interests? How shall we interpret this bloody interlude of history in the transition from barbarism to civilization?

According to Hegel, historical movement at the most critical junctures produces a drama of two opposed rights coming into collision. The one is based upon the traditional right of the established order, the other is charged with the power of a new and higher order striving to free itself from the fetters of the old. The collision between the two is a tragedy in the full sense of the term, for each is right unto itself. This applied to the irreconcilable conflict between mother's brother right and father right that marked the transition from the divided family to the one-father family.

On the one hand, the mother's brother could not easily relinquish his inherited "blood bond" to his sister and sister's children. On the other hand, the father could not easily shed his inherited "blood debt," carried over from the epoch of cannibalism and blood revenge. The "blood gift" or "bloody offering" became the price of liquidating a heritage that no man had been fully aware of, but that all had to pay for.

Apparently there was no other way to sever the Gordian knot of the matrilineal blood line that created the divided two-father family. The very form of the sacrifice is symbolical; it is sometimes called the "partitioning" of the child.

Who was the sacrificer and who the sacrificed? This is an extremely complex question. Since every man was at once a mother's brother to his sister's son and a father to his wife's son, all men were stained with the blood of the slain firstborn sons. Whether the child was the son of a sister or the son of a wife, he was the victim who was partitioned. Finally, since a woman was both the sister of a brother and the wife of a husband, every mother suffered the agony of the sacrifice of her firstborn son. All humanity paid the price for adherence to an outworn kinship system.

At a later stage blood redemption was satisfied through the substitution of a domesticated animal for the firstborn son. In the Passover legend the lamb is the price of redemption; elsewhere other animals came to serve the same purpose. The son lived to become the prized "eldest son" in the newly developing "line of fathers and sons."

A penetrating insight into the part played by sacrifice in the transitional process is given by John Layard in his book *Stone Men of Malekula*. Although this region had emerged from its cannibalistic past relatively recently, it passed through the period of human sacrifice rapidly and had arrived at animal substitutes by the time Layard began his studies in 1914. In Malekula the sacrificial animal is not the lamb but the

carefully raised tusked boar, which is used for both individual
and mass sacrifices. According to Layard, "This sacrifice of
tusked boars is said by the natives to replace the sacrifice
of human beings" (p. 14).

The most important ritual is called "Maki" and is divided
into two parts, Low Maki and High Maki. It appears to be a
composite of "making men" in the low ritual and of making
"lines of fathers and sons" in the high ritual. Mass sacrifices
of pigs are required on both occasions; about a hundred in
Low Maki, double that number or more in High Maki. In
addition to these mass rituals that make and maintain the
patrilineal relationship in general, there are individual rites
and sacrifices that make a man the father of his eldest son.

In Malekula both the son and his pig substitute are called
bete-ram. After the birth of a male child, and at the conclusion of various preliminary ceremonies including sham fights
and gift exchanges, the dedication of the *bete-ram* takes place
and the pig is sacrificed. "Proceedings end with the sounding of
the sacrificial signal on the gongs in honour of the tusked
boar and, through him, of the now officially recognised 'eldest
son'" (p. 183).

There is no ambiguity about the meaning of these sacrifices.
The Maki ritual represents an acknowledgment that "the patriarchal was intruding on the matriarchal system," says
Layard. In South Raga it is explicitly said to be *"on account
of the matrilineal organization* that the sacrifices made to the
ancestral ghosts are given to the mother's brother, and, in
his name, to all the members of his family or clan" (p. 295,
emphasis in the original).

Malekula never made the full transition from matriarchy
to patriarchy. Layard's studies therefore furnish us with a
kind of photograph of an incompleted process. Of particular
importance is the foreshadowing of the disappearance of the
mother's brother, the "matrilineal father." Although in Malekula
he still retains his earthly form, he is already passing over
into the mystical "ancestral ghost." Side by side with the maternal uncle, guardian of his sister's son in real life, we come
upon his spiritual counterpart, the "Guardian Ghost." The
Malekulans make little or no distinction between the two.

This transformation from mother's brother to Guardian Ghost
is mirrored in the legend of Asaor, the major Malekulan myth.
Asaor, a mother's brother, is under terrible pressure to slay
his sister's son to avenge his own son's death. The clash of

loyalties between his allegiance on the one hand to his matrilineal ties, and on the other hand to his new paternal ties, is "like a Greek tragedy," says Layard. Under the matrilineal system uncle and nephew are "of one flesh, indissolubly united." But now Asaor is under mounting pressures to sacrifice his sister's son.

"In the high tragedy of this tale," says Layard, "Asaor is forced to outrage all personal feeling and at the same time the main principle of the old matrilineal order in obedience to the new principle of overt patrilineal descent. . . ." He adds that this typifies the revolutionary change that "turned a man's nearest blood-relative according to the old matrilineal system into a traditional foe" (pp. 604-07).

For a long time Asaor hesitates, drawing back from committing the abominable crime against his own blood kin. But in the end he submits and kills his sister's son. Thereupon, according to the tale, he "took a new name. And the name he took was Le-hev-hev, the name of the Guardian Ghost." The legend ends as follows:

> Henceforth, having committed this crime against his own nature in the interests of the new order of society, he said, "I am Le-hev-hev. I don't care what I do any more, and I shall do what I like." No other man, it is said, has ever dared to take this name, for, though others have since been forced to sacrifice their sisters' sons, none has ever pursued this dread duty with such perseverence as he. (ibid., p. 606)

Thus the mother's brother, for many millennia the guardian of his sister's son, departs from the earth to reappear in supernatural form as the Guardian Ghost. He becomes a respected and somewhat fearsome creature who lives in the sky and governs the land of the dead, demanding not only regular blood offerings but also gifts, emoluments, and tributes of all kinds. Indeed, he has such an unslakable thirst that he must be propitiated over and over again.

As Layard writes, "The natives must for ever keep paying the price due to the matrilineal principle for the outrage done to it through the introduction of overt patrilineal descent." He adds, quoting Tattevin: "'This blood claim, this sacrifice, covers every kind of object: pigs, mats, taro [and nowadays] money and cloth, and lasts throughout a man's whole life. It takes hold of the native in his cradle, and accompanies him to his tomb and even beyond . . .'" (ibid., p. 724).

Despite all this the full transition was not achieved; the matrilineal system was not overthrown, nor was the full-fledged father-family established. Malekula remained a region in limbo between the two social orders.

Layard's study provides a valuable clue to the origin of the more fearsome gods and demons that emerged out of the ancestral ghost. These menacing Baals and Molochs made their appearance a few thousand years ago in the cradle of civilization where the original changeover from matriarchy to patriarchy was achieved. These superhuman beings could hurl death and destruction upon humankind unless sacrifices were offered to appease their wrath. The child sacrifice that arose in connection with such deities reached an extreme pitch before the practice was abandoned altogether.

This confirms Frazer's view that totemism in the epoch of savagery was not a religion and that religion arose only with the more highly developed culture of a later period. In the totemic era men tried to establish peaceful relations with dangerous animals, unaware that some of these were humans like themselves. By providing food and protection to these "animals" they tried to placate them and turn them from foes into friends. These totemic alliances with humans and animals had beneficial results — the expansion of the tribal brotherhood and the domestication of many useful animals.

But in the later period of barbarism these naive attempts to placate animals were supplanted by an equally naive attempt to placate superhuman gods and demons. Unable to explain or control natural disasters such as droughts, famines, and epidemics, or the rising incidence of social conflicts and wars, men paid whatever price they thought was demanded by the wrathful gods and demons plaguing them with these calamities.

This brought about a change in redemptive sacrifice. It had begun as a transaction between men — between mothers' brothers and fathers — in an effort to change the line of blood kinship and descent and achieve a one-father family. But it ended as a transaction between men and superhuman beings, the gods and demons they had themselves invented. How could men gauge the demands of these unseen Baals and Molochs who, after being propitiated with sacrificial offerings, continued to imperil them with famines, wars, and other calamities? They

could only pour out more and more sacrifices to these vora-
cious demons — while the demons could never open a human
mouth to cry "Enough!"

Where formerly offerings had been restricted to the firstborn
son, more and more children came to be slaughtered and
burned to appease the gods and demons. The war god emerges
as the most thirsty of all for sacrifices. This can be seen in two
examples from Frazer. First, the solitary sacrifice:

> Among the Semites of Western Asia the king, in a time
> of national danger, sometimes gave his own son to die
> as a sacrifice for the people. Thus Philo of Byblus, in
> his work on the Jews, says: "It was an ancient custom in
> a crisis of great danger that the ruler of a city or nation
> should give his beloved son to die for the whole people,
> as a ransom offered to the avenging demons; and the
> children thus offered were slain with mystic rites. So Cronus
> whom the Phoenicians call Israel, being king of the land
> and having an only-begotten son called Jeoud (for in the
> Phoenician tongue Jeoud signifies 'only-begotten') dressed
> him in royal robes and sacrificed him upon an altar in a
> time of war, when the country was in great danger from the
> enemy." When the king of Moab was besieged by the
> Israelites and hard beset, he took his eldest son who should
> have reigned in his stead, and offered him for a burnt of-
> fering on the wall. (*The Golden Bough,* Part III, *The Dying
> God,* p. 166)

Mass child sacrifices were also made:

> When the Carthaginians were defeated and besieged by
> Agathocles, they ascribed their disasters to the wrath of
> Baal; for whereas in former times they had been wont
> to sacrifice to him their own offspring, they had latterly
> fallen into the habit of buying children and rearing them
> to be victims. So, to appease the angry god, two hundred
> children of the noblest families were picked out for sacri-
> fice, and the tale of victims was swelled by not less than
> three hundred more who volunteered to die for the father-
> land. They were sacrificed by being placed, one by one,
> on the sloping hands of the brazen image, from which they
> rolled into a pit of fire. Childless people among the Cartha-
> ginians bought children from poor parents and slaughtered

them, says Plutarch, as if they were lambs or chickens; and the mother had to stand by and see it done without a tear or a groan, for if she wept or moaned she lost all the credit and the child was sacrificed none the less. But all the place in front of the image was filled with a tumultuous music of fires and drums to drown the shrieks of the victims. Infants were publicly sacrificed by the Carthaginians down to the proconsulate of Tiberius . . . [and it] still went on secretly in the lifetime of Tertullian. (*The Golden Bough,* Part III, *The Dying God,* pp. 167-68)

Redemptive sacrifice flared up in its most extreme forms shortly before the practice was extinguished. Even female children were swept into the firepits. Frazer cites the Psalmist's lament that the Canaanites "sacrificed their sons and their daughters unto demons, and shed innocent blood . . . and the land was polluted with blood" (ibid., p. 169).

In the Americas a similar pattern of escalated sacrifice is found — among the most advanced peoples, those who stand on the threshold of civilized culture, the Aztecs of Mexico and the Incas of Peru. Lippert writes:

The cult of child sacrifice was enormously developed in ancient Peru and Mexico. The tribes of Quito in the pre-Inca period sacrificed every first child. In Peru it is alleged that at the accession of a new Inca as many as a thousand children were sacrificed, and other cults demanded periodic offerings of children. . . . The Aztec gods also demanded children as sacrifices in order to grant increase to the crops. (*Evolution of Culture,* p. 449)

Homer W. Smith says this on the subject:

It is believed that human sacrifice reached its most elaborate development with the Aztecs. One Spanish historian estimated that the number of victims sacrificed to the god Xipa annually exceeded the number who died a natural death in the entire country of Mexico. Cortez reported 136,000 skulls in the great temple, and Prescott estimated that the yearly toll throughout the Empire exceeded 20,000 and perhaps totaled 50,000 victims. . . .

This wholesale slaughter was not the madness of a demented people, but the logical application of a faith. The

Aztecs gave to their gods whatever they themselves valued; food, clothing, flowers, jewelry, incense, the first-fruits of the harvest, of hunting and fishing, and of the handicrafts. Animal sacrifices were made on a tremendous scale, but the most acceptable, the indispensable offering was human blood. (*Man and His Gods,* p. 133)

W. I. Thomas reports the following mass sacrifice in Mexico only a few hundred years ago:

When the great temple of Huitzilopochtli was dedicated in 1486, the chain of victims sacrificed on that occasion extended for the length of two miles. In this terrible massacre the hearts of no less than 70,000 human beings were offered up! (*Primitive Behavior,* p. 304)

Blood redemption was first and fully conquered in the Old World. This leaves us with the question: By what means was the conquest achieved? Here we must turn our attention to private ownership of property, which first came about in the cradle of civilization; this new development put an end to redemptive sacrifice.

With the rise of private property, humans as well as animals became too valuable to be wantonly slaughtered. Humans as slaves could produce ever-increasing wealth for their masters. Livestock became the first form of property that could be exchanged for other wealth. The new material interests of men thus became a socioeconomic force more powerful than fear of punishment by angry demons.

Once men came into possession of their own disposable property, they could effect the full transition from the matrifamily to the one-father family. Through his own property a man could pay off his blood debt once and for all and eliminate not only the blood offering but also the endless gift-offerings and tribute payments. By the disposition of his own property a man could also secure his wife's son as his own. This transformation is imprinted in the Old Testament. "The father is obliged to redeem his firstborn son from the priest by payment of a ransom of five shekels or its equivalent in goods" (*Encyclopedia of the Jewish Religion,* p. 146).

The Aztecs and Incas could not liberate themselves from blood sacrifice because they did not reach the level of the private ownership of property. Early explorers and travelers, admiring the economic abundance in these regions, made the mistake of viewing this wealth in terms of their own European social system, founded on private property, and wrote many erroneous reports. But by the time of the conquest neither the Mexicans nor the Peruvians had passed over from the last stage of matriarchal society to the first stage of private property, the father-family, and the patriarchal order.

As Engels has explained, patriarchal class society was founded upon the family, private property, and the state. There is an interlocking relationship between the family and private property, which preceded it. The driving necessity to achieve the one-father family and do away with the divided matri-family opened the road to private property. Private property, in turn, became the indispensable means for severing all chains to the old social order and inaugurating the new patriarchal, class-based society. The state, which arose later, consolidated and legalized both private property and the father-family with its line of descent, inheritance, and succession from fathers to sons.

The transition was a protracted and agonizing process. Deep-seated fears and superstitions about cruel and revengeful gods and demons continued to haunt barbaric peoples. Many relapses occurred; under conditions of great stress, frightened people resorted to blood sacrifices to avert disasters and death. Lippert, who views blood redemption as the starting point for inducting children into the patriarchal family, points out that liberation from barbaric practices was not achieved at a single step; battles between the old and the new raged back and forth (*Evolution of Culture,* pp. 434, 483).

The patriarchal epoch opened some six thousand years ago. According to the Old Testament, Abraham was the first patriarch. He is also called the "father" of monotheism, the one-god religion closely associated with the one-father family. The story of Abraham tells of the end of son sacrifice and the substitution of animals. It also records the patriarch's "line of fathers and sons": Abraham begot Isaac of Sarah; Isaac begot Jacob of Rebekah; and Jacob begot Joseph of Rachel.

By the fourth generation the line becomes uncertain and is perhaps broken. According to Greek legends, similar breaks occurred in the early royal houses of Greece. Despite this, the new social order founded upon private property and the father-family vanquished the matriarchy.

Out of child sacrifice there arose the oppressive sense of

sin. In the Greek Orphic mysteries sin is born with the crime of partitioning the body of Dionysus. Freud writes on this point:

> The theory of primal sin is of Orphic origin; it was preserved in the mysteries and thence penetrated into the philosophic schools of Greek antiquity. Men were the descendents of Titans, who had killed and dismembered the young Dionysos-Zagreus; the weight of this crime oppressed them. A fragment of Anaximander says that the unity of the world was destroyed by a primordial crime and everything that issued from it must carry on the punishment for this crime. (*Totem and Taboo,* p. 198)

The sense of sin, however, is not primordial; it did not exist in the epoch of savagery. It came in with the dreadful violation of human feelings evoked by the slaughtering and burning of children to appease the wrath of barbaric demons and gods.

About "Female Infanticide"

Although the origin of infanticide is left unexplained, an occasional vague allusion is made to the biblical account of son sacrifice. Despite this, the impression has grown up that in primitive societies only female children were subjected to infanticide. It is supposed that when some children had to be disposed of owing to lack of food, females were chosen since they were, then as now, an economic liability. Thus "infanticide" has come to be virtually synonymous with "female infanticide." This impression is false.

The abandonment of redemptive sacrifice did not all at once put an end to the practice of child-killing; under conditions of emergency, especially war, men continued for a time to make sacrificial offerings. It is this residue of the former practice that represents infanticide. In the cradle of civilization it evolved into the form known as "exposure." The infant was abandoned alive and thus given a chance to live if it was found and adopted. The most famous foundlings are Moses and the legendary pair who founded Rome — Romulus and Remus. Oedipus was another.

Female infanticide came late in history and was only a faint

echo of the sacrifice of firstborn sons. Even the method of killing female children differed from that used on males, as Robertson Smith describes:

> In Arabia, as among other barbarous peoples, child-murder
> was carried out in such a way that no blood was shed;
> the infant was buried alive, and often, if we may believe
> Zamakhshari on Sur . . . the grave was ready by the
> side of the bed on which the daughter was born. The same
> authority says that girls were sometimes spared till the
> age of six, and then adorned and led forth by their father
> and cast into a pit in the wilderness. . . . the father said
> to the mother, "Dress her up that I may bring her to her
> mothers." (*Kinship and Marriage in Early Arabia,* p. 293)

Smith writes that in Arabia female infanticide is attributed to
the parents' fear that they could not find food for all their offspring or that their daughters might bring shame and dishonor upon them. Smith, agreeing with the *Kamil,* says that
"pride and the fear of disgrace were mere pretexts" and points
to a terrible seven years' drought as the factor that probably
gave new life to infanticide. But this does not explain why females rather than males should have been sacrificed.

Female infanticide is found in the transitional period from
communal ownership to private property. Under the old system
property had been transmitted from mothers to daughters,
the brothers sharing in it. With the rise of patriarchy and
property, this maternal and fraternal line of descent and inheritance created problems — until patriarchal laws were enacted and
state power enforced a permanent line of descent and inheritance
from fathers to sons.

Patriarchy required more than individual fathers begetting
their "own" sons; it needed an unbroken line of fathers and sons
down the generations to secure both the father-family and the
transmission of property through the father-line. Thus men
even resorted to daughter-murder to clear away any maternal
contestants so that they could leave their property to their
sons or, in the absence of sons, to their brothers. Smith cites
a fragment from the *Kamil* on this subject. "A detail in this
story shows a curious connection between child-murder and
the law of inheritance: a father [awaiting the birth of a child]
says, 'If it is a colt we will make it partner in our wealth, but
if it is a filly we will bury it.'" In an earlier footnote he writes,
"That the paternal uncle is the heir as against the daughter is

affirmed in Moslem times in the . . . *Kamil* . . ." (*Kinship and Marriage in Early Arabia,* pp. 294, 66).

Unlike male sacrifice, however, which passed through a prolonged evolution, female infanticide was a short-lived phenomenon. The very same factor, private property, that put an end to son sacrifice also rapidly diminished female infanticide. Female children became desirable because of the "bride price" they could bring at marriage.

This did not alter the trend toward the dispossession of women from the inheritance of property. Men, who had always been the warriors, now had the weapons not only to seize the property of other men as their booty, but to push aside female heirs. Robertson Smith cites the old law of Medina by which "women were excluded from inheritance on the principle that 'none can be heirs who do not take part in battle, drive booty and protect property'. . . ." He adds, "The exclusion of women from inheritance was not therefore confined to Medina, and we shall see . . . that it was probably nearly if not quite coextensive with marriage by contract or purchase" (ibid., pp. 65-66).

The terms "bride price" and "purchase marriage" refer to the practice of exchanging property for a woman in marriage. This transaction marks the great turning point not only toward the patriarchal family but away from sacrifice; it was when "bride price" supplanted "blood price" that men won redemption from blood redemption.

14

'Bride Price'
and the Father-Family

Women reached the apex of their influence and prestige in the first stage of barbarism, which began with agriculture. Although the family had emerged, it was a matrifamily, still tied to the matriclan with its collectivist, egalitarian principles. Women continued to work in groups, applying their "magic" skills to farming, craft production, and social functions. This peak period of female creativity is registered in the many honorific names applied to women, summed up in the terms "goddess" or "fertility goddess."

Frazer describes the Egyptian Isis, earliest goddess of the transition:

> Her attributes and epithets were so numerous that in the hieroglyphics she is called "the many-named," "the thousand-named," and in Greek inscriptions "the myriad-named." . . . Dr. Budge writes that "Isis was the great and beneficent goddess and mother, whose influence and love pervaded all heaven and earth and the abode of the dead, and she was the personification of the great feminine, creative power which conceived and brought forth every living creature and thing, from the gods in heaven to man on earth, and to the insect on the ground; what she brought forth she protected, and cared for, and fed, and nourished, and she employed her life in using her power graciously and successfully, not only in creating new beings but in restoring those that were dead. (*The Golden Bough*, Part IV, *Adonis, Attis, Osiris*, vol. II, p. 115)

How, then, in the later period of barbarism, did women plummet from this highly esteemed position to their degraded

411

status in civilized patriarchal society? Or, to put the question another way, how did men establish their supremacy in society and the family? Doubts about the priority of the matriarchy have persisted because this downfall of the female sex has not been adequately explained.

The basis of woman's downfall lies in the evolution of private property.

The Origin of Private Property

The underlying socioeconomic factors have been delineated by Engels and others. Historically, private property originated with "movable property," objects that could be conveyed from one possessor to another. The institution of immobile property (real estate), consisting of land and its improvements, came much later in history; it began with the recognition of the family dwelling, garden, or orchard as distinct from the common land. But unlike movable goods this petty private domain did not originally enter into the exchange circuit.

The accumulation of the first private wealth was made possible by the higher economy that began with agriculture and stock-raising. The abundance of food led to more concentrated populations and new divisions of social labor. Men who had formerly been hunters now became farmers, herdsmen, and craftsmen. The more productive economy and augmented labor force gave rise to surpluses over and above the immediate consuming needs of the primary producers.

At first these surpluses were used to sustain the village elders who coordinated work on community projects such as irrigation systems. But gradually some men elevated themselves into priest-kings, nobles, and overlords, standing above the common people, exacting foodstuffs, livestock and handicrafts as tribute and later as taxes. Private wealth was now accumulating in the hands of an elite, a ruling class.

The subsequent development of commodity exchange on a larger scale leading toward a money economy speeded up the formation of new strata of wealthy proprietors and traders. In place of the old tribal warriors there appeared soldiers in the service of their warlords, sharing in the booty as a reward for their services. The captives they took were not adopted but put to work as slaves to augment the wealth of their masters.

The introduction of slavery sealed the downfall of women. Removed from productive and social life, they were relegated to the individual home. Although women continued to produce on farms and in home crafts, these were no longer social but family functions. Wealthy women were even more removed from productive activities, becoming little more than breeders of legal heirs to men's property.

All this, however, still leaves certain questions unanswered. How did women's downfall coincide with the rise of private property? And why, when women were at the height of their power and prestige, did this property come into the hands of the men, not the women?

Wilhelm Reich touches on this subject in *The Invasion of Compulsory Sex-Morality*. He agrees with Engels that the advent of private property imposed the need to transmit wealth through children. But "this hypothesis does not show *how* wealth got into the man's hands . . . it does not indicate the mechanism behind the historical process" (p. 89). His own hypothesis calls attention to the "marriage gift" and its development into "purchase marriage" as the mechanism behind the advance from mother right to father right. But the matter goes deeper than this.

The origin of private property and how it came into the hands of men is tied up with the replacement of the matri-family with undivided father right in the one-father family. The process to study, therefore, is the victory of father right over mother's brother right. The defeat of the mothers' brothers also brought about the downfall of the mothers.

As Reich detected, the turning point came with the development of the marriage gift into purchase marriage. Marriage gifts were the primitive interchanges of food and other items to bring hostile groups of men together, a necessary precondition for matrimonial relations. As a certain point in history this gift-giving between men passed over into a new and different kind of transaction—the exchange of what had become personal property. With this the marriage gift became the bride price. Since gift interchange had taken place between men, the bride price likewise became a transaction between men. This was the first factor behind the rise of private property in male, not female hands.

The gift could not become a price until a sufficiently high economic level had been reached. To go beyond the interchange of token items, goods of value such as cattle had to be available for exchange. The first regions in which gift-giving passed over into barter were the pastoral regions of the Old World, and cattle became the first value involved in the transition from the marriage gift to the bride price. Briffault explains this:

> The purchase of a wife is impossible in the most primitive cultural stages, not only because the men have no notion of any commercial exchange, but because they possess no fundable property, and are therefore destitute of purchasing power. . . . Only at a very definite stage of cultural evolution has the man become an owner of transferable and fundable property, and in a position to drive a bargain, and to commute all contributions to the woman's family by a lump payment. That position was attained only when he became an owner of domesticated cattle, his first form of real property. Marriage by purchase in the proper sense is accordingly not found at all in Australia, Melanesia, Polynesia, or in America, where no domesticated cattle and consequently no man-owned wealth, existed. It is in pastoral societies, or in societies that have passed through pastoral stages, in Africa, Asia, and Europe, that the purchasing power of the bride-gift has developed. (*The Mothers*, vol. II, p. 218)

The importance of cattle in the development of private property has long been recognized. Cattle were very valuable in the early period of farming; they served as draft and pack animals, and they provided food for the larder and by-products for craft industries. In addition, livestock reproduced themselves, multiplying all these benefits. These were the reasons cattle became the earliest form of movable property to be bartered for wives.

The connection between cattle and the institution of property at this turning point of history is imprinted in the English language. Hoebel writes:

> The word *chattel*, which means any object of personal ownership, is derived from the Old French *chatel*. The modern Anglo-American word *cattle* has the same origin. *Chatel* has its ultimate etymology in the Latin *caput*, or head. *Chatel* in ancient France referred to property of greatest value, head property. Cattle were so much the chief form of property among our pastoral ancestors that our specialized word for personal property grew from the same root. (*Man in the Primitive World*, pp. 342-43)

Transactions involving the barter of brides for cattle are called "cattle marriage," but they are more fundamentally a "child price" than a bride price.

Cattle Marriage and the "Child Price"

In cattle marriage the husband gave a herd of cattle to secure a wife. The cattle were received by the wife's male kin on behalf of their group. Yet it was not the brothers or mothers' brothers who became the owners of the cattle as property but the husbands and fathers. How did this come about?

This question cannot be answered without tracing the conversion of the marriage gift into the bride price. Cattle marriage falls into both categories; it began as a gift interchange between intermarrying communities and families and ended as the bride price. Some cattle-raising regions up to our times have not passed over from gift interchange to purchase, and others hover between the two. Hoebel notes the difficulties this creates for anthropologists. "The line between gift and purchase is gossamer thin," he writes. "This makes it sometimes difficult to determine whether the social practice in a given tribe is bride purchase or merely gift" (*Man in the Primitive World*, p. 308).

Nevertheless there are ways of making the distinction. In intermarriage arrangements that have not gone beyond interchange, the cattle are not permanently retained by the recipient group or family as their property; they are kept in constant circulation. Writing about the Bantu of Africa, Ralph Piddington quotes Cullen Young's picturesque description of the constant giving and receiving of cattle for brides:

> To those who . . . see at once the little bunch of cattle setting out from one group-settlement to another, and see simultaneously the maiden setting out in the opposite direction and, so to say, passing the animals on the way; who see also those beasts kraaled and tended till a later day, when they again set out from the settlement that had in the first instance been that of a receiving wife-group but has now become that of a paying husband-group, as a young male in the family has reached the stage of taking a wife; who see this process going on endlessly and these cattle always when they set out equating with a maiden likewise setting out to meet and transfer for them; to those alone has the phrase 'bride-wealth' its real meaning. (*Introduction to Social Anthropology*, pp. 140-41)

It is incorrect, however, to refer to this as the bride price. The passing of cattle from group to group upon each marriage simply expresses the fraternal-matrimonial relations between the groups. It is not a purchase transaction. As Piddington himself observes: "The cattle or other wealth obtained in return for a woman are very frequently used at a later date to obtain a wife for her brother, and a progressive series of such transactions links together a whole series of individuals and groups in a complex network of social relationships which is characteristic of primitive society."

George Peter Murdock gives an example from Africa reminiscent of the Trobriand "kula" interchange, even though it is being conducted not with valueless shells but with cattle:

> The Lovedu even group lineages into rings to expedite and stabilize their rule of matrilateral cross-cousin marriage. Within such a ring, women pass from lineage to lineage in one direction, and the cattle received for them in marriage payments circulate in the opposite direction. (*Africa,* p. 388)

Lucy Mair explicitly states that some types of cattle exchange are "analogous to the *kula.*"

> The Turkana of northern Kenya establish, by gifts of cattle, friendships with individuals in remote parts of the country through which they wander with their herds. On his home ground the partner in such an exchange is an ally and protector to his fellow. . . .
> These exchanges maintain partnerships between equals. (*Introduction to Social Anthropology,* p. 166)

So long as these gift interchanges prevailed between men, women did not come under the domination of either brothers or husbands. They retained their important place in productive life, their independence, and their esteem. These were lost only with the rise of bride price and its consolidation in purchase marriage. Whereas a woman previously made the decision about the man she married, with the advent of purchase marriage the woman's wishes were of little or no account. Men made the deals and the marriage contracts. But these transactions were no longer between the brothers and mothers' brothers of different clans; they were made between the husbands and fathers of different families.

How did this occur? In the interchange system the men who passed the cattle in return for a bride were the husbands, and the cattle were received by brothers and mothers' brothers. Why then didn't the brothers and mothers' brothers become the private owners of cattle instead of the husbands? The answer to this seldom-asked question will disclose how the husbands and fathers superseded the brothers and mothers' brothers — paving the way for male supremacy.

Two main factors were responsible: the restricted powers of brothers and mothers' brothers, and the way the bride price functioned as a "child price." Together these represent the "mechanism" that Reich sought as the explanation of how gift marriage became purchase marriage.

The maternal uncle, as the older male in the matriclan or matrifamily, did receive the cattle transferred by the husband in return for a wife. But he was not an independent individual who could take possession of the cattle as his personal property. He was only the male custodian acting in the interests of the whole group. As Lippert puts it, brother right was dependent on mother right, and the transmission of property still followed the mother-line (*Evolution of Culture*, p. 248).

The situation was different with the husband, striving to become the sole father in an undivided family setup. His opportunity came from the fact that the cattle exchanged for his wife gave him claims to her children as his own. Even if the marriage broke up, these claims remained valid and could only be voided through the return of the cattle. This was not always possible if, for example, the cattle had been passed on to secure a wife for the brother of the bride. Cattle that died created further problems in the matter of refunds. It is not difficult to see how the passing of cattle as marriage gifts would falter in the face of claims and counter-claims regarding the possession of children or the refund of cattle. Subtly but inexorably cattle marriage passed over from an interchange relationship to an exchange relationship involving ownership of property. With the advent of the bride price and child price the road was paved for the private ownership of cattle in the hands of the husband and father who, as an individual, could dispose of them as he wished.

Anthropologists have noted that the prime purpose of the bride price was to get possession of the wife's children. Among the Bantu, according to Ralph Piddington, the cattle given are called the *lobola,* and there is a saying that "cattle beget children." He writes:

> It is the lobola payment which establishes the claim of a father to his children and their membership of his patrilineal group. This is most clearly seen in certain Bantu groups where, in case of divorce, the children remain with their father unless the original cattle handed over at marriage are returned, in which case the children belong to the group of their mother. This rule is summed up in the native saying: "The children are where the cattle are not." (*Introduction to Social Anthropology,* p. 140)

Audrey I. Richards points out with respect to the Southern Bantu that the *lobola* payment means the wife's kin "surrender their own claims on the woman's unborn children, who would otherwise belong to her own clan." She further indicates that through the bride price the father not only gets the child from his wife but gets it away from the *malume,* the wife's brother.

> It is clear from the evidence, not only that the father acquires in marriage the sole right over the children, but that this right is acquired through the *lobola* transaction itself. "The delivery of lobolo," says Posselt of Zulu marriage, "*is not an essential part of a valid native marriage, but it is the very essence of the transfer of the custody of the children to their father*; all other considerations, rights or obligations are only ancillary." Among the Bechuana, as long as no *Bogadi,* or bride price, is given, the woman and her offspring remain the property of her family and clan. The same appears to be true of the Metabele, among whom the *lobola* is stated to be a consideration paid by the father for control over the children "without which the *Malume* would claim them.". . . Faye describes the *lobola* as "the purchase price of the bride's prospective progeny from the maternal clan to which it rightly belongs." (*Hunger and Work in a Savage Tribe,* pp. 124-25)

The claims on a woman's children were so much a part of the bride price that if a wife did not bear children for her husband he could demand another wife in her place. Failing that, he could demand the return of the cattle. According to Hoebel, in Africa the bride's family substitutes a younger sister "if no issue is forthcoming from the first daughter for whom they have received bride price." He adds:

> As an alternative, the sum of the bride price may be refunded. This is often difficult, however, because the capital received in payment for the daughter may already have been invested in the purchase of a wife for a son. (*Man in the Primitive World,* p. 208)

It has been noted that the practice of female infanticide is abandoned with the advent of the bride price. Lippert writes that "girls now become objects of high value." He explains, "When the birth of a girl gives the Kaffir father a prospect of acquiring thirty cattle, he will certainly desire many such children, and in the decision as to whether the newborn child shall live or die the economic interest operates more and more in favor of life." The same conversion occurred in Greece:

> Among the Greeks the course of development is particularly clear. . . . this is confirmed by Aristotle's report that the forefathers of the Greeks had bought their wives from each other. As in India, cattle were the characteristic units of value among the Homeric Greeks. With unusual liberality Iphidamas gave a hundred steers for his bride, while in another case four oxen constituted the purchase price of a capable woman. As the Greeks accumulated capital in herds, girls more and more frequently escaped the fate of exposure, long before this was raised to a law. The true nature of the new esteem for the maiden found expression in the praise of Homer, who lauds her because she brings cattle to her father's household. (*Evolution of Culture,* pp. 308-13)

"Child price" was progressive in that it suppressed female infanticide. But it had a retrogressive aspect—the curtailment of the independence and freedom of women. The wife who wanted to leave her husband found it increasingly difficult to do so because the children were involved. Men who had come into ownership of cattle or children were not inclined to part with them merely because a woman wanted her freedom. The only alternative left to the wife, in the absence of a cattle refund, was to give up her children.

This was a difficult decision for a mother to make, however much she longed for her freedom, particularly when more than one child was exacted as the price of her redemption from marriage. Lippert writes that "among certain tribes in Central Africa the birth of five children is said to have given the mother the option of returning to her parental home. Among the Songhay the wife is redeemed by bearing three children" (*Evolution of Culture,* p. 309).

Even women who did not bear children in a marriage were not exempted from the obligations incurred through the bride price. If they married again and bore children in the second marriage, they were obliged to "deed over" the children to the divorced husband in lieu of a refund of the bride price. Hoebel cites the following example:

> Linton's report on the Vezo Sakalava of Madagascar shows to what extent bride price is actually the purchase of a right to children among these people. In the case of divorce, neither a refund of the cattle paid nor the substitution of another woman is socially permissible. The divorced wife may remarry, but only with her former husband's permission. This will be forthcoming upon agreement by the wife and her new husband-to-be that the first children born to them (up to the limit of three) will be deeded over to the first husband, who is the one that paid the bride price to her family. The woman nurses and keeps the children until weaning, whereupon they are turned over to her first husband and become his legal heirs without the formality of adoption. (*Man in the Primitive World,* p. 209)

Thus by degrees the wife came more and more under the dominion of her husband, who had paid the bride price for her and along with it the child price for her children. Through cattle payments the father had taken over possession; the mother's brother now had to relinquish all claims to his sister's children. Once the brothers and mothers' brothers were eliminated, the husbands and fathers could consolidate their supremacy over their wives and children as their "own" families.

It was essential not only for the father-family to win supremacy but to maintain it through an unbroken line of fathers and sons down the generations. Briffault points out what happened if this line were broken: "Under the law of the Twelve

Tables, in the absence of a patriarchal heir, property went to the clan. . . . The absence of a legal heir reduced even the patrician under the law, to the condition of tribal communism as regards the transmission of property" (*The Mothers,* vol. II, p. 345).

From Purchase Marriage to Patriarchal Power

It may come as a surprise to learn that the father-family was founded before the facts about biological paternity became known. In pre-civilized society, as we have seen, physiological paternity was unknown. The first recognition of the father was socially established; the husband who performed certain rituals became officially recognized as the father of his wife's children. Ignorance of paternity continued into the founding stage of the father-family, on the threshold of civilization. At this point the husband became the father not by ritual, but by payment in cattle of the bride price and child price.

The continuing ignorance of genetic relationship between father and child is not often perceived — or believed. C. L. Meek, writing about the peoples of Northern Nigeria, says, "It appears to be immaterial to a husband whether the children borne by his wife were begotten by himself or one of his kindred group. . . . It is hard for a European who believes in the 'instinctive love' of parent for child to allow this point of view" (*Tribal Studies in Northern Nigeria,* vol. I, p. 102). But the evidence is unambiguous; before the facts about paternity became known, a man "begot" a child not through a genetic process but through a property transaction.

Hoebel partially concedes this. After noting that the children born to a woman in her second marriage could be demanded by her first husband who paid the bride price, he says that this illustrates a basic principle: "*viz: among primitives sociological fatherhood is generally of more significance than biological fatherhood"* (*Man in the Primitive World,* p. 209, emphasis in the original). According to this view, men knew about biological paternity but for some unexplained reason gave equal or greater recognition to children who were not their own.

However, there is no evidence to show that men were ever indifferent to biological paternity once they became acquainted with the idea. On the contrary, they have instituted stringent laws and severe punishments for wives suspected of bearing a child that was not related "by blood" to its father. Thus, when men demand the children of other men as their "own" children, this indicates that they are still ignorant of physiological paternity.

When the Bantu say that "cattle beget children" they are not saying that a man begets children by having sexual intercourse with his wife. It is the cattle that beget the children for the man because that is the property he hands over to secure his ownership of them. As Lucy Mair writes:

> Only if the bridewealth is returned can the woman give children to another man. She may conceive in adultery, or even leave her husband and live with another man, but as long as her husband's cattle are with her lineage her children are his. This means that the boys inherit from him and not from their actual father, and he claims the bridewealth that is given for the girls. (*Introduction to Social Anthropology,* p. 84)

Frazer drew the following conclusion from the evidence on the subject:

> Denying, as they do explicitly, that the child is begotten by the father, they can only regard him as the consort, and, in a sense, the owner of the mother, and therefore, as the owner of her progeny, just as a man who owns a cow owns also the calf she brings forth. In short, it seems probable that a man's children were viewed as his property long before they were recognized as his offspring. (*Totemism and Exogamy,* vol. I, p. 167)

Lippert cites the Hindu Laws of Manu to the same effect: "The child belongs to its father just as the owner of a cow becomes the owner of its calf" (*Evolution of Culture,* p. 362). Robertson Smith writes that the Arab idea of paternity is "strictly correlated" to the "nature of the contract in marriage by purchase." He adds, "A man is father of all the children of the woman by whom he has purchased the right to have offspring that shall be reckoned to his own kin" (*Kinship and Marriage in Early Arabia,* p. 132).

Thus a man's own children were the children he owned through payment. How little physiological paternity had to do with the early father-family can be seen in the various ingenious

devices men invented to maintain their ownership and perpetuate the father-son line of descent, inheritance, and succession. These are called "leviratic marriage," "ghost marriage,"
and "woman-to-woman marriage." All are based on payment
of cattle as the child price and have no connection whatever
with physiological fatherhood. And all are designed to guarantee a man a permanent line of sons through the generations
in case he dies before he has begotten a son.

Leviratic marriage is the best known. The term is derived
from the Latin *levir,* meaning "husband's brother." If a husband died before his wife bore him a son, one of his brothers
married his widow to beget a son for him. Lippert points out
that leviratic marriage was "enjoined as a duty by the Laws
of Manu."

Among the ancient Hebrews, the firstborn son succeeded to
the name of the deceased, "that his name not be put out of
Israel" (*Evolution of Culture,* p. 348). In such a marriage
it was only through the father's brother, never the mother's
brother, that the paternal line of descent, inheritance, and succession could be maintained.

In her section on "proxy fathers," Lucy Mair writes:

> In many patrilineal societies a man's heir is his next
> brother, who *succeeds* to his responsibilities and his status
> generally as well as *inheriting* his possessions. He thus
> becomes the guardian of his widows as well as of his chil-
> dren, and is expected, particularly if a widow is young
> and has not yet borne many children, to "raise up seed,"
> in the biblical expression, to his dead brother by cohabiting
> with her. This is an expression of the principle that a mar-
> riage made legal by bridewealth is not dissolved even by
> death; it can only be broken by the return of the marriage
> cattle. This principle operates often in another way; a widow
> who does not want to cohabit with her dead husband's
> brother is often not forced to, but if she chooses to live
> with another man the children she has by him are still
> counted as her husband's. (*Introduction to Social Anthro-
> pology,* pp. 84-85)

"Cohabitation" in the sexual sense was actually irrelevant in
leviratic marriage. Whether the woman cohabited with the living
brother or with a complete stranger, the children she bore
went to the father-line of the deceased man by virtue of the

cattle payment that had been made for them. The dead husband's brother was not so much the guardian of the widow as of the transaction that involved the widow's children.

"Ghost marriage," despite its mystical-sounding name, is a variation of the principle involved in leviratic marriage. In this case there is no need for the living brother to marry his dead brother's widow — nor is she obliged to marry him. He can pay the child price, beget a son from any woman, and credit the son to his dead brother's line. The institution even applied to unmarried men. Piddington writes that among the Nuer "if a man, married or unmarried, dies without male issue, it becomes the duty of one of his kinsmen to marry a wife on his behalf. The sons of such a union are legally the children of the dead man, and inherit social or ritual privileges which he would normally pass on to his sons" (*Introduction to Social Anthropology,* p. 157).

Lucy Mair, citing Evans-Pritchard, shows that ghost marriages are quite common in parts of Africa.

> The Nuer, and some other African peoples, believe that every man has a right to marry and found his own line of descent. It is the duty of his agnatic kin to provide cattle, from the herds which they own in common, to enable him to do so. But sometimes a young man dies before his marriage arrangements have been completed, or a man has only daughters, or his sons die before they grow up. It is then the duty of his nearest kinsman to "marry a wife to his name." The children of this marriage will count as the dead man's children, and since most Nuer cannot afford to marry more than one wife, this husband in his turn will die without heirs, and a kinsman will have to make a "ghost-marriage" for him. Evans-Pritchard reckoned that there must be as many ghost-marriages as ordinary marriages. (ibid., p. 85)

Finally there is woman-to-woman marriage. Not a brother but a kinswoman arranges to carry on a dead man's line. As Piddington describes it, "A woman may sometimes contract a ghost-marriage with another woman on behalf of a dead kinsman. The children of the second woman, begotten by some extraneous man, are legally the offspring of the 'female husband's' dead kinsman." This custom, he says, is found not only among the Nuer but in areas of Africa "as far apart as the Transvaal and Dahomey" (ibid., pp. 157-58).

A transaction that can make a woman a "female husband" can also make her a "female father," as Hoebel points out:

> A unique twist to the bride price as a means of obtaining offspring is found among the Dahomeans of West Africa. A married woman may pay the bride price to obtain a second wife for her husband as a means of providing him with children. These children call their sire's first wife "father," because she, after all, is the one who paid for them. This may seem to be carrying the principle of sociological fatherhood a bit far, but who can deny that it is logical? (*Man in the Primitive World*, p. 209)

All this shows how little physiological paternity, or even sexual relations between husband and wife, had to do with founding the father-family and the paternal line. It also helps correct the widespread misconception that the sexual infidelity or "adultery" of the wife was the cause of the incessant quarrels and feuds among men.

To us the term "adultery" means the sexual cohabitation of a wife with a man who is not her husband, usually on a furtive basis. This is looked upon as a crime against the woman's husband and a sin against her marriage vows. Up to recent times, heavy punishments were inflicted upon an adulterous woman. She could be cast out by her husband, she could have her children taken away from her, or she could be ruined economically and socially. But in pre-civilized society neither the concept nor the punishment existed.

Exactly the contrary was the case. In the numerous examples of so-called wife-lending and similar practices, the wife was not only free but encouraged to give her sexual favors to protect her husband by turning a potential foe into a friend or to safeguard the community from some disaster. As some anthropologists put it, adultery is "permissible" so long as the husband knows about it, or sanctions it, or when it is the custom. But it cannot be called "adultery" if it is neither furtive nor forbidden.

Even after the father-family made its appearance the concept of "adultery" was not connected with the sexual misdeeds of a wife but with the misappropriation of a man's property. Some anthropologists refer to this as "theft." In his Hastings Encyclopedia article on "Adultery" J. A. MacCulloch writes that "in the Torres Straits there is no word for adultery apart from theft . . . and all irregular connexion was called 'stealing a woman'" (vol. I, p. 123). Others have made the same observation.

Wife stealing, like cattle rustling, was originally a matter of property rights. The man who went off with another man's wife without refunding the bride-price cattle was a thief. And the wife who went off without concerning herself about the refund was "unfaithful" not in a sexual but in a property sense. The matter could be amicably settled, however, either through return of the cattle or transfer of the wife's children to the husband who had paid for them.

When ancient quarrels among men over marriage rights are interpreted as sexual jealousy the picture becomes distorted. John Layard, for example, believes that in Malekula "the immediate cause of almost all wars is a sexual one, such as adultery or the elopement of a married woman. . . ." At the same time he observes that the "theft" of pigs, used in this region as the bride price, provokes similar disputes. Although vague about the connection between adultery and theft, he notes that such disputes are settled by "the return of bride-price to a husband whose wife has run away. . . ." Elsewhere he observes that "the procedure for divorce is, theoretically, simple, involving nothing more complicated than the return of the bride-price to the aggrieved husband" (*Stone Men of Malekula,* pp. 588, 201). By his own statements it would be more accurate to say that the quarrels of the men are not so much due to jealousy over the wife's sexual favors as to infringed property rights.

Hardly had men been liberated from the old blood feuds than they were again in conflict with one another, this time over ownership rights to cattle and children. In fact, the dividing line between the two is often imperceptible; in some regions up to our times blood feuds coexist with quarrels over bride price. This is especially true where the transition from marriage gifts to bride price has not been completed.

A hint of this state of affairs is given by Audrey I. Richards in a description of the Southern Bantu:

> . . . the transfer of the *lobola* cattle determines the social status of the wife and legitimacy of the children; and, since these cattle are used to buy a wife for the woman's broth-

er, yet a third family of relatives is united in the same tie. . . . The transfer of *lobola* cattle at marriage, therefore, subjects the two groups of relatives to perpetual strains. Each is anxiously watching to see that its side of the bargain is fulfilled. Jealousies and subjects of conflict constantly occur. A large proportion of the time and energies of the cattle-owning Bantu appears to be given to the endless discussion and debate of *lobola* quarrels, whether of present transactions, or unfulfilled obligations in the past. (*Hunger and Work in a Savage Tribe,* pp. 131-32)

Sexual jealousy—which did not exist in matriarchal society—developed side by side with private property and the patriarchal family. MacCulloch says, "It is especially among peoples with whom polygamy or monogamy is the rule that we see the working of jealousy and the idea of property in the woman existing most emphatically" (*Encyclopedia of Religion and Ethics,* vol. I, p. 123).

The husband now owned his wife and had exclusive rights to her sexual organs as well as her children; they were part and parcel of his property. Severe punishments were meted out to any man who tampered with these property rights, and in the case of infidelity the wife too was severely punished. According to MacCulloch, a man could punish his wife by killing her or cutting off her nose, ears, or hair; and he could kill, emasculate, mutilate, or flog the man who invaded his rights of property.

Thus with the full development of private property and the patriarchal family, women lost control over their lives, their destinies, and even their own bodies. Wives were reduced to economic dependency upon their husbands for support. Divorce was made more and more difficult, until finally it was forbidden altogether to the wife. As the noose of marriage tightened around the necks of women, they were coralled like cattle in the homes of their husbands, under their full domination.

Father-power begins with what Robertson Smith calls "dominion marriage." In this form, he writes, the wife "has lost the right freely to dispose of her person; her husband has authority over her and he alone has the right of divorce." He adds:

Accordingly the husband in this kind of marriage is called, not in Arabia only, but also among the Hebrews and Aramaeans, the woman's "lord" or "owner" (*ba'l, ba'al, be'el*).

. . . It will be convenient to have a short name for the type
of marriage in which these features are combined, and, as
the name Baal is familiar to everyone from the Old Testament, I propose to call it *ba'al* marriage or marriage of
dominion, and to call the wife a *be'ulah* or subject wife.
(*Kinship and Marriage in Early Arabia,* pp. 92-93)

Baal, the lord-deity of the sacrificial era, now takes an earthly,
patriarchal form as the lord and master of livestock, of women
and children, and of other properties. Henceforth, a new posture
is ordained for women. They will be down on their knees in
worship of their lords on earth and in the heavens.

New sexual mores rigidly curtailed the former freedom of
women. Whether these are called sexual "morality," "purity,"
"virginity," or "chastity," they are imposed by men upon wom-
en, not by women upon men. As Sumner spells it out, "Chastity for the unmarried meant — no one; for the married — none
but the husband" (*Folkways,* p. 359).

Briffault demonstrates the drastic change in women's lives
by comparing the Aryan Hindu women of the Vedic period with
their successors under patriarchal rule:

The women of the Vedic period, whether married or single,
moved openly and mixed freely with male company at
festivals and functions. . . . They enjoyed complete liberty
in the choice of lovers and husbands. That contrast between the freedom which they anciently enjoyed and their
position in later times, when they were bound by patriarchal laws, was familiar to the writers of the 'epic' period.
In the 'Mahabharata,' Pandy thus addresses his wife Kunty:
"I shall now tell thee about the practice of old indicated by
illustrious Rishis fully acquainted with every rule of morality. O thou of handsome face and sweet smiles, women
were not formerly immured in houses and dependent upon
husbands and relatives. They used to go about freely,
enjoying themselves as best they pleased. O thou of excellent qualities, they did not then adhere to their husbands
faithfully; and yet, O beauteous one, they were not regarded as sinful, for that was the sanctioned usage of the
times. . . . Indeed, that usage, so lenient to women, hath
the sanction of antiquity. The present practice, however,
of women being confined to one husband for life hath been
established but lately." (*The Mothers,* vol. I, p. 346)

He shows the subordinate and effaced position of women after their downfall as follows:

> It is laid down in the 'Laws of Manu' that "No act is to be done according to her own will by a young girl, a young woman, though she be in her own house. In her childhood a girl should be under the will of her father; in her youth under that of her husband; her husband being dead, under the will of her sons. A woman should never enjoy her own will. Though of bad conduct or debauched, or devoid of all good qualities, a husband must always be worshipped like a god by a good wife." (ibid., p. 345)

With the consolidation of private property and the father-family, not only the matriarchy but the fratriarchy fell in ruins. The mothers' brothers, abandoning their sisters, became the fathers of their own families and the owners of their own property. This left women with no male allies; they were completely at the mercy of the new social forces unleashed by property-based patriarchal society.

How women felt about this can be gleaned from a passage in the Arabian *Kamil*, cited by Robertson Smith. He calls it "a very instructive passage as to the position of married women."

> "Never let sister praise brother of hers; never let daughter bewail a father's death;
> For *they* have brought her where she is no longer a free woman, and *they* have banished her to the farthest ends of the earth."
>
> (*Kinship and Marriage in Early Arabia*, p. 94, emphasis in the original)

In reality women were not banished to the ends of the earth; they were on the contrary cloistered in the private households of their husbands, to serve their needs and bear their legal sons. But to women who were once so free and independent this must indeed have seemed like the end of the world.

With the advent of slavery, which marks the first stage of civilized class society, the degradation of women was completed. Formerly exchanged for cattle, they were now reduced to the chatteldom of domestic servitude and procreative functions. The Roman jurists' definition of the term "family" is a clear expression of this:

Famulus means a household slave and *familia* signifies the totality of slaves belonging to one individual. Even in the time of Gaius the *familia, id est patrimonium* (that is, the inheritance) was bequeathed by will. The expression was invented by the Romans to describe a new social organism, the head of which had under him wife and children and a number of slaves, under Roman paternal power, with power of life and death over them all. (*Origin of the Family, Private Property, and the State,* p. 68)

The downfall of women brought about a sharp reversal in their "value" as wives. In place of the bride price, the payment made by a husband to secure a wife, we now come upon the dowry. "The Athenians," says Briffault, "offered a dowry as an inducement for men to marry their daughters, and the whole transaction of Greek marriage centered around that dowry" (*The Mothers,* vol. II, p. 337).

Tylor, one of the few anthropologists to notice this reversal, found it an "interesting problem in the history of law" to account for this curious transposition of bride price into dowry (*Anthropology,* p. 248). But the law was merely a reflection of the new social reality. Once women lost their place in productive, social, and cultural life, their worth sank along with their former esteem. Where formerly the man paid the price for a valuable wife, now the dependent wife paid the price to secure a husband and provider.

How women felt about this humiliation heaped upon degradation is recorded in Euripides' drama, where Medea mourns:

"Ay, of all living and of all reasoning things
Are women the most miserable race;
Who first must needs buy a husband at great price,
To take him then for owner of our lives."

Even this was not all. After reducing women to economic dependency and to merely procreative functions, the men of early civilized society declared that women were only incidental even in childbearing. No sooner was the paternal line of descent fixed by law than men began to claim that the father alone created the child. According to Briffault, Greek thinkers in the classical period viewed the mother's womb as "but a suitable receptacle"—a bag—for the child; the mother was subsequently its nurse, but "the father was, strictly speaking, the sole progenitor" (*The Mothers,* vol. I, p. 405). Lippert writes that, while "no historian has turned his attention" to this sub,ect, the evidence shows that matrilineal descent gave way to "the opposite extreme," which he describes this way:

> She who for untold thousands of years had been the pillar of the history of young mankind now became a weak vessel devoid of a will of her own. No longer did she manage her husband's household; these services were forgotten in a slave state. She was merely an apparatus, not as yet replaced by another invention, for the propagation of the race, a receptacle for the homunculus. (*Evolution of Culture,* pp. 355, 358)

This idea that men alone created children indicates that even at this late date, the beginning of civilization, men were still ignorant of the facts about reproduction. Whatever vague speculations they engaged in on the subject, genetic fatherhood had played no part in the victory of the father-family and patriarchal power. Men had won on the basis of their private ownership of property. It was not biology but the Roman law that laid down the dictum *patria potestas* — "all power to the father." And, as Briffault's description shows, property was the father of this patriarchal legality.

> The patriarchal principle, the legal provision by which the man transmits his property to his son, was evidently an innovation of the "patricians," that is, of the partisans of the patriarchal order, the wealthy, the owners of property. They disintegrated the primitive mother-clan by forming patriarchal families, which they "led out of" the clan — "familiam ducere." The patricians set up the paternal rule of descent, and regarded the father, and not the mother, as the basis of kinship — "patres ciere possunt." (*The Mothers,* vol. I, p. 428)

The Romans likewise made clear to their male descendants the necessity for maintaining masculine supremacy and above all preventing women from gaining their freedom and independence. Briffault tells us:

> The elder Cato refers in pretty clear terms to that legal establishment of male supremacy. "Our fathers," he says

in his defense of the Lex Oppia, "have willed (voluerunt) that women should be in the power of their fathers, of their brothers, of their husbands. Remember all the laws by which our fathers have bound down the liberty of women, by which they have bent them to the power of men. As soon as they are our equals, they become our superiors. (ibid.)

This triumphant patriarchal father is a roaring lion compared to the Seri husband who sat at the end of the line of mother's brothers when he made his appearance in history. But once the last moved up to first place, he more than made up for his inglorious past. The all-powerful "father figure" presided not only over the civilized world but also over the superworld. In the ironical words of Lord Raglan:

> . . . most Englishmen have at least five fathers. There is the Heavenly Father, who confers immortality upon us at baptism by means of the priest, the Father in God. . . . There is the King, the father of his people, to whom we send our daughters dressed as brides, that he may confer life-essence upon them. . . . Then there is our godfather, who confers upon us his name, and with it no doubt a portion of his life-essence; and finally there are our father-in-law and our mother's husband. (*Jocasta's Crime,* p. 189)

The English missionary-anthropologist Lorimer Fison wittily observed that the introduction of paternal descent is at "the bottom of all aristocratic notions." He wrote:

> Birth comes in as establishing rank, until we get men who are not "born" at all, others who are born but not "fullborn," others who are fullborn but not "wellborn," others who are wellborn but not "highborn" and at last men who are so highborn as to be "godborn." (Quoted in *Lewis Henry Morgan,* by Carl Resek, p. 128)

15

Facts and Fallacies
About Incest

"Incest, the universal crime, violates a taboo that is as forceful among primitives as among sophisticated moderns." This is the opening sentence of the book *Incest Behavior* by S. Kirson Weinberg, a University of California professor of sociology (Citadel Press, 1965, p. 3). To buttress this proposition he cites A. L. Kroeber: "If ten anthropologists were asked to designate one universal institution nine would likely name the incest prohibition; some have expressly named it as the only universal one" (p. 7).

On what documented evidence is this sweeping assertion made? Here it is pertinent to refer to Lord Raglan's comment on the subject: "One of the most surprising things about anthropological literature is the number of utterly unproved assumptions that succeed in passing muster as unquestionable scientific facts" (*Jocasta's Crime,* p. 46). Nowhere is this more true than with regard to the "unquestionable" universality of the incest taboo.

As in the case of cannibalism and sacrifice, there are scattered references but no comprehensive work on incest and its history. The unhistorical anthropologists fall into a curious inconsistency on this subject. They reject the evolutionary approach on the grounds that nothing certain can be known about the institutions and customs of paleolithic humankind; consequently no "universals" can be established — yet they put forward a "universal" fear of incest.

There is no question that an incest taboo exists in modern society throughout the whole world. Under this prohibition members of the same family may not marry or have sexual intercourse with one another. But the question is: How far back in history does this in-family prohibition go? The most obvious point is that *an in-family taboo cannot begin until the father-family unit has come into existence and this, as we have seen, was at the beginning of the civilized epoch.*

In a footnote, Weinberg deals with one theory of the word's origin:

> The term, "incest," is derived from the Latin word, *incestum,* or unchaste. *Incestum* alludes to the cestus or girdle of Venus, which in a lawful marriage was worn by the woman and loosened by the husband as an omen of conjugal and parental happiness; its disuse in an unlawful marriage, rendered it "incestuous or ungirdled." (*Incest Behavior,* p. 7)

This indicates that the term "incest" is no older than the term "family." Both were coined by the Roman jurists who codified the laws on the father-family, property rights, and father-son inheritance at the beginning of patriarchal society.

In its origin the term had reference to the "unchastity" of a wife, the violation of the proprietary rights of a husband who had exclusive sexual possession of the woman he married. But this has nothing to do with incest in our sense of the term.

Today the prohibition applies to the members of the same family; there may be no sexual intercourse between father and daughter, son and mother, brother and sister. Incest involves a great deal more than simply an "unchaste" woman violating her marriage vows. Any woman, married or unmarried, having sexual intercourse with a father or brother or son is guilty of incest. This is regarded as the most abominable of all sexual crimes because the persons involved are "blood relatives" and it is believed that this will "taint" the blood of any resulting child — that is, make it defective.

This is not the meaning of incest when the term came into existence at the beginning of civilization. When and how did the change come about? This largely uninvestigated subject requires an examination of two different concepts of "blood" kinship — ancient and modern — and of the evolution from matriarchal exogamy to the patriarchal incest taboo.

The Ambiguity of "Blood" Kinship

Savages did not know that children were born as the result of the sexual intercourse of a man and a woman with the offspring inheriting traits from both parents. In their view only the matrilineal kin were the blood kin because they were born in the blood of the community of mothers and ate the same food together. Men were "blood brothers" to one another because they ate the same flesh and drank the same blood together, which was a guarantee that they would not assail and eat each other.

Thus the primitive concept of "blood" kinship was totally different from ours; it was based upon considerations connected with food and cannibalism and not with sex, chastity, and incest. This fact deals a stunning blow to the notion that the one universal fear of all humankind has been the dread of incestuous relations between "blood relatives." The savage prohibition was directed against the annihilation of the species through cannibalism while the modern incest prohibition is said to be directed against fear of the degeneration of the human species through inbreeding.

This fear did not exist even at the beginning of the age of civilization, when the term "incest" merely meant "unchaste." The Greek philosophers and scholars, who were among the first investigators of social and natural phenomena, speculated on the part played by sexual intercourse in the generative process. But despite some brilliant flashes of insight, they had only crude ideas on biology. How recently this knowledge was acquired — and only after bitter disputes — is pointed to by Briffault:

> That the contributions of father and mother to the inherited life of the offspring are equal is a piece of knowledge which dates from recent years. It was in the seventeenth century that Swammerdam first discovered that contact of the spermatic fluid with the ovum is a necessary condition of generation. The revolutionary and somewhat heretical discovery gave rise to fierce controversies, and many were reluctant to admit that fertilisation by the male was absolutely essential to conception. The male germ cells were discovered in 1785 only by Spallanzani. That the process of reproduction is initiated by the fusion of the male and female germ cells was first suspected by Barry in the year 1843, and adequately demonstrated for the first time by Herman Fol in 1879. The knowledge of these facts thus dates, so to speak, from yesterday. (*The Mothers,* vol. II, pp. 443-44)

Clearly, our modern concept, with its degrees of blood kinship, came into existence quite recently. Degrees of kinship did not exist within the savage clan where, as Robertson Smith points out, blood ties "rested with absolute and identical force on every member of the clan" (*Religion of the Semites,* p. 273). The need for degrees of kinship arose only after the clan narrowed down to the individual family, and family kin had to be demarcated from more remote "blood" relatives.

What we have today is a chaotic variety of relics reflecting different stages of the narrowing-down process in defining close blood kin. According to the *Columbia Encyclopedia:*

> Christian countries differ as to prohibited degree of relationship; until 1907 the cohabitation of a man with his deceased wife's sister was held to be incestuous in English law; that of a woman with her deceased husband's brother is still so regarded. In the United States incestuous marriages are void; cousin marriage is forbidden in only a few states.

Circumscribing the boundaries of the incest prohibition seems to have taxed the ingenuity of church and state officials over the past few centuries, and the definition is still far from definitive. This is how Raglan described the situation some years ago:

> It is doubtful whether there are two countries in Europe in which the incest laws are exactly the same. . . . The Churches have ceased to insist that the marriage of those who are godparents to the same child is as incestuous as that of brother and sister; it appears that this view . . . now only survives in corners of the Balkans.
>
> The Jewish laws have tended, like those of Christianity . . . to bar marriages which the Mosaic code permitted, such as those between uncle and niece . . . while the chief difference between Romans and Christians was that among the former kinship by adoption was, as it now is among the Hindus, equivalent to blood-relationship.
>
> Among the Chinese persons with the same surname are forbidden to marry, even if they come from opposite ends of the empire. . . . (*Jocasta's Crime,* pp. 100-01)

As Raglan pointed out with respect to the ambiguities of

incest boundaries in the England of his day, "This state of affairs is transitional, and it is transitional in the direction of removing restrictions on marriage, a process the exact opposite of that postulated by the theorists, who suppose all incest laws to be extensions of simple prohibitions either of brother-sister or of parent-child incest" (ibid., p. 99). More exactly, a taboo that was originally directed against cannibalism left a vestige that we know as a prohibition against incest.

Given the short historical memory of humankind through the ages, it probably seemed to people who grew up amid strict family exogamy that this had always been the rule. But sooner or later questions arose as to the source of this in-family sexual taboo, particularly after civilized society advanced toward its age of science. At some point, still unknown, a rationale was developed to explain why "blood relatives" could not marry one another. In popular terms, this produced the "tainted blood" theory—that children born of such close inbreeding would be mentally or physically deformed. By the time anthropology was founded this had become the conventional wisdom.

The assumptions that have been made about incestuous marriages in the past must now be reexamined. This is especially true with respect to the ancient "royal" or "dynastic" marriages in Egypt and in other places where, it is said, brothers regularly married their own sisters. This practice has been held up as a prime example of the evils of in-family marriages.

Was There "Royal Incest" in Egypt?

Egypt stands out as an exception among the cultures of the cradle of civilization, retaining many of its matriarchal features and customs while all around it patriarchal society had become firmly entrenched. Thus Egypt provides the longest view of a continuous matriarchal evolution—a period of five thousand years. As Hartland writes:

It is remarkable that throughout the fifty or more centuries of Egyptian history down to the final fall of the kingdom and the death of Cleopatra, matrilineal institutions were never outgrown, in spite of numerous revolutions and even repeated conquests by foreign invaders. (*Primitive Society,* pp. 118-19)

In the Egyptian royal house the top rulership was vested in the queen, and the throne passed from mother to princess-daughter. This is summed up by Briffault as follows:

> While every Egyptian princess of the Royal House was born a queen and bore the titles and dignities of the office from the day of her birth, a man only acquired them at his coronation, and could do so only by becoming the consort of a royal princess. It was in the queen, and not in the king, that the mystic or divine virtue attaching to the royal office was thought to reside; and the dependence of the male occupants of the throne upon the queen and the queen-mother for the legitimacy of their title was never lost sight of even by the most powerful and ambitious monarchs. (*The Mothers*, vol. I, p. 378)

This preeminence of the women in the royal family was not unique; Egyptian women in general held the most esteemed position in the family, as is characteristic of a matrifamily. Briffault cites well-known Egyptologists on this:

> "The family in Egypt," says Sir William Flinders Petrie, "was based on a matriarchal system[;] the office-holder or farmer who married into a family was a secondary affair; the house and property went with the woman and daughters." "The Egyptian woman of the lower and middle class," says Sir Gaston Maspero, "was more respected, more independent than any other woman in the world. As a wife, she is the real mistress of the house, her husband being, so to speak, merely a privileged guest." "The most important person in the family," says Dr. Hall, "was not the father, but the mother." The Egyptian wife was called the 'Ruler of the House'. . . ; there is no corresponding term for the husband. "There is nothing in Egyptian jurisprudence which bears any resemblance to the power of the husband as head of the household." (ibid., p. 381)

As Briffault points out, many distortions exist in the reports of Egyptologists whose patriarchal outlook and assumptions prevented them from understanding practices and customs that had survived from a former matriarchal epoch. Some were so dismayed by a female line of descent and the freedom and independence of women that they attributed these to "corruption."

Theories of 'corruption' abound. The great Champollion, the founder of Egyptological science, actually imagined that the practice of reckoning descent in the female line was a 'corruption' introduced into Egypt by the Greeks! . . . Even Professor Revillout, who by his translations of Egyptian marriage contracts has done more than anyone to exhibit the legal status of women in Egypt, speaks contemptuously of "the matriarchal theory". . . . M. Paturet, in his excellent monograph, ascribes the power of women in Egypt to "abuse and corruption". . . . (ibid., p. 379)

Egypt was exceptional in the tenacity with which her matriarchal structure survived, despite the rise of private property, royal prerogatives, and a ruling family. Elsewhere these advances produced the patriarchal family and rule by kings. For whatever historical reasons — and some attribute it to the fact that Egypt had primarily an agricultural rather than a pastoral economy — here was a queendom in a world of kingdoms.

The central mistake made by Egyptologists was their assumption that the father-family and patriarchal society had always existed. They were not aware of — or rejected — the prior matriarchal stage of social evolution and therefore could not see that Egypt had fallen short of the transition from matriarchy to patriarchy and from the matrifamily to the father-family. They tried to analyze the royal family according to patriarchal institutions and customs.

In fact, the Egyptian family was a matrifamily and therefore a divided family. Since the line of descent, inheritance, and succession remained matrilineal it was also fratrilineal — the mother, her brother, and her children were the royal line. The husband of the queen did not belong to the royal line; he was only an outsider who had married into the royal family.

Thus, as in all matrifamilies, the queen stood between two men, her brother and her husband. Both men, by virtue of their connection to the queen, were "kings," but in different ways. The queen's brother was king by right of birth and kinship to the queen, which made him undeposable. The queen's husband, on the other hand, as a "commoner," was king only as long as the marriage lasted; he was deposed if it was terminated by the queen. And from the record it appears that there were quite a number of such terminations.

This dual kingship is seldom recognized by Egyptologists and anthropologists. Some confusedly refer only to the queen and her "consort" husband, a "commoner" who is not of high rank but serves her as her "man of business affairs" in the management of the "kingdom." Others refer to the brother as the queen's husband, leaving out of account the "consort" husband. This has led to the notion of "brother-sister marriages" and "royal incest" or "dynastic incest."

In fact, there was no such thing as dynastic incest in Egypt, among the Incas of Peru, or in Greece or anywhere else where the matrifamily had reached the inflated level of a ruling family before giving way to the one-father family and the patriarchal order. In the case of Egypt and Peru, which failed to evolve this far, the change came only after their conquest by patriarchal nations.

The deceptive word in analyzing the Egyptian royal family is "marriage." To us this invariably connotes sexual intercourse along with certain economic, legal, and other features. In our society a woman is married to only one husband, a queen to one king. What shall we say about the Egyptian divided family where the queen was attached to two "kings," her brother and her consort? Was she "married" to both of them in our sense of the term, that is, did she have sexual intercourse with both of them?

There is no evidence that the queen had sexual relations with her brother-king; she did have intercourse with her consort-king (or series of such consorts). The queen was "married" to her brother, assuming the term is appropriate at all, only in the sense that he shared in the inheritance of throne, property, and royal privileges as a member of the matrilineal royal line.

In other words, brother-sister "marriages" involved a property connection, not a sexual one. For sexual intercourse the brother had his wife or wives, the sister her husband or husbands. In neither case were the spouses included in the possession or transmission of the property. This was true not simply in the royal family but in all the families of Egypt in that period. Where formerly clan property had been collectively held and transmitted, now it was held and transmitted by individual matrifamilies. But the transmission belt remained the same: matriliny and fratriliny — not patriliny.

A "marriage" that excludes sexual intercourse cannot be called an "incestuous marriage." There are many indications that property was the only basis for the so-called brother-sister marriages. Sometimes the brother is called "regent," a term that is useful in distinguishing between brother-king and husband-king. While the queen was married, her husband shared her rulership, managing those affairs of the queendom that were in the province of men. But if the queen was unmarried or separated from her husband, her brother became regent, managing affairs until the queen had acquired another consort.

Egyptologists and others have noted that brother-sister "marriages" were connected with property considerations. Under the heading "Incest," the *Columbia Encyclopedia* sums this up: "Only in royal families, as in Egypt and among the Inca, have incestuous marriages (including marriage between brothers and sisters) been customary — perhaps to conserve royal prerogatives and property." Unfortunately, comments of this type do not explain two questions that immediately come to mind: What kind of family is it where property accrues to sisters and brothers and excludes husbands and fathers? And why should it be assumed that a property arrangement of such an odd type should be a "marriage" in our sense of the term, including sexual intercourse?

A royal matrifamily was not essentially different from any other matrifamily; it was a divided family with the mother's brother holding a more important and permanent place in his sister's family than her husband, who was often only her sexual mate. This was true even though the brother did not live in the same house with his sister, her husband, and her children. The very fact that he lived in a separate house — if married, with his own wife and her children — indicates that the marriage was not incestuous.

Survivals of African queendoms shed light on the royal divided family in ancient Egypt. Although a queen-sister and king-brother were members of the ruling family, they did not even occupy the same palace, much less the same bedroom. The following example is given by Frazer:

> The Queen Sister (*Lubuga*) has also her own establishment. . . . she rules her own people and is called a king. The remarkable position occupied by the Queen Sister in Uganda has its parallel among the Barotse or Marotse, an important Bantu tribe on the Upper Zambesi. In the Barotse country, we read, "there are two capitals, Lealouyi and Nalolo. The first of these, a large village of about three thousand inhabitants, is the residence of the king Leouanika; Nalolo is the residence of the king's eldest sister. Like him, she has the title of *morena,* which means 'lord,' 'king,' or 'queen,' without distinction of sex. She is sometimes also called *mokouae* or 'princess,' a general

term applicable to all the women of the royal family, but the *mokouae* of Nalolo is the most important of all. She alone reigns in concert with the king and shares with him the title of *morena*. The same honours that are paid to him are paid to her, and she keeps the same state. Like him, she has her *khotla*, where she sits surrounded by her councillors and chiefs of the tribe. Lastly, she also receives taxes from the most distant parts of the kingdom. Both of them have handsome rectangular houses, very large and high, which form conspicuous features of the landscape."

The existence of this double kingship, a male kingship and a female kingship, in two important Bantu peoples is very remarkable, all the more so, as the writer observes, because in Africa woman generally occupies an inferior position. Yet among the Barotse "this queen is quite independent of her brother. In fact there are two kingdoms quite distinct from each other. But they are closely united, and it often happens that persons are transferred from the service of the king to that of the queen, or reciprocally. Many sons of the chiefs bred at the court of Lealouyi have become vassals of the queen, or on the contrary young people of Nalolo are sent to the king. Messengers are constantly coming and going between the two capitals, in order that the king and queen may be kept informed of what is happening in the country. (*Totemism and Exogamy*, vol. IV, pp. 305-06)

Frazer perceived that "the high rank thus assigned to the king's sister . . . seems to point to a system of mother-kin, whether present or past." But he could not entirely escape his male-oriented viewpoint; he thought that the high position of the sister was endowed upon her by her king-brother, whereas it was just the other way around. The brother was co-ruler with the sister because of the preeminence of the queen.

Unaware that the pre-patriarchal family was a divided family, Frazer did not know how to explain the presence of another man in the life of the queen in addition to her king-brother. He describes this other personage as follows:

The Queen Sister has a husband chosen by herself, who ranks as Prince Consort. He is her representative and man of business; he must salute her humbly like a slave, and when she goes out he walks behind her. Formerly he might not even sit on the same mat with her or share her meals; but of late years the rigour of the custom has been somewhat relaxed, and the "son-in-law of the nation," as the Queen Sister's husband is called, has not to put up with so many affronts as in past days. (ibid., p. 306)

The Egyptian royal family advanced considerably beyond this in wealth, power, and sophistication; the queen's husband was treated more like a king. However, so long as the Egyptian family remained a matrifamily, the permanent ruling pair were the queen-sister and her brother, who acted as regent in the event the queen's husband died or was deposed.

Some investigators, assuming the Egyptian sister-brother co-rulership to be "dynastic incest," have tried to soften the shock of the continuous "inbreeding" this signified. They theorize that a brother could only marry a sister on his father's side, not his mother's side, and consequently she was only a "half" sister. Presumably this produced only half the amount of "tainted" blood in the progeny.

However, the term "half sister" cannot be applied to a period before the father-family and degrees of kinship came into existence. Until then, children were reckoned through the mother-line alone, and all the children born of the mothers of a matriclan or matrifamily were equally sisters and brothers. It is only in father-family terms that they can be called "half" sisters and brothers. But the matter goes deeper than this.

Whether a brother married a full sister, as some say, or a half sister, as others say, there is a conspicuous absence of data on the disastrous consequences to the progeny born of such continuous and systematic inbreeding as that produced by "dynastic incest." In fact, it is difficult to find confirmation that any children at all were born of these sister-brother "marriages." This is further proof — albeit negative — that these were not marriages in our sense of the term. The only children on whom we have reliable data are those born of the queen and her consort or consorts.

Cleopatra, the last queen of the Ptolemaic dynasty, furnishes a conspicuous example. She was "married" first to one younger brother, and after his death to a still younger brother. She had no children by these "marriages"; in fact, there is no evidence that she lived in close proximity to these male kin, much less had sexual intercourse with them. But Cleopatra's sexual affairs or marriages to the foreign rulers from Rome are well known, and she had children by them. She had one son, Caesarion, by Julius Caesar, and two children, a boy and a girl, by Marc Antony.

Some investigators attribute the absence of children to the evil consequences of incest. Sumner accepted the thesis of Sir Francis Galton, who sought to show that the Ptolemies suffered from sterility. "The close intermarriages were sterile. The line was continued by others" (*Folkways,* p. 486). It is more probable that there were no children because there was no sexual intercourse between sisters and brothers despite their co-rulership.

Others present a different version of the evil effects of "dynastic incest." In their imagination the whole Ptolemaic line was so riddled with mentally and physically damaged offspring that it led to the collapse of the Egyptian nation. But as Briffault writes, "The race that produced Seti and Rameses affords no evidence of degeneration," and he adds, "It is easy to call Cleopatra a 'moral degenerate' on the ground that her sexual morality was not in accordance with Victorian standards; but it is difficult to perceive in the brilliant and clever woman, the last scion of the race, any manifestations of evils traceable to dynastic incest." He scoffs at H. R. Hall's statement that the practice of incest "resulted in destroying dynasty after dynasty" (*The Mothers,* vol. I, pp. 222-23).

Although Egypt was ultimately crushed, this was not due to any degeneration of the royal family but to the untenable situation of a matriarchal queendom in the midst of rising patriarchal empires. A divided royal house and a female line were anachronisms that could not survive the rising patriarchal forces determined to win supremacy.

These forces were aided by the corrosion of the three-century-old Ptolemaic dynasty—but it was in-family murder, not in-family breeding, that contributed to its downfall. The matriarchal crime of crimes, shedding the blood of the blood kin, became a commonplace. All the familiar betrayals and murders found in primitive myths were here found in reality, as brothers, uncles, nephews, and sons were murdered by their own kin. Even the unthinkable crime of mother murder made its appearance.

Queen sisters were forced into this game of politics, betrayal, and murder. An earlier Queen Cleopatra who ruled at the time of Ptolemy VII led a revolt against the overambitious king and drove him out of Egypt, although later he was permitted to return, apparently a chastened man. Her descendant, the last Cleopatra and daughter of Ptolemy XI, whose consorts were Caesar and Antony, led an army against her younger brother, Ptolemy XII, and defeated him. It is said he was later drowned in the Nile; some reports implicate his sister in his murder — for the sake of her lover, Antony. Cleopatra is also said to have murdered her still younger brother, to whom she was "married" after the other's death.

According to Margaret A. Murray, neither Caesar nor Antony interfered with the matriarchal customs or rulership of Cleopatra's queendom. That occurred after Octavius defeated Antony and entered Egypt as a conqueror. Cleopatra would not accept him as her king-consort and co-ruler; "that spirited woman preferred death to such a fate," says Murray. Thus the last Egyptian queendom perished along with the queen (*The Splendor That Was Egypt*, pp. 72, 102-103).

Murray writes that the "classical historians, imbued as they were with the customs of patrilineal descent and of monogamy, besides looking upon women as the chattels of their menfolk" misunderstood Egyptian history and have "misinterpreted it to the world." This is the case with "dynastic incest." That thesis was based upon the assumption that the ancient Egyptian family was a father-family when in fact it was an over-developed matrifamily — that is, a divided family.

For a final investigation of mistaken assumptions about incest and the family in the transitional period between matriarchy and patriarchy, let us go from the banks of the Nile to the legendary royal houses of Greece at the dawn of civilization.

16

The Father-Family
in Greek Tragedy

The conflict and turbulence that accompanied the transition from matriarchy to patriarchy left an indelible imprint in Greek mythology. The fifth-century Greek dramatists created their tragedies on the basis of these myth-histories. The most memorable are *Orestes* by Aeschylus, *Oedipus* by Sophocles, and *Medea* by Euripides.

The story of Oedipus, the best known, is believed to be a tragedy of the crime and punishment of incest — an impression introduced by Freud. In the course of his psychoanalytical studies, Freud uncovered a widespread unconscious incestuous desire of boys for their mothers. He seized upon the story of Oedipus, the man who killed his father and married his mother, to buttress his theory that boys from time immemorial had had the secret urge to kill their fathers and marry their mothers.

By extension, other incestuous feelings — between brother and sister, father and daughter — were posited. But the mother-son "Oedipus complex" remained central. Anthropologists picked up the theme, and since Freud's time there have been innumerable references to the "Oedipal" factor at work in the unconscious minds of savages as well as civilized peoples.

Freud unquestionably performed a service in bringing to light a sexual neurosis that afflicts members of the modern family. He went wrong, however, in interpreting this as an everlasting affliction and naming it after an ancient Greek legend. Other psychological theorists have since given more realistic explanations for the phenomenon; they pinpoint its source in the ingrown character of the modern "nuclear" family. An appropriate term for the neurosis would be the

447

"nuclear family complex" because this restricts its application to more recent times.

The term "nuclear family" is of recent coinage and expresses the last stage in the evolution of the father-family. It signifies a family reduced to a molecule consisting of a father, a mother, and their children. The nuclear family differs from the "extended" family, that is, the large farm family characteristic of the pre-industrial era. The extended farm family, which included grandparents and even uncles, aunts, and cousins, was a productive unit; all its members worked to sustain the whole group.

But with the industrial revolution, under the impact of factory work and city life, the family unit narrowed down. The nuclear family no longer had a significant role in production. It was composed of a small group of consumers dependent on the father or mother for their support. This closed-in economic dependence fostered emotional dependence. Added to this was the Judeo-Christian idea of the sinfulness of sex outside marriage. This puritanism meant the suppression of sexual intercourse until it became economically possible for a pair to marry. All this invited the "fixation" of a boy on his mother, with whom he was in intimate association for many years while deprived of other sexual outlets. The inhibitions thus acquired often afflicted a man even long after he became a husband.

The story of Oedipus does not at all fit into the basic premise of the nuclear family sex neurosis. Incest fixation depends upon a boy remaining in prolonged intimate association with his mother. Only in that way would he develop his secret sexual desires for the forbidden woman and conceive the notion that his father was the obstacle standing in the way of mother-son intercourse.

However, Oedipus never knew his father and mother; he was cast out at birth. In earlier times and under other conditions, Oedipus would have been the sacrificial firstborn son. Instead, under the slightly more humane conditions of a higher culture, he was "exposed"; he was lucky enough to be saved by shepherds and finally to be adopted by the childless king and queen of Corinth.

How, under these circumstances, could Oedipus's acts be said to spring from "incestuous" desires for his mother — or an impulse to kill his father in order to have access to her? He grew up believing his foster parents were his real parents. It is true that he killed a man whom he later discovered to be his real father and married a woman who turned out to be his real mother. But at the time these events occurred they were complete strangers to him.

Thus Oedipus was one man who could not possibly have had an "Oedipus complex"; the essentials were absent. Freud's use of the term gives the grossly misleading impression that unconscious incestuous desires occur in the male psyche from time immemorial when in fact they are quite recent.

If the story of Oedipus is not about incest — even though he did marry his mother — what is its message? Here it is instructive to place it in the same context as the stories of Medea and Orestes. These three plays and the myth-histories on which they are based tell us about the family tragedy on a vast scale that attended the crucial change from matriarchy to patriarchy. The story of Oedipus, like the others, emphasizes the price paid in human suffering to achieve an unbroken line of fathers and sons.

In presenting our analysis of these three plays, we begin with Medea, the woman who symbolically took revenge for the degradation of the female sex in the patriarchal family.

Medea: Slayer of Brother and Sons

Medea, a mythological figure, bears a singular resemblance to the historical Cleopatra, the Egyptian queen. Both were of royal houses claiming divine descent. Medea is described as a barbarian princess and sorceress, which suggests her matriarchal heritage. She lived in the distant land of Colchis on the Black Sea and fell in love with Jason, the Greek hero who had sailed there to capture the Golden Fleece. Cleopatra lived in far-off Egypt and fell in love with the Roman rulers who went there to fleece her of her realm, which they coveted as a golden granary for their empire.

In both instances matriarchal women married men from patriarchal cultures. They were tragic figures who committed blood crimes against the matriarchal order to aid their foreign husbands who had married into the royal family. Cleopatra murdered her brother for the sake of her lover, Antony, and Medea murdered her brother to advance the interests of Jason. Subsequently both women were themselves betrayed by the patriarchal forces they had befriended, and their sons were murdered.

Here the similarities end. The historical figure, Cleopatra, was completely defeated by the new patriarchal forces and committed suicide. Octavius then got rid of her daughter, heiress to the throne under Egyptian law, by marrying her off to a kinglet in a distant country. He also killed Cleopatra's two sons, who were claimants to the throne under Roman law (*Splendor That Was Egypt*, pp. 102-03). Egypt was reduced to a province of Rome.

In contrast, Medea fights back and defeats the man who brought about her downfall. She murders the two sons she bore him as a supreme act of revenge. The question is: Why did the mother choose a form of vengeance that must have wounded her as much as the father, and how did this act bring about Jason's total defeat?

In the events leading up to the play, Medea planned to flee with Jason after she had assisted him in capturing the Golden Fleece from her father, King Aeetes. But her father, suspicious of the strangers who had landed on his shores, sent her brother with an armed force to get rid of Jason and his Argonauts. To help Jason escape with the Golden Fleece, Medea killed her brother. In matriarchal terms this was an unforgivable crime, and it marks the beginning of the trail of blood that follows this betrayer of her kin.

There are two versions of how the foul deed was carried out. According to Edith Hamilton, some accounts say Medea sent word to her brother asking him to meet her at a certain spot that night. "He came all unsuspecting and Jason struck him down and his dark blood dyed his sister's silvery robe as she shrank away." The other version seems more appropriate, since Medea hardly qualifies as the shrinking type of woman: "Medea herself struck her brother down, and cutting him limb from limb cast the pieces into the sea." This delayed the pursuers, who had to stop and pick up the pieces for burial (*Mythology*, p. 126).

The pair settled for some years in Jason's kingdom, and Medea bore him two sons. After a time, rival claimants to the throne led Medea to commit another crime for Jason's sake. Rex Warner depicts this episode as follows:

Medea and Jason then settled in Jason's hereditary kingdom of Iolcos, where Pelias, his uncle, still cheated him of his rights. Medea, hoping to do Jason a favour, persuaded the daughters of Pelias to attempt, under her guidance, a magic rejuvenation of their father. The old man was to be killed, cut in pieces and then, with the aid of herbs and incantations, restored to his first youth. The unsuspecting daughters did as they were told and Medea left them with their father's blood upon their hands. However, the result of this crime was no advancement for Jason but rather exile for him, Medea and their two children. (*Three Great Plays of Euripides,* p. 23)

Once again Medea is in flight, but this time Jason is implicated in the crime, which involves the murder of his kin. Now both Jason and Medea are outcasts who must forever live in the lands of strangers. In these circumstances the pair arrives in the kingdom of Corinth, where Euripedes' play opens.

Medea has just been repudiated by Jason in favor of the daughter of King Creon of Corinth. She voices her grief and rage at the fate of a wife confined to domestic servitude in a man's house and then forsaken:

> A man when he's tired of the company in his home,
> Goes out of the house and puts an end to his boredom
> And turns to a friend or companion of his own age,
> But we are forced to keep our eyes on one alone.
> (ibid., p. 33)

That a man is not obligated to keep his eyes on "one alone" is amply demonstrated by Jason's forthcoming marriage to the princess of Corinth. Deserted by her husband, having severed her past ties through blood crimes, Medea is utterly alone:

> But I am deserted, a refugee, thought nothing of
> By my husband — something he won in a foreign land.
> I have no mother or brother, nor any relation
> With whom I can take refuge in this sea of woe.

It is unendurable to Medea that she, who sacrificed everything for Jason, should go down to defeat while he, through a brilliant marriage, rises to the pinnacle of power and founds his own royal line of fathers and sons. This dictates the course her revenge will take: to render Jason childless. In patriarchal terms a man without a son is not fully a man, and to die sonless is to suffer the annihilation of the line.

Medea first destroys the new bride — and with her, Jason's chance to beget more sons. Then, to complete his destruction, she turns around and slaughters her two sons. This act has a twofold meaning. First, out of love for Jason, she had murdered her brother; now out of hate for him she murders his sons begotten of her. Medea is not only avenged — she has redeemed her crime against matriarchal blood with a crime against patriarchal blood. Jason is left without a son, a ruined man.

Although this is not the usual interpretation of the tragedy of Medea, there is ample evidence in the play to sustain it. The ending of the tragedy is prefigured at the beginning when Medea curses her "hateful" children of a hateful father, saying "Let the whole house crash" (p. 30). She means not only her own but Jason's royal house. "I pray that I may see him and his bride and all their palace shattered," she says, while mourning the dishonor she has brought upon her own country by killing her brother (p. 31).

Again, in the bitter reproaches Medea heaps upon Jason when he announces his new marriage, Medea reminds him that she has given him children. "If that had not been, you would have had an excuse for another wedding," she says. Jason counters with the argument that he is not marrying for the sake of having more children. "We have enough already. I am quite content." However, he points out, as a pair of fugitives in a foreign land, their economic prospects are dim and can only get worse. "A man's friends leave him stone-cold if he becomes poor," he says.

He justifies his marriage into the Corinthian royal family on the ground that it will give Medea and her sons the security they need, as well as benefiting him. "What luckier chance could I have come across than this, an exile to marry the daughter of the King?" He promises that, although he expects to "breed a royal progeny" by his new wife, they will be "brothers to the children I now have, a sure defence to us" (pp. 43-44).

"Do you think this is a bad plan?" Jason asks Medea. Then, in exasperation at her stubborn resistance, he lashes out: "It would have been better far for men to have got their children in some other way, and women not to have existed. Then life would have been good" (p. 43). Here we have a frank expression of the insuperable dilemma of patriarchal men. While they could rob women of their former place in productive, social, and cultural life, they could not strip them of their procreative powers. Men desirous of sons could beget them only through women.

Medea knows this. She is the daughter of King Aeetes, son of the sun-god Helios. She has committed abominable blood crimes and sacrificed her own position and prospects for Jason's sake, and she will not become the cast-off dependent of a former husband in a foreign kingdom.

This pride is manifested when the father of Jason's new bride, who distrusts this dangerous barbarian sorceress, asks Medea to leave his kingdom. Jason offers to send her money in exile and provide her with introductions to friends. "I shall never accept the favours of friends of yours,/Nor take a thing from you," she says. "There is no benefit in the gifts of a bad man" (p. 45). But where can this tormented fugitive, already excluded from two kingdoms for her blood crimes and now banished from a third, find security?

By good fortune an old friend, Aegeus, king of Athens, is passing through and visits Medea. He has been desperately searching for some way to have a child before he dies. Medea tells him that chance has brought him to the right person. "I will end your childlessness, and I will make you able to beget children," she assures him. In return, Medea is granted refuge in Athens.

Once her escape is assured, Medea proceeds with her plot to make her husband childless. Although she must steel herself to pick up the sword and murder her children, there is no other way to destroy her husband. She says:

> And when I have ruined the whole of Jason's house,
> I shall leave the land and flee from the murder of my
> Dear children, and I shall have done a dreadful deed . . .
> For those children he had from me he will never
> See alive again, nor will he on his new bride
> Beget another child, for she is to be forced
> To die a most terrible death by these my poisons.

To this she adds, although it hardly seems necessary:

> Let no one think me a weak one, feeble-spirited,
> A stay-at-home, but rather just the opposite,
> One who can hurt my enemies and help my friends,
> For the lives of such persons are most remembered.
> (p. 51)

Upon learning of the death of his bride and her father, Jason rushes to Medea's house to punish her. "Does she imagine that, having killed our rulers, she will herself escape uninjured from this house?" he shouts. Suddenly he discovers that she has committed an even more terrible crime; she has killed his sons. Jason is the defeated one. He cries out, "What! This is it? O woman, you have destroyed me . . . and left me childless." Now it is Jason's turn to become wild with frustrated rage as he declaims: "Oh, my life is over!" (pp. 67-68).

In the last dialogue between them, Medea is about to take her departure in a dragon-drawn chariot that had been given to her by a sun-god ancestor to protect her from enemies. The bodies of her dead children are in the chariot with her. She rejects Jason's plea that he be allowed to take the children to mourn and bury them. He accuses her of being an evil, hateful, and loathsome barbarian. "There is no Greek woman who would have dared such deeds," he says. Medea coolly informs him that she goes to dwell in the palace of the King of Athens, and prophesies that Jason, "as is right, will die without distinction" (p. 70).

And so, cheated of his sons, his line annihilated, Jason was left a broken man. Robert Graves describes the end of the husband who broke faith with Medea. He "wandered homeless from city to city, hated of men."

> In old age he came once more to Corinth, and sat down in the shadow of the *Argo*, remembering his past glories, and grieving for the disasters that had overwhelmed him. He was about to hang himself from the prow, when it suddenly toppled forward and killed him. (*The Greek Myths*, vol. II, p. 257)

Some mythographers see the end of Medea's story in her marriage to King Aegeus of Athens. In other accounts she rose higher to become the wife of a Greek god. Graves writes that "Medea never died, but became an immortal and reigned in the Elysian Fields where some say that she, rather than Helen, married Achilles" (p. 257).

Oedipus: Father-Killer

Greek mythology, upon which the tragic dramatists based their plays, deals with every conceivable kind of crime and bloodshed involving kin — parricide, matricide, fratricide, suicide, infanticide, cannibalism, vengeance killing, and sacrifice. The Oedipus tragedy supposedly introduces a new kind of kinship crime—his "incestuous" marriage to his mother after killing his father. But was it incest or father-killing that brought about his ruin and the destruction of his line?—that is the question.

Oedipus is a fourth-generation descendant of the House of Thebes, founded by Cadmus; his father was King Laius and his mother Queen Jocasta. Cast out at birth because of a prophetic warning that he would grow up to kill his father, he is saved by shepherds and adopted by the childless king and queen of Corinth. On reaching manhood, Oedipus learns of the prophecy and leaves Corinth, since he does not wish to kill the man he believes to be his own father.

His route takes him back to Thebes. On the road he kills a belligerent stranger who, unbeknownst to him, is his real father, King Laius. Arriving at Thebes, he challenges the Sphinx, who is devastating the land by devouring man after man who fails to answer her riddle. Oedipus answers the riddle (with the word "man") and defeats the female dragon. The grateful population want him as their king and he marries widowed Queen Jocasta—who, unbeknownst to him, is his mother.

The married pair live happily for many years and have four children, two boys and two girls. Then a terrible plague descends, afflicting the people, their crops, their herds and flocks. "No one suffered more than Oedipus," writes Edith Hamilton. "He regarded himself as the father of the whole state; the people in it were his children; the misery of each one was his too" (*Mythology,* p. 257).

Sophocles' play opens with an inquiry launched by King Oedipus to discover the reason for the blight and the measures necessary to overcome it. He dispatches Creon, the queen's brother, to the Oracle of Apollo for counsel. Creon returns with the message that a horrible crime has been committed in the realm; a son has murdered his father and remains unpunished. The plague will be lifted only when the killer of King Laius is found and punished.

As a just ruler, Oedipus relentlessly pursues his inquiry, although from the beginning the suspicion creeps through that he is himself the father-killer. Bit by bit, the truth comes out —Oedipus unwittingly murdered his father and married his mother. In self-punishment Jocasta kills herself. Oedipus, after blinding himself, is banished — no longer king and father of his realm.

This is usually interpreted as a punishment for incest. However, some mythographers have pointed out that if the play were about incest, and if incest had really been abhorred in all times as a polluter of heredity, we would expect the sins of the parents to be visited upon the children as physical and mental deformities — a punishment to fit the crime of "tainted blood." But this was not the case. As Edith Hamilton observes, the two sons and two daughters of Oedipus and Jocasta "were very unfortunate young people, but they were far from being monsters all would shudder to look at, as the Oracle had told Oedipus" (*Mythology*, p. 261). Raglan writes on the same point:

> Jocasta was a perfectly innocent and virtuous woman, who believed that her only son was dead; her children by Oedipus, far from being weaklings or imbeciles, were among the most famous heroes and heroines of Greek mythology.
>
> The problem is one which has puzzled theologians, philosophers, and scientists from the earliest times. (*Jocasta's Crime*, p. 2)

To be sure, even in matriarchal terms the man who married his mother was committing a breach of the old law of exogamy. Conscious or not, a violation of this most ancient taboo was a punishable offense — and Oedipus, who violated the taboo unwittingly, was indeed punished. But twenty-five hundred years ago a breach of the law of exogamy, even of family exogamy, was still a long way from the concept of incest. "Incest" as a term did not exist except in its earlier form, referring to an "unchaste" wife.

Far overshadowing Oedipus's breach of exogamy was the horrible act of father-killing — the crime of crimes in patriarchal terms. This brought the plague upon the land. The demand issued by the oracle of the god Apollo — archdefender of the father-family — was to find the son who had shed the blood of his father and exact retribution. Here the punishment to fit the crime was Oedipus's banishment from his kingdom and separation from his children.

This sheds a different light upon the remarks made by Oedipus as he probes his past, trying to uncover his real identity.

He remembers that the oracle blurted out some "disgusting" things, "how mating with my mother I must spawn a progeny to make men shudder." But he gives an odd reason why citizen and alien alike will turn away from him and drive him out of their homes. He has "clasped a dead man's wife with filthy hands; these hands by which he fell" (*The Oedipus Plays of Sophocles,* translated by Paul Roche, pp. 54-55).

For a man to marry a woman when his hands are stained with the blood of her husband — and his father — is enough to make men shudder at the progeny born of such a murderous and unchaste mating. But this has nothing to do with inflicting biological deformities upon children born of incest. At the end, when Oedipus is a blind and broken man, he worries about who will marry his daughters, not because they are ugly or imbeciles but because he wonders "who in this world will face the destiny that dogs our line?" (p. 81).

This destiny is nothing less than its destruction. His two sons, Polyneices and Eteocles, later kill each other in a struggle for power. One daughter, Antigone, is sentenced to death by her mother's brother, Creon, and the other daughter, Ismene, quietly fades away. As Edith Hamilton puts it, "The House of Oedipus, the last of the royal family of Thebes, was known no more" (*Mythology,* p. 264). The kingdom reverts to Creon, the uncle, who becomes regent after the death of his sister Jocasta and the banishment of Oedipus.

Thus the legend of Oedipus is not a story about incest but a reflection of the enormous difficulties involved in consolidating the father-family and the line of descent from fathers to sons. The many setbacks that dog its development through three generations are well summarized by Edith Hamilton. By the time of Oedipus, in the fourth generation, the conditions are ripe for such a consolidation. Oedipus has the obligation to eliminate the ambivalent position of the royal house and establish an unbroken paternal line.

But he fails. He is a victim of the turbulent forces unleashed in the transition from matriarchy to patriarchy. He does not know who he is or where he stands in a drastically changing kinship system. Ignorance of a man's kinship and family ties at this critical juncture, when the father-family must win supremacy over the matriarchal divided family, can result only in disaster.

Oedipus, blindly stumbling between two irreconcilable kinship systems, brings his whole house to ruin. The consequences of his failure to carry through his historical role can be seen in both kinship and social terms. In terms of kinship, who is he? The crucial injunction, "Know Thyself," is inscribed on the temple of the Delphic Oracle that Oedipus visits in search of his identity. Oedipus knows himself to be a "man," and this enables him to answer the riddle of the Sphinx and defeat her. What he does not know is where he stands as a kinsman. That is his tragic dilemma.

Who, then, is Oedipus? Is he, as the son of his mother, the oldest brother among her children? His age category would make him at the same time a mother's brother to her other four children. Or is he, as the husband of the mother, the father of her four other children? If so, he is at once father and son. Here is a man who is simultaneously a father, a son, and a mother's brother. It is not surprising that this riddle has baffled theologians, philosophers, and anthropologists. Oedipus is a man trapped between colliding kinship systems.

His status in society is equally snarled. A man's kinship line determines descent, succession, and inheritance. To which royal family does Oedipus belong — to his own House of Thebes or to the House of Corinth in which he was adopted? Where does he stand as an heir? In rapid succession Oedipus learns first about the death of his foster father, King Polybus of Corinth, and then that he is the son of his dead father, King Laius of Thebes. The deaths of the two fathers make Oedipus heir apparent to two kingdoms. But under the circumstances he can inherit neither. He is not the real son of his Corinthian father and he has killed his real father. The man cast out at birth is now doubly an outcast.

Here we touch the nerve center of the whole baffling situation. A closer look at the Royal House of Thebes discloses its essential vulnerability as a patriarchal family. It has the structure of a matrifamily — a divided family. The undissolvable unit is the sister-brother pair, and the husband is king only through his marriage to the queen. Whether or not Sophocles was aware of this matriarchal structure of the royal house, it comes through clearly in the play.

Queen Jocasta stands between two men, her brother Creon and her husband Oedipus. They are her male co-rulers — and this is the indelible insignia of the divided family. Moreover, as in real life, rivalries and suspicions are easily triggered between these men. Commentators who have focused their attention upon the sexual relations between Jocasta and Oedipus have tended to overlook the strained relations between her husband and her brother. Yet the collision between these two is a prominent part of the story.

The conflict begins early in the play with the inquiry launched by Oedipus to discover the killer of King Laius. Maddened by frustration and premonitory fears, Oedipus wrongly accuses Creon of instigating the rumor that Oedipus is the guilty man. He attributes Creon's treachery to his jealousy of Oedipus and his ambition to snatch the rulership from him. Creon's mild and reasoned response indicates the structure of this divided house; it is a queendom with both men serving as Jocasta's co-rulers:

> *Creon:* Well then, are you married to my sister?
> *Oedipus:* I am. Why should I deny it?
> *Creon:* And reign equally with her over all the realm?
> *Oedipus:* Yes, I do my best to carry out her wishes.
> *Creon:* And of this twosome do I make an equal third?
> *Oedipus:* Exactly! Which is why you make so false a friend.
> (*Oedipus Plays of Sophocles*, p. 46)

Creon then enunciates his own philosophy with respect to his place in the ruling trio to show that he could not possibly be envious of Oedipus or lust for his crown. He explains that Oedipus, the husband of the queen, has all the disagreeable cares and woes that go with serving her as her man of business. Creon, on the other hand, has all the advantages that royal prerogative give him without these drawbacks. "I could not covet kingship for itself when I can be a king by other means," he says (p. 46). In other words, the queen's brother is the permanent ruler by right of birth; the husband is king only through his marriage to the queen and only until her death or his deposition.

It is in the course of this bitter quarrel over the royal rights of the two kings that Jocasta exercises her power as queen. Hurrying out of the house, she issues commands to them: "You wretched men! Out on all this senseless clatter! . . . Get back home sir, you; and Creon you into your house!" (p. 48). In a patriarchal kingdom a queen might have her head cut off for displaying such impudence to the male crowned head.

To be sure, at this stage of the development of the Royal

House of Thebes, Oedipus Rex has acquired considerable powers. In the opening line of the play this "father" of the kingdom addresses the people who have come to beseech him for aid against the plague as "children, children! Scions of the ancient Cadmean line." Nonetheless the brother, Creon, is the male "power behind the throne" for life, always ready to take over the functions of rulership in the event of death or dethronement.

Both contingencies occur. After the death of his sister Jocasta, it is announced to Oedipus that Creon "takes your place as sole custodian of the State" (p. 78). And in the final dialogue between brother and husband, as Oedipus demands his children who are now under the guardianship of their mother's brother, Creon's last words to Oedipus are: "Stop being master now — the mastery you had in life has meant so little" (p. 82). With this, the broken man is led away; the play ends.

Oedipus, the man who failed to "know himself" in the critical turning point of history in which he lived, was caught in the grip of contending social forces he could not control; they crushed him and annihilated his line.

Orestes: Mother-Murderer

George Thomson characterizes the story of Orestes (the *Oresteia*) as "a stratified piece of social history embodying the accumulated deposits" of culture from the primitive tribe to civilization (*Aeschylus and Athens*, pp. 248-49). Indeed, it runs the gamut from cannibalism and sacrifice to the victory of the father-family, recapitulating some five thousand years of evolution from matriachal commune to patriarchal class society.

Orestes belongs to another celebrated Greek family, the House of Atreus. Like Oedipus, he is a fourth-generation scion of his line and stands at the crucial turning point of the social order. Orestes, however, succeeds where Oedipus failed in carrying out the historical task of establishing an unbroken line of fathers and sons. Orestes is the culture-hero of the new patriarchal order, accomplishing his objectives through the bloodiest of crimes — mother-murder.

Orestes is not alone; he is the descendant of a long line of kings guilty of blood crimes. As the myth is summarized by Edith Hamilton (*Mythology*, pp. 236-37), the line goes back to Tantalus, king of Lydia and son of Zeus. Tantalus "had his only son Pelops killed, boiled in a great cauldron and served to the gods." The cannibalistic sacrifice was rejected by the Olympians; Tantalus was punished with an unquenchable thirst, and Pelops was restored to life.

In the next generation Atreus, son of Pelops, secretly murdered the two sons of his brother Thyestes, cut them into pieces, and served them up to their father. Having disposed of his nephews as rival claimants, Atreus seized the power from his brother and established his line. Thus, by combining old practices with the new thirst for property and power, the grandfather of Orestes founded the House of Atreus on blood and wealth. His crime went unpunished for he was the sole king and master of his house.

In the third generation, with Agamemnon, son of Atreus and father of Orestes, all traces of cannibalism and son-sacrifice disappear. But a new version of ancient blood rites makes its appearance — the slaughter of sons has become the sacrifice of a daughter. Agamemnon, leader of the Trojan War, has been assured of success in his expedition if he offers up his daughter, Iphigenia. He sends for the girl on the pretext that she is to be married. Instead of a husband awaiting her at a marriage altar, Iphigenia finds death upon a sacrificial altar. Edith Hamilton describes Iphigenia: "lovely, innocent young thing, trusting her father utterly, and then confronted with the altar, the cruel knives, and only pitiless faces around her" (p. 241). This unprecedented murder of a kinswoman sets off the in-family blood feud that threatens to bring the whole House of Atreus crashing down.

Aeschylus's play opens ten years later with Agamemnon returning victorious from his wars to his wife Clytemnestra. He is unaware of what everyone else knows, that his faithless wife has taken a lover in his absence. And he does not know that she is plotting his death in revenge for the murder of her daughter. Taken off guard, Agamemnon is killed.

Under the matriarchal principle, Clytemnestra has committed no crime. The man she has killed was not her blood kin. He was a stranger who married into the maternal family. Moreover, in accordance with the principle of blood revenge, Clytemnestra has done no more than exact just retribution for the murder of her blood kin, her daughter. As Edith Hamilton depicts the scene after the slaying:

Dark red stains were on her dress, her hands, her face, yet she herself looked unshaken, strongly sure of herself. She proclaimed for all to hear what had been done. "Here lies my husband dead, struck down justly by my hand" . . . She saw no reason to explain her act or excuse it. She was not a murderer in her own eyes, she was an executioner. (p. 243)

The story of Orestes, Clytemnestra's son, begins at this point. As a child he lived away from home and now, grown to manhood, he is confronted by the family tragedy. Formerly, when all members of the matrilineal kin stood together in every act of vengeance, the son would have defended the act since he was of the same blood as his mother and sister. However, times have changed, and the situation is no longer so clear and simple for Orestes.

Orestes, scion of the House of Atreus, is very much tied to his father. His patrimony, social status, rank, and inheritance come down through the father-line. Furthermore, after encountering another sister, Electra, who had lived at home while he was away, he learns that his mother and her lover are squandering the wealth of their dead father, threatening to leave the children destitute. Electra looks to her brother to avenge the death of their father — which can only be done by slaying their mother.

The archaic heritage Orestes must grapple with is not, as with Oedipus, the ancient tribal law of exogamy shrunk to family exogamy. He has to cope with the ancient tribal injunction of blood revenge which has dwindled to a destructive in-family blood feud. "The *Oresteia* is the story of an aristocratic house in the process of destroying itself under a hereditary curse . . . the blood feud," is the way Paul Roche puts it in his introduction to *The Orestes Plays of Aeschylus*.

The blood feud was the last stage of the blood revenge institution, which arose out of the ignorance of natural death. But in civilized Greece this ignorance no longer existed. By the same token the blood feud as a form of justice was not only an anachronism but a deadly obstacle in the path of consolidating a unified father-family and an unbroken line of descent. In the case of Orestes, the social task of replacing blood vengeance with a civilized code of justice is combined with the necessity of maintaining the unified father-family.

The issue posed pointblank before Orestes is: should he side with his mother and preserve a decayed system of matrilineal blood vengeance, or should he kill his mother in defense of his father's line? In matriarchal terms, killing the mother is the crime of crimes, the unthinkable deed. Carried out by the son of the mother, it signified an irrevocable historical deed: the definitive end of the matriarchy.

Orestes wavers and fights against his own hesitations and forebodings, up to the very point where he takes action. In fact, it requires the exhortations and injunctions of Apollo, the patriarchal god and archenemy of the matriarchy, before Orestes is able to summon up the fortitude to carry through the decisive act.

The colossal social upheaval taking place at this juncture is reflected not only in the Olympian superworld but also in the underworld. As Thomson writes, "The feud between mother and son will become a feud between the deities of Heaven and Hell affecting the welfare of all mankind" (*Aeschylus and Athens,* p. 266). Orestes' murder of his mother brings forth the Erinyes, the female Furies who protect matriarchal interests. They hound the son who has shed the blood of his mother, demanding the ultimate penalty for the crime. In answer to the protests of Orestes that they did nothing when his mother killed his father, they reply that the married pair were not of the same blood as were mother and son.

Orestes, on the verge of denying his blood relationship to his mother, turns instead to Apollo and asks him to justify his deed. This brings forth the well-known argument by Apollo:

> The mother is not parent of her so-called child
> but only nurse of the new-sown seed.
>   The man who puts it there is parent;
> she merely cultivates the shoot —
> host for a guest — if no god blights.
>   (p. 186)

For proof of this assertion he points to Athena, the "daughter of Olympian Zeus — never nurtured in the darkness of a womb." She was born of a father but no mother. And this eminent goddess, standing in the Olympian hierarchy above Apollo, confirms his thesis:

> No mother ever gave me birth:
> I am unreservedly for male in everything
> save marrying one—
> enthusiastically on my father's side.
>   I cannot find it in me to prefer
> the fate of a wife who slew her man:
> the master of the house.
>   (p. 190)

Athena, the goddess of wisdom who is credited with advancing society from barbarism to civilization, sets up a court to judge Orestes according to an unprecedented procedure—trial by jury. When the votes for and against Orestes come out even, Athena declares that the mother-murderer is acquitted. She even persuades the Erinyes to change their ways; from the avenging Furies they became the Eumenides, compassionate to the suppliant.

Evolutionary anthropologists have long recognized that the story of Orestes is a story of the transition from matriarchy to patriarchy. In fact all three of these great Greek plays symbolize the turmoil and suffering that accompanied this colossal upheaval. But while the other two lines of fathers and sons are annihilated, Orestes sails through the stormy seas of social change, bringing himself and his house to safe moorings on the patriarchal shores. He represents the victory of the father-family and the triumph of the new social order.

Glossary

AFFILIATED CLANS: A general category including both linked (parallel) clans and allied (cross-cousin) clans.

ANTHROPOIDS: Human-like apes out of which the hominids evolved.

ANTHROPOLOGY: The science of the prehistoric evolution of human society.

ANTHROPOPHAGY: Cannibalism.

ARTIFACT: An object processed by human labor.

AUSTRALOPITHECUS (plural, *AUSTRALOPITHECINES*): The earliest tool-making hominid; birthplace: Africa.

AVOIDANCE, RULES OF: Prohibitions on contact with people and things governed by taboos.

AVUNCULATE: The relationship between mother's brother and sister's son in the last stage of the evolution of the fratriarchy.

BARBARISM: The second and higher level of social evolution after savagery, with an economy based on agriculture and stock raising, and marked in its first stage by the rise of the matrifamily.

BLOOD REVENGE: A primitive system of reciprocal punishment for deaths. Also called vengeance fighting.

BRIDE PRICE: Cattle or other items exchanged for a wife; a transaction that evolved out of gift-interchange.

CHIEF: Another term for headman.

CIVILIZATION: The third and present stage of social evolution, marked by the emergence of private property, class divisions, and the patriarchal family.

CLAN: A group composed of mothers, their brothers, and the children of the mothers; matrilineal kin who are descendants of the same ancestral mothers; an exogamous unit within a tribe.

CLASSIFICATORY KINSHIP: A system of social kinship binding together a large group of people without reference to genetic (family) ties.

COUP: Touching an enemy without injuring or killing him; a deed of valor among the Plains Indians.

COUVADE: A ritual in which a man undergoes "childbirth" and is established as the individual father of a woman's child.

CROSS-COUSINS: Men and women of the same generation belonging to opposite (and formerly hostile) groups; the men of the two sides are "brothers-in-law" and the women and men of the two sides are actual or potential mates.

DIVIDED FAMILY: The matrifamily, in which the mother's brother predominates over the mother's husband in relation to the children.

DUAL ORGANIZATION: Reciprocal relationship between two moieties or phratries of a tribe. They exchange fraternal and matrimonial ties.

ENDOGAMY: A reciprocal relationship between two exogamous communities (moieties) for the interchange of food and mates.

EVOLUTION, SOCIAL: The theory that society has passed through successive stages of development from lower to higher.

EXOGAMY: The "marrying out" rule, which is also a rule of "hunting out." Men belonging to a kinship group must obtain their food and mates outside their own territory.

FATHER-FAMILY: The patriarchal family consisting of a father standing at the head of his wife or wives and their children.

FEMINID: Term used in this book for the female hominid.

FOSSIL: An organic object that has been prevented from perishing by solidification into stone.

FRATRIARCHY: Term used in this book for the primitive brotherhood of men molded in the image of the matriarchy, the sisterhood of women.

FRATRILINEAL KINSHIP: Term used in this book for the male corollary of matrilineal kinship.

FRATRILINY: Term used in this book for the male side of matriliny; male descent traced through the mother's brother.

GENS: Archaic term for clan.

GIFT-GIVING: The interchange of food and other things between groups to create fraternal and matrimonial relations.

HEADMAN: Usually an old man in charge of male affairs such as regulated fighting, rituals, and sports.

HOMINIDS: Various beings above the apes but below *Homo sapiens;* subhumans.

HOMO SAPIENS: The sole species of full-fledged humans.

HORDE: See Primal Horde.

INITIATION: A ritual practiced on young males marking a new status.

INTERCHANGE: Reciprocal social relations involving gift-exchange; distinct from barter and commodity exchange which evolved later.

KULA: Trobriand term for their interchange system.

LINEAGE: Another term for matrilineal clan.

LOBOLA: Term for bride price among Bantu-speaking peoples of southern Africa.

MATRIARCHY: The maternal, communal clan system of social organization that preceded patriarchal society.

MATRIFAMILY: The final stage in the evolution of the maternal clan structure and the first form of family. See Divided Family.

MATRILOCAL MARRIAGE: Residence of a cohabiting pair in the community of the wife.

MOIETY: One of the two sides (phratries) of a tribe.

NEOLITHIC PERIOD: The New Stone Age, the period of barbarism.

NUCLEAR FAMILY: The modern father-family, consisting of husband, wife, and children.

ORUZO: African term for marriage division; also used for food division.

PAIRING FAMILY: Morgan's term for the matrifamily.

PALEOLITHIC PERIOD: The Old Stone Age, the epoch of savagery.

PARALLEL COUSINS: Men and women of the same generation belonging to different but linked clans. The men are "brothers" and the women are "sisters," and sexual relations between them are forbidden.

PATRIARCHY: The supremacy of the father and the male sex in general in social and family life.

PATRILINEAL KINSHIP: Acknowledgment of paternal ties of a child with its mother's husband.

PATRILOCAL MARRIAGE: Residence of a cohabiting pair in the community of the husband and his maternal kin.

PHRATRY: A number of linked (parallel) clans comprising one side or moiety of a tribe.

POTLATCH: Northwest Coast Indian ceremony featuring food and gift interchange.

PRIMAL HORDE: The earliest social group emerging from primate life.

PRIMEVAL PERIOD: The lower stage of savagery.

PRIMITIVE: Term usually applied to the upper stage of savagery, although the first stage of barbarism is also considered "primitive."

PROPERTY, PRIVATE: Wealth possessed by individuals or individual families as opposed to the communal property of primitive society.

RITE OF PASSAGE: Ritual signifying a change in age, status, function, or occupation. See Initiation and Couvade.

SAVAGERY: The earliest, most primitive stage of social evolution, with an economy based on hunting and gathering.

SIB: Alternative term for clan.

SUSU: Dobuan term for a matrilineal clan.

TABOO (TABU): Prohibition or quality of being prohibited.

TALIO, TALION: Law of retribution. Also *lex talionus.*

TOTEM: Species of animal or plant regarded as members of the kinship group; more broadly, the symbol of a totem.

TOTEMISM: The earliest system of social regulation, based on totem relationships and taboos.

TRIBE: An "endogamous" community composed of two phratries, each in turn composed of several linked clans.

VEVE: Melanesian term for maternal clan.

Bibliography

Note: Where a later edition is listed, the date of the original edition is given in parentheses.

Aberle, David F. "Navaho." In *Matrilineal Kinship,* ed. by Kathleen Gough and David M. Schneider. Berkeley and Los Angeles: University of California Press, 1961.

Ardrey, Robert. *African Genesis: A Personal Investigation Into the Animal Origins and Nature of Man.* New York: Dell, 1963 (1961).

Atkinson, J. J. "Primal Law." In *Social Origins and Primal Law,* by Andrew Lang and J. J. Atkinson. London: Longmans Green, 1903.

Bachofen, J. J. *Myth, Religion and Mother Right,* tr. by Ralph Manheim. Princeton, N. J.: Princeton University Press, 1967.

Baegert, Jacob. "An Account of the Aboriginal Inhabitants of the California Peninsula." In *A Reader in General Anthropology,* ed. by Carleton S. Coon. London: Cape, 1950.

Bates, Marston. *The Forest and the Sea.* New York: New American Library, 1961.

Benedict, Ruth. *Patterns of Culture.* New York: New American Library, 1959 (1934).

Boas, Franz. *Race, Language and Culture.* New York: Free Press, 1966 (1940).

—"Ceremony and Economics." In *Primitive Heritage,* ed. by Nicolas Calas and Margaret Mead. New York: Random House, 1953.

Braidwood, Robert J. *Prehistoric Men.* Chicago: Chicago Natural History Museum, Popular Series, Anthropology, no. 37, 1961 (1948).

Brasch, R. *How Did Sports Begin? A Look at the Origins of Man at Play.* New York: McKay, 1970.

Briffault, Robert. *The Mothers: A Study of the Origin of Sentiments and Institutions.* 3 vols. New York: Macmillan; London: Allen and Unwin; 1952 (1927).

— *The Mothers: The Matriarchal Theory of Social Origins* [abridged ed. in 1 vol.]. New York: Macmillan, 1931.

Budge, E. A. Wallis. *Osiris.* New Hyde Park, N. Y.: University Books, 1961 (1911).

Bullough, Vern L., and Bullough, Bonnie. *The Subordinate Sex: A History of Attitudes Towards Woman.* Urbana, Ill.: University of Illinois Press, 1973.

Calverton, V. F., ed. *The Making of Man: An Outline of Anthropology.* New York: Modern Library, 1931.

Carpenter, C. R. "Societies of Monkeys and Apes." In *Primate Social Behavior,* ed. by C. H. Southwick. Princeton, N. J.: Van Nostrand, 1963.

Catlin, George. *North American Indians.* 2 vols. Edinburgh: Grant, 1926.

— *Life Among the Indians.* London: Gall and Inglis, 1874.

Chapple, Eliot D., and Coon, Carleton S. *Principles of Anthropology.* New York: Holt, 1942.

Childe, V. Gordon. *Man Makes Himself.* New York: New American Library, 1951 (1936).

— *What Happened in History.* Harmondsworth, Middlesex: Penguin, 1960 (1936).

Clark, John Grahame Douglas. *From Savagery to Civilization.* Past and Present: Studies in the History of Civilization, vol. 1. London: Corbett, 1946.

Clark, W. E. LeGros. *History of the Primates: An Introduction to the Study of Fossil Man.* 2nd ed. London: British Museum, 1950.

Codrington, R. H. *The Melanesians.* London: Oxford University Press, 1969 (1891).

Colson, Elizabeth. "Plateau Tonga." In *Matrilineal Kinship,* ed. by Kathleen Gough and David M. Schneider. Berkeley and Los Angeles: University of California Press, 1961.

Coon, Carleton S., ed. *A Reader in General Anthropology.* London: Cape, 1950.

Crawley, Ernest. *The Mystic Rose* [2 vols. in 1]. New York: Meridian, 1960 (1902).

Dange, S. A. *India: From Primitive Communism to Slavery.* Bombay: People's Publishing House, 1949.

Dart, Raymond A. *Adventures With the Missing Link.* New York: Harper and Row, 1959.

Davis, Elizabeth Gould. *The First Sex.* Baltimore: Penguin, 1972 (1971).

Darwin, Charles. *The Descent of Man.* 2nd ed., revised. New York: Burt, 1874 (1871).

Diamond, A. S. *Primitive Law.* London: Longmans Green, 1935.

Diner, Helen. *Mothers and Amazons: The First Feminine History of Culture.* Garden City, N. Y.: Doubleday, 1973 (1965).

Driberg, J. H. *At Home With the Savage.* London: Routledge, 1932.

Du Bois, Cora. *The People of Alor: A Social-Psychological Study of an East Indian Island.* New York: Harper and Row, 1961 (1944).

Eggan, Fred. "The Hopi and the Lineage Principle." In *Social Structure,* ed. by Meyer Fortes. New York: Russell and Russell, 1963.

Eliade, Mircea. *Rites and Symbols of Initiation: The Mysteries of Birth and Rebirth.* New York: Harper and Row, 1965 (1958).

Elkin, A. P. *The Australian Aborigines.* Garden City, N. Y.: Doubleday, 1964 (1938).

Engels, Frederick. *The Origin of the Family, Private Property, and the State.* Introduction by Evelyn Reed. New York: Pathfinder, 1972.

Evans-Pritchard, E. E. *Essays in Social Anthropology.* London: Faber and Faber, 1969 (1962).

— *The Nuer.* New York and Oxford: Oxford University Press, 1972 (1940).

—"Nuer Rules of Exogamy and Incest." In *Social Structure,* ed. by Meyer Fortes. New York: Russell and Russell, 1963.

Fallaize, E. N. "The Family." In *Encyclopedia of Religion and Ethics,* ed. by James Hastings [q.v.].

Farber, Seymour M., and Wilson, Roger H. L., eds. *The Potential of Woman.* Man and Civilization Symposium Series. New York: McGraw-Hill, 1963.

Farrington, Benjamin. *Greek Science.* 2 vols. Harmondsworth, Middlesex: Penguin, 1949 (1944).

Firth, Raymond. *We, the Tikopia: Kinship in Primitive Polynesia.* Abridged ed. Boston: Beacon, 1968 (1936).

Forde, C. Daryll. *Habitat, Economy and Society.* New York: Dutton, 1963 (1934).

—, and Radcliffe-Brown, A. R., eds. *African Systems of Kinship and Marriage.* London: Oxford University Press, 1950.

Fortes, Meyer, ed. *Social Structure.* New York: Russell and Russell, 1963 (1949).

—"An Ashanti Case Study." Ibid.

Fortune, R. F. *Sorcerers of Dobu: The Social Anthropology of the Dobu Islanders of the Western Pacific.* New York: Dutton, 1963 (1932).

Frazer, James G. *The Golden Bough.* 12 vols. London and New York: Macmillan, 1907-15.

— *Folklore in the Old Testament.* 3 vols. London and New York: Macmillan, 1919.

— *Folklore in the Old Testament* [abridged ed. in 1 vol.] London and New York: Macmillan, 1923.

— *Garnered Sheaves.* London and New York: Macmillan, 1931.

— *Myths of the Origin of Fire.* London and New York: Macmillan, 1930.

— *Totemism and Exogamy.* 4 vols. London and New York: Macmillan, 1910.

Freuchen, Peter. *Book of the Eskimos,* ed. by Dagmar Freuchen. New

York: World, 1961.

Freud, Sigmund. *Totem and Taboo: Resemblances Between the Psychic Lives of Savages and Neurotics.* New York: Modern Library, 1946 (1918).

Frobenius, Leo. *The Childhood of Man.* New York: Meridian, 1960 (1909).

—"Marriage and Matriarchy." In *The Book of Marriage,* ed. by Count Hermann Keyserling. New York: Harcourt, Brace, 1931 (1920).

Gladwin, Thomas, and Sarason, Seymour B. *Truk: Man in Paradise.* New York: Viking Fund Publications, 1953.

Gluckman, Max. *Custom and Conflict in Africa.* Oxford: Blackwell, 1966.

—"The Role of the Sexes in Wiko Circumcision Ceremonies." In *Social Structure,* ed. by Meyer Fortes. New York: Russell and Russell, 1963.

Goldenweiser, Alexander. *Anthropology: An Introduction to Primitive Culture.* London: Crofts, 1937.

Gough, Kathleen, and Schneider, David M., eds. *Matrilineal Kinship.* Berkeley and Los Angeles: University of California Press, 1961.

Graves, Robert. *The Greek Myths.* 2 vols. Baltimore: Penguin, 1955.

Grey, George. "The Creation According to the Maori." In *Source Book in Anthropology,* ed. by A. L. Kroeber and T. T. Waterman. New York: Harcourt, Brace, 1931.

Grosse, Ernst. *The Beginnings of Art.* New York: Appleton, 1897.

Haddon, Alfred C. *History of Anthropology.* London: Watts, 1945 (1934).

Hamilton, Edith. *Mythology.* New York: New American Library, 1959 (1940).

Harris, Marvin. *The Rise of Anthropological Theory: A History of the Theories of Culture.* New York: Crowell, 1968.

Hartland, E. Sidney. *Primitive Law.* London: Methuen, 1924.

—*Primitive Paternity: The Myth of Supernatural Birth in Relation to History of the Family.* 2 vols. London: Nutt, 1909-10.

—*Primitive Society: The Beginning of the Family and the Reckoning of Descent.* London: Methuen, 1921.

—"Adoption." In *Encyclopedia of Religion and Ethics,* ed. by James Hastings [q.v.].

—"Totemism." Ibid.

—"Matrilineal Kinship and the Question of its Priority." In *Memoirs of the American Anthropological Association,* vol. 4, no. 1, January-March 1917. Lancaster, Pa.: New Era, 1917.

Hastings, James, ed. *Encyclopedia of Religion and Ethics.* 12 vols. Edinburgh: Clark; New York: Scribner's, 1908-21.

Herskovits, Melville J. *Economic Anthropology: The Economic Life of Primitive Peoples.* New York: Norton, 1965 (1940). [Original title: *The Economic Life of Primitive Peoples.*]

—, and Herskovits, Frances S. "The Bush Negro Family." In *Primitive Heritage,* ed. by Margaret Mead and Nicolas Calas. New York:

Random House, 1953.

Hobhouse, L. T. "Class Relations." In *The Making of Man,* ed. by V. F. Calverton. New York: Modern Library, 1931.

Hocart, A. M. *The Progress of Man: A Short Survey of His Evolution, His Customs, and His Works.* London: Methuen, 1933.

— *Social Origins.* London: Watts, 1954.

Hoebel, E. Adamson. *The Law of Primitive Man: A Study in Comparative Legal Dynamics.* New York: Atheneum, 1973 (1954).

— *Man in the Primitive World: An Introduction to Anthropology.* London and New York: McGraw-Hill, 1949.

—; Jennings, Jesse D.; Smith, Elmer D., eds. *Readings in Anthropology.* New York: McGraw-Hill, 1955.

Hogg, Garry. *Cannibalism and Human Sacrifice.* London: Pan, 1973 (1958).

Howells, William W. *Man in the Beginning.* London: Bell, 1956.

— *Mankind in the Making: The Story of Human Evolution.* Garden City, N. Y.: Doubleday, 1959.

— *Mankind So Far.* American Museum of Natural History Science Series. Garden City, N. Y.: Doubleday, 1944.

Howitt, A. W. *The Native Tribes of South-East Australia.* London: Macmillan, 1904.

Huizinga, Johan. *Homo Ludens: A Study of the Play Element in Culture.* Boston: Beacon, 1955 (1950).

Huxley, Julian; Hardy, A. C.; and Ford, E. B., eds. *Evolution As a Process.* New York: Collier, 1958 (1954).

James, E. O. "Sacrifice." In *Encyclopedia of Religion and Ethics,* ed. by James Hastings [q.v.].

Jay, Phyllis C. "The Female Primate." In *The Potential of Woman,* ed. by Seymour M. Farber and Roger H. L. Wilson. Man and Civilization Symposium Series. New York: McGraw-Hill, 1963.

Jevons, Frank Byron. *An Introduction to the History of Religion.* New York: Macmillan, 1911 (1890).

Jones, F. Wood. *Arboreal Man.* London: Arnold, 1926.

Kanter, Emanuel. *The Amazons: A Marxian Study.* Chicago: Kerr, 1926.

Karsten, Rafael. "The Head Trophy of the Jibaro Indians." In *Primitive Heritage,* ed. by Margaret Mead and Nicolas Calas. New York: Random House, 1953.

Kelsen, Hans. *Society and Nature: A Sociological Inquiry.* Chicago: University of Chicago Press, 1943.

Kenny, Michael J. *The Story of Evolution.* New York: Funk and Wagnalls, 1968 (1966).

Kosambi, D. D. *Ancient India.* New York: Pantheon, 1965.

Kroeber, A. L. *Anthropology.* New York: Harcourt, Brace, 1948 (1923).

— *Essays in Social Anthropology.* London: Faber and Faber, 1969.

—, ed. *Anthropology Today: An Encyclopedic Inventory.* Chicago: University of Chicago Press, 1953.

—, and Waterman, T. T., eds. *Source Book in Anthropology.* New York: Harcourt, Brace, 1931.

Kroeber, Theodora. *Ishi in Two Worlds: A Biography of the Last Wild Indian in North America.* Berkeley and Los Angeles: University of California Press, 1969 (1961).

Lang, Andrew. *Myth, Ritual and Religion.* New York: Ams, 1968 (1906).

—"Social Origins." In *Social Origins and Primal Law,* by Andrew Lang and J. J. Atkinson. London: Longmans Green, 1903.

Layard, John. *Stone Men of Malekula.* London: Chatto and Windus, 1942.

Leacock, Eleanor Burke. Introduction to *The Origin of the Family, Private Property and the State,* by Frederick Engels. New York: International, 1972.

—, ed. *Ancient Society,* by Lewis Henry Morgan. New York: World, 1963.

Levi-Strauss, Claude. *The Elementary Structure of Kinship.* Revised ed. Boston: Beacon, 1969 (1967).

— *Totemism.* Boston: Beacon, 1962.

—"The Family." In *Man, Culture and Society,* ed. by Harry L. Shapiro. New York: Oxford University Press, 1960 (1956).

Levy-Bruhl, Lucien. *The "Soul" of the Primitive.* Chicago: Regnery, 1971 (1966).

Linton, Ralph. *The Tree of Culture.* New York: Knopf, 1955.

Lippert, Julius. *The Evolution of Culture.* New York: Macmillan, 1931 (1886).

Lowie, R. H. *The History of Ethnological Theory.* New York: Farrar and Rinehart, 1937.

— *An Introduction to Cultural Anthropology.* New York: Farrar and Rinehart, 1940.

—"The Matrilineal Complex." *American Archaeology and Ethnology,* vol. XVI (1919-20). Berkeley and Los Angeles: University of California Press.

McGee, W. J. *The Seri Indians.* Seventeenth Annual Report of the Bureau of American Ethnology, Part I. Washington, D. C.: Smithsonian Institution, 1898.

McKenzie, Dan. *The Infancy of Medicine.* London and New York: Macmillan, 1927.

MacCulloch, J. A. "Cannibalism." In *Encyclopedia of Religion and Ethics,* ed. by James Hastings [q.v.].

—"Covenant." Ibid.

Mair, Lucy. *An Introduction to Social Anthropology.* New York and Oxford: Oxford University Press, 1970 (1965).

— *Marriage.* London: Penguin, 1971.

Malinowski, Bronislaw. *Argonauts of the Western Pacific.* New York: Dutton, 1961 (1922).

— *Crime and Custom in Savage Society.* Totawa, N. J.: Littlefield, Adams, 1967 (1926).

— *Sex and Repression in Savage Society.* New York: Meridian, 1960 (1927).
— *Sex, Culture and Myth.* New York: Harcourt, Brace, 1962.
— *The Sexual Life of Savages in North-Western Melanesia.* New York: Harcourt, Brace, 1929.
Mason, Otis Tufton. *Woman's Share in Primitive Culture.* New York and London: Appleton, 1911 (1894).
Mauss, Marcel. *The Gift: Forms and Functions of Exchange in Archaic Societies.* New York: Norton, 1967.
Mayr, Ernst. *Animal Species and Evolution.* Cambridge, Mass.: Harvard University Press, 1966 (1963).
Mead, Margaret. *Sex and Temperament in Three Primitive Societies.* New York: Morrow, 1963 (1935).
—, and Calas, Nicolas, eds. *Primitive Heritage: An Anthropological Anthology.* New York: Random House, 1953.
Meek, C. L. *Tribal Studies in Northern Nigeria.* London: Kegan Paul, 1931.
Metraux, Alfred. *La Religion des Tupinamba.* Paris: Leroux, 1928.
—"Tupinamba—War and Cannibalism." In *Readings in Anthropology,* ed. by E. Adamson Hoebel. New York: McGraw-Hill, 1955.
Moret, A., and Davy, G. *From Tribe to Empire: Social Organization among Primitives in the Ancient East.* London and New York: Knopf, 1926.
Morgan, Lewis H. *Ancient Society.* Chicago: Kerr [1877]
— *Houses and House-Life of the American Aborigines.* Chicago and London: University of Chicago Press, 1965 (1881).
— *League of the Iroquois.* New York: Corinth, 1962 (1851).
Murdock, George Peter. *Africa: Its Peoples and Their Culture History.* New York and London: McGraw-Hill, 1959.
Murray, Margaret A. *The Splendor That Was Egypt.* New York: Hawthorn, 1963 (1949).
Oakley, Kenneth P. *Man the Tool-Maker.* London: British Museum, 1950.
— Comments in Chapter XIV, *An Appraisal of Anthropology Today,* ed. by Sol Tax. Chicago: University of Chicago Press, 1953.
Penniman, T. K. *A Hundred Years of Anthropology.* London: Ducksworth, 1952.
Piddington, Ralph. *An Introduction to Social Anthropology.* 2 vols. Edinburgh and London: Oliver and Boyd, 1952, 1957.
Radcliffe-Brown, A. R. *The Andaman Islanders.* New York: Free Press, 1964.
— *Structure and Function in Primitive Society.* New York: Free Press, 1965.
— and Forde, C. Daryll, eds. *African Systems of Kinship and Marriage.* London: Oxford University Press, 1950.
Raglan, R. Fitzroy. *Jocasta's Crime.* London: Methuen, 1933.
Reich, Wilhelm. *The Invasion of Compulsory Sex Morality.* New York: Farrar, Straus and Giroux, 1971.

Resek, Carl. *Lewis Henry Morgan, American Scholar.* Chicago: University of Chicago Press, 1960.

Richards, Audrey I. *Hunger and Work in a Savage Tribe: A Functional Study of Nutrition among the Southern Bantu.* Cleveland and New York: World, 1964 (1932).

— "Some Types of Family Structure Amongst the Central Bantu." In *African Systems of Kinship and Marriage,* ed. by A. R. Radcliffe-Brown and C. Daryll Forde. London: Oxford University Press, 1950.

Rivers, W. H. R. *The History of Melanesian Society.* 2 vols. Cambridge: Cambridge University Press, 1914.

— *Psychology and Ethnology.* New York: Harcourt, Brace, 1926.

— *Social Organization.* New York: Knopf, 1924.

— "Mother Right." In *Encyclopedia of Religion and Ethics,* ed. by James Hastings [q.v.].

Roche, Paul, ed. and tr. *The Oedipus Plays of Sophocles.* New York: New American Library, 1958.

— ed. and tr. *The Orestes Plays of Aeschylus.* New York: New American Library, 1962.

Routledge, W. Scoresby, and Routledge, Katherine. *With a Prehistoric People: The Akikuyu of British East Africa.* London: Arnold, 1910.

Sahlins, Marshall. "The Origin of Society." *Scientific American,* vol. 203, no. 3, September 1960, pp. 76-87.

Schneider, David M., and Gough, Kathleen, eds. *Matrilineal Kinship.* Berkeley and Los Angeles: University of California Press, 1961.

Simoons, Frederick J. *Eat Not This Flesh: Food Avoidances in the Old World.* Madison: University of Wisconsin Press, 1961.

Simpson, George Gaylord. *The Meaning of Evolution.* New Haven: Yale University Press, 1969.

Smith, Homer W. *Man and His Gods.* New York: Grosset and Dunlap, 1957.

Smith, W. Robertson. *The Religion of the Semites: The Fundamental Institutions.* New York: Meridian, 1956 (1889).

— *Kinship and Marriage in Early Arabia.* Boston: Beacon, 1903 (1885).

Spencer, Baldwin, and Gillen, F. J. *The Native Tribes of Central Australia.* London: Macmillan, 1889.

Sumner, William Graham. *Folkways: A Study of the Sociological Importance of Usages, Manners, Customs, Mores, and Morals.* Boston: Ginn, 1906.

Tax, Sol, ed. *Evolution After Darwin.* Evolution of Man Series, vol. 2. Chicago: University of Chicago Press, 1960.

—, et al., eds. *An Appraisal of Anthropology Today.* Chicago: University of Chicago Press, 1953.

Thomas, W. I. *Primitive Behavior: An Introduction to the Social Sciences.* New York and London: McGraw-Hill, 1937.

— *Sex and Society: Studies in the Social Psychology of Sex.* Chicago and London: University of Chicago Press, 1907.

— *Source Book for Social Origins.* Chicago and London: University of Chicago Press, 1909.

Thomson, George. *Aeschylus and Athens: A Study in the Social Origins of Drama.* London: Lawrence and Wishart, 1950 (1941).

— *Studies in Ancient Greek Society.* 2 vols. New York: International Publishers, 1949, 1955.

Tylor, Edward Burnett. *Anthropology.* Abridged ed. Ann Arbor: University of Michigan Press, 1960 (1881).

— *The Origins of Culture* [Part I of *Primitive Culture*]. New York and Evanston: Harper and Row, 1958 (1874).

— *Researches into the Early History of Mankind.* Abridged ed. Chicago and London: University of Chicago Press, 1964 (1878).

— "On a Method of Investigating the Development of Institutions." In *Source Book in Anthropology,* ed. by A. L. Kroeber and T. T. Waterman. New York: Harcourt, Brace, 1931.

Van Gennep, Arnold. *The Rites of Passage.* Chicago: University of Chicago Press, 1964.

Warner, Rex, ed. and tr. *Three Great Plays of Euripedes.* New York: New American Library, 1958.

Washburn, Sherwood L. "Tools and Human Evolution." *Scientific American,* vol. 203, no. 3, September 1960, pp. 63-75.

Webster, Hutton. *Primitive Secret Societies.* New York: Macmillan, 1908.

— *Taboo: A Sociological Study.* Stanford: Stanford University Press, 1942.

Weinberg, S. Kirson. *Incest Behavior.* New York: Citadel, 1965.

Werblowsky, R. J. Zwi, and Wigoder, Geoffrey, eds. *The Encyclopedia of the Jewish Religion.* New York: Holt, Rinehart and Winston, 1966.

Wertheim, W. F. *Evolution and Revolution: The Rising Waves of Emancipation.* London: Penguin, 1974.

Westermarck, Edward. *The History of Human Marriage.* London: Macmillan, 1903 (1891).

Wetmore, Alexander. "Birds." *Warm-Blooded Vertebrates,* Part I. Smithsonian Scientific Series, vol. 9. New York: 1931.

White, Leslie A. *The Science of Culture.* New York: Farrar, Straus, 1949.

— "Ethnological Theory." In *Philosophy for the Future,* ed. by Marvin Farber, F. J. McGill, and Roy W. Sellars. New York: Macmillan, 1949.

Yerkes, Robert M. *The Great Apes.* New Haven: Yale University Press, 1929.

Zuckerman, Solly. *The Social Life of Monkeys and Apes.* London: Routledge and Kegan Paul, 1932.

Index

Abraham, 406

Adoption: and cannibalism, 278; of enemy scalps, 231-32; and interchange system, 247-48; of husbands, 311; kinship by, 436; to replace dead, 247

Adultery, 387, 425-26

Africa: bride price in, 415-20; fathers in, 373; ghost marriages in, 424-25; hostility in, 239-40; husbands in, 323; kinship in, 379; royal family in, 441-42; work competition in, 240. *See also* Ashanti; Bantu; Herero; Kikuyu; Nigeria; Zande

African Genesis (Ardrey), 52-56

Agriculture, 337-38, 412; and men, 312-13; and women, 106-10, 131-32, 148. *See also* Gardening; Digging stick

Akikuyus, *see* Kikuyus

Alliances, *see* Fraternal relationship

Amazons, 298

Andaman Islands: gift-giving in, 212-13; mythology in, 149

Animal behavior: and cannibalism, 25; and cooperation, 45-46; and female sexuality, 61-62; and food, 23; and human behavior, 73-74; and jealousy, 50; and maternity, 45-46; and mating, 9, 23, 44, 49-53, 56, 57, 59-66; misconceptions regarding, 51-53, 55, 56, 59, 65-66; and rape, 61-62, 63-64; and sex roles, 53-56; and sex segregation, 53-54, 58-60, 62

Animals: distinguished from humans, 29-30, 274-76; domestication of, 109-10, 121, 312-13; man as, 277-78, 280-82, 286; sacrifice of, 399-400; and women, 280-82. *See also* Apes and monkeys; Lions; Primates

Anthropologists, xv

—early: on couvade, 343; on endogamy, 203-04; on exogamy, 205-06; on incest, 17, 206; on marriage, 186; on matrilineal kinship, 132, 165; on taboo, 3, 34; on totemism, 35

—modern: on father-family, 75-76, 378; on "Oedipus complex," 447; on totemism, 35

—patriarchal views of, 72-73, 92-93, 97, 100-01, 103-04, 126-27, 131-33, 137-38, 152-54, 264-65, 349, 364, 438-40, 445

Antigone, 364

Antony, Marc, 443, 445

Apes and monkeys: biology of, 43; and canine teeth, 70-71; and cooperation, 45; estrus among,